An American History Reader

Volume I
Colonial to Reconstruction

Edited and Introductions by
John Moretta and Andrew S. Walmsley

Carol Brown, Coordinator
Houston Community College System
History Department

David Aldstadt
Carol Brown
Charles Cook
Carol Davis
Jon Garrett
John Moretta
Don Smith
James Sparks
Andrew S. Walmsley
David Wilcox

KENDALL/HUNT PUBLISHING COMPANY
2460 Kerper Boulevard P.O. Box 539 Dubuque, Iowa 52004-0539

Contents

Preface   v

The Colonial Period   1

Perry Miller, *Errand into the Wilderness*   5
Philip J. Greven, Jr., *Family Structure in Seventeenth-Century
    Andover, Massachusetts*   17
Edmund Morgan, *The Jamestown Fiasco*   29

The American Revolution   43

James Kirby Martin, *A Most Undisciplined, Profligate Crew: Protest
    and Defiance in the Continental Ranks, 1776–1783*   45
Broadus Mitchell, *The War Within*   57
Gordon S. Wood, *Republicanism as a Revolutionary Ideology*   69

Forming a Government   79

Merrill Jensen, *The Problem of Interpretation*   83
Esmond Wright, *The Constitution*   91
Federalist Paper #10 *The Size and Variety of the Union as a Check on
    Faction*   107

The New Nation 1784–1814   115

Forrest McDonald, *Hamiltonianism*   119
John C. Miller, *Thomas Jefferson and the Philosophy of Agrarianism*
    129
Harry Coles, *Prologue to War*   139

The Jacksonian Era   153

James Curtis, *President and Defender*   157
Edward Pessen, *The Jacksonian Character: A Contemporary Portrait
    of American Personality, Traits and Values*   171
Glyndon Van Deusen, *Politics, a Tariff and a Bank*   187

Reform and Antebellum America   201

Merton Dillon, *Goading the Monster*   203
David J. Rothman, *The Well-Ordered Asylum*   219
Gerda Lerner, *The Grimké Sisters from South Carolina*   235

The World of the Slaves   243

Winthrop Jordan, *Enslavement of Africans in America to 1700*   247
Sterling Stuckey, *Through the Prism of Folklore: The Black Ethos in
    Slavery*   263
Peter Kolchin, *Reevaluating the Antebellum Slave Community: A
    Comparative Perspective*   273

Crisis of the 1850s   287

Otis Singletary, *The Coming of the War*   291
David Potter, *The Nature of Southern Separatism*   301
Kenneth Stampp, *The Search for Remedies*   319

The Civil War   329

T. Harry Williams, *Abraham Lincoln: Pragmatic Democrat*   331
Emory Thomas, *Foundations of the Southern Nation*   345
William Barney, *The People's War*   361

Reconstruction   379

Kenneth Stampp, *Radical Reconstruction*   383
T. Harry Williams, *An Analysis of Some Reconstruction Attitudes*
    397
Leon Litwack, *Slaves No More*   409

Questions   419

Preface

This volume of articles in American history originated from a general dissatisfaction with the use of textbooks alone as aids in teaching history. Textbooks are adequate tools in providing students with factual information essential to a general understanding of historical events and ideas. However textbooks often fail to go beyond the confines of narrative history, and thus students are unaware of the variety of interpretations that give history its vitality.

The number of "selected readings in American history" that are available is staggering, but they nevertheless boil down to two types. On the one hand, there are those that present the interpretive approach—a collection of antithetical arguments challenging the prevailing scholarship on a particular historical topic. Then there are the narrative readers that offer interesting insights into for example, the personality of Andrew Jackson or give a graphic account of a particular Civil War battle. Both types have merit. Indeed, many of us would have gladly settled for one type but not necessarily the other. After reviewing numerous available readers we concluded that the type of monograph we wanted simply did not exist. We then decided to create our own reader that would not only match the diversity of our teaching styles but the multiformity as well of our students. Three years and many changes later, we have a finished product which we believe will offer both students and instructors the most recent and enlightening historical scholarship.

Beyond this preface is a ten chapter volume with three selections comprising each chapter. The first two articles of each section are opposing interpretations. These arguments are followed by a narrative that either provides a general overview of the period, or an interesting discussion of a particular personality, event, or idea. Instructors will ask you to read one, two or all three articles. Regardless of how an instructor wishes to use this reader, we are confident that it will not only complement any teaching style and methodology but expose students as well to the wide variety of historical interpretation.

Before each set of articles you will find an introduction to each chapter topic. Each introduction not only provides background information of the chapter's overall theme, but also a brief description of each selection. At the end of each article you will find a set of questions designed to help students interpret the argument presented. These questions may be discussed orally in class, reviewed independently at home, or used as a basis for an essay exam. We hope the questions will be helpful in your understanding of the articles' main theses.

In closing we would like to acknowledge those who have contributed to this project. First, to Dr. Sue A. Cox, Dean of the Social Sciences Division at Houston Community College, whose inspiration and counsel was invaluable in the preparation of this text. To Mr. Phillip Crow, fellow historian and former colleague, we thank for first introducing us to this idea and starting us on our way. Finally, to our HCCS students, past and present, we owe a great deal of thanks. It was your questions, thoughts and desire to want more than the ordinary history course that encouraged us to produce what we feel is a quality historical reader.

John Moretta
History Department
Houston Community College
Houston, Texas

The Colonial Period

The first Europeans to colonize New World territory were the Spanish. Following the trail-blazing voyages of Christopher Columbus (1492 to 1503), agents of Spain's vigorous nationalism rapidly invaded South and Central America with overwhelming single-mindedness, organizational skill, and efficiency. By 1550 Spain had erected a patriarchal empire as impressive in its wealth production as it was in its geographic magnitude. By the end of the sixteenth century Spain was the recognized front-runner among Europe's competing powers.

In contrast with Spain's dynamism, England's sixteenth-century colonization efforts were sluggish, halting, and ultimately unsuccessful. As early as 1497 John Cabot had claimed territory in Newfoundland, Labrador, and Nova Scotia, but his efforts were forgotten in the maelstrom of Henry VIII's turbulent reign. Even as England's search for new markets became more serious during the 1550's, and as Protestant Elizabeth I moved to rival Spain's New World hegemony, still Anglo colonization seemed unenthusiastic. Gilbert's 1578 effort in Nova Scotia failed miserably, soon to be followed by the disaster of Roanoake (1585–87). Disorganized, chaotic, and lacking centralized direction, English colonization paled alongside the glittering successes of the Spanish Conquistadores. But the English persevered. Following the peace with Spain in 1604 a new wave of expansionism captured the imaginations of hundreds of thousands of diverse, ambitious Englishmen, eventually spawning a multitude of distant colonies. Ireland, the Caribbean, Newfoundland, Canada, Nova Scotia, parts of mainland South America, and India all provided sites of permanent seventeenth century English settlements. To this impressive list England's North American colonies may, of course, be added.

The Virginia Company's Englishmen came to Jamestown with high hopes: easily extractible mineral wealth; an easy passage to the magical, and profitable, East; pliant natives, easy to subordinate and exploit. However, as Edmund Morgan's article, "The Jamestown Fiasco", eloquently demonstrates, the realities of life in Virginia during the first decade of settlement forced a

1

drastic revision of these expectations. It seems the early settlers made every mistake possible, the result being that life in Virginia was extremely rigorous, competitive, often brutal, disappointing, tragic, and desolate. Mere survival soon became the overriding goal of the once buoyant colonists. The settlers *had* to adapt or die. In the process of adaptation old ideas had to be jettisoned, replaced by new values forged in the crucible of the charnel house that was the infant Virginia. These new values eventually provided the context for decisions which were fundamental in defining the character of the community of Virginia; for example, the decision to base the economy upon tobacco cultivation, and the decision to accept the slave labor system.

In the lives of the New England Puritans, too, there is a corresponding theme of high expectations, followed by disappointment, followed by adjustment and reconciliation. The second article in this section is Perry Miller's "Errand into the Wilderness" which contends that second generation Puritan writers of the 1660's and 1670's experienced a sense that something had gone wrong in New England. According to Miller, the progeny of the original Puritan settlers of Winthrop's generation perceived a sense of failure of mission, not in a physical or material sense but in a spiritual way. Puritans had settled Massachusetts to be exemplars, to establish a "Modell of Christian Charity", to be witnessed then emulated by England's errant church. But somehow they had failed. God visited Massachusetts with grasshoppers, Indian attacks, hurricanes, and unsatisfactory children to demonstrate His displeasure. But perhaps God was not displeased, suggests Miller. Perhaps the Puritans had succeeded with their Bible Commonwealth and the self-condemnations of the jeremiads convey another, subconscious message. In Miller's view, the intellectual self-flagellations of the jeremiads indicate not so much a failure of the Puritans to live up to their holy covenant, but a sense of betrayal, frustration, and lost identity. The success of the New England experiment hinged upon maintaining the rapt attention of unreformed England. What troubled the second generation was the feeling that they had lost their audience, and that the very *raison d'etre* of their community had disappeared. In Miller's words, "If the due form of government were not everywhere to be saluted, what would New England have upon its hands? How give it a name, this victory nobody could utilize?" The answer, Miller suggests, was for the colonists to look inside themselves for future guidance as their American outpost could no longer be justified by external considerations.

Perry Miller's imaginative thesis rests upon a creative reading of literary sources. In contrast, the final article in the Colonial section provides an example of "the new social history" pioneered in America in the 1960's. Focusing upon the development of the family unit, and employing sources such as probate records, wills and testaments, land deeds, county archives, church and graveyard records, Philip Greven's "Family Structure in Seventeenth

Century Andover, Mass." provides a microscopic, statistical analysis of family structures in early Andover. How many children did people have? At what age did they marry? How much control did fathers have over children? What kept families together? These and others are the kinds of specific, down-to-earth issues, important in the daily lives of ordinary people, with which Greven concerns himself. In doing so he has provided us with an important companion to Miller's work, allowing us to see "from the bottom up" the same society Miller approached "from the top down" via the literature of an articulate minority.

Errand into the Wilderness

Perry Miller

It was a happy inspiration that led the staff of the John Carter Brown Library to choose as the title of its New England exhibition of 1952 a phrase from Samuel Danforth's election sermon, delivered on May 11, 1670: *A Brief Recognition of New England's Errand into the Wilderness.* It was of course an inspiration, if not of genius at least of talent, for Danforth to invent his title in the first place. But all the election sermons of this period have interesting titles; a mere listing tells the story of what was happening to the minds and emotions of the New England people: John Higginson's *The Cause of God and His People In New England* in 1663, William Stoughton's *New England's True Interest, Not to Lie* in 1668, Thomas Shepard's *Eye-Salve* in 1672, Urian Oakes's *New England Pleaded With* in 1673, and Increase Mather's *A Discourse Concerning the Danger of Apostasy* in 1677.

All of these show by their title pages alone a deep disquietude. Something has gone wrong. As in 1662 Wigglesworth already was saying in verse, God has a controversy with New England; He has cause to be angry and to punish it because of its innumerable defections. They say, unanimously, that New England was sent on an errand, and that it has failed.

To our ears these lamentations of the second generation sound strange indeed. We think of the founders as heroic men—of the towering stature of Bradford, Winthrop, and Thomas Hooker—who braved the ocean and the wilderness, who conquered both, and left to their children a goodly heritage. Why then this whimpering?

Some historians suggest that the second and third generations suffered a failure of nerve; they weren't the men their fathers had been, and they knew it. All these children could do was tell each other that they were on probation and that their chances of making good did not seem very promising.

Reprinted by permission of the publishers from ERRAND INTO THE WILDERNESS by Perry Miller, Cambridge, Mass.: The Belknap Press of Harvard University Press, Copyright © 1956 by the President and Fellows of Harvard College.

Since Puritan intellectuals were thoroughly grounded in grammar and rhetoric, we may be certain that Danforth was fully aware of the ambiguity concealed in his word "errand." It already had taken on the double meaning which it still carries with us. Originally, it meant exclusively a short journey on which an inferior is sent to convey a message or to perform a service. In that sense we today speak of an "errand boy"; or the husband says that while in town on his lunch hour, he must run an errand for his wife. But by the end of the Middle Ages, errand developed another connotation: it came to mean the actual business on which the actor goes, the purpose itself, the conscious intention in his mind. In this signification, the runner of the errand is working for himself, is his own boss; the wife, while the husband is away at the office, runs her own errands. Now in the 1660's the problem was this: which had New England originally been—an errand boy or a doer of errands? In which sense had it failed? Had it been despatched for a further purpose, or was it an end in itself? Or had it fallen short not only in one or the other, but in both of the meanings?

If the children were in grave doubt about which had been the original errand—if, in fact, those of the founders who lived into the later period and who might have set their progeny to rights found themselves wondering and confused—there is little chance of our answering clearly. Of course, there is no problem about Plymouth Colony. That is the charm about Plymouth: its clarity. The Pilgrims, as we have learned to call them, were reluctant voyagers; they had never wanted to leave England, but had been obliged to depart because the authorities made life impossible for Separatists. They could, naturally, have stayed at home had they given up being Separatists, but that idea simply did not occur to them. Yet they did not go to Holland as though on an errand; neither can we extract the notion of a mission out of the reasons which, as Bradford tells us, persuaded them to leave Leyden for "Virginia." The war with Spain was about to be resumed, and the economic threat was ominous; their migration was not so much an errand as a shrewd forecast, a plan to get out while the getting was good. True, once the decision was taken, they congratulated themselves that they might become a means for propagating the gospel in remote parts of the world, and thus of serving as steppingstones to others in the performance of this great work.

The great hymn that Bradford, looking back in his old age, changed about the landfall is one of the greatest passages in all New England's literature; yet it does not resound with the sense of a mission accomplished—instead, it vibrates with the sorrow and exultation of suffering, the sheer endurance, the pain and the anguish, with the somberness of death faced unflinchingly:

> May not and ought not the children of these fathers rightly say: Our fathers were Englishmen which came over this great ocean, and were ready to perish in this wilderness; but they cried unto the Lord, and he heard their voyce, and looked on their adversitie. . . .

They came for better advantage and for less danger, and to give their posterity the opportunity of success.

The Great Migration of 1630 is an entirely other story. True, the economic motive frankly figures. Wise men thought that England was overpopulated and that the poor would have a better chance in the new land. But Massachusetts Bay was not just an organization of immigrants seeking advantage and opportunity. It had a positive sense of mission—either it was sent on an errand or it had its own intention, but in either case the deed was deliberate. It was an act of will, perhaps of willfulness. These Puritans were not driven out of England—they went of their own accord.

Why? If we are not altogether clear about precisely how we should phrase the answer, this is not because they themselves were reticent. They spoke as fully as they knew how, and none more magnificently than John Winthrop in the midst of the passage itself, when he delivered a lay sermon aboard the flagship *Arbella* and called it "A Modell of Christian *Charity*." It distinguishes the motives of this great enterprise from those of Bradford's forlorn retreat, and especially from those of the masses who later have come in quest of advancement. Hence, for the student of New England and of America, it is a fact demanding incessant brooding that John Winthrop selected as the "doctrine" of his discourse, and so as the basic proposition to which the errand was committed, the thesis that God had disposed mankind in a hierarchy of social classes, so that "in all times some must be rich, some poor, some highe and eminent in power and dignitie; others mean and in subjeccion." It is as though, sensing what the promise of America might come to signify for the rank and file, Winthrop took the precaution to drive out of their heads any notion that in the wilderness the poor and the mean were ever so to improve themselves as to mount above the rich or the eminent in dignity. Winthrop told them that, although other peoples, lesser breeds, might come for wealth, this migration was specifically dedicated to an avowed end that had nothing to do with incomes. We have entered into an explicit covenant with God, "we haue professed to enterprise these accions vpon these and these ends"; we have drawn up indentures with the Almighty, wherefore if we succeed and do not let ourselves get diverted into making money, He will reward us. Whereas if we fail, if we "fall to embrace this present world and prosecute our carnall intencions, seeking greate things for our selves and our posterity, the Lord will surely breake out in wrathe against us be revenged of such a periured people and make us knowe the price of the breache of such a Covenant."

Well, what terms were agreed upon in this covenant? Winthrop could say precisely—"It is by a mutuall consent through a specially overruleing providence, and a more than ordinary approbation of the churches of Christ to seeke out a place of Cohabitation and Consorteshipp under a due forme of Government both civill and ecclesiasticall." If it could be said thus correctly, why should there be any ambiguity? There was no doubt whatsoever about what Winthrop meant by a due form of ecclesiastical government: he meant the pure Biblical polity set forth in full detail by the New Testament, which later generations would settle down to calling Congregational, but which for Winthrop was the very essence of organized Christianity. A political regime, possessing power, which would consider its main function to be the erecting, protecting, and preserving of this form of polity. This due form would have, at the very beginning of its list of responsibilities, the duty of suppressing heresy,—of being, in short, deliberately, vigorously, and consistently intolerant.

Regarded in this light, the Massachusetts Bay Company came on an errand in the second sense: it was on its own business. About this Winthrop seems to be perfectly certain, as he declares specifically what the due forms will be attempting: the end is to improve our lives to do more service to the Lord, and to preserve our posterity from the corruptions of this evil world, so that they in turn shall work out their salvation under the purity and power of Biblical ordinances. Because the errand was so definable in advance, certain conclusions about the method of conducting it were equally evident: one, obviously, was that those sworn to the covenant should not be allowed to turn aside in a lust for mere physical rewards; but another was, in Winthrop's simple but splendid words, "we must be knit together in this worke as one man, wee must entertaine each other in brotherly affection." This was to say, were the great purpose kept steadily in mind, if all gazed only at it and strove only for it, then social solidarity (within a scheme of fixed and unalterable class distinctions) would be an automatic consequence. A society despatched upon an errand that is its own reward would want no other rewards: it could go forth to possess a land without ever becoming possessed by it; social gradations would remain eternally what God had originally appointed, there would be no internal contention among groups or interests, and though there would be hard work for everybody, prosperity would be bestowed not as a consequence of labor but as a sign of approval upon the mission itself. For once in the history of humanity (with all its sins), there would be a society so dedicated to a holy cause that success would prove innocent and triumph not raise up sinful pride or arrogant dissension.

Or, at least, this would come about if the people did not deal falsely with God, if they would live up to the articles of their bond. If we do not perform these terms, Winthrop warned, we may expect immediate manifestations of divine wrath. And here in the 1660's and 1670's, all the jeremiads (of which Danforth's is one of the most poignant) are castigations of the people for having defaulted on precisely these articles. They recite the long list of afflictions an angry God had rained upon them: crop failures, epidemics, grasshoppers, caterpillars, torrid summers, arctic winters, Indian wars, hurricanes, shipwrecks, accidents, and (most grievous of all) unsatisfactory children. The solemn work of the election day, said Stoughton in 1668, is "Foundation-work"—not, that is, to lay a new one, "but to continue, and strengthen, and beautifie, and build upon that which has been laid." Hence the terms of survival, let alone of prosperity, remained what had first been propounded:

> If we should so frustrate and deceive the Lords Expectations, that his Covenant interest in us, and the Workings of his Salvation be made to cease, then All were lost indeed; Ruine upon Ruine, Destruction upon Destruction would come, until one stone were not left upon another.

Since so much of the literature after 1660—in fact, just about all of it—dwells on this theme of declension and apostasy, would not the story of New England seem to be simply that of the failure of a mission? Winthrop's dread was realized: posterity had not found their salvation amid pure ordinances but had, despite the ordinances, yielded to the seductions of the good land.

This would certainly seem to be the impression conveyed by the assembled clergy and lay elders who, in 1679, met at Boston in a formal synod, under the leadership of Increase Mather. The result of their deliberation, published under the title *The Necessity of Reformation,* was the first in what has proved to be a distressingly long succession of investigations into the civic health of Americans, and it is probably the most pessimistic. The land was afflicted, it said, because corruption had proceeded apace; assuredly, if the people did not quickly reform, the last blow would fall and nothing but desolation be left. It published a long and detailed inventory of sins, crimes, misdemeanors, and nasty habits, which makes, to say the least, interesting reading.

We hear much talk nowadays about corruption. If we ask our current Jeremiahs to descend to particulars, they tell us that the republic is going on the rocks, or to the dogs, because the wives of politicians aspire to wear mink coats and their husbands take a moderate five per cent cut on certain deals to pay for the garments. The Puritans were devotees of logic, and the verb "methodize" ruled their thinking. When the synod felt obliged to enumerate the enormities of the land so that the people could recognize just how far short of their errand they had fallen, it did not, in the modern manner, assume that regeneration would be accomplished at the next election by turning the rascals out, but it digested this body of literature; it reduced the contents to method. The result is a staggering compendium of iniquity, organized into twelve headings.

First, there was a great and visible decay of godliness. Second, there were several manifestations of pride—contention of the churches, insubordination of inferiors toward superiors, particularly of those inferiors who had, unaccountably, acquired more wealth than their betters, and, astonishingly, a shocking extravagance in attire, especially on the part of these of the meaner sort, who persisted in dressing beyond their means. Third, there were heretics, especially Quakers and Anabaptists. Fourth, a notable increase in swearing and a spreading disposition to sleep at sermons (these two phenomena seemed basically connected). Fifth, the Sabbath was wantonly violated. Sixth, family government had decayed, and fathers no longer kept their sons and daughters from prowling at night. Seventh, instead of people being knit together as one man in mutual love, they were full of contention, so that lawsuits were on the increase and lawyers were thriving. Under the eighth-head, the synod described the sins of sex and alcohol, thus producing some of the juiciest prose of the period: militia days had become orgies, taverns were crowded; women threw temptation in the way of befuddled men by wearing false locks and displaying naked necks and arms "or, which is more abominable, naked Breasts"; there were "mixed Dancings," along with light behavior and "Company-keeping" with vain persons, wherefore the bastardy rate was rising. In 1672, there was actually an attempt to supply Boston with a brothel. Ninth, New Englanders were betraying a marked disposition to tell lies, especially when selling anything. In the tenth place, the business morality of even the most righteous left everything to be desired: the wealthy speculated in land and raised prices excessively; "Day-Labourers and Mechanicks are unreasonable in their demands." In the eleventh place, the people showed no disposition to reform, and in the twelfth, they seemed utterly destitute of civic spirit.

Indeed they had been, and thereafter they continued to be even more inculcated. At the end of the century, the synod's report was serving as a kind of handbook for preachers: they would take some verse of Isaiah or Jeremiah, set up the doctrine that God avenges the iniquities of a chosen people, and then run down the twelve heads, merely bringing the list up to date by inserting the new and still more depraved practices in ingenious people kept on devising. I suppose that in the whole literature of the world, including the satirists of imperial Rome, there is hardly such another uninhibited and unrelenting documentation of a people's descent into corruption.

I have elsewhere endeavored to argue that the cultural anthropologist will look slightly askance at these jeremiads; he will exercise caution about taking them at face value. If you read them all through, the total effect, curiously enough, is not at all depressing: you come to the paradoxical realization that they do not bespeak a despairing frame of mind. There is something of a ritualistic incantation about them; whatever they may signify in the realm of theology, in that of psychology they are purgations of soul; they do not discourage but actually encourage the community to persist in its heinous conduct. The exhortation to a reformation which never materializes serves as a token payment upon the obligation, and so liberates the debtors. Changes there had to be: adaptations to environment, expansion of the frontier, mansions constructed, commercial adventures undertaken. These activities were thrust upon the society by American experience; because they were not only works of necessity but of excitement, they proved irresistible—whether making money, haunting taverns, or committing fornication. Land speculation meant not only wealth but dispersion of the people, and what was to stop the march of settlement? The covenant doctrine preached on the *Arbella* had been formulated in England, where land was not to be had for the taking; its adherents had been utterly oblivious of what the fact of a frontier would do for an imported order, let alone for a European mentality. Hence I suggest that under the guise of this mounting wail of sinfulness, this incessant and never successful cry for repentance, the Puritans launched themselves upon the process of Americanization.

However, there are still more pertinent or more analytical things to be said of this body of expression. If you compare it with the great productions of the founders, you will be struck by the fact that the second and third generations had become oriented toward the social, and only the social, problem; herein they were deeply and profoundly different from their fathers. The finest creations of the founders—the disquisitions of Hooker, Shepard, and Cotton—were written in Europe, or proceeded from a thoroughly European mentality, upon which the American scene made no impression whatsoever. The most striking example of this imperviousness is the poetry of Anne Bradstreet: she came to Massachusetts at the age of eighteen, already two years married to Simon Bradstreet; there, she says, "I found a new world and new manners, at which my heart rose" in rebellion, but soon convincing herself that it was the way of God, she submitted and joined the church. She bore Simon eight children, and loved him sincerely, as her most charming poem, addressed to him, reveals:

> If ever two were one, then surely we;
> If ever man were loved by wife, then thee.

After the house burned, she wrote a lament about how her pleasant things in ashes lay and how no more the merriment of guests would sound in the hall; but there is nothing in the poem to suggest that the house stood in North Andover or that the things so tragically consumed were doubly precious because they had been transported across the ocean and were utterly irreplaceable in the wilderness. In between rearing children and keeping house she wrote her poetry; her brother-in-law carried the manuscript to London, and there published it in 1650 under the ambitious title, *The Tenth Muse Lately Sprung Up in America.* But the title is the only thing about the volume which shows any sense of America, and that little merely in order to prove that the plantations had something in the way of European wit and learning, that they had not receded into barbarism. Anne's flowers are English flowers, the birds, English birds, and the landscape is Lincolnshire.

The titles alone of productions in the next generation show how concentrated have become emotion and attention upon the interest of New England, and none is more revealing than Samuel Danforth's conception of an errand into the wilderness. Instead of being able to compose abstract treatises like those of Hooker upon the soul's preparation, humiliation, or exultation, these later saints must, over and over again, dwell upon the specific sins of New England, and the more they denounce, the more they must narrow their focus to the provincial problem. If they write upon anything else, it must be about the halfway covenant and its manifold consequences—a development enacted wholly in this country—or else upon their wars with the Indians. Their range is sadly constricted, but every effort, no matter how brief, is addressed to the persistent question: what is the meaning of this society in the wilderness? If it does not mean what Winthrop said it must mean, what under Heaven is it? Who, they are forever asking themselves, who are we?—and sometimes they are on the verge of saying, who the Devil are we, anyway?

This brings us back to the fundamental ambiguity concealed in the word "errand," that *double entente* of which I am certain Danforth was aware when he published the words that give point to the exhibition. While it was true that in 1630, the covenant philosophy of a special and peculiar bond lifted the migration out of the ordinary realm of nature, provided it with a definite mission which might in the secondary sense be called its errand, there was always present in Puritan thinking the suspicion that God's saints are at best inferiors, despatched by their Superior upon particular assignments. Anyone who has run errands for other people, particularly for people of great importance with many things on their minds, such as army commanders, knows how real is the peril that, by the time he returns with the report of a message delivered or a bridge blown up, the Superior may be interested in something else. If he gets home in time and his service proves useful, he receives a medal; otherwise, no matter what prodigies he has performed, he may not even be thanked. He has been sent, as the devastating phrase has it, upon a fool's errand, than which there can be a no more shattering blow to self-esteem.

The Great Migration of 1630 felt insured against such treatment from on high by the covenant; nevertheless, the God of the covenant always remained an unpredictable Jehovah, a *Deus Absconditus.* When God promises to abide by stated terms, His word, of course, is to be trusted; but then, what is man that he dare accuse Omnipotence of tergiversation? If any such apprehension was in Winthrop's mind as he spoke on the *Arbella,* they could stile the thought, not only because Winthrop and his colleageus believed fully in the covenant, but because they could see in the pattern of history that their errand was not a mere scouting expedition: it was an essential maneuver in the drama of Christendom. The Bay Company was an organized task force of Christians, executing a flank attack on the corruptions of Christendom. These Puritans went in order to work out that complete reformation which was not yet accomplished in England and Europe, but which would quickly be accomplished if only the saints back there had a working model to guide them. It is impossible to say that any who sailed from Southampton really expected to lay his bones in the new world; were it to come about—as all in their heart of hearts anticipated—that the forces of righteousness should prevail against Laud and

Wentworth, that England after all should turn toward reformation, where else would the distracted country look for leadership except to those who in New England had perfected the ideal polity and who would know how to administer it? This was the large unspoken assumption in the errand of 1630: if the conscious intension were realized, not only would a federated Jehovah bless the new land, but He would bring back these temporary colonials to govern England.

In this respect, therefore, we may say that the migration was running an errand in the earlier and more primitive sense of the word—performing a job not so much for Jehovah as for history, which was the wisdom of Jehovah expressed through time. Winthrop was aware of this aspect of the mission— fully conscious of it. "For wee must Consider that wee shall be as a Citty upon a Hill, the eies of all people are uppon us." If we deal falsely with God, not only will He descend upon us in wrath, but even more terribly, He will make us "a story and a by-word through the world, wee shall open the mouthes of enemies to speake evill of the wayes of god and all professours for Gods sake." This errand was being run for the sake of Reformed Christianity; and while the first aim was indeed to realize in America the due form of government, both civil and ecclesiastical, the aim behind that aim was to vindicate the most rigorous ideal of the Reformation, so that ultimately all Europe would imitate New England. If we succeed, Winthrop told his audience, men will say of later plantations, "the lord make it like that of New England." The situation was such that, for the moment, the model had no chance to be exhibited in England; Puritans could talk about it, theorize upon it, but they could not display it, could not prove that it would actually work. But if they had it set up in America—in a bare land, devoid of already established (and corrupt) institutions, empty of bishops and courtiers, where they could start *de novo,* and the eyes of the world were upon it—and if then it performed just as the saints had predicted of it, the Calvinist internationale would know exactly how to go about completing the revolution in Europe.

When we look upon the enterprise from this point of view, the psychology of the second and third generations becomes more comprehensible. It would not perform its errand even when the colonists did erect a due form of government in church and state: what was further required in order for this mission to be a success was that the eyes of the world be kept fixed upon it in rapt attention. If the rest of the world, or at least of Protestantism, looked elsewhere, or turned to another model, or simply got distracted and forgot about New England, then every success in fulfilling the terms of the covenant would become a diabolical measure of failure. If the due form of government were not everywhere to be saluted, what would New England have upon its hands? How give it a name, this victory nobody could utilize? How provide an identity for something conceived under misapprehensions? How could a universal which turned out to be nothing but a provincial particular be called anything but a blunder or an abortion?

If an actor, playing the leading role in the greatest dramatic spectacle of the century, were to attire himself and put on his make-up, rehearse his lines, take a deep breath, and stride onto the stage, only to find the theater dark and empty, no spotlight working, and himself entirely alone, he would feel as did New England around 1650 or 1660. For in the 1640's, during the Civil Wars, the colonies, so to speak, lost their audience.

In other words, New England did not lie, did not falter; it made good everything Winthrop demanded—wonderfully good—and then found that its lesson was rejected by those choice spirits for whom the exertion had been made. By casting out Williams, Anne Hutchinson, and the Antinomians, along with an assortment of Gortonists and Anabaptists, into that cesspool then becoming known as Rhode Island, Winthrop, Dudley, and the clerical leaders showed Oliver Cromwell how he should go about governing England. Instead, he developed the utterly absurd theory that so long as a man made a good soldier in the New Model Army, it did not matter whether he was a Calvinist, an Antinomian, an Arminian, an Anabaptist or even—horror of horrors—a Socinian! Year after year, as the circus tours this country, crowds howl with laughter, no matter how many times they have seen the stunt, at the bustle that walks by itself: the clown comes out dressed in a large skirt with a bustle behind; he turns sharply to the left, and the bustle continues blindly and obstinately straight ahead, on the original course. It is funny in a circus, but not in history. There is nothing but tragedy in the realization that one was in the main path of events, and now is sidetracked and disregarded.

The most humiliating element in the experience was the way the English brethren turned upon the colonials for precisely their greatest achievement. It must have seemed, for those who came with Winthrop in 1630, that the world was turned upside down and inside out when, in June 1645, thirteen leading Independent divines—such men as Goodwin, Owen, Nye, Burroughs, formerly friends and allies of Hooker and Davenport, men who might easily have come to New England and helped extirpate heretics—wrote the General Court that the colony's law banishing Anabaptists was an embarrassment to the Independent cause in England. Opponents were declaring, said these worthies, "that persons of our way, principall and spirit cannot beare with Dissentors from them, but Doe correct, fine, imprison and banish them wherever they have power soe to Doe." There were indeed people in England who admired the severities of Massachusetts, but we assure you, said the Independents, these "are utterly your enemyes and Doe seeke your extirpation from the face of the earth: those who now in power are your friends are quite otherwise minded, and doe professe they are much offended with your proceedings."

We have lately accustomed ourselves to the fact that there does exist a mentality which will take advantage of the liberties allowed by society in order to conspire for the ultimate suppression of those same privileges. The government of Charles I and Archbishop Laud had not, where that danger was concerned, been liberal, but it had been conspicuously inefficient; hence, it did not liquidate the Puritans. Instead, it generously, even lavishly, gave a group of them a charter to Massachusetts Bay, and obligingly left out the standard clause requiring that the document in London, that the grantees keep their office within reach of Whitehall. Winthrop's revolutionaries availed themselves of this liberty to get the charter overseas, and thus to set up a regime dedicated to the worship of God in the manner they desired—which meant allowing nobody else to worship any other way, especially adherents of Laud and King Charles. All this was perfectly logical and consistent. But what happened to the thought processes of their fellows in England made no sense whatsoever. Out of the New Model Army came the fantastic notion that a party struggling for power should proclaim that, once it captured the state, it would recognize the right of dissenters to disagree and to have their own worship, to hold their own opinions. Oliver Cromwell was so far gone in this idiocy as to become a dictator, in order to impose toleration by force! Amid this shambles, the errand of New England collapsed. There was nobody left at headquarters to whom reports could be sent.

A couple may win their way to each other across insuperable obstacles, elope in a blaze of passion and glory—and then have to learn that life is a matter of buying the groceries and getting the laundry done. This sense of the meaning having gone out of life, that all adventures are over, that no heroism lie ahead, is particularly galling when it falls upon a son whose father once was the public hero or the great lover. He has to put up with the daily routine without ever having known at first hand the thrill of danger or the ecstasy of passion. True, he has his own hardships—hauling in the cod during a storm, fighting Indians in a swamp—but what are these compared with the magnificence of leading an exodus of saints to found a city on a hill, for the eyes of all the world to behold? He would be reduced to writing accounts of himself and scheming to get a publisher in London, in a desperate effort to tell a heedless world, "Look, I exist!"

His greatest difficulty would be not the storms, and Indians, but the problem of his identity. In something of this sort, I should like to suggest, consists the anxiety and torment that inform productions of the late seventeenth and early eighteenth centuries. It appears most clearly in *Magnalia Christi Americana,* the work of that soul most tortured by the problem, Cotton Mather: "I write the Wonders of the Christian Religion, flying from the Depravations of Europe, to the American Strand." Thus he proudly begins, and at once trips over the acknowledgment that the founders had not simply fled from depraved Europe but had intended to redeem it. And so the book is full of lamentations over the declension of the children, who appear, page after page, in contrast to their mighty progenitors, about as profligate a lot as ever squandered a great inheritance.

And yet, the *Magnalia* is not an abject book; neither are the election sermons abject, nor is the inventory of sins offered by the synod of 1679. There is bewilderment, confusion, chagrin, but there is no surrender. A task has been assigned upon which the populace are in fact intensely engaged. They seem still to be on an errand, but if they are no longer inferiors sent by the superior forces of the Reformation, to whom they should report, then their errand must be wholly of the second sort, something with a purpose and an intention sufficient unto itself. If so, what is it? If it be not the due form of government, civil and ecclesiastical, that they brought into being, how otherwise can it be described?

The literature of self-condemnation must be read for meanings far below the surface, for meanings of which, we may surmise, the authors were not fully conscious, but by which they were troubled. They looked in vain to history for an explanation of themselves; more and more it appeared that the meaning was not to be found in theology. Thereupon, these citizens found that they had no other place to search but within themselves—even though, at first sight, that repository appeared to be nothing but a sink of iniquity. Their errand having failed in the first sense of the term, they were left with the second, and required to fill it with meaning by themselves and out of themselves. Having failed to rivet the eyes of the world upon their city on the hill, they were left alone with America.

Family Structure in Seventeenth-Century Andover, Massachusetts

Philip J. Greven, Jr.

Surprisingly little is known at present about family life and family structure in the seventeenth-century American colonies. The generalizations about colonial family life embedded in textbooks are seldom the result of studies of the extant source materials, which historians until recently have tended to ignore. Genealogists long have been using records preserved in county archives, town halls, churches, and graveyards as well as personal documents to compile detailed information on successive generations of early American families. In addition to the work of local genealogists, many communities possess probate records and deeds for the colonial period. A study of these last testaments and deeds together with the vital statistics of family genealogies can prove the answers to such questions as how many children people had, how long people lived, at what ages did they marry, how much control did fathers have over their children, and to what extent and under what conditions did children remain in their parents' community. The answers to such questions enable an historian to reconstruct to some extent the basic characteristics of family life for specific families in specific communities. This essay is a study of a single seventeenth-century New England town, Andover, Massachusetts, during the lifetimes of its first and second generations—the pioneers who carved the community out of the wilderness, and their children who settled upon the lands which their fathers had acquired.

The development of a particular type of family structure in seventeenth-century Andover was dependent in part upon the economic development of the community during the same period. Andover, settled by a group of about eighteen men during the early 1640's and incorporated in 1646, was patterned at the outset after the English open field villages familiar to many of the early settlers. The inhabitants resided on house lots adjacent to each other in the

From the *William and Mary Quarterly*, 3rd ser., 23 (1966), pp. 234–256. Reprinted by permission of the *William and Mary Quarterly*.

village center. House lots ranged in size from four to twenty acres, and subsequent divisions of land within the two were proportionate to the size of the house lots. By the early 1660's, about forty-two men had arrived to settle in Andover, of whom thirty-six became permanent residents. During the first decade and a half, four major divisions of the arable land in the town were granted. Cumulatively, these four successive divisions of town land, together with additional divisions of meadow and swampland, provided each of the inhabitants with at least one hundred acres of land for farming, and as much as six hundred acres. During the years following these substantial grants of land, many of the families in the town removed their habitations from the house lots in the town center onto their distant, and extensive, farm lands, thus altering the character of the community through the establishment of independent family farms and scattered residences. By the 1680's, more than half the families in Andover lived outside the original center of the town on their own ample farms. The transformation of the earlier open field village effectively recast the basis for family life within the community.

An examination of the number of children whose births are recorded in the Andover town records between 1651 and 1699 reveals a steady increase in the number of children being born throughout the period. (See Table 1.) Between 1651 and 1654, 28 births are recorded, followed by 32 between 1655 and 1659, 43 between 1660 and 1664, 44 between 1665 and 1669, 78 between 1670 and 1674, and 90 between 1675 and 1679. After 1680, the figures rise to more than one hundred births every five years.

The entire picture of population growth in Andover, however, cannot be formed from a study of the town records alone since these records do not reflect the pattern of generations within the town. Looked at from the point of view of the births of the children of the first generation of settlers who arrived in Andover between the first settlement in the mid-1640's and 1660, a very different picture emerges, hidden within the entries of the town records and genealogies. The majority of the second-generation children were born during the two decades of the 1650's and the 1660's. The births of 159 second-generation children were distributed in decades as follows: 10 were born during the 1630's, either in England or in the towns along the coast of Massachusetts where their

Table 1 The Number of Sons and Daughters Living at the Age of 21 in Twenty-nine First Generation Families

Sons	0	1	2	3	4	5	6	7	8	9	10
Families	1	2	7	1	6	6	3	3	0	0	0
Daughters	0	1	2	3	4	5	6	7	8	9	10
Families	0	2	7	6	11	2	0	0	0	1	0

parents first settled; 28 were born during the 1640's; 49 were born during the 1650's; 43 were born during the 1660's; declining to 21 during the 1670's, and falling to only 8 during the 1680's. Because of this pattern of births, the second generation of Andover children, born largely during the 1650's and the 1660's, would mature during the late 1670's and the 1680's. Many of the developments of the second half of the seventeenth century in Andover, both within the town itself and within the families residing there, were the result of the problems posed by a maturing second generation.

From the records which remain, it is not possible to determine the size of the first-generation family with complete accuracy, since a number of children were undoubtedly stillborn, or died almost immediately after birth without ever being recorded in the town records. It is possible, however, to determine the number of children surviving childhood and adolescence with considerable accuracy, in part because of the greater likelihood of their names being recorded among the children born in the town, and in part because other records, such as church records, marriage records, tax lists, and wills, also note their presence. Evidence from all of these sources indicates that the families of Andover's first settlers were large, even without taking into account the numbers of children who may have been born but died unrecorded. An examination of the families of twenty-nine men who settled in Andover between 1645 and 1660 reveals that a total of 247 children are known to have been born to these particular families. Of these 247 children whose births may be ascertained, thirty-nine, or 15.7 per cent, are known to have died before reaching the age of 21 years. A total of 208 children or 84.3 per cent of the number of children known to be born thus reached the age of 21 years, having survived the hazards both of infancy and of adolescence. This suggests that the number of deaths among children and adolescents during the middle of the seventeenth century in Andover was lower than might have been expected.

In terms of their actual sizes, the 29 first-generation families varied considerably, as one might expect. Ten of these twenty-nine families had between 0 and 3 sons who survived to the age of 21 years; twelve families had either 4 or 5 sons surviving, and six families had either 6 or 7 sons living to be 21. Eighteen of these families thus had four or more sons to provide with land or a trade when they reached maturity and wished to marry, a fact of considerable significance in terms of the development of family life in Andover during the years prior to 1690. Fewer of these twenty-nine families had large numbers of daughters. Fifteen families had between 0 and 3 daughters who reached adulthood, eleven families had 4 daughters surviving, and three families had 5 or more daughters reaching the age of 21. In terms of the total number of their children born and surviving to the age 21 or more, four of these twenty-nine first-generation families had between 2 and 4 children (13.8 per cent), eleven families had between 5 and 7 children (37.9 per cent), and fourteen families had between 8 and 11 children (48.3 per cent). Well over half of the first-generation families thus had 6 or more children who are known to have survived adolescence and to have reached the age of 21. The average number of children known to have been born to these twenty-nine first-generation families was 8.5, with an average of 7.2 children in these families being known to have reached the age of 21 years. The size of the family, and particularly the number of sons who survived adolescence, was a matter of great importance in terms of the problems which would arise later over the settlement of the second generation upon land in Andover and the division of the estates of the first generation among their surviving children. The development of a particular type of family structure within Andover during the first two generations depended in part upon the number of children born and surviving in particular families.

Longevity was a second factor of considerable importance in the development of the family in Andover. For the first forty years following the settlement of the town in 1645, relatively few deaths were recorded among the inhabitants of the town. Unlike Boston, which evidently suffered from smallpox epidemics throughout the seventeenth century, there is no evidence to suggest the presence of smallpox or other epidemical diseases in Andover prior to 1690. With relatively few people, many of whom by the 1670's were scattered about the town upon their own farms, Andover appears to have been a remarkably healthy community during its early years. Lacking virulent epidemics, the principal hazards to health and to life were birth, accidents, non-epidemical diseases, and Indians. Death, consequently, visited relatively few of Andover's inhabitants during the first four decades following its settlement. This is evidence in the fact that the first generation of Andover's settlers was very long lived. Prior to 1680, only five of the original settlers who came to Andover before 1660 and established permanent residence there had died. The longevity of the first-generation fathers was to have great influence on the lives of their children. The second generation, in turn, was almost as long lived as the first generation had been. The average age of 138 second-generation men at the time of their deaths was 65.2 years, and the average age of sixty-six second-generation women at the time of their deaths was 64.0 years. (See Table 2.) Of the 138 second-generation men who reached the age of 21 years and whose lifespan is known, only twenty-five or 18.1 per cent, died between the ages of 20 and 49. Forty-two (30.3 per cent) of these 138 men died between the ages of 50 and 69; seventy-one (51.6 per cent) died after reaching the age of 70. Twenty-five second-generation men died in their eighties, and four died in their nineties. Longevity was characteristic of men living in seventeenth-century Andover.

The age of marriage often provides significant clues to circumstances affecting family life and to patterns of family relationships which might otherwise remain elusive. Since marriages throughout the seventeenth century and

Table 2 Second-generation Ages at Death

Ages	Males		Females	
	Numbers	Percentages	Numbers	Percentages
20–29	10	7.3	4	6.1
30–39	9	6.5	4	6.1
40–49	6	4.3	6	9.1
50–59	16	11.5	10	15.2
60–69	26	18.8	13	19.7
70–79	42	30.4	16	24.2
80–89	25	18.1	8	12.1
90–99	4	3.1	5	7.5
Total	138	100.0%	66	100.0%

Table 3 Second-generation Female Marriage Ages

Age	Numbers	Percentages	
under 21	22	33.3	24 & under = 69.7%
21–24	24	36.4	25 & over = 30.3%
25–29	14	21.2	29 & under = 90.9%
30–34	4	6.1	30 & over = 9.1%
35–39	1	1.5	
40 & over	1	1.5	
	66	100.0%	Average age = 22.8 years

the early part of the eighteenth century were rarely fortuitous, parental authority and concern, family interests, and economic considerations played into the decisions determining when particular men and women could and would marry for the first time. The age of marriage both of men and of women in the second generation proved to be much higher than most historians hitherto have suspected.

Traditionally in America women have married younger than men, and this was generally true for the second generation in Andover. They were not as young in most instances as one might have expected if very early marriages had prevailed, but they were relatively young nonetheless.

The age of marriage for second-generation men reveals a very different picture, for instead of marrying young, as they so often are said to have done, they frequently married quite late. (See Table 4.) The average age for ninety-four second-generation sons of Andover families at the time of their first marriages was 27.1 years. No son is known to have married before the age of 18,

Table 4 Second-generation Male Marriage Ages

Age	Numbers	Percentages	
Under 21	4	4.3	24 & under = 39.4%
21–24	33	35.1	25 & over = 60.6%
25–29	34	36.2	
30–34	16	17.2	29 & under = 75.6%
35–39	4	4.3	30 & over = 24.4%
40 & over	3	2.9	
	94	100.0%	Average age = 27.1 years

and only one actually married then. None of the ninety-four second-generation men whose marriage ages could be determined married at the age of 19, and only three married at the age of 20. The contrast with the marriages of the women of the same generation is evident, since only 4.3 per cent of the men married before the age of 21 compared to 33.3 per cent of the women. The majority of second-generation men married while in their twenties, with thirty-three of the ninety-four men marrying between the ages of 21 and 24 (35.1 per cent), and thirty-four men marrying between the ages of 25 and 29 (36.2 per cent). Nearly one quarter of the second-generation men married at the age of 30 or later, however, since twenty-three men or 24.4 per cent delayed their marriages until after their thirtieth year. In sharp contrast with the women of this generation, an appreciable majority of the second-generation men married at the age of 25 or more, with 60.6 per cent marrying after that age. This tendency to delay marriages by men until after the age of 25, with the average age being about 27 years, proved to be characteristic of male marriage ages in Andover throughout the seventeenth century.

Marriage negotiations between the parents of couples proposing marriage and the frequent agreement by the father of a suitor to provide a house and land for the settlement of his son and new bride are familiar facts. But the significance of this seventeenth-century custom is much greater than is sometimes realized. It generally meant that the marriages of the second generation were dependent upon their fathers' willingness to let them leave their families and to establish themselves in separate households elsewhere. The late age at which so many sons married during this period indicates that the majority of first-generation parents were unwilling to see their sons married and settled in their own families until long after they had passed the age of 21. The usual age of adulthood, marked by marriage and the establishment of another family, was often 24 or later. Since 60 per cent of the second-generation sons were 25 or over at the time of their marriage and nearly one quarter of them were 30 or over, one wonders what made the first generation so reluctant to part with its sons?

At least part of the answer seems to lie in the fact that Andover was largely a farming community during the seventeenth century, structured, by the time that the second generation was maturing, around the family farm which stood isolated from its neighbors and which functioned independently. The family farm required all the labor it could obtain from its own members, and the sons evidently were expected to assist their fathers on their family farms as long as their fathers felt that it was necessary for them to provide their labor. In return for this essential, but prolonged, contribution to their family's economic security, the sons must have been promised land by their fathers when they married, established their own families, and wished to begin their own farms. But this meant that the sons were fully dependent upon their fathers as long as they remained at home. Even if they wanted to leave, they still needed paternal assistance and money in order to purchase land elsewhere. The delayed marriages of second-generation men thus indicates their prolonged attachment to their families, and the continuation of paternal authority over second-generation sons until they had reached their mid-twenties, at least. In effect, it appears, the maturity of this generation was appreciably later than has been suspected hitherto. The psychological consequences of this prolonged dependence of sons are difficult to assess, but they must have been significant.

Even more significant of the type of family relationships emerging with the maturing of the second generation than their late age of marriage is the fact that paternal authority over sons did not cease with marriage. In this community, at least, paternal authority was exercised by the first generation not only prior to their sons' marriages, while the second generation continued to reside under the same roof with their parents and to work on the family farm, and not only at the time of marriage, when fathers generally provided the economic means for their sons' establishment in separate households, but also *after* marriage, by the further step of the father's withholding legal control of the land from the sons who had settled upon it. The majority of first-generation fathers continued to own the land which they settled their sons upon from the time the older men received it from the town to the day of their deaths. All of the first-generation fathers were willing to allow their sons to build houses upon their land, and to live apart from the paternal house after their marrage, but few were willing to permit their sons to become fully independent as long as they were still alive. By withholding deeds to the land which they had settled their sons upon, and which presumably would be theirs to inherit someday, the first generation successfully assured the continuity of their authority over their families long after their sons had become adults and had gained a nominal independence. Since the second generation with a few exceptions, lacked clear legal titles to the land which they lived upon and farmed, they were prohibited from selling the land which their fathers had settled them upon, or from alienating the land in any other way without the consent of their fathers, who continued to own it. Being unable to sell the land which they expected to inherit, second-generation sons could not even depart from Andover without their fathers' consent, since few had sufficient capital of their own with which to purchase land for themselves outside of Andover. The family thus was held together not only by settling sons upon family land in Andover, but also by refusing to relinquish control of the land until long after the second generation had established its nominal independence following their marriages and the establishment of separate households. In a majority of cases, the dependence of the second-generation sons continued until the deaths of their fathers. And most of the first generation of settlers was very long lived.

The characteristic delays in the handing over of control of the land from the first to the second generation may be illustrated by the lives and actions of several Andover families. Like most of the men who wrested their farms and their community from the wilderness, William Ballard was reluctant to part with the control over his land. When Ballard died intestate in 1689, aged about 72 years, his three sons, Joseph, William, and John, agreed to divide their father's estate among themselves "as Equally as they could." They also agreed to give their elderly mother, Grace Ballard, a room in their father's house and to care for her as long as she remained a widow, thus adhering voluntarily to a common practice for the provision of the widow. The eldest son, Joseph, had married in 1665/6, almost certainly a rather young man, whereas his two brothers did not marry until the early 1680's, when their father was in his mid-sixties. William, Jr., must have been well over 30 by then, and John was 28. Both Joseph and William received as part of their division of their father's estate in Andover the land where their houses already stood, as well as more than 75 acres of land apiece. The youngest son, John, got all the housing, land, and meadow "his father lived upon except the land and meadow his father gave William Blunt upon the marriage with his daughter," which had taken place in 1668. It is unclear whether John lived with his wife and their four children in the same house as his parents, but there is a strong likelihood that this was the case in view of his assuming control of it after his father's death. His two older brothers had been given land to build upon by their father before his death, but no deeds of gift had been granted to them, thus preventing their full independence so long as he remained alive. Their family remained closely knit both by their establishment of residences near their paternal home on family land and by the prolonged control by William Ballard over the land he had received as one of the first settlers in Andover. It was a pattern repeated in many families.

Some Andover families were less reluctant than Nicholas Holt to let their sons marry early and to establish separate households, although the control of the land in most instances still rested in the father's hands. The Lovejoy family, with seven sons, enabled the four oldest sons to marry at the ages of 22 and 23. John Lovejoy, Sr., who originally emigrated from England as a young indentured servant, acquired a seven-acre house lot after his settlement in Andover during the mid-1640's, and eventually possessed an estate of over 200 acres in the town. At his death in 1690, at the age of 68, he left an estate worth a total of £327.11.6, with housing and land valued at £260.00.0, a substantial sum at the time. Although he himself had waited until the age of 29 to marry, his sons married earlier. His eldest son, John, Jr., married on March 23, 1677/8, aged 22, and built a house and began to raise crops on land which his father gave him for that purpose. He did not receive a deed of gift for his land, however; his inventory, taken in 1680 after his premature death, showed his major possessions to consist of "one house and a crope of corn" worth only twenty pounds. His entire estate, both real and personal, was valued at only £45.15.0, and was encumbered with £29.14.7 in debts. Three years later, on April 6, 1683, the land which he had farmed without owning was given to his three year old son by his father, John Lovejoy, Sr. In a deed of gift, the elder Lovejoy gave his grandson, as a token of the love and affection he felt for his deceased son, the land which John, Junior, had had, consisting of fifty acres of upland, a piece of meadow, and a small parcel of another meadow, all of which lay in Andover. Of the surviving Lovejoy sons only the second, William, received a deed of gift from the elder Lovejoy for the land which he had given them. The others had to await their inheritances to come into full possession of their land. In his will dated September 1, 1690, shortly before his death, Lovejoy distributed his estate among his five surviving sons: Christopher received thirty acres together with other unstated amounts of land, and Nathaniel received the land which his father had originally intended to give to his brother, Benjamin, who had been killed in 1689. Benjamin was 25 years old and unmarried at the time of his death, and left an estate worth only £1.02.8, his wages as a soldier. Without their father's land, sons were penniless. The youngest of the Lovejoy sons, Ebenezer, received his father's homestead, with the house and lands, in return for fulfilling his father's wish that his mother should "be made comfortable while she Continues in this world." His mother inherited the east end of the house, and elaborate provisions in the will ensured her comfort. With all the surviving sons settled upon their father's land in Andover, with the residence of the widow in the son's house, and with the fact that only one of the sons actually received a deed for his land during their father's lifetime, the Lovejoys also epitomized some of the principal characteristics of family life in seventeenth-century Andover.

Exceptions to the general pattern of prolonged paternal control over sons were rare. The actions taken by Edmund Faulkner to settle his eldest son in

Andover are instructive precisely because they were so exceptional. The first sign that Faulkner was planning ahead for his son came with his purchase of a twenty-acre lot from the town at the annual town meeting of March 22, 1669/70. He was the only first-generation settler to purchase such a lot, all of the other purchasers being either second-generation sons or newcomers, and it was evident that he did not buy it for himself since he already had a six-acre house lot and more than one hundred acres of land in Andover. The town voted that "in case the said Edmond shall at any time put such to live upon it as the town shall approve, or have no just matter against them, he is to be admitted to be a townsman." The eldest of his two sons, Francis, was then a youth of about nineteen years. Five years later, January 4, 1674/5, Francis was admitted as a townsman of Andover "upon the account of the land he now enjoyeth," almost certainly his father's twenty acres. The following October, aged about 24, Francis married the minister's daughter. A year and a half later, in a deed dated February 1, 1676/7, Edmund Faulkner freely gave his eldest son "one halfe of my Living here at home" to be "Equally Divided between us both." Francis was to pay the town rates on his half, and was to have half the barn, half the orchard, and half the land about his father's house, and both he and his father were to divide the meadows. Significantly, Edmund added that "all my Sixscore acres over Shawshinne river I wholly give unto him," thus handing over, at the relatively young age of 52, most of his upland and half of the remainder of his estate to his eldest son. The control of most of his estate thereby was transferred legally and completely from the first to the second generation, Edmund's second and youngest son, John, was still not married at the time Francis received his gift, and waited until 1682 before marrying at the age of 28. Eventually he received some land by his father's will, but his inheritance was small compared to his brother's. Edmund Faulkner's eagerness to hand over the control of his estate of his eldest son is notable for its rarity and accentuates the fact that almost none of his friends and neighbors chose to do likewise. It is just possible that Faulkner, himself a younger son of an English gentry family, sought to preserve most of his Andover estate intact by giving it to his eldest son. If so, it would only emphasize his distinctiveness from his neighbors. For the great majority of the first-generation settlers in Andover, partible inheritances and delayed control by the first generation over the land were the rule. Faulkner was the exception which proved it.

Embedded in the reconstructions of particular family histories is a general pattern of family structure unlike any which are known or suspected to have existed either in England or its American colonies during the seventeenth century. It is evident that the family structure which developed during the lifetimes of the first two generations in Andover cannot be classified satisfactorily according to any of the more recent definitions applied to types of family life in the seventeenth century. It was not simply a "patrilineal group of extended kinship gathered into a single household," nor was it simply a "nuclear independent family, that is man, wife, and children living apart from relatives." The characteristic family structure which emerged in Andover with the maturing of the second generation during the 1670's and 1680's was a combination of both the classical extended family and the nuclear family. This distinctive form of family structure is best described as a *modified extended family*—defined as a kinship group of two or more generations living within a single community in which the dependence of the children upon their parents continues after the children have married and are living under a separate roof. This family structure is a *modified* extended family because all members of the family are not "gathered into a single household," but it is still an *extended* family because the newly created conjugal unit of husband and wife live in separate households in close proximity to their parents and siblings and continue to be economically dependent in some respects upon their parents. And because of the continuing dependence of the second generation upon their first-generation fathers, who continued to own most of the family land throughout the better part of their lives, the family in seventeenth-century Andover was *patriarchal* as well. The men who first settled the town long remained the dominant figures both in their families and their community. It was their decisions and their actions which produced the family characteristic of seventeenth-century Andover.

One of the most significant consequences of the development of the modified extended family characteristic of Andover during this period was the fact that remarkably few second-generation sons moved away from their families and their community. More than four fifths of the second-generation sons lived their entire lives in the town which their fathers had wrested from the wilderness. The first generation evidently was intent upon guaranteeing the future of the community and of their families within it through the settlement of all of their sons upon the lands originally granted to them by the town. Since it was quite true that the second generation could not expect to acquire as much land by staying in Andover as their fathers had by undergoing the perils of founding a new town on the frontier, it is quite possible that their reluctance to hand over the control of the land to their sons when young is not only a reflection of their patriarchalism, justified both by custom and by theology, but also of the fact that they could not be sure that their sons would stay, given a free choice. Through a series of delays, however, particularly those involving marriages and economic independence, the second generation continued to be closely tied to their paternal families. By keeping their sons in positions of prolonged dependence, the first generation successfully managed to keep them in Andover during those years in which their youth and energy might have led them to seek their fortunes elsewhere. Later generations achieved their independence earlier and moved more. It remains to be seen to what extent the family life characteristic of seventeenth-century Andover was the exception or the rule in the American colonies.

The Jamestown Fiasco

Edmund Morgan

The first wave of Englishmen reached Virginia at Cape Henry, the southern headland at the opening of Chesapeake Bay, on April 26, 1607. The same day their troubles began. The Indians of the Cape Henry region (the Chesapeakes), when they found a party of twenty or thirty strangers walking about on their territory, drove them back to the ships they came on. It was not the last Indian victory, but it was no more effective than later ones. In spite of troubles, the English were there to stay. They spent until May 14 exploring Virginia's broad waters and then chose a site that fitted the formula Hakluyt had prescribed. The place which they named Jamestown, on the James (formerly Powhatan) River, was inland from the capes about sixty miles, ample distance for warning of a Spanish invasion by sea. It was situated on a peninsula, making it easily defensible by land; and the river was navigable by oceangoing ships for another seventy-five miles into the interior, thus giving access to other tribes in case the local Indians should prove as unfriendly as the Chesapeakes.

Captain Christopher Newport had landed the settlers in time to plant something for a harvest that year if they put their minds to it. After a week, in which they built a fort for protection, Newport and twenty-one others took a small boat and headed up the river on a diplomatic and reconnoitering mission, while the settlers behind set about the crucial business of planting corn. Newport paused at various Indian villages along the way and assured the people, as best he could, of the friendship of the English and of his readiness to assist them against their enemies. Newport gathered correctly from his attempted conversations that one man, Powhatan, ruled the whole area above Jamestown, as far as the falls at the present site of Richmond. His enemies, the Monacans, lived above the falls (where they might be difficult to reach if Powhatan proved unfriendly). Newport also surmised, incorrectly, that the

Chesapeake Indians who had attacked him at Cape Henry were not under Powhatan's dominion. He accordingly tried to make an alliance against the Chesapeakes and Monacans with a local chief whom he mistook for Powhatan. At the same time, he planted a cross with the name of King James on it (to establish English dominion) and tried to explain to the somewhat bewildered and justifiably suspicious owners of the country that one arm of the cross was Powhatan, the other himself, and that the fastening of them together signified the league between them.

If the Indians understood, they were apparently unimpressed, for three days later, returning to Jamestown, Newport found that two hundred of Powhatan's warriors had attacked the fort the day before and had only been prevented from destroying it by fire from the ships. The settlers had been engaged in planting and had not yet unpacked their guns from the cases in which they were shipped. That was a mistake they were not likely to repeat. But for the next ten years they seem to have made nearly every possible mistake and some that seem almost impossible. It would take a book longer than this to recount them all, and the story has already been told many times. But if we are to understand the heritage of these ten disastrous years for later Virginia history, we should look at a few of the more puzzling episodes and then try to fathom the forces behind them.

Skip over the first couple of years, when it was easy for Englishmen to make mistakes in the strange new world to which they had come, and look at Jamestown in the winter of 1609–10. It is three planting seasons since the colony began. The settlers have fallen into an uneasy truce with the Indians, punctuated by guerrilla raids on both sides, but they have had plenty of time in which they could have grown crops. They have obtained corn from the Indians and supplies from England. They have firearms. Game abounds in the woods; and Virginia's rivers are filled with sturgeon in the summer and covered with geese and ducks in the winter. There are five hundred people in the colony now. And they are starving. They scour the woods listlessly for nuts, roots, and berries. And they offer the only authentic examples of cannibalism witnessed in Virginia. One provident man chops up his wife and salts down the pieces. Others dig up graves to eat the corpses. By spring only sixty are left alive.

Another scene, a year later, in the spring of 1611. The settlers have been reinforced with more men and supplies from England. The preceding winter has not been as gruesome as the one before, thanks in part to corn obtained from the Indians. But the colony still is not growing its own corn. The governor, Lord De la Warr, weakened by the winter, has returned to England for his health. His replacement, Sir Thomas Dale, reaches Jamestown in May, a time when all hands could have been used in planting. Dale finds nothing planted except "some few seeds put into a private garden or two." And the people he finds at "their daily and usuall workes, bowling in the streetes."

It is evident that the settlers, failing to plant for themselves, depend heavily on the Indians for food. The Indians can finish them off at any time simply by leaving the area. And the Indians know it. One of them tells the English flatly that "we can plant any where . . . and we know that you cannot live if you want [i.e., lack] our harvest, and that reliefe we bring you." If the English drive out the Indians, they will starve.

With that in mind, we look back a year on a scene in the summer following the starving, cannibal winter. It is August, when corn is ripening. The governor has been negotiating with Powhatan about some runaway Englishmen he is thought to be harboring. Powhatan returns "noe other than prowde and disdaynefull Answers," and so the governor sends George Percy "to take Revendge upon the Paspeheans and Chiconamians [Chickahominies]," the tribes closest to Jamestown. Percy, the brother of the Earl of Northumberland and the perennial second in command at Jamestown, takes a group of soldiers up the James a few miles by boat and then marches inland three miles to the principal town of the Paspaheghs. They fall upon the town, kill fifteen or sixteen Indians, and capture the queen of the tribe and her children.

Percy then has his men burn the houses and "cutt downe their Corne groweinge about the Towne." He takes the queen and her children back to his boats and embarks for Jamestown, but his men "begin to murmur becawse the quene and her Children weare spared." Percy therefore obliges them by throwing the children overboard "and shoteinge owtt their Braynes in the water." Meanwhile he sends another party under Captain James Davis to attack another Indian town (presumably a Chickahominy town), where again they cut down the corn and burn the houses. Upon returning to Jamestown, Percy hears that the governor is displeased that the queen of the Paspaheghs has been spared. Davis wants to burn her, but Percy, "haveinge seene so mutche Bloodshedd that day," insists that she merely be put to the sword. So she is led away and stabbed.

Thus the English, unable or unwilling to feed themselves, continually demanding corn from the Indians, take pains to destroy both the Indians and their corn.

One final scene. It is the spring of 1612, and Governor Dale is supervising the building of a fort at Henrico, near the present site of Richmond. He pauses to deal with some of his men, Englishmen, who have committed a serious crime.

It is not easy to make sense out of the behavior displayed in these episodes. How to explain the suicidal impulse that led the hungry English to destroy the corn that might have fed them and to commit atrocities upon the people who grew up? And how to account for the seeming unwillingness or incapacity of the English to feed themselves? Although they had invaded Indian territory and quarreled with the owners, the difficulty of obtaining land was not great. The Indians were no match for English weapons. Moreover, since the Indians could afford to give up the land around Jamestown as well as Henrico without seriously endangering their own economy, they made no concerted effort to drive the English out. Although Indian attacks may have prevented the English from getting a crop into the ground in time for a harvest in the fall of 1607, the occasional Indian raids thereafter cannot explain the English failure to grow food in succeeding years. How, then, can we account for it?

The answer that comes first to mind is the poor organization and direction of the colony. The government prescribed by the charter placed full powers in a council appointed by the king, with a president elected by the other members. The president had virtually no authority of his own; and while the council lasted, the members spent most of their time bickering and intriguing against one another and especially against the one man who had the experience and the assurance to take command. The names of the councillors had been kept secret (even from themselves) in a locked box, until the ships carrying the first settlers arrived in Virginia. By that time a bumptious young man named John Smith had made himself unpopular with Captain Christopher Newport (in command until their arrival) and with most of the other gentlemen of consequence aboard. When they opened the box, they were appalled to find Smith's name on the list of councillors. But during the next two years Smith's confidence in himself and his willingness to act while others talked overcame most of the handicaps imposed by the feeble frame of government. It was Smith who kept the colony going during those years. But in doing so he dealt more decisively with the Indians than with his own quarreling countrymen, and he gave an initial turn to the colony's Indian relations that was not quite what the company had intended.

Smith, the son of a yeoman, was a rare combination of actor and man of action. He had already won his spurs fighting against the Turks in Hungary, where, as he tells it, he won all the battles except the last, in which he was captured, enslaved, and then rescued by a fair princess. With her assistance he made his escape, then trekked across Europe and was back in England to join the Jamestown expedition at the age of twenty-seven. In spite of his youth, he may have had more experience than anyone else at Jamestown in making war, in living off the land, and in communicating with people whose language he did not know. Certainly he showed more aptitude than anyone else in all these matters. And it was probably his ability to deal with the Indians that prevented them from destroying or starving the settlement.

When the supplies ran out in the first autumn, Smith succeeded in trading with the Indians for corn. Then, on an exploring expedition up the Chickahominy River, he was made a prisoner and brought before Powhatan. This was the point at which another fair princess, Pocahontas, stepped in to save his life—or so Smith later told it; and in spite of the skepticism engendered by the larger-than-life view of himself that Smith always affected, there seems to be no good reason to doubt him. In any case, he returned unharmed; and while he remained in Virginia (until the fall of 1609), he conducted most of the colony's relations (both with Powhatan and with the tribes under Powhatan's dominion.

Smith took a keener interest in the Indians than anyone else in Virginia for a century to come. The astonishingly accurate map he made of the country shows the locations of the different tribes, and his writings give us most of the information we will ever have about them. But his interest in them was neither philanthropic nor philosophic. As he came to know them, he was convinced that they could be incorporated into the English settlement, but he scorned the notion that gentleness was the way to do it. Although Smith looks a little like a latter-day Drake or Hawkins, he did not see the Indians as Drake saw the Cimarrons. His own model seems to have been Hernando Cortez, and he would gladly have made Powhatan his Montezuma. He was disgusted when orders came from the company requiring that the settlers give the old chief a formal coronation, designed to make him a proper king, ally, and in some sense a vassal of King James. Smith witnessed the ceremony with undisguised contempt. Powhatan himself submitted with ill grace to the dignity thus thrust upon him and made it plain that he did not consider himself anybody's vassal and that he needed none of the proffered English assistance against his enemies.

Smith was sure that kindness was wasted on savages, and within weeks he was successfully bullying and browbeating Powhatan out of hundreds of bushels of corn. Years later, as he reflected in England on the frustrations that continued to beset Virginia, he was sure he had been right, that the Spanish had shown the way to deal with Indians. The English should have learned the lesson of how the Spanish "forced the treacherous and rebellious Infidels to doe all manner of drudgery worke and slavery for them, themselves living like Souldiers upon the fruits of their labours." John Smith's idea of the proper role of the Virginia Indians in English Virginia was something close to slavery. Given the superiority of English arms, he had no doubt of his ability to conquer the lot of them with a handful of men, just as Cortez had conquered the much more populous and formidable Aztecs. Once conquered, they could forthwith be put to work for their conquerors.

Smith was not afraid of work himself; and in the absence of Indian slaves he bent his efforts as much toward getting work out of Englishmen as he did toward supplying their deficiencies from Indian larders. In these first years many Englishmen perceived that the Indians had a satisfactory way of living without much work, and they slipped away "to live Idle among the Savages." Those who remained were so averse to any kind of labor, Smith reported, "that had they not beene forced nolens volens perforce to gather and prepare their victuall they would all have starved, and have eaten one another." While the governing council ruled, under the presidency of men of greater social prestige than Smith, he could make little headway against the jealousies and intrigues that greeted all his efforts to organize the people either for planting or for gathering food. But month by month other members of the council died or returned to England; and by the end of 1608 Smith was left in complete control. He divided the remaining settlers into work gangs and made them a little speech, in which he told them they could either work or starve: "Howsoever you have bin heretofore tolerated by the authoritie of the Councell from that I have often commanded you, yet seeing nowe the authoritie resteth wholly in my selfe; you must obay this for a law, that he that will not worke, shall not eate (except by sicknesse he be disabled)." He did not except himself from the rule and assured them that "every one that gathereth not every day as much as I doe, the next daie shall be set beyond the river, and for ever bee banished from the fort, and live there or starve." And lest this only produce a general exodus to the Indians, Smith used his influence with the neighboring tribes to apply the same discipline to any settler who dared choose that course. As a result, in the winter of 1608–9 he lost only seven or eight men.

Had Smith been left in charge, it is not impossible that he would have achieved a society which, in one way or another, would have included the Indians. They might have had a role not much better than the Spanish assigned them, and they might have died as rapidly as the Arawaks from disease and overwork. But it is unlikely that the grisly scenes already described would have taken place (they all occurred after his departure). In spite of his eagerness to subdue the Indians, Smith was in continual contact and communication with them. He bullied and threatened and browbeat them, but we do not read of any atrocities committed upon them under his direction, nor did he feel obliged to hang, break, or burn any Englishman who went off to live with them.

But the Virginia Company in 1609 was not yet ready to abandon its goal of making its own way in Virginia and sharing the country with the Indians on more favorable terms than Smith would have allowed them. The members of the council who returned to England complained of Smith's overbearing ways, with Englishmen as well as Indians. So the company decided not to leave the colony in the hands of so pushy a young man. At the same time, however, they recognized that the conciliar form of government was ineffective, and that a firmer authority was necessary to put their lazy colonists to work. They accordingly asked, and were given, a new charter, in which the king relinquished his government of the colony. Henceforth the company would have full control and would rule through a governor who would exercise absolute powers in the colony. He would be assisted by a council, but their advice would not be binding on him. In fact, he would be as much a military commander as a governor, and the whole enterprise would take on a more military character.

For the next eight or nine years whatever evils befell the colony were not the result of any diffusion of authority except when the appointed governor was absent—as happened when the first governor, Lord De la Warr, delayed his departure from England and his deputy, Sir Thomas Gates, was shipwrecked en route at Bermuda. The starving winter of 1609–10 occurred during this interval; but Gates arrived in May, 1610, followed by De la Warr himself in June. Thereafter Virginia was firmly governed under a clear set of laws, drafted by Gates and by De la Warr's subsequent deputy, Sir Thomas Dale. The so-called *Lawes Divine, Morall and Martiall* were mostly martial, and they set the colonists to work with military discipline and no pretense of gentle government. They prescribed that the settlers be divided into work gangs, much as Smith had divided them, each of which would proceed to its assigned tasks at regular hours. At the beating of a drum, the master of each gang would set them to work and "not suffer any of his company to be negligent, and idle, or depart from his worke" until another beat of the drums allowed it.

The *Laws* prescribed death for a variety of crimes, including rape, adultery, theft, lying, sacrilege, blasphemy, or doing or saying anything that might "tend to the derision" of the Bible. On a more practical level, in order to increase the livestock which had by this time been brought over, the *Laws* made it death to kill any domestic animal, even a chicken. It was also death, in weeding a garden, to take an ear of corn or a bunch of grapes from it, death too to trade privately with anyone on the ships that came to the colony. And the punishments were inflicted with an arbitrary rigor that became a scandal. For stealing two or three pints of oatmeal a man had a needle thrust through his tongue and was then chained to a tree until he starved.

The *Laws* did not even contemplate that the Indians would become a part of the English settlement. Though the company had frowned on Smith's swashbuckling way with Indians, it was disenchanted with Powhatan and convinced that he and those under his dominion did need to be dealt with more sternly. Sir Thomas Gates was instructed to get some Indian children to bring up in the English manner, free of their parents' evil influence. And he was also told to subjugate the neighboring tribes, to make them pay tribute, and to seize the chiefs of any that refused. If he wanted to make friends with any Indians, they must be "those that are farthest from you and enemies unto those amonge whom you dwell." The company's new attitude was incorporated in several provisions of the *Laws*. When Indians came to Jamestown to trade or visit, they were to be placed under guard to prevent them from stealing anything; no inhabitant was to speak to them without the governor's permission; and the settlers were forbidden on pain of death to "runne away from the Colonie, to Powhatan, or any savage Werowance else whatsoever." The company's desire to bring the Indians into the community had given way to an effort to keep settlers and Indians apart.

In their relations to the Indians, as in their rule of the settlers, the new governing officers of the colony were ruthless. The guerrilla raids that the two races conducted against each other became increasingly hideous, especially on the part of the English. Indians coming to Jamestown with food were treated as spies. Gates had them seized and killed "for a Terrour to the Reste to cawse them to desiste from their subtell practyses." Gates showed his own subtle practices by enticing the Indians at Kecoughtan (Point Comfort) to watch a display of dancing and drumming by one of his men and then "espyeinge a fitteinge oportunety fell in upon them putt fyve to the sworde wownded many others some of them beinge after fownde in the woods with Sutche extreordinary Lardge and mortall wownds that itt seemed strange they Cold flye so far." It is possible that the rank and file of settlers aggravated the bad relations with the Indians by unauthorized attacks, but unauthorized fraternization seems to have bothered the governors more. The atrocities committed against the queen of the Paspaheghs, though apparently demanded by the men, were the work of the governing officers, as were the atrocities committed against the Englishmen who fled to live with the Indians.

John Smith had not had his way in wishing to reduce the Indians to slavery, or something like it, on the Spanish model. But the policy of his successors, though perhaps not with company approval, made Virginia look far more like the Hispaniola of Las Casas than it did when Smith was in charge. And the company and the colony had few benefits to show for all the rigor. At the end of ten years, in spite of the military discipline of work gangs, the colonists were still not growing enough to feed themselves and were still begging, bullying, and buying corn from the Indians whose lands they scorched so deliberately. We cannot, it seems, blame the colony's failures on lax discipline and diffusion of authority. Failures continued and atrocities multiplied after authority was made absolute and concentrated in one man.

Another explanation, often advanced, for Virginia's early troubles, and especially for its failure to feed itself, is the collective organization of labor in the colony. All the settlers were expected to work together in a single community effort, to produce both their food and the exports that would make the company rich. Those who held shares would ultimately get part of the profits, but meanwhile the incentives of private enterprise were lacking. The work a man did bore no direct relation to his reward. The laggard would receive as large a share in the end as the man who worked hard.

The communal production of food seems to have been somewhat modified after the reorganization of 1609 by the assignment of small amounts of land to individuals for private gardens. It is not clear who received such allotments, perhaps only those who came at their own expense. Men who came at company expense may have been expected to continue working exclusively for the common stock until their seven-year terms expired. At any rate, in 1614, the year when the first shipment of company men concluded their service, Governor Dale apparently assigned private allotments to them and to other independent "farmers." Each man got three acres, or twelve acres if he had a family. He was responsible for growing his own food plus two and a half barrels of corn annually for the company as a supply for newcomers to tide them over the first year. And henceforth each "farmer" would work for the company only one month a year.

By this time Gates and Dale had succeeded in planting settlements at several points along the James as high up as Henrico, just below the falls. The many close-spaced tributary rivers and creeks made it possible to throw up a palisade between two of them to make a small fortified peninsula. Within the space thus enclosed by water on three sides and palisaded on the fourth, the settlers could build their houses, dig their gardens, and pasture their cattle. It was within these enclaves that Dale parceled out private allotments. They were affirmations of an expectation that would linger for a century, that Virginia was about to become the site of thriving cities and towns. In point of fact, the new "cities" scarcely matched in size the tiny villages from which Powhatan's people threatened them. And the "farmers" who huddled together on the allotments assigned to them proved incapable of supporting themselves or the colony with adequate supplies of food.

According to John Rolfe, a settler who had married John Smith's fair Pocahontas, the switch to private enterprise transformed the colony's food deficit instantly to a surplus: instead of the settlers seeking corn from the Indians, the Indians sought it from them. If so, the situation did not last long. Governor Samuel Argall, who took charge at the end of May, 1617, bought 600 bushels from the Indians that fall, "which did greatly relieve the whole Colonie." And when Governor George Yeardley relieved Argall in April, 1619, he found the colony "in a great scarcity for want of corn" and made immediate preparations to seek it from the Indians. If, then, the colony's failure to grow food arose from its communal organization of production, the failure was not overcome by the switch to private enterprise.

Still another explanation for the improvidence of Virginia's pioneers is one that John Smith often emphasized, namely, the character of the immigrants. They were certainly an odd assortment, for the most conspicuous group among them was an extraordinary number of gentlemen. Virginia, as a patriotic enterprise, had excited the imagination of England's nobility and gentry. The shareholders included 32 present or future earls, 4 countesses, and 3 viscounts (all members of the nobility) as well as hundreds of lesser gentlemen, some of them perhaps retainers of the larger men. Not all were content to risk only their money. Of the 105 settlers who started the colony, 36 could be classified as gentlemen. In the first "supply" of 120 additional settlers, 28 were gentlemen, and in the second supply of 70, again 28 were gentlemen. These numbers gave Virginia's population about six times as large a proportion of gentlemen as England had.

Gentlemen, by definition, had no manual skill, nor could they be expected to work at ordinary labor. They were supposed to be useful for "the force of knowledge, the exercise of counsell"; but to have ninety-odd wise men offering advice while a couple of hundred did the work was inauspicious, especially when the wise men included "many unruly gallants packed thether by their friends to escape il destinies" at home.

What was worse, the gentlemen were apparently accompanied by the personal attendants that gentlemen thought necessary to make life bearable even in England. The colony's laborers "were for most part footmen, and such as they that were Adventurers brought to attend them, or such as they could perswade to goe with them, that never did know what a dayes worke was." Smith complained that he could never get any real work from more than thirty out of two hundred, and he later argued that of all the people sent to Virginia, a hundred good laborers "would have done more than a thousand of those that went."

The company may actually have had little choice in allowing gentlemen and their servants to make so large a number of their settlers. The gentlemen were paying their own way, and the company perhaps could not afford to deny them. But even if unencumbered by these volunteers, the colony might have foundered on the kind of settlers that the company itself did want to send. What the company wanted for Virginia was a variety of craftsmen. Richard Hakluyt had made up a list for Walter Raleigh that suggests the degree of specialization contemplated in an infant settlement: Hakluyt wanted both carpenters and joiners, tallow chandlers and wax chandlers, bowstave preparers and bowyers, fletchers and arrowhead makers, men to rough-hew pikestaffs and other men to finish them. In 1610 and again in 1611 the Virginia Company published lists of the kind of workers it wanted. Some were for building, making tools, and other jobs needed to keep the settlers alive, but the purpose of staying alive would be to see just what Virginia was good for and then start sending the goods back to England. Everybody hoped for gold and silver and jewels, so the colony needed refiners and mineral men. But they might have to settle for iron, so send men with all the skills needed to smelt it. The silk grass that Hariot described might produce something like silk, and there were native mulberry trees for growing worms, so send silk dressers. Sturgeon swam in the rivers, so send men who knew how to make caviar. And so on. Since not all the needed skills for Virginia's potential products were to be found in England, the company sought them abroad: glassmakers from Italy, millwrights from Holland, pitch boilers from Poland, vine dressers and saltmakers from France. The settlers of Virginia were expected to create a more complex, more varied economy than England itself possessed. As an extension of England, the colony would impart its variety and health to the mother country.

If the company had succeeded in filling the early ships for Virginia with as great a variety of specialized craftsmen as it wanted, the results might conceivably have been worse than they were. We have already noticed the effect of specialization in England itself, where the division of labor had become a source not of efficiency but of idleness. In Virginia the effect was magnified. Among the skilled men who started the settlement in 1607 were four carpenters, two bricklayers, one mason (apparently a higher skill than bricklaying), a blacksmith, a tailor, and a barber. The first "supply" in 1608 had six tailors, two goldsmiths, two refiners, two apothecaries, a blacksmith, a gunner (i.e., gunsmith?), a cooper, a tobacco pipe maker, a jeweler, and a perfumer. There were doubtless others, and being skilled they expected to be paid and fed for doing the kind of work for which they had been hired. Some were obviously useful. But others may have found themselves without means to use their special talents. If they were conscientious, the jeweler may have spent some time looking for jewels, the goldsmiths for gold, the perfumer for something to make perfume with. But when the search proved futile, it did not follow that they should or would exercise their skilled hands at any other tasks. It was not suitable for a perfumer or a jeweler or a goldsmith to put his hand to the hoe. Rather, they could join the gentlemen in genteel loafing while a handful of ordinary laborers worked at the ordinary labor of growing and gathering food.

The laborers could be required to work at whatever they were told to; but they were, by all accounts, too few and too feeble. The company may have rounded them up as it did in 1609 when it appealed to the mayor of London to rid the city of its "swarme of unnecessary inmates" by sending to Virginia any who were destitute and lying in the streets.

The company, then, partly by choice, partly by necessity, sent to the colony an oversupply of men who were not prepared to tackle the work essential to settling in a wilderness. In choosing prospective Virginians, the company did not look for men who would be particularly qualified to keep themselves alive in a new land. The company never considered the problem of staying alive in Virginia to be a serious one. And why should they have? England's swarming population had had ample experience in moving to new areas and staying alive. The people who drifted north and west into the pasture-farming areas got along, and the lands there were marginal, far poorer than those that awaited the settlers of tidewater Virginia. Though there may have been some farmers among the early settlers, no one for whom an occupation is given was listed as a husbandman or yeoman. And though thirty husbandmen were included in the 1611 list of men wanted, few came. As late as 1620 the colony reported "a great scarcity, or none at all" of "husbandmen truely bred," by which was meant farmers from the arable regions. In spite of the experience at Roanoke and in spite of the repeated starving times at Jamestown, the company simply did not envisage the provision of food as a serious problem. They sent some food supplies with every ship but never enough to last more than a few months. After that people should be able to do for themselves.

The colonists were apparently expected to live from the land like England's woodland and pasture people, who gave only small amounts of time to their small garden plots, cattle, and sheep and spent the rest in spinning, weaving, mining, handicrafts, and loafing. Virginians would spend their time on the more varied commodities of the New World. To enable them to live in this manner, the company sent cattle, swine, and sheep: and when Dale assigned them private plots of land, the plots were small, in keeping with the expectation that they would not spend much time at farming. The company never intended the colony to supply England with grain and did not even expect that agricultural products might be its principal exports. They did want to give sugar, silk, and wine a try, but most of the skills they sought showed an expectation of setting up extractive industries such as iron mining, smelting, saltmaking, pitch making, and glassmaking. The major part of the colonists' work time was supposed to be devoted to processing the promised riches of the land for export; and with the establishment of martial law the company had the means of seeing that they put their shoulders to the task.

Unfortunately, the persons charged with directing the motley work force had a problem, quite apart from the overload of gentlemen and specialized craftsmen they had to contend with. During the early years of the colony they could find no riches to extract. They sent back some cedar wood, but lumber was too bulky a product to bear the cost of such long transportation to market. Sassafras was available in such quantities that the market for it quickly collapsed. The refiners found no gold or silver or even enough iron to be worth mining. Silk grass and silk proved to be a will-o'-the-wisp.

The result was a situation that taxed the patience both of the leaders and of the men they supervised. They had all come to Virginia with high expectations. Those who came as servants of the company had seven years in which to make their employers rich. After that they would be free to make themselves rich. But with no prospect of riches in sight for anybody, it was difficult to keep them even at the simple tasks required for staying alive or to find anything else for them to do.

The predicament of those in charge is reflected in the hours of work they prescribed for the colonists, which contrast sharply with those specified in the English Statute of Artificers. There was no point in demanding dawn-to-dusk toil unless there was work worth doing. When John Smith demanded that men work or starve, how much work did he demand? By his own account, "4 hours each day was spent in worke, the rest in pastimes and merry exercise." The governors who took charge after the reorganization of 1609 were equally modest in their demands.

To have grown enough corn to feed the colony would have required only a fraction of the brief working time specified, yet it was not grown. Even in their free time men shunned the simple planting tasks that sufficed for the Indians. And the very fact that the Indians did grow corn may be one more reason why the colonists did not. For the Indians presented a challenge that Englishmen were not prepared to meet, a challenge to their image of themselves, to their self-esteem, to their conviction of their own superiority over foreigners, and especially over barbarous foreigners like the Irish and the Indians.

If you were a colonist, you knew that your technology was superior to the Indians'. You knew that you were civilized, and they were savages. It was evident in your firearms, your clothing, your housing, your government, your religion. The Indians were supposed to be overcome with admiration and to join you in extracting riches from the country. But your superior technology had proved insufficient to extract anything. The Indians, keeping to themselves, laughed at your superior methods and lived from the land more abundantly and with less labor than you did. They even furnished you with the food that you somehow did not get around to growing enough of yourselves. To be thus condescended to by heathen savages was intolerable. And when your own people started deserting in order to live with them, it was too much. If it came to that, the whole enterprise of Virginia would be over. So you killed the Indians, tortured them, burned their villages, burned their cornfields. It proved your superiority in spite of your failures. And you gave similar treatment to any of your own people who succumbed to the savage way of life. But you still did not grow much corn. That was not what you had come to Virginia for.

By the time the colony was ten years old and an almost total loss to the men who had invested their lives and fortunes in it, only one ray of hope had appeared. It had been known, from the Roanoke experience, that the Indians grew and smoked a kind of tobacco; and tobacco grown in the Spanish West Indies was already being imported into England, where it sold at eighteen shillings a pound. Virginia tobacco had proved, like everything else, a disappointment; but one of the settlers, John Rolfe, tried some seeds of the West Indian variety, and the result was much better. The colonists stopped bowling in the streets and planted tobacco in them—and everywhere else that they could find open land. In 1617, ten years after the first landing at Jamestown, they shipped their first cargo to England. It was not up to Spanish tobacco, but it sold at three shillings a pound.

To the members of the company it was proof that they had been right in their estimate of the colony's potential. But the proof was bitter. Tobacco had at first been accepted as a medicine, good for a great variety of ailments. But what gave it its high price was the fact that people had started smoking it for fun. Used this way it was considered harmful and faintly immoral. People smoked it in taverns and brothels. Was Virginia to supplement England's economy and redeem her rogues by pandering to a new vice? The answer, of course, was yes. But the men who ran the Virginia Company, still aiming at ends of a higher nature, were not yet ready to take yes for an answer.

The American Revolution

No event in the history of the United States is more surrounded by patriotic mythology than the American Revolution. Traditionally we have been told that:

> In America a new people had risen up without King or princes . . . knowing nothing of titles and little of landlords, the plough being for the most part in the hands of free holders of the soil. They were sincerely religious, better educated, of serener minds and of purer morals than the men of any former republic. (Words of George Bancroft from E. Wright, CAUSES AND CONSEQUENCES, p. 23).

These virtuous, "new people", so the story goes, in a single-minded, united effort marched to expel the tyrannical British in the name of self-determination, liberty, equality, and justice for all. The Founding Fathers who engineered this great movement were not mere politicians but unselfish patriots of exceptional talent, foresight, and compassion. Epitomized by George Washington, the Founders opposed the British at great personal risk for the benefit of liberty-loving Americans whose freedom was jeopardized by the sword of British dictatorship. Following logically from the Revolution, according to this tradition, came the federal constitution, guaranteeing free government and equality for everyone. As the following articles attempt to demonstrate, this highly romantic view of the Revolution may not be credible. Modern objective scholarship has presented a more complex and more plausible look at these important events.

Gordon Wood's article "Republicanism As a Revolutionary Ideology" sees political theory as the locomotive force behind the Revolution. Behind Wood's thesis is the question of what made the average American rise up in rebellion against the British. After all, despite what may have been said about George III's administration, evidence that the British fundamentally circumscribed the traditional freedoms and privileges of the colonial masses was lacking. According to Wood, the Revolution rested upon the belief in republican ideology. As this article explains, colonial political leaders argued that if the British were expelled, American society would somehow be free to realize a utopian republican goal which involved not merely a change in government but a change in American character and social relations. In short, Wood argues that the Revolution has less to do with the injustices of British rule (no taxation without representation) than with the inexorable ambitions of a politicized section of American society concerned with regenerating colonial life with a spirit of republican virtue.

The next article is James Kirby Martin's revealing look inside the Continental Army. "A Most Undisciplined, Profligate Crew: Protest and Defiance in the Continental Ranks, 1776 to 1783" clearly disproves the old myth that the colonial military effort was united, enthusiastic, and resolute. Martin shows us an army of severely underpaid and disgruntled officers, line mutinies in several states, insensitive state legislatures, an uncaring populace, bounty jumping, soldiers forced to loot to survive, and so on. Under these circumstances the old question of how the colonies managed to emerge victorious from the war again becomes relevant.

The final article in this section is Broadus Mitchell's "The War Within". Concerning himself with the differences between the revolutionaries and the Loyalists, Mitchell reveals a society with deep internal divisions equally as distressing as the formal war. Not only were the colonists at war with Great Britain but, as often happens in a revolutionary crisis, American society was also involved in a bitter civil war. What these two sides of colonial society meant to the 30% of American society who remained indifferent to the conflict and the Revolution, how deep their differences ran, and what the longer term consequences of this division were are the kinds of issues with which Mitchell is concerned. Not only is this selection revealing as it demonstrates the degree to which colonial society was racked by this split, but it also offers important insights into how early American society dealt with the thorny problem of how to treat a substantial dissenting group.

A "Most Undisciplined, Profligate Crew":
Protest and Defiance in the Continental Ranks, 1776–1783

James Kirby Martin

A sequence of events inconceivable to Americans raised on patriotic myths about the Revolution occurred in New Jersey during the spring of 1779. For months the officers of the Jersey brigade had been complaining loudly about everything from lack of decent food and clothing to pay arrears and late payments in rapidly depreciating currency. They had petitioned their assembly earlier, but nothing had happened. They petitioned again. Using "the most plain and unambiguous terms," they stressed that "unless a speedy and ample remedy be provided, the total dissolution of your troops is inevitable." The Jersey assembly forwarded the petition to the Continental Congress without comment. After all, the officers, although from New Jersey, were a part of the Continental military establishment.

The assembly's behavior only further angered the officers, and some of them decided to demonstrate their resolve. On May 6 the brigade received orders to join John Sullivan's expedition against the Six Nations. That same day, officers in the First Regiment sent forth yet another petition. They again admonished the assembly about pay and supply issues. While they stated that they would prepare the regiment for the upcoming campaign, they themselves would resign as a group unless the legislators addressed their demands. Complaints had now turned into something more than gentlemanly protest. Protest was on the verge of becoming nothing less than open defiance of civil authority.

When George Washington learned about the situation, he was appalled. "Nothing, which has happened in the course of the war, . . . has given me so much pain." It upset him that the officers seemingly had lost sight of the "principles" that governed the cause. What would happen, he asked rhetorically, "if their example should be followed and become general?" The result would be the "ruin" and "disgrace" of the rebel cause, all because these officers had *"reasoned wrong about the means of obtaining a good end."*

From R. Hoffman and P. J. Albert, editors: ARMS AND INDEPENDENCE. Copyright © 1984 by University of Virginia Press, Charlottesville, Virginia. Reprinted with permission.

So developed a little known but highly revealing confrontation. Washington told Congress that "the causes of discontent are too great and too general and the ties that bind the officers to the service too feeble" to force the issue. What he did promise was that he would not countenance any aid that came "in [such] a manner extorted. On the other hand, the officers had been asking the assembly for relief since January 1778, but to no avail. They, too, were not about to be moved.

The New Jersey legislature was the political institution with the ability to break the deadlock. Some of the legislators preferred disbanding the brigade. The majority argued that other officers and common soldiers might follow the First Regiment's lead and warned that the war effort could hardly succeed without a Continental military establishment. The moment was now ripe for compromise. The assemblymen agreed to provide the officers with whatever immediate relief could be mustered in return for the latter calling back their petitions. That way civil authorities would not be succumbing to intimidation by representatives of the military establishment, and the principle of subordination of military to civil authority would remain inviolate. The assembly thus provided an immediate payment of £200 to each officer and $40 to each soldier. Accepting the compromise settlement as better than nothing, the brigade moved out of its Jersey encampment on May 11 and marched toward Sullivan's bivouac at Easton, Pennsylvania. Seemingly, all now had returned to normal.

The confrontation between the New Jersey officers and the state assembly serves to illuminate some key points about protest and defiance in the Continental ranks during the years 1776–83. Most important here, it underscores the mounting anger felt by Washington's regulars as a result of their perceived (and no doubt very real) lack of material and psychological support from the society that had spawned the Continental army. It is common knowledge that Washington's regulars suffered from serious supply and pay shortages throughout the war. Increasingly, historians are coming to realize that officers and common soldiers alike received very little moral support from the general populace. As yet, however, scholars have not taken a systematic look at one product of this paradigm of neglect, specifically, protest and defiance. The purpose of this essay is to present preliminary findings that will facilitate that task.

A second purpose of this essay is to outline those basic patterns of protest and to indicate why protest and defiance did not result in serious internal upheaval between army and society.

During the past twenty years, historians have learned that there were at least two Continental armies. The army of 1775–76 might be characterized as a republican constabulary, consisting of citizens who had respectable amounts of property and who were defending hearth and home. They came out for what they believed would be a rather short contest in which their assumed virtue and moral commitment would easily carry the day over seasoned British regulars not necessarily wedded to anything of greater concern than filling their own pocketbooks as mercenaries.

The first army had a militialike appearance. There was not much discipline or rigorous training. These early soldiers had responded to appeals from leaders who warned about "our wives and children, with everything that is dear to us, [being] subjected to the merciless range of uncontrolled despotism." They were convinced that they were "engaged . . . in the cause of virtue, of liberty, of *God*." Unfortunately, the crushing blows endured in the massive British offensive of 1776 against New York undercut such high-sounding phrases about self-sacrifice. The message at the end of 1775 had been "Persevere, ye guardians of liberty." They did not.

The second Continental establishment took form out of the remains of the first. Even before Washington executed his magnificent turnabout at Trenton and Princeton, he had called for a "respectable army," one built on long-term enlistments, thorough training, and high standards of discipline. The army's command, as well as many delegates in Congress, now wanted soldiers who could stand up against the enemy with more than notions of exalted virtue and moral superiority to upgird them. They called for able-bodied men who could and would endure for the long-term fight in a contest that all leaders now knew could not be sustained by feelings of moral superiority and righteousness alone.

To assist in overcoming manpower shortages, Congress and the states enhanced financial promises made to potential enlistees. Besides guarantees about decent food and clothing, recruiters handed out bounty moneys and promises of free land at war's end (normally only for long-term service). Despite these financial incentives, there was no great rush to the Continental banner. For the remainder of the war, the army's command, Congress, and the states struggled to maintain minimal numbers of Continental soldiers in the ranks.

In fact, all began to search diligently for new recruits. Instead of relying on propertied freeholders and tradesmen of the ideal citizen-soldier type, they broadened the definition of what constituted an "able-bodied and effective" recruit. For example, New Jersey in early 1777 started granting exemptions to all those who hired substitutes for long-term Continental service—and to masters who would enroll indentured servants and slaves. The following year Maryland permitted the virtual impressment of vagrants for nine months of regular service. Massachusetts set another kind of precedent in 1777 by declaring blacks (both slave and free) eligible for the state draft. Shortly thereafter, Rhode Islanders set about the business of raising two black battalions.

The vast majority of Continentals who fought with Washington after 1776 were representative of the very poorest and most repressed persons in Revolutionary society. A number of recent studies have verified that a large proportion of the Continentals in the second establishment represented ne'er-do-wells, drifters, unemployed laborers, captured British soldiers and Hessians, indentured servants, and slaves. Some of these new regulars were in such desperate economic straits that states had to pass laws prohibiting creditors from pulling them from the ranks and having them thrown in jail for petty debts. (Obviously, this was not a problem with the unfree.)

The most important point to be derived from this dramatic shift in the social composition of the Continental army is that few of these new common soldiers had enjoyed anything close to economic prosperity or full political (or legal) liberty before the war. As a group, they had something to gain from service. If they could survive the rigors of camp life, the killing diseases that so often ravaged the armies of their times, and the carnage of skirmishes and full-scale battles, they could look forward to a better life for themselves at the end of the war. Not only were they to have decent food and clothing and regular pay until the British had been irrevocably beaten, they had also been promised free land (and personal freedom in the cases of indentured servants, black slaves, and criminals). Recruiters thus conveyed a message of personal upward mobility through service. In exchange for personal sacrifice in the short run, there was the prospect of something far better in the long run, paralleling and epitomizing the collective rebel quest for a freer political life in the New World.

To debate whether these new Continentals were motivated to enlist because of crass materialism or benevolent patriotism is to sidetrack the issue. A combination of factors was no doubt at work in the mind of each recruit or conscript. Far more important, especially if we are to comprehend the ramifications of protest and defiance among soldiers and officers, we must understand that respectably established citizens after 1775 and 1776 preferred to let others perform the dirty work of regular, long-term service on their behalf, essentially on a contractual basis. Their legislators gave bounties and *promised* many other incentives. Increasingly, as the war lengthened, the civilian population and its leaders did a less effective job in keeping their part of the agreement. One significant outcome of this obvious civilian ingratitude was protest and defiance coming from Washington's beleaguered soldiers and officers.

That relations between Washington's post-1776 army and Revolutionary society deteriorated dramatically hardly comes as a surprise to those historians who have investigated surviving records. Widespread anger among the rank and file became most demonstrable in 1779 and 1780, at the very nadir of the war effort. Gen. John Paterson, who spoke out in March 1780, summarized feelings among many officers when he said, "It really gives me great pain to think of our public affairs; where is the public spirit of the year 1775? Where are those flaming *patriots* who were ready to sacrifice their lives, their fortunes, their all, for the public?" These statements indicate that the army had come to believe that Revolutionary civilians had taken advantage of them—and had broken their part of the contract for military services.

There were real dangers hidden behind these words. With each passing month beginning in 1777, Washington's regulars, especially that small cadre that was signing on for the long-term fight, became more professional in military demeanor. Among other things, the immediate thoughts of individual soldiers, whether recruited, dragooned, or pressed into service, became attached to their respective primary units in the army, such as the particular companies or regiments in which they served. The phenomenon was nothing more than a developing comradeship in arms. Any threat or insult thus became an assault on the group. The bonding effect of unit cohesion suggests that collective protest and defiance would become more of a danger to a generally unsupportive society with each passing month, unless civilians who had made grand promises started to meet their contractual obligations more effectively.

Indeed, the most readily observable pattern in Continental army protest and defiance was that it took on more and more of a collective (and menacing) character through time. At the outset, especially beginning in 1776, most protest had an individual character. Frequently it was the raw recruit, quite often anxious for martial glory but quickly dissillusioned with the realities of military service once in camp, who struck back against undesirable circumstances. Protest could come through such diverse expressions as swearing, excessive drinking, assaulting officers, deserting, or bounty jumping. One source of such behavior was the dehumanizing, even brutal nature of camp life. Another had to do with broken promises about pay, food, and clothing. A third was a dawning sense that too many civilians held the soldiery in disregard, if not utter contempt.

It must be remembered that middle- and upper-class civilians considered Washington's new regulars to be representative of the "vulgar herd" in a society that still clung to deferential values. The assumption was that the most fit in terms of wealth and community social standing were to lead while the least fit were to follow, even when that meant becoming little more than human cannon fodder. Perhaps James Warren of Massachusetts summarized the social perceptions of "respectable" citizens as well as any of the "better sort" when he described Washington's troops in 1776 as "the most undisciplined, profligate Crew that were ever collected" to fight a war.

While civilians often ridiculed the new regulars as riffraff, troublemakers, or mere hirelings (while conveniently ignoring the precept that military service was an assumed obligation of all citizens in a liberty-loving commonwealth), individual soldiers did not hold back in protesting their circumstances. In many cases, they had already acknowledged the personal reality of downtrodden status before entering the ranks. Acceptance of these circumstances and the conditions of camp life did not mean, however, that these new soldiers would be passive. Thus it may be an error to dismiss heavy swearing around civilians or repeated drunkenness in camp as nothing more than manifestations of "time-honored military vices," to borrow the words of one recent student of the war period.

Only over time did individual acts of protest take on a more collective character. That transition may be better comprehended by considering the phenomenon of desertion. While it is true that a great many soldiers did not think of desertion as a specific form of protest, they fled the ranks with greater frequency when food and clothing were in very short supply or nonexistent, as at Valley Forge. However, primary unit cohesion worked to militate against unusually high desertion levels. Sustained involvement with a company or regiment reduced the likelihood of desertion. Hence as soldiers came to know, trust, and depend upon one another, and as they gained confidence in comrades and felt personally vital to the long-term welfare of their primary group, they were much less likely to lodge a statement of individual protest through such individualized forms as desertion.

The first few days and weeks in the ranks were those in which these poor and desperate new regulars asked themselves whether vague promises of a better lot in life for everyone, including themselves, in a postwar republican polity was worth the sacrifice now being demanded. Many enlistees and conscripts concluded that it was not, and they fled. Since they had little proof that they could trust the civilian population and its leaders, they chose to express their defiance through desertion. Unit cohesion, in turn, helped sustain those who read the equation differently, and it eased the pain of enduring a long war in return for the remote prospect of greater personal freedom, opportunity, and prosperity.

Then there were those individuals who neither deserted nor became hardcore regulars. By and large, this group defied civil and military authority through the practice of bounty jumping. The procedure, which Washington once referred to as "a kind of business" involved enlisting, getting a bounty, and deserting, then repeating the same process with another recruiting agent in another location. Some of the most resourceful bounty jumpers got away with this maneuver seven, eight, or even nine times, if not more.

Bounty jumping was invariably the act of protesting individuals; looting and plundering (like desertion) combined individual with collective protest. Certainly there were numerous occasions when hungry soldiers looted by themselves. Just as often, groups of starving men "borrowed" goods from civilians. Even before the second establishment took form, looting had become a serious problem. One sergeant, for example, described how he and his comrades, searching desperately for food, "liberated" some geese belonging to a local farmer in 1776 and devoured them "Hearty in the Cause of Liberty of taking what Came to their Hand."

Above all else, two patterns stand out with respect to common soldier protest. First, as the war effort lengthened, defiance became more of a collective phenomenon. Second, such protest had a controlled quality. While there was unremitting resentment toward civilians who were invariably perceived as insensitive and unsupportive, protest rarely metamorphosed into wanton violence and mindless destruction. Soldiers looted and pillaged, but they rarely maimed, raped, or murdered civilians. Pvt. Joseph Plumb Martin attempted to explain why. Even though "the monster Hunger, . . . attended us," he wrote, and the new regulars "had borne as long as human nature could endure, and to bear longer we considered folly," he insisted that his comrades had become, in the end, "truly patriotic." They were persons who "loved their country, and they had already suffered everything short of death in its cause." The question by 1779 and 1780 was whether these hardened, cohesive veterans would be willing to endure even more privation.

In reflecting positively on the loyalty of his comrades, Martin was commenting on a near mutiny of the Connecticut Line in 1780. Indeed, the specter of collective defiance in the form of line mutinies had come close to reality with the near insubordination of the New Jersey officers in 1779. They had not demonstrated in the field, but they had made it clear that conditions in the army were all but intolerable—and that civil society, when desperate to maintain a regular force in arms, could be persuaded to concede on basic demands. Washington had used the phrase "extorted"; he had also pointed out that, "notwithstanding the expedient adopted for a saving appearances," this confrontation "cannot fail to operate as a bad precedent."

Among long-term veterans, anger was beginning to overwhelm discipline. There had been small-scale mutinies before, such as the rising of newly recruited Continentals at Halifax, North Carolina, in February 1776. In 1779 Rhode Island and Connecticut regiments threatened mutinies, but nothing came of these incidents. Then in 1780 another near uprising of the Connecticut Line occurred. Invariably, the issues had the same familiar ring: lack of adequate civilian support as demonstrated by rotten food, inadequate clothing, and worthless pay (when pay was available). On occasion, too, the heavy hand of company- and field-grade officers played its part. The near mutiny of the Connecticut Line in 1780 had been avoided by a fortuitous shipment of cattle and by promises from trusted officers of better treatment. In the end, the Connecticut Line calmed itself down, according to Martin, because the soldiery was "unwilling to desert the cause of our country, when in distress." Nevertheless, he explained that "we knew her cause involved our own, but what signified our perishing in the act of saving her, when that very act would inevitably destroy us, and she must finally perish with us."

By the end of 1780, there were some veterans who would have disputed Martin's reasoning. They had all but given up, let come what might for the glorious cause. On January 1, 1781, the Pennsylvania Line proved that point.

Suffering through yet another harsh winter near Morristown, New Jersey, the Pennsylvanians mutinied. Some one thousand determined comrades in arms (about 15 percent of the manpower available to Washington) ostensibly wanted nothing more to do with fighting the war. On a prearranged signal, the Pennsylvanians paraded under arms, seized their artillery, and marched south toward Princeton, their ultimate target being Philadelphia. These veterans had had their fill of broken promises, of the unfulfilled contract. They maintained that they had signed on for three years, not for the duration. If they were to stay in the ranks, then they wanted the same benefits (additional bounty payments, more free land, and some pay in specie) that newer enlistees had obtained.

Formal military discipline collapsed as the officers trying to contain the mutineers were brushed aside. The soldiers killed one and wounded two other officers, yet their popular commander, Anthony Wayne, trailed along, attempting to appeal to their sense of patriotism. Speaking through a committee of sergeants, the soldiers assured Wayne and the other officers that they were still loyal to the cause, and they proved it by handing over two spies that Sir Henry Clinton had sent out from New York to monitor the situation. Moreover, the mutineers, despite their anger and bitterness, behaved themselves along their route and did not unnecessarily intimidate civilians who got in their way.

Later checking demonstrated that many of the mutineers were duration enlistees, yet that was a moot point. When the soldiers reached Trenton, representatives of Congress and the Pennsylvania government negotiated with them and agreed to discharge any veteran claiming three years in rank. Also, they offered back pay and new clothing along with immunity from prosecution for having defied their officers in leaving their posts. Once formally discharged, the bulk of the mutineers reenlisted for a new bounty. By late January 1781 the Pennsylvania Line was once more a functioning part of the Continental army.

These mutineers won because Washington was in desperate need of manpower and because they had resorted to collective defiance, not because their society wanted to address what had been grievances based on the contract for service. Unlike their officers, who had just won a major victory in driving for half-pay pensions, they were not in a position to lobby before Congress. Hence they employed one of the most threatening weapons in their arsenal, collective protest against civil authority, but only after less extreme measures had failed to satisfy their claims for financial justice. They were certainly not planning to overthrow any government or to foment an internal social revolution against better-placed members of their society. They had staked their hopes on a better life in the postwar period and had already risked their lives many times for the proposed republican polity. All told, the extreme nature of this mutiny demonstrated, paradoxically, both that Washington's long-term Continentals were the most loyal and dedicated republican citizens in the new nation, and that they were dangerously close to repudiating a dream that far too often had been a personal nightmare because of the realities of societal support and of service in the Continental army.

More worrisome in January 1781 than the matter of appropriate appreciation of the soldiers' actions was whether this mutiny, and its stillborn predecessors, would trigger further turbulence in the ranks. Also camped near Morristown during the winter of 1780–81 were veteran soldiers of the New Jersey Line. Their officers were aware that the Jersey regulars sympathized with the Pennsylvanians and had been in constant communication with them. Then, on January 20, 1781, the New Jersey Line, having witnessed the success of its comrades, also mutinied. The soldiers had each recently received $5 in specie as a token toward long overdue pay, but they were bothered by the better bounties and terms of enlistment offered newer recruits. Their leaders urged them on by shouting: "Let us go to Congress who have money and rum enough but won't give it to us!"

Within a few days, the Jersey Line had won acceptable concessions and was back under control. Washington, however, had decided that enough was enough. "Unless this dangerous spirit can be suppressed by force," he wrote to Congress, "there is an end to all subordination in the Army, and indeed to the Army itself." To back up his strong words, the commander ordered Gen. Robert Howe and about five hundred New England troops near West Point to march to the Jersey camp at Pompton to make sure that the mutineers were back in line and summarily to execute the most notorious leaders. Howe did as instructed. He reached Pompton on January 27, three days after grievances had been redressed. Deploying his men around the campsite just before dawn, Howe caught the Jersey soldiers off guard. He ordered them to fall in without arms, then singled out three ringleaders and ordered their summary execution, to be shot to death by nine of their comrades. A Jersey officer intervened in one case, but the other two were put to death by firing squad.

It was a brutal ending for men who had dreamed of a better future despite all of society's violations of the contract. Perhaps because of the calculated coldheartedness of Washington's orders, or perhaps because the war picture began to brighten in 1781, there were no major uprisings among Washington's regulars after the mutiny of the New Jersey Line. Then again, the soldiery may have been too worn down physically and mentally to continue their protest and defiance in the name of financial justice, humane treatment, and psychological support.

An important question that must be raised in conclusion has to do with political perceptions and fears: given real concerns in Revolutionary society that a regular army could obtain too much power, could corrupt the political system, and could threaten the civilian sector with some form of tyranny, such as a military dictatorship, why did officers and soldiers never unite effectively and put maximum pressure on the frail Revolutionary political structure by protesting in unison? They could have easily played on fears of a coup. But about the closest such union was the Jersey officers' defiance of 1779. Thus, while common soldiers got drunk, deserted, looted, or mutinied, officers pursued their own (and largely separate) avenues of protest. This is curious, especially since the officers too worried about the personal financial cost of service; they too came to resent civilian indifference, ineptitude, and greed; and they too were dismayed over society's inability to treat them with respect. They feared that their virtuous behavior and self-sacrifice would go unappreciated if not completely unrecognized and unrewarded. Having so much in common with their brethren in the rank and file, then, it is worth considering why the officers almost never aligned with them. For if they had, the alliance might have been powerful enough to have fomented something truly menacing to the vitals of Revolutionary society.

The officer corps developed its own forms of protest, and the pattern paralleled that of the common soldiers. The movement was from a dominant expression of individual defiance (resignations in 1776 and 1777) to collective protest (the drive for half-pay pensions which began in earnest during the fall of 1777 and climaxed with the Newburgh Conspiracy of 1782–83). Like common soldiers, the officers had collectivized their protest. In that sense, unit cohesion among comrades had come into play, but such cohesion never broke through the vertical hierarchy of military rank.

Part of the reason lay in the social gulf separating the two groups. As befit the deferential nature of their times as well as their concern for maintaining sharp distinctions in rank as a key to a disciplined fighting force, officers, many of whom were drawn from the "better sort" in society, expected nothing less than steady, if not blind obedience to their will from the rank and file. In their commitment to pursuing the goals of the Revolution, the officers were anything but social levelers. Indeed, many of them feared that the Revolution might get out of hand and lead to actual internal social upheaval, particularly if the "vulgar herd" gained too much influence and authority, whether in or out of the army. They hesitated to turn their troops against society because these same soldiers could always turn against them as well and, through brute force, undermine all assumed claims to economic and social preeminence in Revolutionary America.

Washington's veteran officers, even though they complained and protested with vehemence, also willingly accepted their responsibilities as the army's leadership cadre. The officers administered harsh discipline to deserters, looters, bounty jumpers, and mutineers whenever it seemed necessary—and sometimes when it was not. They generally supported Washington's desire to set the legal limit for lashes at 500 strokes, and many of them often sanctioned whippings of more than 100 lashes, despite the Articles of War of 1776. For example, officers took with relish to Washington's general orders at Morristown in 1780 to inflict 100 to 500 lashes on duly tried plunderers and to administer up to 50 lashes on the spot, even before formal hearings, when soldiers were caught breaking military laws.

Many officers thus used their authority with impunity and rarely expressed sympathy for the plight of common soldiers in the ranks. They were much more concerned with societal stability and the protection of property, as well as with military decorum and hierarchy, all of which precluded the officer corps from working in harmony with the soldiery when protesting common grievances against the civilian sector.

Washington's officers, in reality, were caught between the rank and file, for which they had little sympathy, and the larger society, which had little sympathy for them. They pursued their half-pay pension demands, resorting to such defiant acts as threatening to resign en masse during the late summer of 1780. Later they became even more extreme as some toyed with the idea of a full mutiny, if not the possibility of a coup, during the Newburgh crisis. In the end, they failed in their short-term quest for pensions or commutation, as the soldiery fell short in its drive for minimal levels of respectable support. Perhaps those quests would have been more successful had officers and regulars been able to unite.

The War Within

Broadus Mitchell

"The animosity between the Whigs and Tories, renders their situation truly deplorable. The Whigs seem determined to extirpate the Tories, and the Tories the Whigs. Some thousands have fallen in this way, in this quarter, and the evil rages with more violence than ever. If a stop cannot be soon put to these massacres, the country will be depopulated in a few months more, as neither Whig nor Tory can live." Thus witnessed General Nathanael Greene in South Carolina.

The Tory-Whig, or loyalist-patriot, conflict was civil war, Americans against Americans. On both sides the hostility shaded from regular military action, under army control, down to neighborhood, even personal clashes. Between these extremes were partisan bands that were more or less organized; generally they had commissioned officers, often rank and file were enlisted, but also frequently the followers were volunteers who came and went. The fights and raids of these guerrilla parties were usually against enemies, though they were guilty of pillage, burnings, and executions which carelessly victimized friends as well as foes. The local sporadic forays, under no military government—was more cruel, indiscriminate, and widespread.

In the fury of factions against each other there was not much to choose, except that alleged legal authority permitted the patriots to impose all sorts of penalties (among them, imprisonment, confiscation, banishment) on the Tories. Such punishments were not in the power of the loyalists except in the limited areas that were under British military occupation or domination. Had the loyalists controlled the governmental machinery, they probably would not have been any more tender toward their opponents.

It is correct to speak of the patriots as composing the popular party. Not that they were clearly more numerous in the colonies as a whole, but that they included more of those of lower income and less recognized social position.

From *The Price of Independence: A Realistic View of the American Revolution* by Broadus Mitchell. Copyright © 1974 by Oxford University Press, Inc. Reprinted by permission.

The term "Tory," borrowed from England, was accurate in America in implying economic and political conservatism associated with privilege, superior status, and wealth. Of course, individuals and entire communities crossed these lines. Still, on the whole, those who felt they had nothing to gain by a change of regime adhered to the Crown. The allegiance of royal officials, from Governors down to minor functionaries, was to be taken for granted. The clergy of the Church of England were disposed against the Revolution, as were the members of the other learned professions. Men with extensive landholdings or invested funds, and merchants of the port cities, were apt to be on the King's side. Roughly, there was a cleavage between patriot Presbyterians and loyalist Episcopalians, though this difference was as much economic and social as religious; the dissenters were democratic, the Anglicans aristocratic.

Between the definable groups, patriots and loyalists, fell perhaps a third of the population. They were neutral or indifferent to the issue of the struggle. The weight of this large passive party favored the loyalists, since the champions of the Revolution needed to rouse the people to positive action. "Those who are not for me are against me" was the applicable saying in the midst of rebellion. The Quakers, who were especially strong in Pennsylvania, were on the fence because of their moral commitment against warfare.

The Americans' internal struggle was as distressing as the formal war. Actually the two conflicts were intimately connected, for the contest between colonies and Crown was itself a civil war. The strife between patriots and loyalists was the more bitter because the antagonists were neighbors, kindred, former friends. The patriots hated the "Hessians," but those mercenaries fought on command of their princes in Europe and were not concerned with the justice or injustice of the cause they defended. On the other hand, the contending parties of Americans each blamed the other for faithlessness to the best interest of their country; each looked on the other as traitorous. Furthermore, the attacks that most excited rage were not inflicted upon soldiers, but upon helpless civilians, and they often took the form of robbery, arson, and worse.

The grave differences between rebels and loyalists were in the main expressed in the realm of reasoned argument until the minute men were killed on Lexington common; then more, on both sides, fell at Concord; and finally, Bunker Hill earned the name of real battle. If a few months more had gone by without a resort to arms, the colonies might have been willing to remain within the British Empire. But the mother country offered terms a little too late. Revolution, on the part of all but the most fervent, was a reluctant recourse. The patriots and their followers, until the moment of the Declaration of Independence, wanted redress of grievances, not separation with all of its hazards and costs. This was the testimony of leaders whose knowledge and integrity it is impossible to question. Most Americans today are unaware that New York did not endorse the Declaration until several days after it was promulgated by the other twelve states. True, American nationhood would have developed sooner or later, from several causes, and, one would have hoped, peaceably. The menace of the French on this continent had been removed a dozen years earlier; the resources of the country invited exploitation, which could have occurred only under native initiative; the British colonial system, as practiced on a people of similar language and culture, was nearing the end of its era. In any case, time and circumstance were working to produce American self-determination, and if they had been allowed to operate, the results might have been preferable to those achieved by rebellion.

The loyalists were content with the present rather than anticipating the future for America, just as patriots resented current restraints more than they envisioned the national maturity that lay ahead. But abstract rights were cried up, and they obscured both British responsibilities and American opportunities. The revolution was more than an economic struggle, but the appeal to political principles, as with other excitants, contained poison as well as tonic.

The language of both Whigs and Tories became exaggerated as the conflict intensified. This was inevitable. Americans under British sovereignty did not suffer "chains and slavery," nor did loyalists oppose Congress even at the expense of being "quartered or cut into inch pieces." Orators and essayists in both camps exhausted the vocabulary of vilification. Sam Adams used his talents as a propagandist to bring on a hysteria. However, even allowing for the disturbed state of the public mind, and mutual fears, the conduct of extreme Tories and Whigs betrayed a moral depravity. Dr. Benjamin Rush wrote Richard Henry Lee, in December 1776, that "every particle of my blood is electrified with revenge." When Cornwallis was overrunning the Carolinas, civil government there almost ceased to exist, which gave rein to outrages. But everywhere the restraints of law were relaxed. Legislative acts permitted arrest, detention, and punishment on the basis of suspicion. In the inflamed state of mind that prevailed, vague terms in statutes were turned to the injury of persons accused. Before the end, all of the states, in one form or another, passed acts for the seizure and trial of anyone who by word or deed brought discredit on Congress, the state legislature, the Commander in Chief, or the paper money. If the accused were found guilty, half of the fine imposed went to the informer.

The legislatures of the states decreed test oaths to determine who supported the Revolutionary government and who retained his allegiance to Britain. The signer testified before God and the world that the war of the colonies was just, promised not to aid the forces of Great Britain, and renounced all obedience to King George III, his heirs, and his abettors. One who refused was held to be outside the law. One purpose of the test oath was to persuade the wavering to declare for the break with the mother country. If unwillingly taken, to protect property or avoid persecution, compliance often covered a secret enemy. Persons appearing before a justice of the peace were given time to consider whether to sign or not, but patriot committees and their agents frequently used force.

Without a certificate stating that he had pledged obedience to the new government, a man was fair game for patriot restrictions and penalties. Few means of injuring him were left untried. If he did not support the government that protected him, what else could he expect? He was denied the vote, service on juries, the holding of any public office of trust or profit, and access to the courts for any purpose. He could neither buy nor sell land, nor could he leave it to his heirs. Several states forbade lawyers who had not taken the test oath from practicing their profession. The same prohibition was extended to teachers and druggists, on the ground that one poisoned the mind, the other the body. Physicians were not included, but the known loyalist doctor saw his practice dwindle and disappear. To prevent spies from gathering and transmitting information, travelers had to show certificates. Freedom of speech and press were interdicted to prevent "honest and well-meaning but misinformed people" from being "deceived and drawn into erroneous opinion." For example, a humble man might abandon the colonies' cause if he believed, when told by wicked Tories that the King, next campaign, would send to America 50,000 Russian Cossacks, led by "masterpieces of inhumanity," along with 90,000 Hessians, Negroes, Laplanders, Fiji Islanders, Japanese, Moors, "Esquimaux," and Persian archers.

It would seem unnecessary to disabuse even the most ignorant of the truth of tales told in Rivington's *Gazette*. This was the main Tory newspaper, published in British-occupied New York, and it was beyond patriot censorship. Before the British came, Rivington's shop was assaulted and his types were scattered in the street. The fanciful rumors that writers in his columns attempted to spread were pathetic evidence of the impotence of the loyalists, shut up in their haven of refuge. News of the French alliance shocked the Tories. The best they could do was to start reports that Louis XVI was preparing to impose Catholicism on America. For this purpose, the French fleets were bringing casks of holy water and consecrated oil, chests of rosaries, crucifixes, and relics to be venerated. For any Americans who proved stubborn against embracing the foreign faith, Louis was providing thumbscrews and racks. Priests were on the way to officiate in confessional or torture chamber. If the Puritan conscience did not revolt at these terrors, the plain patriot countryman would be offended by the promised import of French dancing masters, *friseurs,* and dehydrated frogs and garlic soup.

Where it was not possible to prevent the Tory from mischievous influence, he was confined to his own house or farm or was removed to a distant place in the state or to another state. Some exiles were put on farms; others were held in jail. Families deprived of the breadwinner were thrown on local charity. The formalities of condemning a man to exile were loose compared to the severity of the punishment. Political exile was bad enough, but imprisonment of Tories for alleged criminal acts was worse, especially if the accused was immured in the Simsbury copper mine in Connecticut, a seventy-foot-deep dungeon.

Some loyalists were sent within the British lines; more fled there, especially to New York. In the beginning they told themselves that the British would soon put down the rebellion, but as time wore on their spirits fell, the money they brought with them was exhausted, and they lived poorly on public allowances. They finally formed the Associated Loyalists, which petitioned the military government of the city on behalf of sufferers, and also directed refugee raids into near-by patriot territory. As months passed into years, those who were loyalists from the beginning showed their jealousy of latecomers, whom they believed were acting from policy rather than principle.

Loyalists who could afford the voyage, or whose official positions in America promised them support in England, went there. Reception and reactions of these exiles in the mother country varied widely. Not a few were disgusted by the undemocratic discriminations in English society and resented the low esteem in which American colonials appeared to be held. They were pained when their hosts rejoiced at American defeats. As their money gave out, the government sustained them with small pensions, though a few dignitaries were well provided for.

One Hessian officer, Captain Johann Ewald of the *Jaegers,* was astonished at the thousands of Negroes following Cornwallis' army in the South. They had responded to promises of freedom and protection. Those who performed some camp duties were "followed by about 4,000 more Negroes of every age and sex. The regions through which this train passed were eaten barren, like a field that has been attacked by a swarm of locusts. I don't know what these people lived on. It was fortunate that the army seldom stopped longer than one day or one night."

Captain Ewald's pity was aroused by the sudden expulsion of the Negroes when Cornwallis found himself besieged at Yorktown. "On the same day that we were attacked by the enemy, all our black friends, who had been freed and dragged away to prevent them from working in the fields, and who had served very well in making entrenchments, were chased towards the enemy. They trembled at having to go back to their former owners. I had to make a secret patrol last night and met many of these unhappy ones, who were desperate because of hunger and who sought help because they were between the two firing lines. This act of cruelty became necessary because of lack of food, but one should have thought earlier to save them."

An American sergeant, Joseph Plumb Martin of the Light Corps at Yorktown, confirmed this picture. "During the siege," he wrote, "we saw in the woods herds of Negroes which Lord Cornwallis (after he had inveigled them from their proprietors), in love and pity to them, had turned adrift, with no other recompense for their confidence in his humanity than the smallpox for their bounty and starvation and death for their wages. They might be seen scattered about in every direction, dead and dying, with pieces of ears of burnt Indian corn in their hands and mouths, even of those that were dead."

For a time the substance of loyalists was nibbled away by discriminatory taxes, double or triple what patriots paid. Then Congress, in 1777, recommended that the states confiscate loyalist property. Abandoned estates first invited seizure, but soon the homes and lands of all who would not take the test oath fell under the auctioneer's hammer or were disposed of at private sale.

Not all of the confiscating of estates was done by patriots. Where the British military controlled an area, offending patriots were similarly expropriated. At Charleston, South Carolina, on September 6, 1780, a proclamation by the Right Honorable Charles Earl Cornwallis, Lieutenant General of His Majesty's forces, etc., sequestered "the estates, both real and personal, in this province, belonging to the wicked and dangerous traitors," who were then named. The list of thirty-three men who had abandoned their plantations to join the enemies of Great Britain was headed by Christopher Gadsden, Lieutenant Governor, et al. . . .

Loyalists who joined the King's forces or were otherwise conspicuous in giving aid to the British were convicted of treason and sentenced to death, but few suffered the extreme penalty; they remained absent, or proved themselves innocent of the charges, or were pardoned. Washington wisely urged leniency, lest the British retaliate on captured British-born soldiers in American service.

The Tories, content to have things stay as they were, relied too much on the British armies and fleets to keep them so. Still, theirs was not a negative role. It is estimated that, from first to last, 50,000 loyalists served in the royal army and navy. An English historian of the war estimated that New York alone furnished 15,000 men to the army and navy, and 8000 militiamen. Loyalist troops figured importantly in Burgoyne's invasion force in 1777, in the defense of Savannah against French and patriots in 1779, and in the capture of Charleston and the defeat of Gates at Camden the next year. Tarleton raised his Legion in New York, Lord Rawdon recruited his Volunteers of Ireland in Pennsylvania, and other ranger outfits were Tory manned. Benedict Arnold ravaged Connecticut towns and the James River valley in Virginia with Tory troops.

The fiercest single conflict between Tories and patriots, and the largest in scale, was the battle of King's Mountain, fought in October 1780. Some 2000 men were engaged on both sides, and all were Americans save the British Commander, Major Patrick Ferguson. Thus King's Mountain, including its preface and sequel, was an event in the civil war.

Sir Henry Clinton, the Commander in Chief of British land forces in America, was more cautious than Lord Cornwallis, whom he had left in charge in the South after the capture of Charleston, South Carolina. Clinton's operations were all on the seaboard. He had no taste for invasion of the interior. For example, when he abandoned Philadelphia he did not march into the backcountry of Pennsylvania, but took his large force straightaway to New York City.

Clinton ordered Cornwallis to dominate South Carolina and Georgia, but he did yield, without enthusiasm, to his aggressive subordinate's ambition to possess himself of North Carolina as well. Cornwallis went further. He argued that the whole tier of Southern states right up to Pennsylvania would have to be conquered if South Carolina and Georgia were to remain secure.

From his interior posts in South Carolina Cornwallis would thrust northward and westward. Major Patrick Ferguson was to subdue the upcountry of South Carolina and move in an arc northeastward, to join Cornwallis and Tarleton at Charlotte, North Carolina. Ferguson was the boldest of the British partisan leaders, with the possible exception of Tarleton. He attracted to his command a large number of South Carolina Tories. Many of them were Scots, traditionally pledged to the King's standard, while others were emboldened by the fall of Charleston and the total American defeat at Camden. Ferguson's recruiting was as much by threat as by persuasion. A backwoodsman had to be stouthearted to cling to his patriotism while his house was plundered or burned and he and his family were abused. The stories of outrages committed by Ferguson's parties lost nothing in the telling as they flew through the district, though the truth was bad enough. These tales reached over the mountains and fired resistance in those parts.

Ferguson made the mistake of further exciting patriotism by his proclamation to the western mountain men. Citing a recent Whig atrocity, he challenged, "if you choose to be degraded forever by a set of mongrels, say so at once and let your women turn their backs on you, and look for real men to protect them." If they refused to be real men—loyal British subjects—he would march his army over the mountains and punish them for their weakness.

These were the wrong things to say to those particular patriots. Frontier hunters and Indian fighters, they were proud and self-reliant. Settled in the district where the states of Virginia, North Carolina, and Tennessee now meet, they were cut off from the seaboard by the Appalachians and had developed their own habits of community defense. With one accord, they resolved to go after Ferguson and his band of 1300 Tories before he could come into their country.

Colonels Shelby, Sevier, Williams, Cleveland, McDowell, Campbell, and others led their neighbors to the place of rendezvous, Sycamore Flats on the Watauga (now Elizabethton, Tennessee). The various companies numbered from fewer than 200 to twice as many, and made a total of 1400, all mounted. In frontier hunting shirts, leggings, and moccasins, they traveled light, each man carrying no more equipment than a blanket, a pouch of parched corn, and a long-barreled rifle. The mountain passes through which they rode in chilling rains and clinging mists are today identified by historic markers, for theirs was the eruption of the West into the American Revolution.

At the Cowpens, in northwest South Carolina, they took a brief rest and food, and decided that 900 of the fittest would press ahead to find Ferguson. The leaders invited any who flinched from the danger to back out. None did so, though many were youngsters in their teens. The battle orders were simple: each man was to be his own officer, and each was to fight Indian style, without waiting for commands.

The advance horsemen rode all night and half the next day to come up to Ferguson's force, which was perched on a mountain spur that rose sixty feet above the plain. The flat summit was a third of a mile long. At the outer end, where Ferguson had his camp, it widened out to 120 yards. The steep sides were covered with rocks and trees. Of the 1100 Tories on this eminence (200 of Ferguson's corps were off on a foraging expedition), 100 were rangers, regulars, from New York and New Jersey; the others were well-disciplined militia, mostly from South Carolina. Their muskets were fitted with bayonets or, serving the same purpose, long knives thrust into the barrels.

Ferguson's position was strong, except that his tongue-like hill could be assailed on three sides at once. The patriot frontiersmen tied their horses in the woods and clambered upward with menacing yells. As they approached the top they were forced backward by solid ranks of stabbing bayonets. In hand-to-hand fighting the mountaineers, who had no bayonets, were at a disadvantage. But their rifles, aimed from cover at the red-coated defenders, were more deadly than the musket fire from above. After each repulse the patriots returned to the attack. Themselves half-concealed, they thinned the lines of the exposed Tories. The riflemen worked up closer on all sides. Then Sevier's men were at the top. Ferguson concentrated on them, but so weakened his defense elsewhere that in minutes three more companies of attackers reached the summit.

Soon the redcoats, massed in the open plateau, were easy targets for the rifles in the forest. Ferguson dashed about, now here, now there, furiously facing his men to their assailants. But the end was near. A white flag was raised in the turmoil of sound and smoke, and Ferguson, with a slash of his sword, cut it down. Then he fell in a fusillade of bullets. His troops, now demoralized, huddled behind the camp wagons.

Captain Abraham dePeyster took command, promptly surrendered, and begged for quarter. He got none, for the blood of the mountain men was up. They fired away at their helpless enemies. Finally Colonel Campbell and Colonel Shelby stopped the murder.

Every Tory on that hilltop was killed, left to die of wounds, or captured. What could be done with 700 prisoners? The victors, an impromptu corps, had no continuing organization and were eager to return to their homes. On the march back, Colonel Campbell had to issue orders to stop "the disorderly manner of slaughtering and disturbing the prisoners." On the following day the "manner of slaughtering" took the semblance of form. Patriot officers who were magistrates summoned a (not impartial) jury; after "trial," thirty-six of the captured were found guilty of robbery, arson, and murder. Nine were hanged forthwith, chiefly in retaliation for alleged crimes of the British and Tories against patriots. Soon thereafter, practically all of the remaining prisoners were allowed to escape.

After King's Mountain, the passions of the divided Americans, loyalists and rebels, did not cool. However, British commanders put less dependence than ever on inhabitants who opposed the colonies' cause. Major Ferguson had been their best recruiter and leader, and he, wrapped in a bull's hide, lay in a shallow grave on his battlefield.

The loyalists, besides going into standup fights, marauded up the Hudson, on Long Island, along the Jersey coast, and, incessantly, in the Carolinas. These forays against open villages and individual farms hardly had the dignity of foraging expeditions, for the horses, cattle, sheep, and hogs driven off were frequently the booty of private bands. Naturally, the patriots replied in kind. Even the recognized patriot partisans—Sumter, for example—supported themselves on plunder.

One would not expect pillage of a loyalist by troops selected for General Washington's bodyguard. In October 1778, Alijah Fisher returned to camp after a short furlough to find some of his comrades had new clothes, though they had received no money from home. It transpired that John Herrin had been out with a horse and a pass "to bye things for the Generals Famely . . . he Come to an old Tory's house and they would not Let him have any thing and he see several things that he wanted so when he Come home he go to his messmates and tales them and they goes and robed him." The thieves "ware all blacked." Howlen, the Tory, complained; John Herrick, one of the messmates, turned state's evidence; and Herrin, Moses Walton, and Elias Brown were sentenced to be hanged. Herrick got off with a hundred lashes.

The Tories distributed counterfeit continental and state currency, quantities of which were supplied by the British in New York. The intent was to damage the economy; however, the patriots were already doing so by spewing paper money from their own presses.

In March 1782 loyalists compelled the surrender of a blockhouse at Tom's River, New Jersey. The events that followed caused formidable resentment in America and extreme anxiety in Europe. Captain Joshua Huddy was first imprisoned in New York, then returned to New Jersey by the loyalists and, without trial, summarily hanged. With the approval of his chief officers and of Congress, Washington ordered the selection, by lot, of an English Captain in

American hands. He was to be executed in retaliation for the murder of Huddy. The choice fell on Captain Charles Asgill, nineteen years old, the only son of a titled family. Before proceeding further, General Washington demanded of Sir Henry Clinton the punishment of Captain Lippincott, whom Americans held responsible for the outrage.

Lady Asgill implored the King and Queen of France to intercede to save her son. Washington submitted their entreaty to Congress, but the insensitive legislators took ten days to get around to their order for young Asgill's release. This was after he had been held in jeopardy for more than six months. Washington expressed his own profound relief to Captain Asgill, to Lady Asgill, and to Their Majesties of France.

During the war thousands of loyalists—the banished, the proscribed, the voluntary exiles—made their way to Canada. They chose the parts they could reach from the port of New York or through the northern counties: either Nova Scotia (which then included New Brunswick) or the Ontario frontier. These wartime expatriates were mostly poor people who were colonized ("staked") by the British government. When the last hope of military success vanished with the coming of peace, there was a mass exodus of loyalists, who feared their fate at the hands of the victorious Whigs. Sir Henry Clinton, in the King's name, promised that when the troops left the refugees would not be abandoned. Ten thousand went from Savannah and Charleston when those towns were evacuated; many of them were planters, bound for Florida or the Caribbean, but others joined the throngs in New York. Loyalist families fleeing the country were supplied by the British government with clothing, tools, and food sufficient for a year; the King's ships transported them and their belongings, chiefly to Nova Scotia. As a result, Canada received about 60,000 *emigres*.

Making a start in a northern wilderness was a severe trial. Abundant land was granted, but clearing the forests was a heartbreaking task and not all of the pioneers were fit for the toilsome life. Whole regiments of Tories who had enlisted in the British army went together, which ensured community cooperation. Able individuals, trained in public life, were available to set up simple governmental machinery. However, years were needed, and much suffering was endured, before these Canadian provinces were well established, much less prosperous.

In the peace negotiations, the British Commissioners tried in vain to secure the return of confiscated estates to their loyalist owners. The Americans conceded only that Congress would recommend this to the states. The recommendation had no effect, nor was the promise against future confiscation kept, for seizures of loyalist property continued for years. Parliament accepted the responsibility of compensating those who had suffered losses because they had supported the King's cause. Including the sums for settlement in Canada, the British government spent $30 million in restitution to the loyalists.

However much the Revolution was an irreparable stroke to the expatriates, their expulsion was a greater deprivation to the United States. Had the peace been followed by generous reconciliation instead of continued bitter hostility, the valuable talents, experience, and industry of the loyalists would have been preserved to the young Republic. The years of faltering government under the Confederation might have been ameliorated, and prosperity under the Constitution would have been aided by the cooperation of the thousands expelled. This was foreseen by wise patriot leaders, but they could not prevail against the public rancor. Nor the least cost of the Revolution was the civil strife, the war within the war, and its aftermath.

Republicanism as a Revolutionary Ideology

Gordon S. Wood

In many ways the American Revolution was unlike any other revolution in modern western history. But in one important, even crucial, respect it was similar. The one identifying feature of a revolutionary movement, is the presence of an ideology, a set of ideas involving a fundamental shift in values which is used to mobilize the society into revolution. Apart from what may have happened politically or socially, in this one essential characteristic the American Revolution resembled every other major revolution in western history: it possessed a comprehensive and utopian revolutionary ideology with profound and even extravagant social implications. It is probably not too much to say that this American revolutionary ideology was just as much a system of ideas for fundamentally reshaping the character of the society as were the ideologies of those other revolutions. This ideology, this plan for changing the basic values of American society, was summed up by the conception of republicanism.

The intellectual sources of this republican ideology were diverse and complicated. Americans' ideas were drawn from their own indigenous Puritan heritage, from classical antiquity, and perhaps most important from the Commonwealth tradition of English Whiggism—all set within a framework of 18th century Enlightenment rationalism. It is this Enlightenment framework—the 18th century's attempt to formulate a science of human behavior that would match that of the natural world—that connects and relates the various strands of thought and that ultimately explains the revolutionary significance of the Americans' venture into republicanism.

Republicanism meant more for Americans than a political system, more than merely elective governments; it necessarily involved a particular kind of social system as well. At the heart of this 18th century political sociology was the belief that the form of government must be adapted to the manners and customs of the people. There was nothing unusual about Montesquieu's notion

This paper was first delivered before the Organization of American Historians, April, 1967, and is reprinted with permission of the author.

69

that the various ideal types of governments were related to different social and cultural characteristics. Of all the various kinds of government a republic was acknowledged by most liberal intellectuals to be by far the most desirable, because it rested totally on the suffrages of the people and had by definition, *res publica,* no other end than the welfare of the people. Yet precisely because it was so utterly dependent on the people it was also the state most sensitive to changes in the character of its society and hence the most fragile kind of polity. In a word, a republic was the state most liable to premature political death.

To the 18th century mind the decay and death of states seemed as scientifically grounded as the decay and death of human beings. Indeed, for all of its talk of contracts, the 18th century generally still conceived of the state in organic terms: "It is with states as it is with men," was a commonplace of the day; "they have their infancy, their manhood, and their decline." The history of particular nations and peoples, whatever may have been the history of civilization as a whole, was not a linear progression, but a variable cycle of birth, maturity and death, in which bodies politic, like the human body, carried within themselves the seeds of their own dissolution, "which ripen faster or slower," depending on the changing character of the society. The study of this life cycle in states, particularly focusing on political disease, was of central concern to the Enlightenment, for through such "political pathology," as one American aptly called it, men could hopefully further their knowledge of political medicine and retard the process of decay.

With these kinds of concerns the whole world, including the past, became a kind of laboratory in which the sifting and evaluating of empirical evidence would lead to an understanding of social sickness and health. Political science thus became a kind of diagnostics, which helps to explain the Americans' remarkable attempt to determine the state of Britain's health in the mid-18th century. In a like way history became a kind of autopsy of past, bodies politic which had died, of which the most important were obviously the great republics of antiquity. The decline and fall of the ancient republics was a fascinating subject to the 18th century, the kind that commencement speakers at American colleges in the 1770's could scarcely resist. For "the moss-grown columns and broken arches of those once renowned empires," as one American put it, "are full with instruction" for a people attempting to rebuild a republican world. Out of their reading of the Latin classics, mingled with ideas drawn from the English classical republican tradition and 17th century Puritanism, all firmly grounded in Enlightenment science, the Americans put together a conception of the ideal society they would have to have if they would sustain their republican revolution.

It was not the force of arms which had made the ancient republics great, nor was it military might which had destroyed them. It was rather the spirit of their people which was ultimately responsible both for the prosperity and

the eventual misery of the classical republics. The Roman Republic had attained the heights it did because its people, "instructed from early infancy to
deem themselves the property of the State," had continually been willing to
surrender their private interests and pleasures to the greater good of the whole
society. This spartan spirit of self-sacrifice for the common welfare—this compelling love of country or patriotism—the 18th century called public virtue,
the most vital quality a people could possess. Every state like England in which
the people participated required some public virtue, but a republic which rested
solely on the people absolutely required it. Although a particular structural
arrangement of the government in a republic, like a bicameral legislature and
a strong governor, might temper the necessity for public virtue, ultimately "no
model of government whatever can equal the importance of this principal, nor
afford proper safety and security without it."

In a monarchy the complicated texture of the society and the vigor of the
unitary authority, often with the aid of a standing army and an established
religious hierarchy, reduced the need for virtue; fear and force alone could be
used to restrain each man's desire to do what was right in his own eyes. In a
republic, however, which possessed no intricate social pattern and where the
elected rulers were "in fact the servants of the public" and known by all "to
be but men," there was no place for fear or sustained coercion from above.
Each man must somehow be persuaded to submerge his selfish wants into the
greater good of the whole. In a republic, said John Adams, "all things must
give way to the public." "Every man in a republic," wrote Benjamin Rush, "is
public property. His time and talents—his youth—his manhood—his old age—
nay more, life, all belong to his country." In a republic then "each individual
gives up all private interest that is not consistent with the general good, the
interest of the whole body," the public good, as it was generally called.

No phrase except liberty was invoked more often by the Revolutionaries
than this term the public good. It, as much as liberty, defined the goals of the
Revolution. It was a central tenet of the Whig faith, shared not only by Hamilton and Paine at opposite ends of the Whig spectrum, but by any American
bitterly opposed to a system which held "that a Part is greater than its whole;
or, in other Words, that some Individuals ought to be considered, even to the
Destruction of the Community, which they compose." This emphasis on the
collective welfare as the goal of politics helps to explain the Revolutionary
generation's aversion to faction. And it also makes sense of the Revolutionaries' belief in the impossibility of maintaining a republic over a large area
and a heterogeneous population. For politics in a republican state was conceived to be not the reconciling but the transcending of the different interests
of the community; it was the discovery and promotion of the unitary common
interest, like Rousseau's general will, which only a relatively small homogeneous community could sustain.

Republicanism thus emphasized a morality of social cohesion and promised the kind of organic state where men were indissolubly linked one to another in harmony and benevolence. "The public good is, as it were, a common bank in which every individual has his respective share; and consequently whatever damage that sustains, the individual unavoidably partakes of that calamity." Public virtue or unselfish devotion to this collective good represented all that men of the 18th century, from Edwards to Franklin, sought in social behavior. The "grand source" of this public virtue, "this endearing and benevolent passion," lay in the attitudes and actions of the individuals who made up the society. In other words, those who would be most willing to forego their selfish interests for the public good were those who individually practiced what were a mixture of classical and Protestant virtues—temperance, industry, frugality, simplicity, and charity—the virtues of the classical patriot, the Puritan saint, and the sturdy rustic yeoman, all intermingled. While some men of the 18th century could see public virtue arising out of the individual's pride and need for approbation, few endorsed Mandeville's paradoxical view that private vices produced public virtue. For most Americans in 1776 vicious behavior by an individual could have only disastrous results for the community. A man racked by the selfish passions of greed, envy, and hate lost his conception of order; "his sense of connection with the *general* system—his benevolence—his desire and freedom of *doing good* ceased." Only men who were industrious and content in their mediocrity, only men who had no desire to set themselves off from their fellow citizens by refinements and wealth, would be willing to sacrifice their individual desires for the common good.

While the Romans for example, as American orators and writers repeatedly explained, maintained their simplicity of manners, their scorn of artificial distinctions, and their recognition of true merit, they raised their state to the heights of glory. But they stretched their conquests too far, and their Asiatic wars brought them wealth they had never known before. "From that moment virtue and public spirit sunk apace: dissipation vanished temperance and independence." Men became obsessed with luxury, with "Grandeur and Magnificance in Buildings, of Sumptuousness and Delicacy in their Tables, of Richness and Pomp in their Dress, of Variety and Singularity in their Furniture." Such love of luxury widened the gap between rich and poor and tore the society with faction and violence. It was no longer merit that raised men up to the first employments of the state, but "the chance of birth, and the caprice of fortune." From an austere and hardy people, "accustomed to the Forts of War, and Agriculture," the Romans, as Sallust and Plutarch only too grimly described, became a soft and effeminate people, concerned only with "a pretended fine taste for all the Refinements of a voluptuous Life." When a republic reached this point when its people were no longer willing or able to serve the state, then dissolution had to follow.

The lesson then for the Americans was obvious: not only did the fall of the ancient states explain the fate of Britain in the mid-18th century but it warned the Americans of the extraordinary kind of people they would have to be if they would establish and maintain their new republic governments. Their revolution thus necessarily involved a radical social adjustment as well as a political transformation—an alteration in their very behavior, "laying the foundation in a constitution not without or over, but within the subject." When the Americans of 1776 talked about their intention to "form a new era and give a new turn to human affairs" by becoming the "eminent examples of every divine and social virtue," they meant that they would become the special kind of unselfish, egalitarian, and virtuous people that history and social science said was needed to sustain a republic. The moral quality of their social character thus became the measure of the success of their Revolution.

However chimerical such hopes for American virtue may seem in retrospect, the Revolutionaries in 1776 had reason for confidence, in fact had reason to believe that they were "aptly circumstanced to form the best republicks, upon the best terms that ever came to the lot of any people before us." Throughout the 18th century the Americans had been repeatedly told by European intellectuals that they were a peculiarly virtuous people, especially fit for republicanism. In the minds of French Philosophes and English radicals alike the New World had become "a mirage in the West," a symbol of their dream of new order and a weapon in their fight against the decadence of the ancient regimes. America seemed to consist, wrote Richard Price, "of only a body of yeomanry supported by agriculture, and all independent, and nearly upon a level." England, in contrast, was old and withered; "inflated and irreligious; enervated by luxury; encumbered by debts, and hanging by a thread." When in the controversy with England Americans were forced to search their souls to find out the kind of people they were, they could not help but be dazzled by the portrait, so "very flattering to us," that these "many worthy patrons beyond the Atlantic" had painted of them. Everywhere they looked there was confirmation of what the philosophes and English radicals had said about them.

All through the 60's and 70's Americans told themselves over and over that they were a sober, egalitarian, industrious people, who were "strangers to that luxury which effeminates the mind and body." "The Americans," said William Henry Drayton, "now live without luxury. They are habituated to despise their yearly profits by agriculture and trade. They engage in war from principle. . . . From such a people everything is to be hoped for, nothing is to be doubted of." Everywhere the colonists were suffering personal injuries and depravations for the cause of their country, moreso, said the Rev. Isaac Mansfield, "than in any given term of time before; no threatening quarrels, or animosities have subsisted; but harmony and internal peace have ever reigned, and one soul has inspired the body politic." And all this at a time,

John Page told Jefferson, "when they were free from the Restraint of Laws." By obeying the nonimportation agreements and the resolves of the Continental and provincial congresses, although they lacked the force of law, the Americans were amply demonstrating, said Peter Thacher, "that a spirit of public virtue may transcend every private consideration." James Iredell, no fanatic, was astonished at the peace and order of the people during the long suspension of the courts, "an instance of regularity," he believed, "not to be equalled, in similar circumstances, by any other people under heaven." This, he could only hope, was "a happy presage of that virtue which is to support our present government." This period of great self-denial and order without formal governments, those years just prior to the Declaration of Independence, marked the time and spirit which best defined the aims of the Revolutionaries and to which they looked back with increasing nostalgia.

For all of this confidence in the peculiarity of their virtue, however, Americans were well aware that their colonial society had not been all that the Enlightenment believed it to be, that they had not really been free of the vices and luxury of the Old World. Indeed, even to those who dwelled on America's distinctiveness, it appeared quite the contrary. America, declared some on the eve of the Revolution, "never was, perhaps, in a more corrupt and degenerate State than at this Day." In the eyes of many Americans, whether Southern planters or New England clergy, the society was far from virtuous and in fact seemed to be approaching some sort of crisis in its development. But the prevalence of vice and corruption that many Americans saw in their midst did not work to restrain their desire to be republican. It became in fact a stimulus, perhaps in the end the most important stimulus, to revolution. What ultimately convinced Americans that they must revolt in 1776 was not that they were naturally and inevitably republican. Rather it was the pervasive fear that they might not be pre-destined to be a virtuous and egalitarian people after all that finally drove them into revolution in 1776. It was this fear, and not their confidence in the peculiarity of their character, that made them so readily and so remarkably responsive to Thomas Paine's warning that the time for independence was at hand and that delay would be disastrous. By 1776 it had become increasingly evident that if they were to be a virtuous people they must become free of Britain.

What we would call the signs of the maturation of colonial society in the middle 18th century seemed to many Americans to be symptoms of regression. "To increase in numbers, in wealth, in elegance and refinements, and at the same time to increase in luxury, profaneness, impiety, and a disesteem of things sacred, is to go backward and not forward." Never before had corruption and the scramble for luxury seemed so prevalent, especially since the war with France. Everywhere men appeared to be seeking the preferment of royal authority, eager to sell their country "for a smile, or some ministerial office." The effects of an expanding capitalistic economy and the apparent emergence of an artificial intercolonial aristocracy springing ultimately from the honors and benefits bestowed by the Crown—were described in frightened tones. Throughout all the colonies and rising to a fever pitch by 1775–76 were strident warnings in newspapers, pamphlets, and sermons of the great social changes threatening American virtue and equality that were sweeping the land.

While some Americans found the source of these social changes in their own wantonness as a people, others increasingly came to attribute what was happening to their society to their connection to the corrupted English monarchy. "Alas! Great Britain," declared one Virginian in 1775, "their vices have even extended to America! . . . By the 60's and 70's the multiplication of wealth and luxury, the attempts to harden the social hierarchy, particularly the efforts of those who considered themselves socially superior to set themselves off from the rest of American society by aping the "Asiatic amusements" of English court life—all seemed to be part of the Crown's conspiracy to numb and enervate the spirit of the American people. England, it seemed, was encouraging American "dissipation and extravagance" both to increase the sale of her manufactures and geegaws and to perpetuate American subordination. "In vain," recalled David Ramsay in 1778, "we sought to check the growth of luxury, by sumptuary laws; every wholesome restraint of this kind was sure to meet with the royal negative." If Americans had not eventually revolted, concluded Ramsay, "our frugality, industry, and simplicity of manners, would have been lost in an imitation of British extravagance, idleness, and false refinements."

Since these social developments threatened the Americans' very capacity to be a free people, the controversy with England assumed a particular timeliness and the call for independence took on a tone of imperativeness. In August 1776 Charles Thompson told John Dickinson that he was fully persuaded, from the prevailing "prejudices" and from "the notions of honor, rank and other courtly ideas so eagerly embraced," that "had time been given for them to strike deeper root, it would have been extremely difficult to have prepared men's minds for the good seed of liberty." "Let our harbours, our doors, our hearts, be shut against luxury" became the common exhortation of Calvinist preachers and Enlightenment rationalists alike. The clergy could not help noting with obvious satisfaction that their traditional Puritan jeremiads were now being reinforced by the best social science of the 18th century. So as "pride, prodigality, and extravagance" were vices "contrary to the spirit of religion, and highly provoking to Heaven, so they also, in the natural course of things, tend to bring poverty and ruin upon a people." Hence, "the light of nature and revelation," Enlightenment rationalism and Christian theology—perhaps for a final moment at the end of the 18th century—were firmly united in their understanding of what was needed for the reformation of American society.

Religion and republicanism would work hand in hand to create frugality, honesty, self-denial and benevolence among the people. The city upon the hill assumed a new republican character. It would now hopefully be, in Samuel Adams' revealing words, "the Christian Sparta."

Republicanism, however, was to be more than just a response to this promised reformation of American society; it was itself to be an agent of regeneration. There was, the 18th century believed, a reciprocating relationship between the form of government and the spirit of its society. It was this belief in the mutual influence, the feedback and interplay, between the character of the government and the character of the people that makes many 18th century intellectuals like Montesquieu so subtle and elusive. On one hand, there was no doubt that the nature of the government must be adapted to the customs and habits of the people. Yet on the other hand politics was not simply a matter of social determinism; the form of government was not simply a passive expression of what the spirit of the people dictated. "It is the Form of Government," said John Adams, "which gives the decisive colour to the Manners of the People, more than any other thing." Hence if the Americans wanted to be a hardy virtuous and egalitarian people, a republican government would be the best means for becoming so.

Not only would republican governments promise a new emphasis on education, a new didactic iconography, and the right kinds of laws against entail, primogeniture, and monopoly, and perhaps even excessive wealth itself, but they would inevitably alter the structure of American society. Under the electoral system of republicanism American society would be governed, as it had not been in the past, by the principle of equality—the very "life and soul" of republicanism David Ramsay called it. Equality to most Americans in 1776 was not a social levelling, although it did presume an absence of legal privilege and of great distinctions of wealth and rank. Rather it was more "an equality which is adverse to every species of subordination beside that which arises from the difference of *capacity, disposition* and *virtue.*" With the Revolution most Americans intended only to change the origin of social and political preeminence, not to do away with such preeminence altogether. "In monarchies," said Ramsay, "favor is the source of preferment; but in our new forms of government, no one can command the suffrages of the people, unless by his superior merit and capacities." Republicanism would mean careers open to talent and distinctions naturally and not artificially based. The republican society, said Charles Lee, would still possess "honour, property, and military glories," but they now would "be obtain'd without court favor, or the rascally talents of servility." Only in such an egalitarian society where, in John Adams' words, "Capacity, Spirit and Zeal in the cause, supply the Place of Fortune, Family, and every other Consideration, which used to have Weight with Mankind," only in such a society would the people willingly follow their leaders and voluntarily surrender their private desires for the good of the whole.

Equality thus represented the social source from which the anticipated harmony and public virtue of America would flow. "It is this principle of equality . . . ," as one Virginian said in 1776, "which alone can inspire and preserve the virtue of its members, by placing them in a relation to the publick and to their fellow citizens, which has a tendency to engage the heart and the affections to both."

It was therefore not just a break from the British empire that the Americans intended in 1776, but a revolution promising extensive changes in the character and structure of their society, changes that republicanism both required and sustained at the same time. These promised changes were not simply the eccentric illusions of overly zealous clergymen or starry-eyed demagogues, but were the scientifically-based expectations of anyone in the 18th century who would establish a republican system. Different men of course expected different degrees of change and their variations in expectations were in fact a measure of their eagerness to revolt, distinguishing a confident Richard Henry Lee from a skeptical Robert Morris. There were apprehensions in 1776, many of them. Running through the correspondence of the Whig leaders are fearful suggestions of what republicanism might mean, of levelling, of licentiousness, of "the race of popularity." A sense of anxiety was never lost, even among the most optimistic like Jefferson. It was a grandiose and dangerous experiment, for they all knew how delicate a polity a republic was. Indeed, it is only in the context of this sense of uncertainty and risk that the Revolutionaries' obsessive concern with their social and moral character can be properly appreciated. They knew only too well where the real source of danger lay. "We shall succeed if we are virtuous," Samuel Adams told John Langdon in 1777. "I am infinitely more apprehensive of the Contagion of Vice than the Power of all other Enemies." Benjamin Rush in 1777 even hoped that the war would not end too soon: "A peace at this time would be the greatest curse that could befall us. . . . Liberty without virtue would be no blessing to us." Several more military campaigns were needed, he said, in order "to purge away the monarchical impurity we contracted by laying so long upon the lap of Great Britain."

Yet for all of this anxiety what in the last analysis remains extraordinary about 1776 is the faith not the doubts of the Revolutionary leaders, the faith they had in their ability to create a truly virtuous society in which the individual was important only in so far as he served the state. It was this hope of regenerating the American character and eliminating individualism and selfishness that made the Revolution such a utopian movement and gave to it its revolutionary ideology. The revolution the Americans eventually achieved was not precisely the revolution they intended and it may in fact have been more revolutionary than the original aim. But the aim itself, the ideology of republicanism, promised in 1776 such a radical transformation of American society as to make the American Revolution one of the truly great revolutions in Western history.

Forming a Government

Following the Declaration of Independence in 1776 the USA experienced thirteen years of unprecedented intense political debate. As British influence waned, obvious power vacuums existed to be filled, and Americans were anxious to fulfill the republican promises of their Revolution. First, new state constitutions were hammered out stressing state and individual rights and minimizing executive influence. Next came the controversial Articles of Confederation, America's first "national" government, though never secure or universally accepted. Finally came the Federal Constitution of 1787 marking the climax of this remarkable national political gestation priod. As the following articles attempt to show, the journey from 1776 to 1789 was by no means an uncomplicated one.

Merrill Jensen's revisionist The Articles of Confederation (1959) is the source for the first article. As its title suggests, "The Problem of Interpretation" is concerned with how we have traditionally come to see the Confederation and what sense we should make of it. Approved by Congress in November 1777, though not ratified until 1781, America's first national governmental document authorized only a loose confederation of states, locating political authority unequivocally in the various state legislatures. The Articles provided for a single representative legislative body selected by state assemblies. There was no national executive office as well as no taxation prerogative. Financial support was expected to be forthcoming on a voluntary basis. Conducting foreign affairs, overseeing Indian and military matters, and resolving inter-state disputes, e.g., land claims, were the prime responsibilities of the national government. Duties beyond these were exclusively state, local, or individual concerns.

Traditionally this loose confederation has been seen as a miserable failure, the young republic's economic difficulties and problems enforcing the 1783 Paris peace providing the usual evidence. However, Jensen disagrees. It is Jensen's view that the Articles have been unfairly maligned by historians and that this tradition goes all the way back to the Founding Fathers. According to

Jensen, in 1787 an elite group who opposed the decentralized, states-oriented, voluntary republicanism of the Articles, and favored a strong, central government relying less on virtue than on strength, emerged to undermine the Confederation. This Federalist group, believing that "the men who own the country ought to govern it", engineered the demise of the Confederation by over-emphasizing its weaknesses and persuading Americans that the Federal Constitution of 1787 was the answer to the nations' ills. In Jensen's view the Articles consistently enshrined the republican principles of the American Revolution which was as much about the political haves against the have-nots within America as it was about America against Britain. In this sense the Confederation represented a victory for American agrarian and proletarian political radicals, in so much as it protected state sovereignty, resisted executive control, and rejected compulsory taxation. The Articles seemed entirely consistent with the ideological rhetoric of the spirit of '76.

Be that as it may, the victory was short-lived. By 1785 America seemed to be foundering. The value of money was declining, threatening the status of creditors; state legislative debates sometimes descended into chaos or culminated in petty legislation. Daniel Shays' mob profoundly shocked the ruling class and they suggested that anarchy lay around the corner. Gradually an elite consensus emerged determined to abolish the Confederation. Concerned to protect their status as property owners and to realize their nationalistic vision of America, the 55 Founding Fathers met in Philadelphia to discipline their errant offspring. The product of their deliberation was the Federal Constitution of 1787 which represented a profound shift in the direction of American government. Concentrated executive power replaced legislative authority; state sovereignty capitulated to federal supremacy in judicial as well as legislative matters; a powerful, indirectly elected Senate guarded the interests of the property owners, and a Bill of Rights was flagrantly omitted. The debate and the document are discussed by Esmond Wright in his article "The Constitution."

The last article in this section helps demonstrate how the Founding Fathers secured ratification of their creation. Despite the protests of such popular figures as Patrick Henry, who called the document "counterrevolutionary" and a threat to the "spirit of republicanism", the Constitution was accepted. The process of ratification provides an exemplary lesson in the arts of political maneuver and propaganda. Originally published as a series of newspaper articles under the pseudonym "Publius" in 1787, The Federalist Papers were written by the leading Constitutionalists Alexander Hamilton, James Madison, and John Jay. Taken together the *Papers* provide an erudite, persuasive, and sometimes elegant case for Constitutional adoption. Madison's Federalist #10 is here recreated for two reasons. It is the most original piece, competently dismantling Montesquieu's belief that large states cannot support a republican structure. Second, this article is brilliantly ironic in that the Founding Fathers succeeded in doing exactly what Madison here argues could not happen; have a single faction control the operation of a large republic. Political persuasion aside, the elite assuaged their anti-Federalist opponents by agreeing to demands for a Bill of Rights which was finally added to the Constitution in 1791. The final Federalist maneuver to secure acceptance of the Constitution concerned the ratifying conventions. Specially convened to vote upon the document, only 160,000 eligible voters participated in the process; this represents about 20% of the white, adult, male property holders who could vote and offers powerful evidence for the argument that the Federal Constitution was not the popular choice of Americans as prescribed by patriotic mythology. Clearly acceptance of the Federal Constitution was not a natural culmination of the American Revolution as that event appears in the rhetoric of the day. Rather, while all Americans may ultimately have benefited by the adoption of the Constitution, the colonial American elite benefited more directly and immediately than the masses whose freedoms and political representation remained largely unaltered.

The Problem of Interpretation

Merrill Jensen

The articles of Confederation have been assigned one of the most inglorious roles in American history. They have been treated as the product of ignorance and inexperience and the parent of chaos; hence the necessity for a new constitution in 1787 to save the country from ruin. In so interpreting the first constitution of the United States and the history of the country during its existence, historians have accepted a tradition established by the Federalist Party. They have not stopped to consider that the Federalist Party was organized to destroy a constitution embodying ideals of self-government and economic practice that were naturally abhorrent to those elements in American society of which that party was the political expression. The Federalist Party, as none knew better than John Adams, was the party of "the education, the talents, the virtues, and the property of the country." As such it had no faith in the democracy made possible by the Articles of Confederation.

In the Convention of 1787 Edmund Randolph pointed out that the framers of the Confederation were wise and great men, but that "human rights were the chief knowledge of the time." Since then, he said, "our chief danger arises from the democratic parts of our constitutions. It is a maxim which I hold incontrovertible, that the powers of government exercised by the people swallows up the other branches. None of the constitutions have provided sufficient checks against the democracy. The feeble Senate of Virginia is a phantom. Maryland has a more powerful senate, but the late distractions in that State, have discovered that is not powerful enough. The check established in the constitution of New York and Massachusetts is yet a stronger barrier against democracy, but they all seem insufficient."

Alexander Hamilton was in profound agreement, and his views are equally illuminating of the character and purpose of the Federalist Party. "All communities," he said in the convention, "divide themselves into the few and the

From THE NEW NATION, by Merrill Jensen. Copyright 1950 by Alfred A. Knopf, Inc. Reprinted by permission of the publisher.

83

many. The first are the rich and well-born, the other the mass of the people";
if the rich and the well-born are given a permanent share in the government,
they will ever after oppose any change in its form. He had only contempt for
the popular belief that the voice of the people was the voice of God. The people,
he said, seldom judge rightly.

John Jay did not elaborate his beliefs to the same extent as did his fellow
Federalists, but contented himself with his favorite maxim that "the people
who own the country ought to govern it."

Men who believed thus undertook to convince their countrymen of the
inadequacies of the Articles of Confederation. They pictured the Confederation period as one of chaos, born solely of the existing form of government.
Many contemporaries were so convinced, and posterity has seldom questioned
their partisan interpretation. The Federalist papers were only one portion of
the propaganda for the Constitution of 1787 which later historians have accepted not as propaganda but as the true history of this so-called "Critical
Period." Thus the "great office" of the Confederation, as it has been por-
trayed, was to demonstrate the need for a more perfect union. The American
people, having progressed slowly through disaster and trial, had made "great
discoveries," which led the way to the Constitution. Faced with the decay of
public virtue, the conflict of sectional interests, the almost total dissolution of
the bonds that held society together, and the threat of anarchy, they had come
to realize the futility of federal union and the necessity of national power. Even
the historians who have seen the Revolution as a "social movement" have not
tied that movement to the political history of the times. A recent essay in
American constitutional history adds nothing to the old interpretation; on the
contrary, it lays new emphasis upon the weakness and inadequacy of the Articles of Confederation. Such analyses differ only in phraseology from sentiments expressed in the Convention of 1787, the more measured indictment in
The Federalist, and the violent attacks in contemporary newspapers.

To approach the Articles of Confederation from the point of view of the
difficulties and tribulations that followed the Revolution, real as these were,
is to miss largely their true significance. Logically they can be approached
only from the point of view of the social-political turmoil out of which came
the Revolution and the independence of the colonies. With such a perspective
the problems involved in their formulation and the ends sought by their adoption appear in a quite different light from that cast on them by hindsight and
a too facile and willing acceptance of Federalist propaganda as historical fact.

The American Revolution was far more than a war between the colonies
and Great Britain; it was also a struggle between those who enjoyed political
privileges and those who did not. Ordinarily the Revolution is treated as the
end of one age and the beginning of another; a new country was born; political
parties sprang into being; political leaders, full of wisdom learned during the

Revolution, sought to save the new nation from the results of ignorance and inexperience. So runs the story.

But the story is true only in an external sense. The basic social forces in colonial life were not eliminated by the Declaration of Independence. There was no break in the underlying conflict between party and party representing fundamental divisions in American society. Those divisions had their roots in the very foundation of the colonies, and by the middle of the eighteenth century there had arisen broad social groupings based on economic and political conditions. More and more, wealth and political power were concentrated along the coast, in the hands of planters in the South and of merchants in the North. There were exceptions, of course, but by and large the colonial governments were in the hands of the economic upper classes. Exceedingly conscious of its local rights, the ruling aristocracy was willing to use democratic arguments to defeat the centralizing policies of Great Britain, but it had no intention of widening the base of political power within the colonies to accord with the conclusions which could be, and were, drawn from those arguments. On the contrary, it had kept itself in power through the use of a number of political weapons. As wealth accumulated and concentrated along the coast, as the frontier moved westward and became debtor and alien in character, and as the propertyless element in the colonial towns grew larger, the owners of property demanded "a political interpretation of their favored position"—that is, political supremacy—as a protection against the economic programs of debtor agrarians and the town poor.

But the economic-political aristocracy which Jefferson hoped to abolish had not always been characteristic of the American colonies. In early Virginia and Maryland every free man, whether holding property or not, could vote. The first serious attempt to impose a property qualification for the suffrage came with the Restoration and it met with bitter opposition. One of the significant acts of Bacon's Assembly in 1676 was the abolition of the property qualification imposed by the Berkeley regime. But the victory of the poorer elements was short-lived at best, and in Virginia, as elsewhere in the colonies by the end of the seventeenth century, the property qualification was an integral part of the political system. During the eighteenth century the tendency was in the direction of ever higher qualifications, and colonial assemblies continued to refuse adequate representation to the expanding West. By the middle of the century a small minority of the colonial population wielded economic and political powers which could not be taken from them by any legal means. This political oligarchy was able to ignore most of the popular demands, and when smoldering discontent did occasionally flare up in a violent outburst, it was forcibly suppressed. Thus democracy was decreasingly a characteristic of constitutional development in the American colonies.

Opposition to the oligarchical rule of the planters and merchants came from the agrarian and proletarian elements which formed the vast majority of the colonial population. Probably most of them were politically inert, but from their ranks nevertheless came some of the effective leadership and much of the support for revolutionary activity after 1763. In the towns the poorer people, although a small part of the colonial population, far outnumbered the large property-owners. Most of them—laborers, artisans, and small tradesmen—were dependent on the wealthy merchants, who ruled them economically and socially. Agrarian discontent, too, was the product of local developments: of exploitation by land speculators, "taxation without representation," and the denial of political privileges, economic benefits, and military assistance. The farmer's desire for internal revolution had already been violently expressed in Bacon's Rebellion and in the Regulator Movement, events widely separated in time but similar in cause and consequence.

To a large extent, then, the party of colonial radicalism was composed of the masses in the towns and on the frontier. In Charleston, Philadelphia, New York, and Boston the radical parties were the foundation of the revolutionary movement in their towns and colonies. It was they who provided the organization for uniting the dispersed farming population, which had not the means of organizing, but which was more than ready to act and which became the bulwark of the Revolution once it had started. Located at the center of things, the town radicals were able to seize upon issues as they arose and to spread propaganda by means of circular letters, committees of correspondence, and provincial congresses. They brought to a focus forces that would otherwise have spent themselves in sporadic outbursts easily suppressed by the established order.

Colonial radicalism did not become effective until after the French and Indian War. Then, fostered by economic depression and aided by the bungling policy of Great Britain and the desire of the local governing classes for independence within the empire, it became united in an effort to throw off its local and international bonds. The discontented were given an opportunity to express their discontent when the British government began to enforce restrictions upon the colonies after 1763. The colonial merchants used popular demonstrations to give point to their more orderly protests against such measures as the Stamp Act, and it was only a step from such riots, incited and controlled by the merchants, to the organization of radical parties bent on the redress of local grievances which were of far more concern to the masses than the more remote and less obvious effects of British policy. Furthermore, there arose, in each of the colonies, leaders of more than ordinary ability, men who were able to create issues when none were furnished by Great Britain, and who seized on British acts as heaven-sent opportunities to attack the local aristocracy—too strongly entrenched to be overthrown on purely local issues—under the guise of a patriotic defense of American liberties. Thus, used as tools at first, the masses were soon united under capable leadership in what became as much a war against the colonial aristocracy as a war for independence.

The American Revolution thus marks the ascendancy of the radicals of the colonies, for the first time effectively united. True, this radical ascendancy was of bried duration, but while it lasted an attempt was made to write democratic ideals and theories of government into the laws and constitutions of the American states. Fulfillment was not complete, for the past was strong and in some states the conservatives retained their power and even strengthened it. And once independence was won, the conservatives soon united in undoing, so far as they could, such political and economic democracy as had resulted from the war. Nevertheless it is significant that the attempt at democratization was made and that it was born of colonial conditions. The participation of the radicals in the creation of a common government is all-important, for they as well as the conservatives believed that a centralized government was essential to the maintenance of conservative rule. Naturally the radicals who exercised so much power in 1776 refused to set up in the Articles of Confederation a government which would guarantee the position of the conservative interests they sought to remove from power.

The conservatives gradually became aware that internal revolution might be the result of continued disputes between themselves and Great Britain, but they were not agreed on the measures necessary to retain both "home rule" and the power to "rule at home." Some of them, like Joseph Galloway, sought to tighten the bonds between the colonies and the mother country and thus to consolidate the power and bulwark the position of the colonial aristocracy. Other conservatives, like John Dickinson, denied that Parliament had any authority over the colonies and cared little for a close tie with the mother country; what they demanded was a status that was in effect home rule within the British Empire. Complete independence was to be avoided if possible, for it was fraught with the danger of social revolution within the colonies. As these men became aware that conservative rule had as much or more to fear from the people of the colonies as from British restrictions, they sought more and more for reconciliation with the mother country, in spite of her obvious intention to enforce her laws by means of arms. But they made the fatal yet unavoidable error of uniting with the radicals in meeting force with force. They made themselves believe that it was neither traitorous nor illegal to resist with arms the British measures they disliked.

When independence could no longer be delayed, the conservatives were forced to choose between England and the United States. Some became "Tories," or "Loyalists." Others, the victims of circumstances partly of their own creation, fearfully and reluctantly became revolutionists. But in so doing they did not throw away their ideals of government. They were too cool, too well versed in checkmating radicalism and in administering governments in their own interest, to be misled by the democratic propaganda of the radicals. Not even John Adams, one of the few conservatives who worked for independence, was willing to stomach the ideas of Tom Paine when it came to the task of forming governments within the American colonies.

The continued presence of groups of conservatives in all the states, weakened though they were by the Revolution, is of profound importance in the constitutional history of the United States. They appeared in strength in the first Continental Congress. In it their ideas and desires were expressed. They were still powerful at the beginning of the second Continental Congress, but gradually their hold was weakened by the growing revolutionary movement in the various states. They were strong enough, however, to obstruct the radical program during 1775 and to delay a declaration of independence in 1776 until long after the radicals believed that independence was an accomplished fact. In the bitter controversies which occurred the conservatives stated their ideas of government. In its simplest form their objection to independence was that it involved internal revolution. When forced to accept independence, they demanded the creation of a central government which would be a bulwark against internal revolution, which would aid the merchant classes, which would control Western lands, which would, in short, be a "national" government. In this they were opposed by the radicals, who created a "federal" government in the Articles of Confederation and who resisted the efforts of the conservatives to shape the character of those Articles while they were in process of writing and ratification.

It is against such a background of internal conflict that the Articles of Confederation must be considered. Naturally any statement of the issues or principles of the Revolution, however broad the terminology, is likely to be misleading, for, as John Adams wrote, "the principles of the American Revolution may be said to have been as various as the thirteen states that went through it, and in some sense almost as diversified as the individuals who acted in it." There are inconsistencies and contradictions that cannot be forced into a logical pattern. Generalizations must therefore be understood as statements of tendencies and of presumed predominance rather than as unexceptionable statements of fact. Thus when the Revolution is interpreted in the following pages as predominantly an internal revolution carried on by the masses of the people against the local aristocracy, it is not without recognition of the fact that there were aristocratic revolutionists and proletarian loyalists; that probably the majority of the people were more or less indifferent to what was taking place; and that British policy after 1763 drove many conservatives into a war for independence.

Any interpretation of the American Revolution is subject to such qualifications, discomforting as it is to those who want complexities reduced to simple formulas. Any collection of facts must, however, be grouped around a theme, and particularly is this true of a movement having so many aspects as the American Revolution. Such grouping is unavoidable if one seeks to understand how the course of events, how the course of social revolution within the several states, often played a far more important role in determining political attitudes than did the more remote dangers of British policy.

In spite of the paradoxes involved one may still maintain that the Revolution was essentially, though relatively, a democratic movement within the thirteen American colonies, and that its significance for the political and constitutional history of the United States lay in its tendency to elevate the political and economic status of the majority of the people. The Articles of Confederation were the constitutional expression of this movement and the embodiment in governmental form of the philosophy of the Declaration of Independence.

The Constitution

Esmond Wright

The Federal Convention of May 1787 had a somewhat accidental origin. The Mount Vernon Conference of 1785, called to discuss the navigation of the Potomac, had adjourned its meetings to a second conference at Annapolis in 1786, attended by representatives of five states. Two of these representatives, Alexander Hamilton and James Madison, persuaded their colleagues that bound up with commerce were many other questions; the time had come for the creation of a "Constitution of the Federal Government adequate to the exigencies of the Union." A conference was needed of a more fundamental sort. Technically the task of such a conference was to draft amendments to the Articles, but all interested had hopes of devising a completely new document. The body that met in the Philadelphia State House was thus not strictly legal, nor was it very punctual. Rhode Island was not represented. The New Hampshire delegation arrived too late. But in the end fifty-five delegates attended, and thirty-nine of them signed the final draft.

Even allowing for retrospective piety, Jefferson was justified in speaking of them as "an assembly of demi-gods." Thirty-two of them were to become front-rank figures, with among them two Presidents, two Chief Justices, and six future state governors. A number of them had served in the Army; nearly three fourths in Congress and in state governments; thirty were college graduates; they were relatively young (average age forty-two) and traveled—a considerable number had lived abroad or at least in a state other than that they represented; the majority were men of means, and some of great wealth, and from the seaboard; over half were lawyers and all but four nationalists. The Philadelphia Convention, in a rare piece of elective good fortune, contained many of those who were the accepted leaders of their states, and many who sought a stronger regime. Their achievement is familiar enough, and well

Reprinted by permission of Hill and Wang, a division of Farrar, Straus and Giroux, Inc. from THE FABRIC OF FREEDOM 1763–1800 by Esmond Wright. Copyright © 1961, 1978 by Esmond Wright.

chronicled. Yet it was chronicled only with difficulty. The official secretary, William Jackson, was far from efficient. His notes were not published until 1819, and when they appeared, James Madison of Virginia proceeded, in accordance with them, to alter his own notes, which had been much more fully kept. These were themselves not issued until 1840, four years after his death, by which time fiction about the Founders bulked as large as fact. And Madison's notes, now transformed, were far from reliable. Not until Max Farrand's *The Records of the Federal Convention* appeared in 1911 was it possible to see clearly just what had occurred in Philadelphia.

Among the records not the least vivid are the comments of one delegate on another, and particularly those of William Pierce of Georgia on all the rest.

The Virginia delegation was punctual and very strong. Its most prominent figure was Washington, who had already expressed the view that the confederation was "shadow without substance," "a rope of sand." With a canniness more appropriate to a Yankee than a Virginian, he hesitated about going lest the Convention fail. He went, in the end, and since he was in the chair could keep his own counsel. The delegation included George Mason, who had drafted the Virginia Declaration of Rights, ambitious young Governor Edmund Randolph, and lawyer George Wythe, "remarked," said Pierce, "for his exemplary life." Its directing intelligence, however, was James Madison, "the best informed Man of any point in debate . . . a Gentleman of great modesty—with a remarkable sweet temper."

From New York came Yates, Lansing, and Hamilton—"of small stature and lean. His manners are tinctured with stiffness, and sometimes with a degree of vanity that is highly disagreeable." From Massachusetts came Rufus King and Elbridge Gerry—"A hesitating and laborious speaker . . . goes extensively into all subjects that he speaks on, without respect to elegance or flower of diction." From Connecticut came shoemaker-politican Roger Sherman—"extremely artful in accomplishing any particular object"—and Oliver Ellsworth.

There was William Paterson from New Jersey ("a Classic, a Lawyer and an Orator"), and from Delaware John Dickinson, the Sicyès-turned-conservative among constitution-makers, to whom Pierce was antipathetic—"With an affected air of Wisdom he labors to produce a trifle,—his language is irregular and incorrect,—his flourishes (for he sometimes attempts them), are like expiring flames, they just shew themselves and go out." Luther Martin and James McHenry were there from Maryland; orator John Rutledge, proud Pierce Butler, and the cousins Pinckney from South Carolina; and, not least, the Pennsylvania delegation, in talent matching Virginia's. It included the "financier of the Revolution," Robert Morris—"he never once spoke on any point"—who ended in a debtors' prison; and the Scots-educated jurist James Wilson—"no great Orator"—who did likewise. There was Gouveneur Morris, who "charms, captivates and leads away the senses of all who hear him. . . .

But with all these powers he is fickle and inconstant—never pursuing one train of thinking—nor ever regular." A crippled arm and lack of a leg did not prevent Morris from seeing himself as the *beau sabreur* of the American, as he was to seek to be of the French, Revolution; in his zest and wit a d'Artagnan, Percy Blakeney, and Münchausen rolled into one. Accompanied wherever he went by two French valets, he was rightly called "exotic" by Hamilton. And there was his only rival as Münchausen, Dr. Franklin, to Pierce "the greatest phylosopher of the present age . . . the very heavens obey him, and the Clouds yield up their lightning to be imprisoned in his rod. But what claim he was to the politican posterity must determine."

Posterity was to be kinder to all of them—Blount from North Carolina apart—even than was William Pierce. The majority of them certainly represented the Federalist viewpoint. Those most obviously identified with a radical point of view were absent. Jefferson and Paine were in Europe, as was John Adams. Patrick Henry, though elected, refused to attend. Samuel Adams was not elected. There was more than a decade of political difference between 1776 and 1787.

A group, then, of unusually talented men, able to debate in secret and keep secret what they said; a basic agreement on what needed to be done to strengthen the government; and small concern, in contrast with the men of 1774–76, with the "why" of political action. The lawyers, Madison and Hamilton preeminently, were now concerned with the mechanics of state-building. To Madison, as a student of constitutions, and to Hamilton, with his taste for executive energy in government, this was a congenial task. The American Constitution was, of course, in Professor Farrand's phrase, "a bundle of compromises"; in the fact that controversy could be resolved by compromise lay its political strength. Again and again recourse was had to statements that sought to reconcile opposing viewpoints, or to a deliberately evasive form of words; thus, the two-year term for congressmen was a compromise between one year and three. Yet in essence there was only one compromise. The Great, the Connecticut, or the Sherman Compromise—since it was largely his doing—was fundamental; it determined the shape of the central government: the decision on Federalism.

Arriving early, the Virginians had prepared, or had listened to Madison's elaboration of, a plan whereby there was to be a legislature of two houses, the lower to be elected by the people and the upper to be elected by the lower. Both houses—one directly, the other indirectly—would thus reflect population rather than statehood; this Virginia Plan was, therefore, acceptable to the larger states. There were also to be a single executive and judiciary, both chosen by the legislature. There was bitter feeling on this point, for the disparity of the states in size was striking. Delaware had 60,000 people; Rhode Island 68,000; Virginia, excluding Kentucky, had 750,000, of whom 300,000 were slaves; and Massachusets, excluding Maine, 380,000, very few of whom were slaves.

New Jersey countered Virginia's Plan with its own, one much closer to the Articles, presented by William Paterson: a legislature of one house, elected by the states regardless of population, and with a plural executive elected by Congress.

The compromise reached after a month's debate gave the states equal representation in the Senate while maintaining the national principle—representation by population—in the House. This was an important result, not merely because it became the basis of the American government but also because it saved the Convention from dissolution. Yet it is possible to argue that, important though it was as a reconciliation of federal and national principles, it was designed to meet a dilemma—the rivalry of great and small states—that was largely illusory. Maryland, a small state, and Virginia, a large one, shared on the Chesapeake a common economy of tobacco plantations and slave labor. Similarly, Connecticut and Massachusetts were alike in their commercial interests. The rivalry of state against state has never been as important in American history as the clash of sections.

The other compromises were at the time less important but were subsequently to become matters of controversy, largely because they reflected economic and sectional tensions. The first concerned the method whereby slaves were to be counted for both representation and taxation. The Northern states wanted slaves excluded from representation, since they were neither citizens nor voters, but included for tax purposes, since they were property. This Yankee subtlety the South could not appreciate. The result was the adoption of the so-called three-fifths compromise whereby a slave was counted as three fifths of a person for both purposes. But this solution was not the result of a compromise in the Convention. It had first been proposed as an amendment to the Articles in 1783 and had been ratified by eleven states before the Convention met. There was here material for future trouble, as there was, also, in the South's fear that Congress might use the commerce power to interfere with the importation of slaves or to levy export duties on her staple products.

That these problems did not arouse the excitement then that they were to do in 1828 or 1861 was due precisely to the legalism and practicality of the delegates. Indeed, the coincidence of the publication of Madison's notes in 1840 with the rise of the slavery question gave an impression that it had been a major issue in 1787. It was not. As John Rutledge put it, "Religion and humanity have nothing to do with the question. Interest alone is the governing principle with nations. . . . If the Northern States consult their interests, they will not oppose the increase of slaves, which will increase the commodities of which they will become the carriers." They did consult their interests and a series of agreements followed: no interference with slave importation until 1808; Congress to be granted the power to regulate foreign and interstate commerce but, to protect the South, all treaties to require for ratification a two-thirds vote of the Senate; Congress to be forbidden to levy export taxes. But none of these matters was very controversial. The most bitter attack on slavery at the Convention came in fact from a Virginian.

On the final problem, the shape and the power of the federal government and its popular base, there was less controversy and less need for compromise, for the Fathers spoke and thought with remarkable unanimity. They declared that the Constitution was the supreme law of the land. The Tenth Amendment, declaring that the powers not expressly delegated to the federal government stayed with the states, has received so much attention that one is apt to minimize that to the Founders the central feature was the creation of this supreme power, as expressed in Article VI, Section 2. The new government shoud be strong, unlike the Congress of the Articles, and should be clearly sovereign. It was to be national rather than federal. It should act not on the states but on the people. It should legislate for all individuals in all the states. It should be empowered to levy taxes and to coin money; to declare war and make peace; to regulate commerce between the states; it should be able to admit new states on terms of absolute equality with the old; and, not least, have authority to make all laws "which shall be necessary and proper" in order to execute its powers (Art. I, Sec. 8). The state issue of paper money and legislation impairing the obligation of contracts were prohibited. The new government was something more than "a firm league of friendship" between the states. In many ways it was at once the apogee of the Revolution and its Thermidor.

Accompanying this firmness were expression of opinion critical of democracy that recalled the debate of 1744–76. Democracy was, said Gerry, the worst of all evils. The people, said Sherman, "should have as little to do as may be about the government." And Hamilton went further than most in devising plans for an executive sitting for life, indirectly elected and with an absolute veto on legislation; for a senate for life also chosen indirectly; and for a three-year assembly. Despite these views, there was nevertheless a political caution; Federalism as thus voiced did not go unopposed. Franklin, though he spoke little and was thought by some to be senile, noted that "some of the greatest rogues he was ever acquainted with were the richest rogues." Mason became overtly critical. And so again compromise was reached: a House to be elected directly, the suffrage being governed by the state suffrage; the Senate elected indirectly by the state legislatures; the President elected still more indirectly, by a cumbrously chosen electoral college. The last was the most academic device of all in an otherwise very practical document. It was hit upon in the closing stages of the Convention by a special committee set up to settle a number of questions on which agreement had not been reached. It survives now, emasculated by the growth of political parties, as a curious relic of eighteenth-century political mechanics. The judiciary was to be appointed by the President, subject to senatorial approval but quite beyond popular control.

Yet in all the rich variety of their processes of election, the three branches of government were nicely balanced one against the other. They were to be equal, coordinate, and, so far as could be contrived, harmoniously interlocked. None could for long be seized by either democrats or potential tyrants. The strong government so patiently manufactured was still as weak and as divided as could safely be managed. The very first Article, like the Articles being "amended," took pains to list at length the powers that the federal government did not have. Least of all did the Fathers attempt, either explicitly or implicitly, to define the government. The omissions again are significant; and wars and near wars were to be needed to resolve the question whether they were building a nation or a federation, and just what "We the people" implied.

The nation has been built, in 1787 as since, not by federal or judicial enactment, but by the common life lived and chosen by its members. This, too, the Fathers sensed; paper constitutions, they knew, had to be brought to life. They produced, therefore, a short document—four thousand words in length after four hundred hours of debate through a hot summer—whose ambiguities and vagueness it was left to the future to clarify. As Madison said, ambiguity was the price of unanimity. They wrought well, not primarily because they were constitutionalists—they were after all overturning one with some casualness—but because they had supreme faith in their own handiwork, in the new country, in the revolution they had led to victory, and in the future they glimpsed of their own resources and fortune. They were politicians of whom some were scholars, like Madison; some creative thinkers, like Hamilton; some, and not the least important, party managers and manipulators like John Beckley of Philadelphia; and like good politicians they had faith, most of all, in themselves. It was for the politicians that Franklin spoke on the last day of the Convention. There had been criticism of the omission of a Bill of Rights, defining the area in which an individual lived a life free from governmental constraint. There was criticism of the powers given to the central government. There was talk of summoning yet another and more representative Convention. Franklin met these challenges in a famous and characteristic plea:

> I confess that there are several parts of the Constitution which I do not at present approve, but I am not sure I shall never approve them. For having lived long, I have experienced many instances of being obliged by better information or fuller consideration, to change opinions even on important subjects, which I once thought right but found to be otherwise. It is therefore that, the older I grow, the more apt I am to doubt my own judgment and to pay more respect to the judgment of others. . . . Thus I consent, sir, to this Constitution because I expect no better, and because I am not sure that it is not the best. . . . On the whole, sir, I cannot help expressing a wish that every member of the Convention who may still have objection to it, would with me, on this occasion, doubt a little of his own infallibility, and to make manifest our unanimity, put his name to this instrument.

The major problem, however, on which compromise would be all but impossible, was the ratification of the Constitution. This involved a public debate outside the State House in Philadelphia and the approval of popularly elected state conventions. As we have seen, the Convention was, although in name only, amending the Articles. To do so required the unanimity of all thirteen states. In the absence of Rhode Island this was clearly unattainable. The Convention therefore took the highhanded view that the new document would become effective when ratified by nine states in specially summoned conventions.

The debate in the country was far more bitter than that in Philadelphia, and much less amenable to control. It was now that the "democratic" issue was most clearly raised and in the course of the debate that faction and party first appeared. Yet the opposition to the new document did not challenge its main themes; the Republic and its balanced government were fully accepted. Nor could it provide a clear leadership: Randolph hesitated and became a Federalist; Hancock in Massachusetts was won over by the expectation of rewards; Samuel Adams was impressed by the support for the Constitution he found among the shipwrights of Boston at a carefully arranged meeting at the Green Dragon, and by the final compromise to include in it a Bill of Rights. The central theme of the Anti-Federalists was the fear of an encroachment on the rights of the states and on "liberty." This fear was stronger in the larger and more "democratic" states than in the smaller. The Delaware convention ratified promptly and unanimously; New Jersey a little less promptly but also unanimously. It took Pennsylvania a month of debate and some rather rough practices to come to accept it. It did so by 46 votes to 23; but the minority claimed that in the elections of delegates only 13,000 freemen voted out of 70,000 entitled to do so; here was still a sharp divergence between the interests of Federalist Philadelphia and Anti-Federalist western Pennsylvania. In Massachusetts the Federalist victory was narrow; 19 votes out of 355. Not until June 1788 did the ninth state, New Hampshire, give its approval. At that point it was not clear that the two key states, Virginia and New York, had agreed to support the Constitution. In fact, Virginia had approved it by a narrow majority of ten votes, 89 to 79, before learning of the action of New Hampshire. New York's majority was even smaller—30 to 27—when it came to its decision in July.

This result in New York was once again evidence of Alexander Hamilton's energy, political flair, and persuasive power. At Philadelphia he had been in a minority in his delegation; he attended only occasionally and his theories of centralization made him suspect. His colleagues, Yates and Lansing, who had finally withdrawn from the Convention on the grounds that it had exceeded its authority, were friends of George Clinton, governor of the state and a leading Anti-Federalist. Clinton expressed his fears in a series of articles under the pen name Cato. New York's politics were personal and peculiar, and they were largely the mercantile politics of the City of New York. It commanded the trade of the whole country, and in 1787—as in 1776 and earlier—it preferred neutrality or even independence to coming down on the wrong side. To these motives of fear, of cupidity, and of commercial risk and profit as well as of public spirit, Hamilton appealed in the series of eighty-five essays that became, along with Madison's and Jay's, the *Federalist Papers*. There was small hope, he believed, for the future of the country so long as the government was powerless and was scorned by foreign trades, so long as it was handicapped by varied and conflicting state laws and currencies, and so long as it was incapable of paying its own debts or compelling the states to meet theirs. He won the New York convention to his views by the sheer force of his arguments.

The victory in New York was narrow. The nation as a whole, had it been polled individually, might well have been opposed to the Constitution. Charles A. Beard's figures, suspect though they now are, showed that only one in four of the adult males voted for delegates to the state ratifying conventions; probably not more than one in six of them ratified it. Hamilton thought that four sevenths of the people of New York were against the Constitution. Neither Rhode Island, which submitted it to its town meetings, nor North Carolina adopted the Constitution until the new government was in operation, when they had little choice. The extent of the opposition led seven states to accompany acceptance by a series of amendments, and in the first session of the new Congress twelve of these were agreed upon and submitted to the states. Ten were ratified and became the Bill of Rights. This was a concession by the Federalist leaders to their critics.

The Constitution was drafted and enacted by a group of determined men, very much a minority among their fellows and acting without legality; so it had been with the Revolution, and so it is with most great developments in human history. Neither the document nor the methods whereby it was made the fundamental law were the work of a majority; nor were they tributes to democracy, still an ideal of the future. The Federalists were nationalists; in nothing were they so skillful as in the name they chose, for their intention was unitary rather than federal. They were led by two masterful politicians, Hamilton and Madison. If Hamilton appears, in print as in his subsequent legislation, an apologist for the economic royalists, it is impossible not to see in his handiwork, as in his consistent purpose, a policy that had about it, at this stage at least, courage, foresight, and idealism. If Madison supplied the scholarship and the draftsmanship, Hamilton provided the drive and combative power that were even more necessary.

Of all aspects of the Revolutionary period, the motives that led to the drafting of the Constitution have become the most controversial. As the United States grew and prospered, it was natural that the Constitution as its basic law should become revered, and that its Founding Fathers should be seen as men of remarkable wisdom. This view was natural but has not gone uncontested in American history. The crisis of 1814, the Civil War of 1861, and the controversies over the legality of the New Deal were indications that the compromises of 1787 had not been final solutions for all problems. There has been in fact no "consensus," to use today's fashionable word, on the central theme of the American story—whether it is a *plures* or a *unum,* a federation or a centralized nation. Yet once the Civil War was won and nationalism was triumphant, Hamilton emerged as the patron saint of the American entrepreneur, and the Constitution was seen once more as a work of great prescience. It came to win approval abroad in the eloquent encomiums of Gladstone and of Bryce. Nationalist historians such as Bancroft praised it still more lavishly. John Fiske, writing in 1888, accepted the Federalist arguments of a century before, to compose his study of *The Critical Period* and to portray the Founders as inspired and dedicated men who had brought order and security out of chaos.

It was natural that there should be a reaction from this patriotic view. And of it Charles Beard became the spokesman. Product of a Midwest that was then passing through the Populist and Progressive phase and of British politics in its Fabian heyday, Beard's *Economic Interpretaiton of the Constitution* (1913) was, as much as Fiske's book, a product of its time. To use a phrase used six years before by one of Beard's mentors, J. Allen Smith, in his *The Spirit of American Government,* Beard saw the Constitution as "a reactionary document," or at least as one that was counterrevolutionary. It was the product, Smith had said, not of democracy but of men who feared democracy, a "scheme of government . . . planned and set up to perpetuate the ascendancy of the property-holding class leavened with democratic ideas." Or, as Burke had said of 1688, it was a revolution not made but prevented.

Beard argued, as did Merrill Jensen later, that the Federalists, the conservatives or nationalists of their day, had exaggerated the weakness of government in the decade before 1787, and that Fiske et al. had accepted their partisan indictments as statements of permanent truth. He pointed to the many fears the Federalists expressed of "democracy," their provisions guarding contracts and debts, their concern with a strong judiciary and the separation of powers as checks on majority rule. And he substantiated his argument by a massive analysis of the economic interests of the Founders, drawing heavily on the Treasury Department on lines that anticipated the cumulative-biography approach of Sir Lewis Namier toward British eighteenth-century politics. Not one of the Founders, he argued, was a farmer or an artisan; and five sixths of them stood to gain from the Constitution, since they owned securities or slaves or land for speculation. Far from being disinterested men, the patriots who came to the rescue of their country, Washington and Randolph, James Wilson and Rufus King, Oliver Ellsworth and Alexander Hamilton,

Robert Morris and John Dickinson, had such a large stake in its property and society that the document they drafted was inevitably biased toward their own economic interest. Their motive was the safeguarding of property rights. The value of their bond holdings appreciated by some $40 million when supported by the credit of the new government. Moreover, they were not popularly chosen and were a small but highly influential group. By controlilng elections and manipulating conventions they put through an undemocratic document to which the majority of Americans were in fact opposed.

If Beard's analysis represents a piece of historical debunking, an expression in fact of militant Jeffersonian populism, it was brilliantly done and has left a profound mark on all subsequent writing on this period. It stimulated many state-by-state analyses; it greatly influenced the attitude of all later writers, some of whom, like V. L. Parrington, made contributions to American historical writing quite as significant as Beard's; it reinforced the trend toward the "new" and social emphasis in historical writing, evidence in the work of Carl Becker, J. Franklin Jameson, and Arthur Schlesinger, Sr.; and, not least, many of the Founding Fathers at last emerged as explicable and human figures. They were not only human, they were capitalists and speculators. Beard was seeking to portray what he called the true "inwardness" of the Constitution. This was needed, he thought, expressly because the document gives no outward recognition of any economic groups in society, mentions no special privileges, and, as he puts it, "betrays no feelings." "Its language is cold, formal and severe." It could hardly be said to be either cold or noncontroversial after he had written.

The extent of Beard's impact is best evidenced by the scale on which his work has recently been attacked. For it was equally bitterly censured in his own time, not only for its economic determinism, but for its demonstration that a work believed to be of near-divine ordering had been in fact the product of a very mundane self-interest. And much of the criticism then made was as weighty as that of our own day. E. S. Corwin in 1914 criticized Beard's exaggerations and faulted his figures; and he pointed out that one of the biggest property-owners of the Convention was Elbridge Gerry, who refused to sign the Constitution and opposed its adoption. R. L. Schuyler, in his excellently balanced study of the Constitution, while accepting that the two main groups were based principally on economic interests, stresses that there were many other motivse; among the Federalists it was impossible to exclude patriotism, the wish to see the new country playing a dignified role in international affairs, the belief that only a strong and vigorous government would preserve the Union, experience in and respect for the Army rather than the Continental Congress; among critics, there was fear for liberty, strong state-right sentiments, and much sectional jealousy. The leaders, it was pointed out, were as much lawyers as businessmen and speculators; they were politicans also playing for power. It was Franklin who spoke of the United States as a "Nation of Politicans," and none could speak of the profession with more authority. Yet they were also, in some measure, idealists. They were affected, says Charles Warren, "by pride in country, unselfish devotion to the public welfare, desire for independence, inherited sentiments and convictions of right and justice."

Economic determinism is persistent and unfashionable in the United States. And in recent years a new political attack has been launched on Beard's interpretation of the Constitution. Robert E. Brown has examined Beard's thesis in great detail and denied not only its validity but the research on which it was based. The records that Beard used date, he has argued, from several years after the Constitutional Convention. The holdings of the Founding Fathers were in land far more than in securities. If their property was adversely affected by the situation before 1787, so were the property interests of the great majority of people, for the ownership of property was widespread. If they were selected by their state legislatures rather than popularly elected, such a method was the constitutional form under the Articles. If a man refrained from voting for delegates to the ratifying convention, this was more from indifference, and therefore presumably from contentment with the status quo, than from disfranchisement. And if both the Founders and the people acted as they did, it was as much for reasons of conviction as for reasons of economic self-interest.

The same author in his *Middle-Class Democracy and the Revolution in Massachusetts 1691–1780* argues that there was no large working class denied the vote in Massachusetts and that the farmers in the western part of the state had as full representation in the legislature as the merchants of the east. Massachusetts, he believes, was already a democratic state. And even more bravely he holds that the same arguments can be sustained for Virginia. Not all the latest research accords with this interpretation, and it would indeed be revolutionary if simliar views were to obtain of the Southern states. But the emphasis is clear.

It has been driven home even more ruthlessly by Forrest McDonald in a name-by-name analysis of the Fathers and of the states, proving that they represented agriculture far more than commerce or securities, that many of them were lawyers with many varied clients to represent, and that their interests were far more diverse than Beards's categories revealed. Clearly, there was no sharp division between the interests of real and personal property.

At this point one is tempted to recall Louis Hartz's remark: "But after all is said and done Beard somehow stays alive, and the reason for this is that, as in the case of Marx, you merely demonstrate your subservience to a thinker when you spend your time attempting to disprove him." What the critics are asserting, however, is partly the superiority of recent research to Beard's avowedly "fragmentary" methods, and still more the viewpoint of the mid-twentieth century. The Fathers, they remind us, were patriots after all, men with principles as well as pocketbooks. If they represented property, they spoke for many constituents, for there were many property owners. They sought to create a strong government not only, and perhaps not mainly, to curb democracy but also to create a new nation and preserve the gains of the Revolution. For they had pride in both achievements. The fashion today is to revere the Constitution almost as did Bancroft and Fiske, and to see it as conserving a society that had already gone far toward becoming a property-owning democracy. The most remarkable characteristic of the political theory of the Revolution, says Clinton Rossiter, was "its deep-seated conservatism." "The American future was never to be contained in a theory," writes Daniel Boorstin. "The Revolution was . . . a prudential decision taken by men of principle rather than the affirmation of a theory." Beard, despite his errors, has, it seems, been legitimized; the Founders were not selfish; they were only wise. The United States has come a long way, not only since 1776, but since 1913.

In his *Politics and the Constitution in the History of the United States,* William W. Crosskey goes much further and contends that the members of the Convention were in fact seeking deliberately to create a unitary national government which would have the power of direct legislation in the fields of commerce and welfare. The power to regulate commerce in its eighteenth-century usage included, he contends, the whole range of economic activity. The Supreme Court was to be a national judicial body which would create a uniform system of national law. In his view, the Fathers were unsympathetic to state rights and sought salvation in the centralizing of power. Moreover, the "United States," he holds, existed as a body politic before the states acquired what was, wrongly, called "sovereignty." This is an interpretation that has not yet won general acceptance.

Does any consensus emerge, then, from these conflicting views?

In contrast with the states of contemporary Europe, American society of 1787 was small in numbers, reasonably unified, and strongly democratic. If there were classes, they were much closer to each other than in Europe, and careers in America had long been open to talents, before the phrase became a slogan of European revolution. There was, as the French troops saw, a much greater degree of economic equality than in Europe. There prevailed in America what Franklin called a "happy mediocrity." If there were conservatives and radicals, they were not yet completely aligned in 1787, and not recruited from the same groups in every state. As Oscar and Mary Handlin have shown, the Federalists and Anti-Federalists of 1788 in Massachusetts do not correspond either politically or socially with the conservatives and radicals of a decade before. Opinion was in flux. The revolutionary Patrick Henry ended up a conservative. Wealthy landowner George Mason was a radical who feared aristocracy, yet he opposed the suggestion that the President be directly elected, on the unradical grounds that "it would be as unnatural to refer the choice of a proper character for chief magistrate to the people, as it would to refer a trial of colours to a blind man"; the people, he said, had not "the requisite capacity to judge." And the proposal that the chief executive should be directly elected was made by the conservative jurist James Wilson. Randolph, who helped to draft the Constitution, refused to sign it, then campaigned for its ratification on his return to Virginia. Individuals can rarely be reduced to a pattern either of economic or of any other determinism. Nor indeed can states. The wealthy states like New York and Virginia hesitated longest over adoption. As Washington noted, the opposition to the Constitution came from "the men of large property in the South," not from "the genuine democratical people of the east."

Americans in 1787 were engaged in a great debate on government that had been in progress at least since the Albany Plan of 1754—if not since 1620 itself—of which the *Federalist Papers* and the Constitution were in a sense merely the latest expression. It is impossible to accept the gloomy view of V. L. Parrington when he says that little abstract political speculation accompanied the making and adoption of the Constitution, for the *Federalist Papers* are a classic statement of the issues that the Fathers faced, and of the ideals of the Whig style of politics. They enshrined a century and a half of experience, and much reflection on classical parallels.

But, in one sense, Beard and Parrington are right. The Fathers were lawyers and practical men, dealing with the problems of their day. They had discovered that, with Britain now removed and themselves facing acute local problems and frontier threats, there was need in America for a strong native executive power and for a President who was also Commander-in-Chief. A reading of Professor Farrand's compilation of the views of the framers of the Constitution reveals clearly that they saw their task as that of correcting the weakness of the Articles. But the appeals they were making were to interests much wider than Beard seems to have realized: to the public creditor, certainly, but also to the soldier, paid in bounty land that he could not obtain without a strong government, or in paper scrip that was almost worthless; to citizens as well as speculators in the West, who alike wanted protection from Indians and from foreign intrigues; to merchants trading abroad as well as manufacturers and workers seeking economic protection and security. "An assembly of the states, alone, by the terror of its power, and the fidelity of its engagements, can preserve a perpetual peace with the nations of Europe." The words were "Harrington's" in *The American Musuem,* June 1787. There were very many who by 1787 had a stake in America's stability and its future, who in Hamilton's words were "anxious for the respectability of the nation." America was, he said, a "representative democracy"; Americans were, in other words, good Whigs.

Equally, the Founders accepted the other dominant aspect of their world, that it was one of sectional interests. Federalism was not an invention but the translation into political form of geographic and economic facts, an expression of social and political reality. Not the least of the miracles wrought in Philadelphia was the settlement of the rivalry between small states and large— an issue that never again became a major problem. Localism remained, of course, a major issue. There was, in 1787, still little sentiment of nationalism to buttress the work of the architects in Philadelphia. And there was great variation. The democratic upthrust that occurred in Pennsylvania was not in evidence in Delaware or Maryland.

The greatest achievement, however, less willed by the Fathers' reason than product of their century and a half of political experience, was popular sovereignty and the principle of representation. As Gordon Wood has brilliantly demonstrated, given the need for a strong central government, whether for economic, nationalist, or idealistic reasons, or perhaps because they were simply persuaded of its necessity, both their history and their revolution taught them that it would be acceptable only if its roots went deep in some formula of consent. The higher the pyramid the deeper must be the local roots and the broader the base. In this sense, what Federalists and Anti-Federalists accepted as common ground was far more striking than the controversy between them. There was no Thermidorean reaction; it was not needed. The men of property formed a party, although only slowly; they sought a stronger union than many, perhaps the majority, may have wanted. They sought it, however, as conservators of the Revolution. They came to Philadelphia from thirteen distinct states, but many had found in the Army a forcing-house of nationalism. The strongest statement heralding Federalism had come from Washington in June 1783, in his last circular as Commander-in-Chief. It was a plea for "An indissoluble Union of the States under One Federal Head." As Washington had again made plain at Newburgh, the Federalists were as dedicated to republicanism as their opponents. They accepted, even accentuated, the separation of powers: they erected barriers against potential executive tyranny with quite as much zeal as the radicals. They did so, however, less from principle or from a reading of Montesquieu or Locke than from practice: it was but the form of colonial government, of governor versus aseembly, to which they were accustomed.

Equally, the "democratic" movement was far removed from Jacobinism. There was no need for any cry of "The land to the peasants," for the land was abundant and was already fairly extensively owned; and few would have accepted the term *peasant*. The seizure of Loyalist land was the closest approximation in American history to the expropriation of the expropriators. They did not need to go further. They were not expropriators but inheritors. And their faith in what men could do with their own property made some of them also—not always successfully—entrepreneurs.

To some aspects of the modern state, of course, almost all Americans in 1787 were quite blind. Some of their modern admirers approve of their "principles." But what were they? They were far from explicit in 1787. It is easier to define them negatively; for they knew more clearly what they were against than what they were for. They were hostile to tyranny, in all its forms—of one man or of many, hostile to the concentration of authority in any one man or institution, hostile to any unbalanced government. The essence of their fears was seen in the bills of rights, incorporated in the state constitutions and by 1790 in the federal document. The liberties for which they had fought were listed there, and the written documents gave them precise form, protection, and, over the years, increasingly sanctity. But despite all its revolutionary advance, there is much that is missing, much that the Constitution did not say. It was not clear where lay the power to regulate industry, as Crosskey shows. Nothing was said on the acquisition of new territories, as Jefferson was to find. Political parties were not mentioned, apparently not even foreseen, despite the threat of faction. Least of all was anything said or glimpsed of the rights of a member state to secede from the new Union.

This is, however, but to say that the Constitution was drafted by politicans seeking to settle, if not to solve, the problems of their own age. "Experience must be our only guide," said John Dickinson. "Reason may mislead us." The work of lawyers, and of men influenced by their own British traditions, the strength of the document was its realism. There was little evidence in it of humanitarian sentiments and no nonsense about a world crusade. "Symbols of a world revolution," says Louis Hartz, "the Americans were not in truth world revolutionaries." Those with foreign experience, like Paine and Franklin, and those without it alike accepted the wisdom of isolation. Nearly all the constitutions, state and federal, contained some statement about equality, but none of them suggested crusading for it abroad—or at home. There was little concern with the rights of man, and when Rufus King did use the phrase, it was in a less exciting fashion than the French. There was no stress on tolerance; indeed, many "democrats" were markedly intolerant men; in Pennsylvania and in the back country clearly so. None of them proclaimed the abolition of slavery or the granting of equal rights, in law or suffrage, to women as well as men. Some Protestants sought to limit the rights of non-Protestants. In Pennsylvania the radicals tried to curb the free expression of opinion. And by equality what was meant was equality before the law, not social justice or economic rights.

Extensive property-owning, then, meant a wide franchise; this in itself did not produce democracy. *Democracy* as a term was little used and in general greatly feared. It was a term completely absent from the Declaration of Independence and from the state and federal constitutions. Even Jefferson avoided it. Nor was a majority vote seen as a safeguard against tyranny. In the form of unicameral legislatures it was particularly feared. Under the Constitution there was to be, locally and at the center, a series of checks on arbitrary power, whether the power came from above or below. Elections were to be as indirect as possible, to allow time for reflection and for passions to cool. Few of the constitution-makers had any faith in simple majority rule.

The great debate of 1787 was successful in its outcome expressly because both groups held so many postulates and so many fears in common. There were men of property, as Beard argued, in the Federal Convention. There were many more outside it, as Brown argues. The Revolution over, all now had much to conserve.

The Size and Variety of the Union as a Check on Faction

Federalist Paper #10

To the People of the State of New York:

Among the numerous advantages promised by a well-constructed Union, none deserves to be more accurately developed than its tendency to break and control the violence of faction. The friend of popular governments never finds himself so much alarmed for their character and fate, as when he contemplates their propensity to this dangerous vice. He will not fail, therefore, to set a due value on any plan which, without violating the principles to which he is attached, provides a proper cure for it. The instability, injustice, and confusion introduced into the public councils, have, in truth, been the mortal diseases under which popular governments have everywhere perished; as they continue to be the favorite and fruitful topics from which the adversaries to liberty derive their most specious declamations. The valuable improvements made by the American constitutions on the popular models, both ancient and modern, cannot certainly be too much admired; but it would be an unwarrantable partiality, to contend that they have as effectually obviated the danger on this side, as was wished and expected. Complaints are everywhere heard from our most considerate and virtuous citizens, equally the friends of our most considerate and virtuous citizens, equally the friends of public and private faith, and of public and personal liberty, that our governments are too unstable, that the public good is disregarded in the conflicts of rival parties, and that measures are too often decided, not according to the rules of justice and the rights of the minor party, but by the superior force of an interested and overbearing majority. However anxiously we may wish that these complaints had no foundation, the evidence of known facts will not permit us to deny that they are in some degree true. It will be found, indeed, on a candid review of our situation, that some of the distresses under which we labor have been erroneously charged on the operation of our governments; but it will be

Federalist Paper No. 10 with thanks to Random House, Inc.

found, at the same time, that other causes will not alone account for many of our heaviest misfortunes; and, particularly, for that prevailing and increasing distrust of public engagements, and alarm for private rights, which are echoed from one end of the continent to the other. These must be chiefly, if not wholly, effects of the unsteadiness and injustice with which a factious spirit has tainted our public administrations.

By a faction, I understand a number of citizens, whether amounting to a majority or minority of the whole, who are united and actuated by some common impulse of passion, or of interest, adverse to the rights of other citizens, or to the permanent and aggregate interests of the community.

There are two methods of curing the mischiefs of faction: the one, by removing its causes; the other, by controllings its effects.

There are again two methods of removing the causes of faction: the one, by destroying the liberty which is essential to its existence; the other, by giving to every citizen the same opinions, the same passions, and the same interests.

It could never be more truly said than of the first remedy, that it was worse than the disease. Liberty is to faction what air is to fire, an aliment without which it instantly expires. But it could not be less folly to abolish liberty, which is essential to political life, because it nourishes faction, than it would be to wish the annihilation of air, which is essential to animal life, because it imparts to fire its destructive agency.

The second expedient is as impracticable as the first would be unwise. As long as the reason of man continues fallible, and he is at liberty to exercise it, different opinions will be formed. As long as the connection subsists between his reason and his self-love, his opinions and his passions will have a reciprocal influence on each other: and the former will be objects to which the latter will attach themselves. The diversity in the faculties of men, from which the rights of property originate, is not less an insuperable obstacle to a uniformity of interests. The protection of these faculties is the first object of government. From the protection of different and unequal faculties of acquiring property, the possession of different degrees and kinds of property immediately results; and from the influence of these on the sentiments and views of the respective proprietors, ensues a division of the society into different interests and parties.

The latent causes of faction are thus sown in the nature of man; and we see them everywhere brought into different degrees of activity, according to the different circumstances of civil society. A zeal for different opinions concerning religion, concerning government, and many other points, as well of speculation as of practice; an attachment to different leaders ambitiously contending for pre-eminence and power; or to persons of other descriptions whose fortunes have been interesting to the human passions, have, in turn, divided mankind into parties, inflamed them with mutual animosity, and rendered them much more disposed to vex and oppress each other than to co-operate for their common good. So strong is this propensity of mankind to fall into mutual animosities, that where no substantial occasion presents itself, the most frivolous and fanciful distinctions have been sufficient to kindle their unfriendly passions and excite their most violent conflicts. But the most common and durable source of factions has been the various and unequal distribution of property. Those who hold and those who are without property have ever formed distinct interests in society. Those who are creditors, and those who are debtors, fall under a like discrimination. A landed interest, a manufacturing interest, a mercantile interest, a moneyed interest, with many lesser interests, grow up of necessity in civilized nations, and divide them into different classes, actuated by different sentiments and views. The regulation of these various and interfering interests forms the principal task of modern legislation, and involves the spirit of party and faction in the necessary and ordinary operations of the government.

No man is allowed to be a judge in his own cause, because his interest would certainly bias his judgment, and, not improbably, corrupt his integrity. With equal, nay with greater reason, a body of men are unfit to be both judges and parties at the same time; yet what are many of the most important acts of legislation, but so many judicial determinations, not indeed concerning the rights of single persons, but concering the rights of large bodies of citizens? And what are the different classes of legislators but advocates and parties to the causes which they determine? Is a law proposed concerning private debts? It is a question to which the creditors are parties on one side and the debtors on the other. Justice ought to hold the balance betewen them. Yet the parties are, and must be, themselves the judges; and the most numerous party, or, in other words, the most powerful faction must be expected to prevail. Shall domestic manufactures be encouraged, and in what degree, by restrictions on foreign manufactures? are questions which would be differently decided by the landed and the manufacturing classes, and probably by neither with a sole regard to justice and the public good. The apportionment of taxes on the various descriptions of property is an act which seems to require the most exact impartiality; yet there is, perhaps, no legislative act in which greater opportunity and temptation are given to a predominant party to trample on the rules of justice. Every shilling with which they overburden the inferior number, is a shilling saved to their own pockets.

It is in vain to say that enlightened statesmen will be able to adjust these clashing interests, and render them all subservient to the public good. Enlightened statesmen will not always be at the helm. Nor, in many caes, can such an adjustment be made at all without taking into view indirect and remote considerations, which will rarely prevail over the immediate interest which one party may find in disregarding the rights of another or the good of the whole.

The inference to which we are brought is, that the *causes* of faction cannot be removed, and that relief is only to be sought in the means of controlling its *effects*.

If a faction consists of less than a majority, relief is supplied by the republican principle, which enables the majority to defeat its sinister views by regular vote. It may clog the administration, it may convulse the society; but it will be unable to execute and mask its violence under the forms of the Constitution. When a majority is included in a faction, the form of popular government, on the other hand, enables it to sacrifice to its ruling passion or interest both the public good and the rights of other citizens. To secure the public good and private rights against the danger of such a faction, and at the same time to preserve the spirit and the form of popular government, is then the great object to which our inquiries are directed. Let me add that it is the great desideratum by which this form of government can be rescued from the opprobrium under which it has so long labored, and be recommended to the esteem and adoption of mankind.

By what means is this object attainable? Evidently by one of two only. Either the existence of the same passion or interest in a majority at the same time must be prevented, or the majority, having such coexistent passion or interest, must be rendered, by their number and local situation, unable to concert and carry into effect schemes of oppression. If the impulse and the opportunity be suffered to coincide, we well know that neither moral nor religious motives can be relied on as an adequate control. They are not found to be such on the injustice and violence of individuals, and lose their efficacy in proportion to the number combined together, that is, in proportion as their efficacy becomes needful.

From this view of the subject it may be concluded that a pure democracy, by which I mean a society consisting of a small number of citizens, who assemble and administer the government in person, can admit of no cure for the mischiefs of faction. A common passion or interest will, in almost every case, be felt by a majority of the whole; a communication and concert result from the form of government itself; and there is nothing to check the inducements to sacrifice the weaker party or an obnoxious individual. Hence it is that such democracies have ever been spectacles of turbulence and contention; have ever been found incompatible with personal security or the rights of property; and have in general been as short in their lives as they have been violent in their deaths. Theoretic politicans, who have patronized this species of government, have erroneously supposed that by reducing mankind to a perfect equality in their political rights, they would, at the same time, be perfectly equalized and assimilated in their possessions, their opinions, and their passions.

A republic, by which I mean a government in which the scheme of representation takes place, opens a different prospect, and promises the cure for which we are seeking. Let us examine the points in which it varies from pure democracy, and we shall comprehend both the nature of the cure and the efficacy which it must derive from the Union.

The two great points of difference between a democracy and a republic are: first, the delegation of the government, in the latter, to a small number of citizens elected by the rest; secondly, the greater number of citizens, and greater sphere of country, over which the latter may be extended.

The effect of the first difference is, on the one hand, to refine and enlarge the public views, by passing them through the medium of a chosen body of citizens, whose wisdom may best discern the true interest of their country, and whose patriotism and love of justice will be least likely to sacrifice it to temporary or partial considerations. Under such a regulation, it may well happen that the public voice, pronounced by the representatives of the people, will be more consonant to the public good than if pronounced by the people themselves, convened for the purpose. On the other hand, the effect may be inverted. Men of factious tempers, of local prejudices, or of sinister designs, may, by intrigue, by corruption, or by other means, first obtain the suffrages, and then betray the interests, of the people. The question resulting is, whether small or extensive republics are more favorable to the election of proper guardians of the public weal; and it is clearly decided in favor of the latter by two obvious considerations:

In the first place, it is to be remarked that, however small the republic may be, the representatives must be raised to a certain number, in order to guard against the cabals of a few; and that, however large it may be, they must be limited to a certain number, in order to guard against the confusion of a multitude. Hence, the number of representatives in the two cases not being in proportion to that of the two constituents, and being proportionally greater in the small republic, it follows that, if the proportion of fit characters be not less in the large than in the small republic, the former will present a greater option, and consequently a greater probability of a fit choice.

In the next place, as each representative will be chosen by a greater number of citizens in the large than in the small republic, it will be more difficult for unworthy candidates to practise with success the vicious arts by which elections are too often carried; and the suffrages of the people being more free will be more likely to centre in men who possess the most attractive merit and the most diffusive and established characters.

It must be confessed that in this, as in most other cases, there is a mean, on both sides of which inconveniences will be found to lie. By enlarging too much the number of electors, you render the representative too little acquainted with all their local circumstances and lesser interests; as by reducing it too much, you render him unduly attached to these, and too little fit to comprehend and puruse great and national objects. The federal Constitution forms a happy combination in this respect; the great and aggregate interests being referred to the national, the local and particular to the State legislatures.

The other point of difference is, the greater number of citizens and extent of territory which may be brought within the compass of republican than of democratic government; and it is this circumstance principally which renders factious combinations less to be dreaded in the former than in the latter. The smaller the society, the fewer probably will be the distinct parties and interests composing it; the fewer the distinct parties and interests, the more frequently will a majority be found of the same party; and the smaller the number of individuals composing a majority, and the smaller the compass within which they are placed, the most easily will they concert and execute their plans of oppression. Extend the sphere, and you take in a greater variety of parties and interests; you make it less probable that a majority of the whole will have a common motive to invade the rights of other citizens; or if such a common motive exists, it will be more difficult for all who feel it to discover their own strength, and to act in unison with each other. Besides other impediments, it may be remarked that, where there is a consciousness of unjust or dishonorable purposes, communication is always checked by distrust in proportion to the number whose concurrence is necessary.

Hence, it clearly appears, that the same advantage which a republic has over a democracy, in controlling the effects of faction, is enjoyed by a large over a small republic,—is enjoyed by the Union over the States composing it. Does the advantage consist in the substitution of representatives whose enlightened views and virtuous sentiments render them superior to local prejudices and to schemes of injustice? It will not be denied that the representation of the Union will be most likely to possess these requisite endowments. Does it consists in the greater security afforded by a greater variety of parties, against the event of any one party being able to outnumber and oppress the rest? In an equal degree does the increased variety of parties comprised within the Union, increase this security. Does it, in fine, consist in the greater obstacles opposed to the concert and accomplishment of the secret wishes of an unjust and interested majority? Here, again, the extent of the Union gives it the most palpable advantage.

The influence of factious leaders may kindle a flame within their particular States, but will be unable to spread a general conflagration through the other States. A religious sect may degenerate into a political faction in a part of the Confederacy; but the variety of sects dispersed over the entire face of it must secure the national councils against any danger from that source. A rage for paper money, for an abolition of debts, for an equal division of property, or for any other improper or wicked project, will be less apt to pervade the whole body of the Union than a particular member of it; in the same proportion as such a malady is more likely to taint a particular county or district, than an entire State.

In the extent and proper structure of the Union, therefore, we behold a republican remedy for the diseases most incident to republican government. And according to the degree of pleasure and pride we feel in being republicans, ought to be our zeal in cherishing the spirit and supporting the character of Federalists.

Publius

The New Nation
1784–1814

The Constitution created only the outline of the new government; it remained for Americans to give it vitality and purpose. During the 1790's the government's leaders, the Federalists, who clung to the name used by the Constitution's supporters, sought to build a consolidated nation that few Americans had envisioned in 1776. As soon as the Federalists took control, they were perceived to be standing in the way of democracy as it was emerging in the country. No sooner were their policies implemented than everything seemed to turn against them. They despised political parties, yet parties inevitably appeared, shattering the remarkable harmony of 1787 and producing one of the most divisive and passionate eras in the Republic's history.

In foreign affairs, the Federalists sought desperately to avoid conflict with England—an effort which ultimately contributed to their downfall. Intensely desiring to maintain American neutrality, they were even willing to go so far as to negotiate with their former nemesis. However, like everything else the Federalists attempted, Jay's Treaty only reaffirmed the suspicions of many Americans that their country was in the hands of Anglophiles too willing to compromise the nation's honor and independence. Perhaps the despairing conclusion of Alexander Hamilton, the quintessential Federalist, "that this American world was not for me," best sums up the heroic dreams of the age.

As Forrest McDonald observes in the first selection of this chapter, no individual embodied the elitist spirit of the Federalist more than Alexander Hamilton, Washington's brilliant yet imperious Secretary of the Treasury. Given the task by Washington to establish the Republic's financial foundation, Hamilton believed the foremost responsibility of the national government to be to secure the nation's economic well-being by promoting diversification. It was Hamilton's opinion that while Americans remained attached to agrarianism, the United States would remain economically dependent and politically vulnerable, as well, to foreign whims. He perceived an obligation on the part of the federal government to do all in its power to stimulate the growth of a capitalist class to promote diversification, commercial prosperity, and political independence.

115

However, as Professor McDonald also points out, Hamilton's fiscal schemes were often more political than economic. Hamilton was a nonpareil elitist, who had nothing but contempt for the masses and the idealistic notion that American society could be held together by its citizens' innate virtue. Instead of virtue and man's "natural sociability," Hamilton contended that individuals were motivated by self-interest; thus, realistic social stability required the harnessing of an individual's selfish pursuits. Thus, Hamilton and his Federalist compatriots attempted to use Hamiltonianism as a means not only to crush the power of the state governments, but to manipulate society into paying allegiance to the central government.

Hamilton's programs generated considerable opposition. John C. Miller, in the second reading of this section, discusses how the antagonists to Hamilton's policies rallied around Thomas Jefferson's philosophy of agrarianism. By 1792, Jefferson and his "Republican faction" had become the most outspoken and vitriolic critics of Hamiltonianism. The Jeffersonians not only politically challenged the elitist and centralist notions of the Federalists, but perhaps, more important, were determined to preserve what they believed to be the essence of American virtue and democracy: agrarianism. The Jeffersonians maintained that the common man possessed an "honest heart," and believed that his character was the result of his independent freeholding status. To the Jeffersonians, democracy and republicanism were synonymous with agrarianism. If Americans hoped to remain a moral and free people, they must avoid the miseries, corruption, and social divisions of the concentrated urban working classes of Europe. Only by keeping America a simple society—a society of independent yeoman farmers—could the ideals of the Revolution flourish.

The United States' acceptance as a viable, respected nation by the European powers had to wait until 1814, two years after the country had haphazardly but successfully challenged the supremacy of Great Britain. England's defeat in the War of 1812 brought notice to the European nations that the new Republic would fight to preserve her sovereignty. Perhaps more important than the external respect was the infusion of the nation with an intense national pride and confidence that enabled Americans to embark on an unprecedented drive of internal expansion, development, and consolidation.

Harry L. Coles observes in the third reading of this section, the impetus for war between the United States and England sprang from the latter's exercise of her maritime power. Through the loss of seamen, ships, and cargoes, America suffered greatly from impressment, blockades, and the Orders in Council. The spirit and self-respect of the nation was injured every time a seaman was removed from beneath the Stars and Stripes or a merchant vessel was dragged before an admiralty court that paid scant heed to international law.

By 1812 the nation had been taxed by British attitudes and actions beyond endurance. Professor Coles points out that from 1810 on, Anglo-American relations deteriorated rapidly. The war spirit in the United States was intensified by Indian uprisings on the Northwestern frontier, allegedly incited by British officials. In addition, a new group of militant young Congressmen, the "War Hawks", stiffened the will of the Madison Administration. An embargo enacted in April of 1812 was both a preparation of hostilities and a last warning to England. Then, at Madison's request, a declaration of war followed in June. Professor Coles concludes, with a little luck, the United States could have avoided one of its most unpopular and least successful wars. This does not mean, however, that the decision in 1812 was made precipitantly or for inconsiderable reasons. It climaxed almost two decades of humiliation and recurring crises. For a majority of Americans the price of peace had become too high. The War of 1812 was just what it purported to be—a defense of national honor.

Hamiltonianism

Forrest McDonald

For Forms of Government let fools contest;
Whate'er is best administered is best.

Hamilton's assigned duty, upon becoming minister of the nation's finances, would be to devise a way of managing the Revolutionary War debts so as to place public credit upon firm foundations. Formidable though the task was, Hamilton conceived of it not as a goal but as a vehicle for reaching a larger goal. In a sense his objective was a fairly common one in the eighteenth century, though hardly one for commoners. Like the enlightened despot Charles Frederic of Baden, Hamilton proposed to make his countrymen into "free, opulent, and law-abiding citizens, whether they liked it or not"; Hamilton set for himself "the task of making the citizens in every regard more well-behaved, healthier, wiser, richer, and more secure." Specifically, he proposed to use his administration of the public finances as an instrument for forging the American people into a prosperous, happy, and respected nation.

Had Hamilton been a despot such an undertaking would have been arduous enough. Within the framework of a republic, wherein government rested upon the consent of the governed, the barriers were well-nigh insurmountable. The greatest general obstacle was inertia: the American people, who tended to think of themselves as God's chosen, had no urge to be remade in Alexander Hamilton's image. The greatest specific obstacle was interest: the oligarchs who dominated the American republic by the grace of the existing rules were of no mind to have those rules changed.

The existing rules defined "the people" in a fashion that excluded most of them. Of the roughly 4 million Americans, nearly 700,000 were slaves; of the remainder half were female and half were children under sixteen. Slaves, women, and children had legal rights to life, but slaves had almost no rights to liberty or property, women and children had few, and all three groups were denied a voice in politics. Nor was every white adult male allowed to participate in choosing those who governed him. Nearly half were disfranchised by property qualifications, and others were effectively disfranchised by distance from polling places, which were often located in county seats, a day's travel over primitive roads and trails. In the most important elections Americans had ever known, those for delegates to the state ratifying conventions, about 160,000 people voted—one-twenty-fifth of the population.

And the limitations on rights and on voting were only the beginninng. More important were the structure of power and the restrictions upon access to it. Despite the lip service paid to the theory of checks and balances, power was in fact exercised directly in most places. In state governments it resided with the legislatures, and locally it was the province of magistrates—boards of selectmen in the towns of New England and justices of the peace in the counties of the South. Pennsylvania permitted all "taxpayers" to hold such offices, but elsewhere the property restrictions were larger, ranging from twenty-five acres of improved land for eligibility for a seat in Virginia's assembly to £2,000 ($8,560) for a seat in the South Carolina senate.

Thus were status and power monopolized, in most American communities, by a handful of intermarried families which, for the most part, were closed to newcomers: except through birth or marriage, precious few entered the ranks of the squirearchy that dominated rural New England, the manor-lord aristocracy of New York, or the slave-plantation gentries of Maryland, Virginia, and South Carolina. A generation or two earlier, American society had been more nearly fluid, but except in the cities the gates to wealth and power had long been closing. In Virginia, for instance, nearly all members of the richest hundred or two hundred families who dominated state and local government in 1790 bore the same names as the people in power in 1750.

The key to this political situation lay in ownership of the land and in American attitudes about land. Most Americans shared Chancellor Robert R. Livingston's view that land was the legitimate source of wealth and status, and their laws and institutions reflected that view. The property qualifications for voting and officeholding were not just any property; normally what was required was "real" property, land and improvements. Moreover, the value of land, for purposes of taxation as well as politics, was not its market or appraised value but its "fair" or intrinsic value—a concept rooted in feudalism. It is true that most American families, possibly 80 percent of the nonslaves, owned their own farms. It is also true that in the United States, in contrast to Europe, land could be bought and sold as a commodity, and that during and after the Revolution many states liberalized their land laws, ridding them of feudal vestiges and making the buying and selling of land still easier. Except in parts of New England, however, most of the land belonged to the few; in the older areas of the South, 10 or 15 percent of the white families owned upwards of two-thirds of the land. As for the legal reforms designed to make a freer market in lands, those did not serve to redistribute land to smaller holders. On the contrary, they mainly helped landed people gain larger quantities of it.

Hamilton had nothing against a hierarchical and deferential social order. He thought such an order natural, desirable, and, in any politically free society, inevitable. Furthermore, he abhorred the leveling spirit. But his detestation of dependency and servility was stronger yet, for those were contrary to his very idea of manhood, and the American system of pluralistic local oligarchies made everyone dependent upon those born to the oligarchy. He hated the narrow provincialism that the system nourished and fed upon; and he resented, as only a natural-born outsider can, the clannishly closed quality of the system. Most objectionable of all was that the system failed to reward industry—industry in the sense of self-reliance and habitual or constant work and effort. Accordingly, though Americans everywhere were prone to praise the virtue of hard work, the fact was, as Hamilton said, they "labour less now then any civilized nation of Europe." Certainly devotion to work was not to be found among slaveowners, nor among their slaves, nor among the Scotch-Irish herdsmen who dominated the interior uplands, nor among the majority of yeoman farmers. Orderly and systematic attention to business was likewise missing among the great majority; when Hamilton attempted to gather information about the relative profitability of agriculture and manufacturing, he was able to find few farmers who knew even approximately how much they had planted, their crop yields, their revenues, or their costs.

Hamilton's method for bringing about the monetization of American society, against its preference and yet with its approval, eluded his contemporaries: otherwise it could not have been done. To be sure, some of his techniques were fairly obvious. He solicited cooperation by appealing to self-interest, on the ground that it was easier to harness human nature than to fight it, check it, or change it. He applied the stick as well as the carrot—the people, he said, must feel the sting as well as the benefits of government—for he understood that an excess of nominal freedom in America, meaning a want of lawful government, perpetuated a social system in which most people were actually less than free. Again, he managed things through an artful mixture of action, example, and illusion. But these were only techniques. The genius of his system lay far deeper, in his idea of establishing the procedures by which people interacted, rather than attempting to ordain what they should do.

His conception was elegant in its simplicity. He would construct efficient fiscal machinery, make it beneficial to everyone, and interlock its operations into the workings of the economy. Imperceptibly, the people would come to find it a convenient, a useful, and finally a necessary part of their daily lives, and a stimulus to industry as well. That accomplished, everyone must comport himself in accordance with the rules by which the machinery of government itself functioned, and it would be almost impossible to dismantle the machinery short of dismantling the whole society.

At every step along the way, Hamilton paid meticulous attention to the details of how things were done. The first step, the writing and ratification of the Constitution, had been taken. The next three were to ensure that Washington became president, for the aegis of his prestige would be essential; to see that the Treasury Department was properly constituted, for otherwise the ministerial function could not be performed; and to obtain his own appointment as ahead of the Treasury. Once Hamilton was in office, his real work would begin, and that, too, would unfold in three major phases. He would work out a way of servicing the public debts that would stabilize their value and thus make them liquid capital; he would use some of that capital to establish a national banking system; and he would direct the flow of the remaining capital into permanently productive channels, lest it be dissipated in the purchase of consumer goods or in land speculation.

To the unthinking there was no need for concern about Washington's election, since Washington was everybody's choice; indeed, had there been no Washington in whom to entrust it, the presidency could scarcely have been created. But there were two nice points on which serious snags could develop. The Constitution originally provided that presidential electors, instead of voting separately for president and vice-president, should cast two ballots, the candidate with the most votes becoming president and the runner-up becoming vice-president. Federalists agreed to support Washington and John Adams for the two offices, but Hamilton foresaw that if all the electors did so the result would be an awkward and embarassing tie. The obvious solution was for a few electors to waste their second ballots by casting them for nonentities, but there was a potential danger in that tactic. It was rumored that anti-Federalists were planning to support George Clinton for the vice-presidency; if they did, and if Federalists wasted too many of their second ballots, the result could be the humiliating one of having the foremost opponent of the Constitution in a position to succeed to the presidency. (The danger of the possibility would be dramatized when, during his first few weeks in office, Washington came close to dying from a malignant pustule in his leg, diagnosed as anthrax, and again a month or two later when he nearly died of pneumonia.) Taking no chances, Hamilton wrote to Federalist leaders in several states and helped orchestrate an appropriate distribution of the electoral votes.

The other possible snag involved a matter of personal delicacy. Upon surrendering his command in 1783, Washington had declared that he was unequivocally and unalterably retiring from public life. Few men but Washington, under the new circumstances that prevailed six years later, would have given a moment's thought to the idea that his retirement had constituted an inviolable promise to the public. Hamilton, knowing his old chief, anticipated that Washington might be concerned about the matter and wrote a circumspect letter urging the general to heed the call when it came. As it turned out, Washington was grateful to Hamilton for raising the problem—which no one else had had the consideration to do. He had wanted to discuss the matter with someone, but, he said, "situated as I am, I could hardly bring the question into the slightest discussion, or ask an opinion even in the most confidential manner; without betraying, in my judgment, some impropriety of conduct, or without feeling an apprehension that a premature display of anxiety, might be construed into a vain-glorious desire of pushing myself into notice as a Candidate." After a further exchange of letters Hamilton was able to overcome Washington's scruples, partly through a challenge to hazard the glory he had already won, partly through an appeal to the duty of giving unqualified support to the Constitution he had signed. Incidentally, the exchange served the additional purpose of reestablishing the relationship between the two men on a footing of intimacy and affection.

Since there were not yet any laws to execute nor any appointments to make, the first subject on which Washington needed and sought advice was purely ceremonial. Washington had a social dilemma. On the one side he was besieged by hordes of strangers who felt free to wander into his house at any hour, to meet and chat with the people's president. Upon inquiry he learned that the presidents of the old Congress had been "considered in no better light than as a maître d'hôtel . . . for their table was considered as a public one and every person who could get introduced conceived that he had a *right* to be invited to it." On the opposite side, many persons including the vice-president and most members of the Senate were insisting that the presidency should be characterized by royal pomp, ceremony, and unapproachability. Neither extreme was acceptable to Washington, and he asked Hamilton and the others for advice on rules of behavior that would strike a balance between "too free an intercourse and too much familiarity," which would reduce the dignity of the office, and an "ostentatious show" of monarchical aloofness, which would be improper in a republic.

Though the matter contained a comic dimension, the problem was in fact an important one, and Hamilton treated it as such. Running through all his writings on the presidency is an implicit awarenness that the presidency is inherently dual in nature, entailing two functions so different that only a rare individual could perform them both well. One is that of the head of state: the president is expected to be chief magistrate, chief administrator, and chief policy formulator. The other is ritualistic and ceremonial: the president is expected to be the symbolic incarnation of the Union. Hamilton recognized that the second function was as vital as the first, and his doubts as to the feasibility of an executive branch founded on republican principles derived from doubts as to whether an elected official could ever command the necessary respect. Knowing British history, he knew that the development of a stable executive branch had been difficult enough in the mother country, for the British had gone through centuries of civil wars and regicides and usurpations before they became able to reconcile the dual aspects of the office. Their solution, which they stumbled across during the reigns of the first two Hanoverian kings, George I and George II, had been to divide the functions. Those functions that had to do with the exercise of power—defending the nation against alien enemies, enforcing domestic order and justice, and formulating and implementing governmental policy—became the province of the ministry, headed by a "prime minister" who doubled as an active member of Parliament and as the chancellor of the exchequer. The ritualistic and ceremonial functions remained the province of the Crown. Largely removed from the actual work of government, the English Crown became the symbol of the nation—its mystical embodiment—and as such the object of reverence, awe, veneration, even love; a people formerly given to killing their kings now became willing to fight and die for them. At the same time, their government, for all its bungling and corruption, became the most effectively administered one in Europe.

The American presidency lent itself to just such a division of functions. The possibilities were wide open, for the framers had been so squeamish about establishing an executive branch at all that they sketched it only in broad outlines in the Constitution, entrusting the evolution of its details to the early occupants of the office. Circumstances also favored the development of a modified ministerial system. Washington was perfect for the ceremonial role, for nearly every American revered him and already regarded him as the symbol of nationhood.

Washington clearly did not think of himself as a symbolic king. Indeed, though he always wanted the esteem of his countrymen, he thought they carried the matter too far: it made him downright uncomfortable to receive the adulation normally due to royalty. He was also genuinely afraid of such treatment, for his popularity, unlike that of a king, rested ultimately on performance, and as he took office the people were expecting miracles. If the constitutional experiment failed, extravagant praise could become equally extravagant censure. Nor was he being falsely modest when he protested, in his inaugural address, that his talents were not up to the tasks before him. Most of the problems with which he would have to deal as president were beyond his experience, and—harsh fact—many of them were beyond his ken as well. He determined that his only hope was to surround himself with able men, supervise them as closely as possible, and pray for the best.

Just when Washington decided upon Hamilton for secretary of the treasury is not definitely known, but it was doubtless early. There is an old story, based on secondhand recollections, that before his inauguration Washington asked Robert Morris what was to be done about the public debts, and Morris replied, "There is but one man in the United States who can tell you; that is, Alexander Hamilton." Hamilton had been preparing himself to be the nation's financier, and he had acted as if he were confident that the appointment would be forthcoming. In 1788 he was extremely active politically but avoided running for any office. In 1789, a few days after Washington's inauguration, he told Troup that the president had asked him to accept the secretaryship, and Hamilton asked Troup to be prepared to take over his law practice. On May 27, 1789, less than four weeks after the inauguration, Madison wrote Jefferson that Hamilton would probably be appointed as soon as the office was created. Yet two months later Hamilton was apparently not sure, for in late July he accepted John Adams's son as an apprentice in his law office—which was quite incompatible with service as secretary of the treasury.

His hesitancy to make a final commitment, despite his preparation and his dreams, derived from a determination that the conditions of his appointment must be compatible with the success of his grand plan. From his point of view three conditions were vital. One he took for granted: that he would have the support of his friend and erstwhile collaborator James Madison, the ablest and most powerful man in the House of Representatives. The second, of which he was less confident, was that the treasury must be under the control of a single person with ample powers—unlike, for example, the impotent three-man Treasury Board that had attempted to administer the Confederation's meager finances since 1784. The third, most important, and least certain condition was that the office must have some measure of independence from the executive and permit direct dealings with Congress. Hamilton knew from experience that Washington would supervise his administration closely, requiring of his subordinates daily written reports on every item of business they transacted, requiring frequent written opinions and compilations of information as well, and not allowing even a routine letter to go out without his having seen it. Such a system would leave Hamilton limited room for creativity and none at all for becoming a genuine minister of finance; it would have amounted to resuming a role as aide-de-camp. The system would have other shortcomings, too. Washington was seasoned and knowledgeable in areas of concern to two of the three original departments, state and war, but he knew next to nothing about fiscal management, taxation, commerce, and other subjects in the purview of the Treasury Department. Moreover, the mere administration of treasury affairs would be so complex and exacting that full compliance with Washington's procedures would have been paralytic.

Hamilton's management of the Treasury Department was subject to four kinds of checks: the law, politics, his position as a member of the executive branch, and his personal standards. The legal restraints, just mentioned, proved highly advantageous and in a way even liberating. Politics came to bear heavily a bit later on, but during his first few months in office, when he was organizing his administrative machinery and setting it in motion, political pressure was virtually nonexistent. The other two sources of restraint, Washington and himself, were much more potent.

Hamilton had those qualities and scrupulously tried to conduct his operations in accordance with their dictates. So, too, did he act in regard to three guiding principles. First, the minister must be attentive at all times to the interests of the people, especially the common people, and thus he must see to it that all laws concerning finance were made as simple as possible and that the main burden of new taxes should always fall upon "objects of luxury and splendor" rather than upon necessities. Second, the financier must be guided by a strict and punctual adherence to promises, for there could be neither public credit nor justice otherwise. Third, he insisted on "the infinite importance of making the state of the finances publicly known." Hamilton followed these dicta with exactitude—and often made enemies in the process.

Otherwise, propriety was Hamilton's polestar. Characteristically, the standards he required of himself were higher than those he required of others. The nearly hysterical fears expressed during the debates over the creation of the Treasury made it clear, as Necker had repeatedly warned, that suspicions would attend his every move as secretary. His sensitivity to the problem was revealed in an exchange with his old army friend Henry Lee. After Hamilton had been in office about two months, Lee wrote him asking information about the prospects for investments in public securities, if it were proper for Hamilton to tell him. Actually, Hamilton could not have divulged information of any real value even had he wanted to. Inside information about the government's prospective financial operations was useful to speculators only if it was specific—only if, for example, a speculator could learn just what securities were to be provided for, on what terms, and when—and Hamilton did not have such information at his command: though he would make specific recommendations to Congress, he was in no better position to forecast what Congress would do with his recommendations than was Lee's brother, Congressman Richard Bland Lee.

But that was not the position Hamilton took in writing his answer. "I am sure you are sincere," he wrote, "when you say, you would not subject me to an impropriety. Nor do I know that there would be any in my answering your queries. But you remember the saying with regard to Caesar's Wife. I think the spirit of it applicable to every man concerned in the administration of the finances of a Country. With respect to the Conduct of such men—*Suspicion* is ever eagle eyed, And the most innocent things are apt to be misinterpreted."

Hamilton also made sure his personal finances would bear hostile scrutiny. He did retain a small investment he had made in the Ohio Company in 1787, and that organization had purchased a million acres of western lands from the Congress; but since the transaction had been completed neither he nor anyone else saw any conflict of interest in such a holding. As to public paper, he owned no securities, having long since disposed of the various certificates he had received in military pay; and he even declined to collect substantial bonuses lawfully due him. Moreover, by totally surrendering his law practice, he cut off all his private sources of income—which neither Washington nor any other man in the national government except Hamilton saw fit to do. His salary as secretary was $3,500 a year. That was a considerable sum for the times, but far less than he had been earning as a lawyer and not enough to support himself and his family in their accustomed style. In 1789 his affairs were so prosperous that he was able to make personal loans to friends in amounts as high as $2,000. When he left the treasury five years later, he was himself deep in debt.

It was toward the creation of smooth-working, self-regulating administrative machinery, not the mere setting of examples, that Hamilton particularly directed his labors. Given his gifts for orderly and systematic management, he could accomplish a great deal of this with minimal efforts. For routine activities that lent themselves to standardized procedures, such as the calculation and collection of customs duties, he prescribed uniform procedures and devised forms that customs officers were required to follow. To prevent standardization from degenerating into the kind of bureaucratic stupidity in which mindless form-filling is substituted for substance, he employed a number of techniques. One was to grant a measure of discretion to collectors in the larger ports, who could usually be counted on to be more intelligent and better informed than those in small outlying ports; but he did that only when he personally knew the collector to be honest and responsible. More importantly, he provided for an efficient two-way flow of information. To that end, he kept Treasury officers apprised of all developments that concerned them, required weekly reports of their collections and payments (which incidentally kept him informed of the volume of business and the movements of shipping in every American port), and invited reports on other matters. He especially solicited observations that "may serve to discover the merits or defects" of the revenue system—in other words, what worked effectively as well as what did not—so as "to point out the means of improving it." He also asked to be told of complaints of merchants, which "always merit attention" though they were by no means "infallible indications of defects."

The gathering of information was crucial, for without it Hamilton's grand conception was useless. He was acutely aware that to redirect the channels through which human activities shall flow, one must first obtain an accurate and thoroughly detailed understanding of the ways in which they are already flowing. No one man had such knowledge, though many had parts of it. To gather it, Hamilton more or less invented a research technique: he conducted a large-scale socioeconomic research project using questionnaires. The first, dated October 15, 1789, was concerned with shipping and consisted of seven broad questions, each of which invited an essay as well as hard facts and figures. It went out to the customs collectors and to everyone else Hamilton had reason to believe had useful information on the subject. The replies poured in, providing him a wealth of data and practical wisdom, much of which was contrary to common assumptions. When all the returns were in and Hamilton had studied and digested them with his usual alacrity, he knew more about the ordinary business of his fellow citizens than anyone else possibly could have.

There was, however, a problem inherent in being so well informed. A number of powerful, influential, and strong-willed men in government, foremost among them James Madison, failed to perceive that Hamilton's newly acquired storehouse of information placed his understanding qualitatively beyond their reach; like Hamilton's friend Troup, they underestimated his capacity for research and were therefore inclined to mistake his depth for facility. That mistake, together with Hamilton's facile manner, his unwillingness to suffer fools gladly, and his natural combativeness, was certain to generate misunderstanding and probably conflict.

An example of the potential friction is seen in the 1789 tariff act, passed about two months before Hamilton took office. The legislation, which provided the main source of the national government's revenues, was largely the work of Madison and Congressman Thomas Fitzsimons of Pennsylvania. Madison's understanding of international trade was broad but wholly theoretical. That of Fitzsimons, a Philadelphia importing merchant, was practical but narrow. Madison, deeply hostile toward Great Britain, thought the tariff should discriminate severely against British ships and goods so that Britain would be forced to relax the commercial restrictions it had imposed on Americans since independence. (Hamilton, from conversation with Beckwith, had learned that this was precisely the wrong way to get anything from the ministry of William Pitt. Pitt would meet friendly overtures with friendship, but to get tough with him was to ensure that he would get many times tougher. Madison never learned that; indeed, he tended to regard the British government as a monolith, as if it made no difference whose ministry was in power. Hamilton explained to Beckwith that Madison was uncorrupted and incorruptible but, though he was " a clever man, he is very little Acquainted with the world." He was soon to become aware that that was an understatement, that Madison's approach was unsound for a hundred additional reasons.)

Thomas Jefferson and the Philosophy of Agrarianism

John C. Miller

In March, 1790, when Jefferson assumed the post of Secretary of State, his support of the main objectives of the Washington administration seemed assured. During the period of the Articles of Confederation, he had been among the first to urge that the Continental Congress be given powers commensurate with its obligation of paying the national debt and upholding American dignity and rights abroad. He had distinguished himself as a champion of American commercial interests and he had advocated the creation of a navy, "the only weapon," he said, "by which we can act on Europe." He wished to see the Federal judiciary made supreme over the state judiciaries in order that it might prevent the states from encroaching upon the authority of the Federal government. His experience as United States minister to France had deeply impressed upon him the necessity of "firmness and tone" in the central government. Although he had objected to the indefinite re-eligibility of the President and the absence of a Bill of Rights, he had favored the adoption of the Constitution. In 1788, he had pronounced *The Federalist* to be one of the greatest treatises on government ever written.

Notwithstanding, Jefferson never admitted to being a Federalist, least of all a Hamiltonian Federalist. Even prior to 1790 he had revealed how little he sympathized with many of the ideals and policies laid down by his colleague at the treasury: while he was of the opinion that the "tyranny of the legislature" was more to be feared than the ambition and lust for power of the executive, he asserted that "the jealousy of the subordinate governments" toward the exercise of power by the national government was the most "precious reliance" that freedom would endure in the United States. At this time, Jefferson was more inclined than was Madison to trust to "the good sense of the people." Far from sharing the Federalists' panic when Shays rose in rebellion,

Jefferson calmly accepted the event as a natural effervescence of popular feeling: when one sailed upon the "boisterous sea of freedom," he said, one expected a little rough going. Shays' Rebellion and other manifestations of what the Federalists called "democratic license" Jefferson attributed to want of information upon the part of the people. There was nothing in the country so radically wrong, he often said, that it could not be cured by good news-papers and sound schoolmasters. For Jefferson had a boundless faith in edu-cation: since man was "a rational animal, endowed by nature with rights, and with an innate sense of justice," he had only to be apprised of the truth to act wisely, moderately, and justly.

Because Jefferson made no effort to conceal his opinions, however unpop-ular they might be in the polite circles of Philadelphia, he was set down by some Federalists in 1790 as "greatly too Democratic for us at present; he left us in that way, but we are infinitely changed, and he must alter his principles." The Federalists who undertook to wean Jefferson from democracy soon dis-covered that he was a hopeless case.

Jefferson's experience under the "energetic government" administered by Alexander Hamilton revived all of the fears of strong government the Vir-ginian had conceived during the American Revolution. What was occurring in the United States seemed to confirm his earlier conviction that "the natural progress of things is for liberty to yield and government to gain ground." While he never lost confidence in the people's devotion to republicanism, he feared that Hamilton and the "Monocrats," solidly entrenched in office, disposing of great wealth, and in a position to mold public opinion through the newspapers, would prove too powerful for the "republican interest." And so Jefferson be-came the champion of minimal government—"a few plain duties to be per-formed by a few servants." He considered Adam Smith's *Wealth of Nations* to be the best book ever written on economics and, eagerly embracing the philosophy of laissez faire, he contended that government could best con-tribute to the public prosperity by letting individuals, businessmen included, manage for themselves.

So distrustful of the Federal government did Jefferson become that in 1791 he even denied it the power to aid agriculture by incorporating an Agricultural Society. If the power to erect corporations were conceded to the government, he predicted, "it would soon be used for no other purpose than to buy with sinecures useful partisans." To the proposal that the Federal government con-struct roads, Jefferson objected that it would open up "the richest provision for jobs to favorites that has ever yet been proposed. . . . The mines of Peru would not supply the monies which would be wasted on this object." Mani-festly, during the Federalist era, Jefferson was so intent upon circumscribing the powers of the Federal government that he ignored its potentialities as a constructive force for the public welfare.

In part, Jefferson's abiding fear of strong government stemmed from his determination to preserve the American farm from the heavy hand of organized business, which, to his way of thinking, always attempted to convert government into an instrument for extracting money from the mass of the people, especially farmers. Jefferson loved farming with an ardor which, to city-bred Federalists, passed understanding. Of course, as the owner of thousands of acres of land and of a considerable number of slaves, he was happily spared the more onerous side of an agriculturalist's life. In his eyes, farming was not simply a matter of grubbing a living from intractable soil; it was a way of life ordained by God for his "Chosen People," the school of "substantial and genuine virtue . . . the focus in which he [the Creator] keeps alive that sacred fire, which otherwise might escape from the face of the earth." For Jefferson, the pursuit of happiness ended on a farm; the true Republican was the man with the hoe and a hundred acres besides. He could conceive of no more ennobling or enduring joy than for a man to look upon his land and say: "This is mine and it will be my children's."

The worst that could happen, in Jefferson's opinion, was for Americans to rush into the Industrial Revolution, exchanging their farms for factories and the open countryside for the slums of large cities. Jefferson never doubted that Americans had created as nearly perfect a society as mankind had yet achieved; to him, the industrialization of the United States was comparable to the exodus from Paradise. Nevertheless, much as he wished to see factories and "the mobs of great cities" confined to their natural habitat in Europe, he recognized that he could not indulge his partialities and prejudices when they ran counter to the aspirations and interests of the majority of the American people. He was prepared to acquiesce in the will of that majority even when it was at variance with his better judgment: if the American people wished to sail the seas, congregate in cities, and labor in factories, he believed that it was the duty of a statesman to yield to their wishes. In consequence, Jefferson altered his policy, but not his predilections, in accord with changing circumstances and the popular will. After the War of 1812, for example, he called for "an equilibrium of agriculture, manufactures and commerce"—the very objective that Hamilton had held in view. And yet, to the end, Jefferson hoped that household manufactures would triumph over the factory system. At Monticello he established a small nail factory operated by slave children.

Always his main point of reference was the quality rather than the number of the inhabitants of the United States. What did it profit a nation, Jefferson asked, if, even though it were rich and powerful, the mass of its citizens was an illiterate, poverty-stricken, mutinous proletariat? He attached paramount importance to farming because he believed that it produced the kind of citizens best qualified to meet the exacting demands of republican government. The choice between shipping and manufactures resolved itself in his mind into a question of the relative desirability of the type of citizen begotten by these occupations. His own preference was for shipping rather than for manufactures because, he said, "comparing the characters of the two classes I find the former[mariners] the most valuable citizens." Seamen, he admitted, were anything but models of propriety, but they seemed respectable and even virtuous in comparison with the factory workers of large cities. Here, Jefferson exclaimed, were found the real enemies of republicanism, "the panders of vice and the instruments by which the liberties of a country are generally overturned."

Where agriculture was concerned, it is apparent that Jefferson was as much concerned with the social as with the economic conditions it created. Nor did he exclude political considerations: he never strayed far from his main point—that agriculture, "the great American interest," constituted the most solid bond of union of the diverse sections of which the American Union was constructed. He recognized that if the farmers could be organized politically, nothing—not even the Hamiltonian "phalanx" of bankers, speculators, and businessmen—could stand against them. Furthermore, as a political leader, Jefferson displayed a flexibility hardly to be expected in one who cleaved so self-righteously to principles. "He who would do his country the most good he can," he said, "must go quietly with the prejudices of the majority until he can lead them into reason." When victory depended upon the support of the "degraded," "vicious," "debauched," and "mobbish" workingmen of the eastern cities, Jefferson welcomed them as allies. He even permitted bankers to squeeze through the needle's eye and to wear the raiment of "true republicans."

Conscious that the mass of the people were on his side, Jefferson enjoyed a serenity of mind and a cheerful confidence in the future which were denied Hamilton. In the Virginian's humanistic optimism all things were possible for an enlightened people; the beneficent Intelligence that had created and governed the world on a rational plan had merely begun to open the doors to man's enquiring mind. He regarded the people, particularly the educated and landowning part thereof, as "the most honest and safe, though not the most wise depository of the public interest"; but, while the people could be fooled some of the time, their folly was less pernicious than the wisdom of oligarchs. If the people were rightly informed, Jefferson was confident that they would do right, even to the extent of electing the best men to political office.

As regards the national debt, Jefferson demanded that it be liquidated forthwith, not only because he had a horror of debt—he held it to be a mortgage unjustly imposed by one generation upon posterity—but because he believed that Hamilton wished "it never to be paid, but always to be a thing with which to corrupt and manage the legislature." Like Madison, Jefferson detected "a sympathy between the speeches and the pockets of all those members of Congress who held certificates." Despite Hamilton's roseate view of the country's financial position, Jefferson insisted that the debt was increasing steadily and that it had already reached a point "beyond the possibility of payment." Moreover, the Virginian was certain in his own mind that the Secretary of the Treasury deliberately made his financial reports intricate and confusing in order to mislead the public, and that he had involved himself in such complexities that he himself could not find a way out of this self-created labyrinth. The only way of putting the country on the right track, said Jefferson, was to adhere religiously to the maxim that "the accounts of the United States ought to be, and may be made as simple as those of a common farmer, and capable of being understood by common farmers."

While Jefferson took it for granted that "absolute acquiescence in the decisions of the majority" was "the vital principle of republics," he excepted majorities created by corruption. He did not doubt that Hamilton owed his influence in Congress less to the rectitude of his policies than to the finesse with which he played upon the acquisitive instinct of his followers. As Jefferson visualized it, Hamilton presided over a Great Barbecue, otherwise known as the funding system, and by dint of cutting choice slices for his friends he assured himself of a majority in Congress. But the evil did not end here: as a result of this unholy alliance between businessmen and government, said Jefferson, "natural aristocrats"—the men of virtue and talent to whom power rightfully belonged—where excluded from public office while "tinsel aristocrats" swarmed into high places. Jefferson estimated that fourteen out of fifteen of these artificial aristocrats were rogues and predators. In Europe, he had seen society divided into "two classes, wolves and sheep." He was resolved that it should not happen here.

To save republicanism from these evildoers, Jefferson urged that all holders of government securities and bank stock be excluded from holding seats in Congress. Not until the legislature had been thoroughly purged of this "corrupt element" was he prepared to accept its acts as a bona fide expression of the majority voice. It is significant, however, that much as Jefferson reprobated the acquisitive instinct as it manifested itself in businessmen, stock speculators, and bankers, he withheld his strictures when that instinct took the form of land speculation. Nor did he ever propose that the owners of slaves, together with the owners of stocks and bonds, be denied admittance to Congress.

Jefferson did not rest his case against Hamilton with the charge of aiding and abetting the rise of a plutocracy in the United States; in the eyes of the Secretary of State, his adversary was guilty of the even more heinous crime of seeking to subvert republicanism and to erect a monarchy in its stead. Every Report which emanated from the office of the Secretary of the Treasury struck Jefferson as part and parcel of an insidious monarchical "plot." As he saw it, Hamilton lived for the day when he could place a diadem upon the brow of George Washington and acclaim him "Highness." In that event, Jefferson felt certain that although the voice which issued from the American throne would be that of George Washington, the script would be the work of Alexander Hamilton.

His suspicions nurtured by John Beckley, the clerk of the House of Representatives and an indefatigable scandalmonger, Jefferson concluded that Hamilton was "a man whose history from the moment at which history can stoop to notice him, is a tissue of machinations against the liberty of the country which . . . has heaped it's honors on his head." Where his rival was concerned, Jefferson's credulity was unbounded: he even gave credit to a report that Hamilton was the author of *Plain Truth,* a pamphlet written in 1776 to oppose American independence.

Particularly in Hamilton's efforts to aggrandize the power and prestige of the Presidency did Jefferson see the monarchical leaven at work. Since the Constitutional Convention, where Hamilton had delivered a speech in praise of monarchy, he seemed to have become more subtle, not more republican: if he could not make Washington a king in name, he would make him a king in fact, leaving only the semblance of republican government to beguile the people into believing that they were still free. But, as Jefferson well knew, a monarchy required the prop of a privileged aristocracy. It was painfully obvious to him from whence this aristocracy was to come: the stockjobbers, merchants, and bankers were being groomed by Hamilton to play the part of members of an American House of Lords. From that eminence they would presumably occupy themselves in keeping the "swinish multitude" in order.

Thus Jefferson recognized no differences between "stock-jobbers and king makers": those who worshiped Mammon were prepared to bend the knee before a king. While he did not suppose that the "monarchical conspiracy" had sunk its roots deep into the body politic—"the bulk below," he remarked, "is sound and pure"—it was not until he attained the Presidency that he proclaimed the doctrine that Federalists and Republicans were brothers under their party labels. During the period of Federalist ascendancy, he declared repeatedly that Hamilton and his followers were dedicated to the overthrow of the Constitution and the creation of a monarchy in the United States. Between monarchism and republicanism, he saw no middle ground. "I hold it as honorable to take a firm and decided part," he said in 1796, "and as immoral to pursue a middle line, as between the parties of Honest men, & Rogues."

No doubt Jefferson and his Partisans sincereley believed in the existence of a "monarchical conspiracy." But no politicans, however pure—and the Jeffersonians arrogated to themselves the full measure of "republican purity"—could have overlooked the enormous possibilities of attaching the name "monarchists" to their political opponents. As a Federalist wryly observed, the word was an epithet—"a substitute for argument, and its overmatch."

Applied to the Federalists, it did violence to the facts. If any real danger of monarchy existed in the United States, it was during the period of the Articles of Confederation, when conservatives were alarmed by the precarious position of property rights. But these troubles were now past and the new government afforded ample protection to property. In the funding-assumption measures adopted in 1790, men of wealth had received a financial windfall calculated to endear them to the general government; even Jefferson was compelled to admit that the beneficiaries of Hamilton's fiscal policies were not likely to bite the hand that fed them. Nor did their personal predilections impel them toward monarchy. In the Constitutional Convention, Franklin had observed that there was "a natural inclination" in the mass of mankind toward kingly government because, he said, "it gives more the appearance of equality among citizens; and that they like." But that the Federalist grandees emphatically did not like: high-spirited, independent-minded, and domineering men, they could not easily bring themselves to acknowledge a master. As Gouverneur Morris pointed out, it was absurd to suppose "that the upper ranks of society will, by setting up a king, put down themselves." Their taste ran much more strongly toward an oligarchic republic than toward a monarchy.

What Jefferson stigmatized as incipient monarchy was in actuality "energetic" government and burgeoning capitalistic enterprise. When he reported in 1790 that he often stood alone at Philadelphia dinner parties as "the only advocate on the republican side of the question," it was his brand of republicanism that he was defending. His opponents in these debates were not monarchists but men who wished to render the republican form of government "competent to its purposes" to strengthen the position of commerce and manufacturing in the American economy, and to wield political power in the interests of the businessmen in the United States.

As for Hamilton himself—the moving spirit, by Jefferson's reckoning, of the monarchical plot—he complained that by accusing him of trying to subvert the established government, his enemies not only impugned his republicanism but cruelly insulted his intelligence. For, he said, only a man far gone in folly could suppose that monarchism was possible in a country where the people were so democratic in their ideas and so egalitarian in their tastes as to raise grave doubts whether they would long remain and submit to the restraints imposed upon them by the Federal Constitution. He regretted that he was compelled to deal with this singularly cross-grained breed of men who balked at deferring to rank, birth, or merit. But Hamilton always took a realistic rather than a romantic view of human nature—his romanticism was reserved for the nation, not for its citizens—and he resigned himself early in his career to making the best of the strange republican world in which his destiny was cast. Robert Troup, one of his most intimate friends, declared that Hamilton "never had the least idea that we had materials, in the country, at all suitable for the construction of a monarchy; and consequently he never harboured any intention whatever of attempting that form of government."

However he might appear to his enemies, Hamilton always visualized himself as the one man who could make republicanism a success. In his opinion this entailed, among other things, protecting popular government from its friends and well-wishers. For republicans seemed to Hamilton to have a peculiar weakness for killing the thing they loved. If monarchy were ever established in the United States, for example, Hamilton felt sure that it would eventuate "from convulsions and disorders, in consequence of the arts of popular demagogues." Here Hamilton believed that he had touched upon the weakest spot of republicanism—its tendency to produce demagogues and the proclivity of the people to follow these Pied Pipers of democracy. The road to political office in the United States, Hamilton decided, was by "flattering the prejudices of the people, and exciting their jealousies and apprehensions, to throw affairs into confusion." While he absolved Jefferson and Madison of any intention of bringing such disaster upon the country, he believed that it would be the inevitable result of their actions.

Considered solely as a theory, republicanism had a strong appeal for Hamilton. "I desire above all things," he said, "to see the equality of political rights, exclusive of all hereditary distinction, firmly established by a practical demonstration of its being consistent with the order and happiness of society." But when it came to reducing this prepossessing theory to practice, Hamilton felt grave doubts and misgivings. The question uppermost in his mind—and it was never answered fully to his satisfaction during his lifetime—was whether republican government was compatible with order, stability, and the maintenance of the Union. Nevertheless, he was resolved to give popular government a fair trial. Everything he did during his tenure of the Secretaryship of the Treasury was intended to contribute to the success of the "republican experiment."

At certain times during his career, Hamilton gave evidence of possessing the ability—rare in a man so deeply comitted in the issues of the day—of viewing himself and his adversaries objectively. On one such occasion, Hamilton's insight led him to discern the real nature of his difference with Jefferson. "One side appears to believe that there is a serious plot to overturn the State governments, and substitute a monarchy to the present republican system," he wrote in 1792. "The other side firmly believes that there is a serious plot to overturn the general government and elevate the separate powers of the States upon its ruins. Both sides may be equally wrong. . . ."

In at least one particular, Jefferson was right: Hamilton was resolved to make the executive department the nerve center of the government, the "cement of the union," the chief stabilizing influence and the checkrein upon demagoguery. By thus exalting the Chief Executive, Hamilton did not believe that liberty would be endangered, for he had learned from history that republics were destroyed not by executive encroachments but by "the licentiousness of the people." Unless the "executive impulse" were made the mainspring of the Federal government, he saw no prospect of success for the "republican experiment": good government, he said, must always naturally depend on the energy of the executive department." Under this conviction, he construed the President's powers as broadly as the Constitution permitted and assigned to the Chief Executive the duty of leading and informing the people.

Hamilton branded as "malignant and false" Jefferson's charge that ownership by congressmen of government securities or stock in the Bank of the United States constituted prima facie evidence of corruption. "It is a strange perversion of ideas," he observed, ". . . that men should be deemed corrupt and criminal for becoming proprietors in the funds of their country. . . . As to improper speculations on measures depending before Congress, I believe never were any body of men freer from them." But he had long since ceased to be surprised by anything Jefferson and his friends said or did—they seemed to consider themselves to be the only honest men in the country, and every man who differed from them in opinion "an ambitious despot or a corrupt knave."

At no time in his career did Hamilton attempt to violate the Constitution, nor has his interpretation of the powers granted the Federal government under that document been nullified by subsequent decisions of the Supreme Court of the United States. The truth is, at the very time that Jefferson was accusing him of planning the overthrow of the Constitution, Hamilton was holding it up to veneration as a sacred ark. But when Jefferson took over the Presidency, Hamilton was prepared to give up the Constitution for lost: in such hands, "the frail and worthless fabric," he said, would never carry the American people to national power and greatness.

Hamilton's achievement was not merely that he had set the finances of the country in order. The Constitution had created a government of three distinct branches, each of which was protected from the encroachments of the others by a system of checks and balances. In 1790, the question was: Could a government so constrained by its internal organization function effectively or was it condemned to inaction produced by deadlock between the departments? Certainly it is true that if the doctrine of the separation of powers were applied in its full rigidity, there was little hope that the new government would prove more effective in meeting emergencies than had the Articles of Confederation. Hamilton demonstrated that the Federal government was capable of fulfilling one of the cardinal objectives of the "more perfect union" created in 1787—the direction of the financial and economic concerns of the country.

Prologue to War

Harry Coles

The War of 1812 resulted from the unsuccessful efforts of the United States to maintain its interests and its honor in a world divided into two armed camps. Both in its origins and in the way it was fought, the war was an outgrowth of a general European conflict that raged from 1793 to 1815, with one brief recess, 1801–1803.

From the founding of the American Republic peace was a cornerstone of its foreign policy. Though President Washington had serious difficulties with both the chief antagonists, Great Britain and France, he somehow managed to maintain the neutrality of the United States. President John Adams had little difficulty with England, thanks to Jay's Treaty, but he was obliged to engage in an undeclared naval war with France. Under the efficient leadership of the Federalists both the army and the navy were built up to respectable, if not formidable, forces. But while preparing for war John Adams worked for peace and, disregarding the advice of some of the militarists in his party, he made a treaty with France in 1800 that cost him a second term.

After Jefferson became President in 1801 France and England concluded the Peace of Amiens; and the Republicans took relish in quietly dismantling the military system of the Federalists. When general war broke out again in 1803 Jefferson attempted to maintain the neutral rights of the United States not by force, but rather by diplomatic negotiation and economic coercion. The same general policy was pusued by President Madison when he assumed office in 1809. By the autumn of 1811, however, a widespread, though by no means universal, demand for war arose. During the session of 1811–12, Congress passed certain measures providing for military preparation while President Madison made some last-ditch efforts to bring about a peacable solution. Unable, however, to accomplish anything on the diplomatic front, President Madison finally recommended a declaration of war against Great Britain which was passed by Congress in June, 1812.

From THE WAR OF 1812 by Harry L. Coles, The University of Chicago Press, 1965. Reprinted by permission.

The Experiment of Economic Coercion

The reasons for the coming of the war are many and complicated. And though historians are by no means in agreement on the relative weight to be attributed to various factors, they have in general discussed two sets of causes: maritime grievances and western aims. Let us examine the maritime grievances first.

In resisting Napoleon, whom many regarded as the devil incarnate, Englishmen honestly thought they were fighting for the liberties of the entire world. Ironically, as the struggle became longer and harder, liberties were increasingly suppressed in Britain while the sense of world mission became ever more potent. Since Britain fought for the right, it was plainly the duty of other nations, particularly the United States, which owed its very existence to Britain, to subordinate national goals to the interests of the struggle which was being waged in behalf of mankind.

But if Englishmen felt that right was on their side, Americans talked about their rights. Though there was some shifting in emphasis and in detail over the years, the United States adhered fairly consistently to certain broad principles. One of these was summed up in the slogan, "Free ships make free goods." England could not countenance this doctrine in all its implications. Had she done so she would have permitted French-owned goods to move unmolested on American ships. One of the problems involved the definition of contraband. The United States wanted the list limited to those articles that would directly help the French war effort. It was, of course, to England's interest to make the list as broad as possible. Americans contended, furthermore, that the only legal blockades were those that named specific ports or areas and stationed ships off the coast to seize ships as they attempted to enter or leave. England proclaimed blockades of hundreds of miles of coastline and did not hesitate to capture ships on the high seas presumed to be headed for a blockaded port. The British never insisted that paper blockades were legal; to have done so would have created precedents not to their long-term interests. They contended that their blockades, while sweeping, were enforceable and therefore legal.

Impressment, on the other hand, involved not only the right to search for deserters but the right of any officer of the Royal Navy to make a decision on the spot. Whenever conditions seemed to warrant it, the British government issued Orders-in-Council authorizing the Lord High Admiral or the Commissioners of the Admiralty to issue press warrants to officers of the navy. These officers in turn were expected to keep their ships manned—no easy task in view of the conditions prevailing in the Royal Navy. Poor food, hard work, and harsh discipline caused British sailors to desert by the thousands. A British seaman wishing to place himself under the protection of the American flag could do so legitimately by taking out naturalization papers. Often, however, deserters simply obtained "protection" papers, which could be purchased, sometimes for as little as one dollar. In view of the heavy traffic in fraudulent papers, it is little wonder that the British refused to recognize any form of naturalization. "Once an Englishman always an Englishman" was the principle on which the press gangs operated. Britain never claimed the right to impress native-born Americans or to search naval vessels for deserters.

One June 22, 1807, a vessel of the U.S. Navy, the "Chesapeake," set sail from Norfolk, Virginia, and when she was about ten miles to sea was hailed by the British frigate, "Leopard." Assuming that the British ship was merely asking him to carry dispatches to Europe, Commodore Barron allowed a British officer to board. This officer produced a copy of an order from Vice-Admiral Sir George Berkeley, Commander-in-Chief of the American station, to search the ship for deserters. Though his guns were not yet in firing order, Commodore Barron refused, whereupon the "Leopard" subjected the defenseless "Chesapeake" to a ten-minute cannonade that killed three men and wounded eighteen. After firing a single shot in honor of his flag, Commodore Barron submitted to the search. A second boarding party removed four members of the crew, all of them allegedly deserters.

When the "Chesapeake" hobbled back to Norfolk with her tale of woe, the response was immediate and loud. Protests from all parts of the country denounced the incident as an outrageous violation on American sovereignty. American opinion not only supported but demanded war.

Though he issued a proclamation forbidding supplies to British ships, President Jefferson did not want the situation to get out of control. What he really hoped to do was to capitalize on the war feeling to force a diplomatic settlement. "They have often enough . . . given us cause for war before," he wrote his minister, James Monroe, in London, "but it has been on points which would not have united the nation. But now they have touched a chord which vibrates in every heart. Now . . . is the time to settle the old and the new." Monroe was to demand not only restoration of the seamen taken from the "Chesapeake" but also, as security for the future, "the entire abolition of impressment from vessels of the United States." Since the British never claimed the right to search American naval vessels, they offered to indemnify the wounded and the families of the killed. Though reparation was eventually made, it was tardy and in poor spirit: the "Chesapeake" incident remained an open sore until 1812.

Instead of war, Jefferson resorted to economic pressure and launched one of the boldest experiments in the history of American foreign policy. In December, 1807, he recommended, and Congress passed, the Embargo Act which forbade any ship of the United States to sail from a U.S. port for any foreign port.

What were Jefferson's motives and objectives? Although economic pressure was by no means new, never before—and never since for that matter— had a President seized the American economy root and branch to wield it as an instrument of policy. It must be remembered that antipathy to war was deeply rooted both in national tradition and in Republican doctrine. All the founding fathers, whether Federalist or Republican, agreed on a policy of non-involvement in European conflicts. They felt that a period of isolation was desirable in order that the United States achieve and maintain freedom of action, freedom to choose, as Washington put it, war or peace as their interests might dictate. The founding fathers disagreed, however, on the best means of achieving this freedom of action. The Federalists had given their answer: adequate preparation for war. The Republicans could not accept this because armies and navies meant encouraging militarism, contracts for private business at public expense, and high taxes, all of which they loathed. Republican doctrine demanded an alternative to war.

Though all parts of the country and all segments of the economy were affected by the embargo, the New England shipping interests felt the impact most directly. It was not long before many coastal towns were scenes of desolation. In the South, with cotton falling nearly 50 per cent in price, many planters were ruined or nearly so. The only part of the country that actually benefitted was along the Canadian border where a thriving smuggling trade arose.

That the embargo brought the domestic economy to near paralysis there can be little doubt. Did it likewise have a profound effect on those countries it was supposed to coerce? France seems to have been helped more than hindered by the measure. In fact, the embargo complemented France's continental system. Napoleon said repeatedly that, though he preferred that the United States declare war against Great Britain, the embargo was the next best thing. England lost a part of her American market but this was offset temporarily by the opening of alternate markets in the Spanish colonies, hitherto closed to the British. Loss of supplies, which the authors of the embargo had thought would be particularly effective, caused some inconvenience but no crucial shortages in Britain. When William Pinkney, the American minister, tried to use the embargo to wring concessions from the British government, he met with a perfect squelch. "The embargo is only to be considered as an innocent municipal regulation which affects none but the United States themselves," George Canning, the foreign secretary told him. "His Majesty does not conceive that he has the right to make any complaint of it; and He has made none. . . ."

The repeal of an old law and the accession of a new President might have provided the occasion for a new departure in foreign policy, but such was not the case. By refusing to prepare militarily the Republicans failed to preserve the options. Limited or all-out war were less realistic alternatives in 1809 than in 1807, because the Army and Navy were even weaker and the embargo had sapped the internal strength and unity of the nation. The only feasible option was to continue the policy of peaceable coercion. This was done in the form of the Nonintercourse Act of 1809 which opened up commerce with all the world except France and England and their dependencies. The President was authorized to suspend the operations of the act in favor of either belligerent that repealed its restrictions on American trade.

In a mood approaching desperation, the Americans attempted to find a way out. They still could not bring themselves to accept war as a solution, both because the United States was less than ever prepared and because the French seizures had caught up with and even surpassed British interference with commerce. Was there any form in which economic pressure might be made to work? After long debate Congress took the old Non-intercourse Act and turned it inside out. The new law, known as Macon's Bill No. 2, restored trade with all the world but offered to renew non-intercourse against England if France repealed her decrees. Likewise if England would repeal her decrees, the United States would restore non-importation against France. Economic coercion had originally been undertaken with the idea of securing concessions while at the same time preserving neutrality. By the time of Macon's Bill No. 2 a subtle transition had taken place. In return for concessions the United States was really offering an alliance.

Historians have repeatedly said that Madison was duped, hoodwinked, and bamboozled by Napoleon. The critics who have dealt so harshly with Madison have failed to appreciate the desperate straits to which he was reduced. It seems unlikely that he was taken in. By pretending, however, to regard the note as genuine, he hoped to win concessions from Britain—not sweeping concessions, necessarily, but some relaxation, even if only of a face-saving kind. When the American minister in London informed the government that the French had repealed the Berlin and Milan Decrees the British demanded proof. Repeated efforts to get some evidence of repeal came to nothing. Soon American policy became hopelessly ambivalent. In London the United States was insisting that repeal was genuine, while in Paris they pleaded in vain for evidence of such repeal. President Madison is to be criticized not so much for his original gamble as for persisting in a position that became increasingly untenable.

In spite of the fact that relations with both France and Great Britain continued to deteriorate, the Eleventh Congress did nothing to prepare for war. The financial strength of the country was in fact weakened by the refusal of Congress to recharter the Bank of the United States and also its refusal to adopt Secretary of the Treasury Albert Gallatin's plans for new taxes which were designed to make up for the loss of revenue that would result from the non-importation of British goods. Naval appropriations were slightly increased over 1810 but provided for no significant increment of strength. A bill to raise a military force of fifty thousand volunteers was allowed to die. Though nothing was done to prepare for war, there were men in the Eleventh Congress who expressed their growing exasperation at the old policy of peacable coercion. Those advocating sterner measures, however, lacked effective leadership.

The Road to War

In the elections of 1810–11 nearly half of the incumbents lost their seats. Energetic candidates often denounced what they considered the do-nothing policies of past Congresses and promised a bold new approach to foreign policy. In some cases old men were replaced by young ones. But neither in the average age of its membership nor in the percentage of new members was the twelfth Congress especially different from other early Congresses. What distinguished the new Congress was the quality of its leadership.

One of the leading lights of the new take-over generation was Henry Clay. Born and educated in Virginia, Clay had moved to the West as a young man and had both drawn and contributed to the vibrant, go-ahead spirit of that region. Though only thirty-four years old in 1811, he was no novice in politics. Schooled in the rough and tumble of the frontier, he had served parts of two terms in the Senate of the United States. Switching to the House, Clay was elected Speaker in his first term and proceeded immediately to make something of the office. Heretofore the Speaker had been merely a presiding officer; by appointments, patronage, and clever management Clay made it a position of true party leadership.

So incommodious was the capital city of the early nineteenth century that most congressmen did not subject their families to the inconveniences of its crude facilities. Instead they became bachelors for a portion of the year and lived in one or another of the city's numerous boardinghouses. Clay shared his quarters with a group that was described as "the strongest war mess in Congress." This group, and others of like mind, have gone down in history as the "war hawks." The term was coined by the Federalists, who wished to imply, of course, that their opponents were heedlessly and recklessly determined on war. Roger Brown, in his recent book, *Republic in Peril,* maintains that "no Republican ever really answered this description." He suggests furthermore that the phrase, "war hawks of 1812," be relegated "to the realm of partisan misunderstanding and historical mythology." The same author admits, however, that "men did wax belligerent, they did ignore or minimize the evils of war, and they did predict quick and easy victory." Through long usage the term has lost much of its original sting and it is used here as a matter of convenience to designate those Republicans who took a lead in advocating new and stronger measures that led ultimately to war.

In making his committee assignments, Clay made little effort to reflect the views of the minority party, the Federalists, or even the wide spectrum of views within his own party, the Republicans (Democrats of a later day). He boldly packed the most important committees with war hawks. Peter B. Porter, a Connecticut Yankee who had moved to the Niagara frontier and settled at Blackrock, near Buffalo, was made chairman of the Foreign Affairs Committee. He was to be assisted by twenty-nine-year-old John C. Calhoun, recently elected on a pro-war platform in South Carolina; Felix Grundy, an Anglophobe from a frontier settlement at Nashville, Tennessee; and John Adams Harper, a thirty-two-year-old firebrand from New Hampshire. The committee also included two moderate Republicans who generally went along with the majority, a sole Federalist, and John Randolph of Roanoke, an old-line Republican unalterably opposed to war. Other committee chairmanships included Langdon Cheves of the strongly pro-war delegation of South Carolina, Naval Affairs; David R. Williams of South Carolina, Military Affairs; and Ezekiel Bacon of Massachusetts, Ways and Means. Though some of these men, notably Williams and Porter, were to disappoint Clay, they were selected with the hope of carrying out a new departure.

The necessities of the times as they were felt by the Committee on Foreign Relations were set forth on November 29. After reviewing Britain's misdeeds over the years, the report recommended bringing the army up to authorized strength, adding ten thousand regulars and fifty thousand volunteers, arming merchantmen, and outfitting existing warshipos. By December 19 every one of the committee's resolutions had been carried by comfortable majorities. The reasons for the heavy pro-war votes were various. A wing of the Federalists, led by Josiah Quincy, voted for the resolutions because they felt that war would be disastrous, would result in the repudiation of the Republicans, and would put the Federalists in the position to make the peace. Many moderate Republicans voted for the resolutions in the hope of inducing a change in British policies. Their motive, in other words, was not to fight a war but to deter one, and it was in this hope that the "Hornet" was sent to Europe laden with the resolutions, the newspapers advocating war, and the record of the debates in Congress.

After dealing with the regular army to its satisfaction, the House considered a bill authorizing the President to accept fifty thousand volunteers, to be officered by state authorities, and called into service by the President when needed. Immediately the question arose whether the President had the authority under the Constitution to send the militia outside the boundaries of the United States. Even some of the most ardent war hawks argued that he could not. It was decided finally to omit mention of the question, and the bill was approved on February 6, 1812. Having raised the constitutional problem and failed to resolve it, Congress accentuated an inherent weakness of the military system of the United States.

Probably Madison made up his mind that there was only war or submission in the summer of 1811. Still he was unwilling to take a strong pro-war stand. This was partly owing to his Republican scruples—the Constitution left the war-making power to Congress. But also Madison seems to have clung to the hope that some development would make war unnecessary. "Our President though a man of amiable manners and great talents," said Calhoun, "has not I fear those commanding talents, which are necessary to control those around him. . . . He reluctantly gives up the system of peace."

Constantly prodding the administration, in March Clay suggested a thirty-day embargo to be followed by a declaration of war. Secretary of State Monroe went to the Hill to confer with the Foreign Affairs Committee. He informed them that he still considered the country ill prepared and that the war legislation was largely "an appeal to the feelings of foreign governments." Though he did not oppose the embargo, he suggested it be extended to sixty days in order to allow time for the "Hornet" to return with news of European developments. In the Senate the embargo was extended to ninety days and went into effect April 4. One of the last excuses for delay was removed when the "Hornet" returned on May 22. The vessel brought supplementary instructions to Foster, but they merely repeated what the British had said time and again before: obviously the French had not repealed their decrees and "America can never be justified in continuing to resent against Us that failure of Relief, which is alone attributable to the insidious Policy of the Enemy." Faced with what seemed to be final refusal of any concession, Madison began composing his war message.

President Madison submitted his war message on June 1. Reviewing Anglo-American relations since 1803 in roughly chronological order, the document was an indictment of British policy under five main heads. First was impressment. Madison has been criticized by Henry Adams on the ground that "this was the first time that the Government had alleged impressment as its chief grievance, or had announced, either to England or America, the intention to fight for redress." The President put impressment first, not because he necessarily thought it was the chief grievance, but because it was the oldest. It is true that the United States did not press the point in negotiations just before the war. But relative silence was the result of a conviction that it was hopeless to pursue the issue rather than indifference toward it. Furthermore, American consular agents had carried on a steady correspondence with the Admiralty about the matter and the practice had by no means abated. It has been conservatively estimated that from 750 to 1,000 men were taken every year from 1809 onward. Next in Madison's catalogue was the practice of British cruisers hovering near American ports and harassing entering and departing commerce. Third were the blockades that were, said Madison, illegal even according to definitions issued by the British themselves.

Fourth were the Orders-in-Council. Assuming the purpose of the message was to arouse sympathy in Britain and indignation at home, it was here that Madison made his most telling point. It has become certain, Madison charged, "that the commerce of the United States is to be sacrificed, not as interfering with the belligerent rights of Great Britain; not as supplying the wants of her enemies, which she herself supplies; but as interfering with the monopoly which she covets for her own commerce and navigation." Though the charge may seem extreme, Madison was saying no more than some Englishmen were saying themselves. George Canning, a staunch adherent of strict blockades, charged in Parliament that the Orders-in-Council had been transformed from a blockade into "a measure of commercial rivalry." This had been done through the use and the abuse of a system of special licenses. The Board of Trade had the power to issue licenses exempting ships and cargoes from the effects of the blockade. It is not difficult to see that the interests of the empire might be well served by a judicious use of such power. The issue of licenses, however, became honeycombed with favoritism, corruption, and fraud. Many an Englishman who would have supported his government to the death on impressments and legitimate blockades blushed at the traffic in special licenses.

Madison's fifth, and only non-maritime grievance, referred to the renewal of Indian warfare on the western frontier. No specific charge was made, but the President found it difficult to believe that the latest uprisings were unconnected with British officers and agents in Canada whose past activities among the Indians were well known.

In a war filled with irony, nothing was more ironical than the timing of the declaration. From April to June the British, who had remained adamant for nearly a decade, moved toward conciliation, while the Americans, who though they had been patient under extreme provocation, hastened toward war. Since 1807 England had been ruled by the Tories and since 1809 Spencer Perceval had been Prime Minister. Under Perceval the war against Napoleon had been prosecuted vigorously and, in general, the shipping interest had been favored over manufacturing. Beginning in 1810 a depression hit the manufacturing areas of the British Isles, and Parliament was soon besieged with petitions for repeal of the Orders-in-Council. On April 21, 1812, the British government announced that if France would publish an official repeal of her decrees, the cabinet would withdraw the Orders-in-Council.

The Problem of Causation

For nearly a hundred years after the outbreak of the War of 1812, American historians took Madison's message more or less at face value. That the war was brought on by Great Britain's impressment of American seamen and her Orders-in-Council seemed self-evident. With the rise of a more critical and professional generation of historians near the end of the nineteenth century, the causes were probed more deeply. For one thing, the nature of the vote on war began to be examined critically. Why should a war for maritime rights be opposed by the Northeast whose rights were allegedly being ignored, and supported by the South and West which had neither ships nor sailors?

During the course of the debate on the war, John Randolph accused his opponents of a variety of base motives. Among other things he charged: "Agrarian cupidity, not maritime right, urges the war." Louis M. Hacker, in an article published in 1924, took up the hint thrown out by Randolph. Pointing out that American agriculture was terribly exploitative, he maintained that by 1812 most of the good lands in the Old Northwest, with the exception of the prairies, were exhausted. Since the prairies at that time were considered unfit for cultivation, the land-hungry farmers wanted the good lands of Canada. This thesis was soon attacked by Julius W. Pratt, who showed that there were still plenty of good agricultural lands left, exclusive of the prairies. Though agreeing that western aims were important, Pratt felt there was a better foundation on which to base the case.

The true picture of western aims, as Pratt saw them, was set forth in his book, *The Expansionists of 1812,* published in 1925. Pratt states that war was declared as a result of a sectional bargain between the South and the West. A general desire to annex Canada had existed since the War for Independence, and this desire became strongly activated with the outbreak of Indian unrest all along the western border in 1811. "The rise of Tecumseh, backed, as was universally believed, by the British, produced an urgent demand in the Northwest that the British be expelled from Canada. This demand was of primary importance in bringing on the war." The South was indifferent about Canada but wished to annex Florida for a variety of strategic and economic reasons. By linking Canada and Florida together in a general program of expansion that would maintain a rough equilibrium in the sectional balance, enough votes were mustered for war.

Based on much original research and written with great clarity and perception, Pratt's book was, and is, widely influential. Although he was careful to say that he was dealing with one set of causes only (western aims), his explanation has often been accepted as the whole story. Before Pratt's book the western aims were sometimes noted as contributing causes; after his book was published, they were often accepted as the main, and sometimes as the only, real causes.

Emphasis on western factors soon received further confirmation from another source. In 1931 George R. Taylor published two articles on prices and economic conditions in the Mississippi Valley in the period just prior to the war. Agreeing with Pratt that the Indian menace was a contributing cause, he pointed out that this matter was of concern to only restricted areas of the West. The whole area, on the other hand, was affected by agricultural prices. Taylor showed that prices had declined in the period before the war and that a general economic depression had hit the whole area. Hitherto it had been assumed that westerners had talked about maritime rights and national honor only to shield their expansionist ambitions. Taylor showed the real connection between western problems and maritime rights. Though the westerners were not sailors and did not own ships, they produced goods that were carried in ships. And though the real causes of economic distress lay primarily within the area, the western farmers and planters blamed British restrictions on neutral commerce for their ills and eventually supported a war to obtain relief.

The timely addition of economic motives in the early thirties immensely strengthened the position of what we might call the western school of causation. Though they differed greatly among themselves, their case now rested on four legs: land hunger, the Indian menace, northern and southern expansionism, and economic depression. For several years the western school gained ground steadily and almost succeeded in ousting the old school of maritime grievances. But just when victory seemed complete, a reaction set in. In recent years the pendulum has been swinging back in favor of maritime causes. In 1941 Warren H. Goodman published an article in the *Mississippi Valley Historical Review* which, after reviewing various interpretations that had been offered down to that time, concluded: "One can no longer doubt that nineteenth century writers overestimated the significance of maritime matters, but contemporary historians are perhaps committing an equally serious error in the opposite direction." He maintained that there was need for a comprehensive account, based on sources, to synthesize the various sets of causes.

The defect of which Goodman complained was soon remedied. A comprehensive survey had in fact already been completed but was probably unavailable at the time Goodman completed his study. In 1940 A. L. Burt published a book entitled *The United States, Great Britain, and British North America from the Revolution to the Establishment of Peace after the War of 1812.* Burt was probably more familiar with the documentary record on both sides of the controversy than any writer since Henry Adams. After tracing the many complicated threads of the story of Anglo-American relations, he examined the Pratt thesis in some detail and concluded by rejecting it outright. Swinging back to maritime grievances, he found the real causes of the war in the cumulative frustration of the American government.

The path hewn by Burt was followed by Reginald Horsman, who in *Causes of the War of 1812,* published in 1962, evaluated both sets of causes. Horsman develops in detail an idea merely suggested by Burt, that in the plans of the war hawks Canada was to be seized as a hostage rather than a prize. While rejecting Pratt's thesis of a sectional bargain on expansionism, he accepts western concern over the Indian problem and depression as contributing causes. The fundamental cause, however, was the British maritime policy which hurt both national pride and the commerce of the United States.

The economic arguments, originally put forth by Taylor and generally accepted by Horsman, received further confirmation in an article by Margaret

Kinard Lattimer, which appeared in 1956. Using the same concepts that Taylor had applied to the Mississippi Valley, Miss Lattimer found that the South too was suffering from declining prices and general depression. Pointing out that South Carolina was even more directly dependent on the European trade than the West, she concluded that "whether or not fighting a war with England was the logical step, the South Carolinians of 1812 were convinced that a war would help."

The Taylor-Lattimer thesis remained unchallenged until 1961, when Norman K. Risjord published his article "Conservatism, War Hawks, and the Nation's Honor." Taking a look at the Middle Atlantic states, Risjord found no economic depression. The prices of beef, corn, and flour, the main exports of the Middle Atlantic states, increased over the decade preceding the war, while the prices of pork declined only slightly. Risjord maintained that Pennsylvania, which in the House voted 16 to 2 for war with Great Britain, could hardly have been following the dictates of economic interest. "The only unifying factor, present in all sections of the country," he concluded, "was the growing feeling of patriotism, the realization that something must be done to vindicate the national honor."

The swing back to maritime grievances and national honor was given another massive push in 1961 by the appearance of a thick volume by Bradford Perkins entitled *Prologue to War*. Henry Adams, A. L. Burt, and Reginald Horsman had all made use of British as well as American sources. Perkins, however, went beyond any of his predecessors or contemporaries in searching out archival and manuscript collections on both sides of the Atlantic. Though he attempts to deal with the whole problem of causation, the great bulk of Perkins' book is devoted to a re-examination of diplomatic relations with Great Britain. To a greater extent than other American historians, Perkins examines internal politics in England in the decade before the war. His general conclusion is: "While the policy of England was far less rigid than Americans often suggested, the self-righteous spirit of messianism engendered by the Napoleonic wars and a woeful underestimation of the price of American good will combined to prevent a reconciliation Jefferson and Madison eagerly desired." Although he blames British statesmen to a degree, Perkins blames American statesmen even more: ". . . the Republican chieftains must bear primary responsibility for the war. . . . Whereas Washington and Adams kept objectives and means in harmony with one another, their successors often committed the United States to seek absolute right with inadequate weapons. . . . In a state of military and psychological unpreparedness, the United States of America embarked upon a war to recover the self respect destroyed by Republican leaders."

What then is the present status of the various explanations that have been advanced? Obviously the war came not as a result of any one cause but the interplay of several. In exploring various avenues historians have not been guilty of hair-splitting. The declaration was carried by a narrow margin and the alteration of even one factor in a complicated equation might have affected the outcome significantly. Historians are justified therefore in investigating the large number of factors entering into the picture, even though it may sometimes seem that their researches complicate rather than clarify the picture. Both sets of causes, the maritime grievances and the internal factors, are necessary to explain the coming of the war, but recent historians are right to give primary weight to the maritime factors.

Though of less importance in the total picture, the internal factors are more difficult to evaluate. Since the land-hunger thesis has not been sustained by recent investigations, it can be dismissed as of little substance. The Indian menace was certainly a factor in the minds of many westerners, but those areas most directly concerned, namely, Mississippi, Indiana, Illinois, and Michigan, were still territories and had no vote in Congress. Economic depression was of more general concern than the Indian problem, but even this factor was operative primarily in the West and South.

Expansionism still has its advocates, but Burt, Horsman, Perkins, have all rejected the idea of a sectional conspiracy to enlarge the boundaries of the United States. Among these historians there is a consensus that the war hawks were interested in Canada primarily as a means of waging war rather than an object of war. This is not to deny, of course, that what was originally a means could not easily have become an object of war. To use a modern expression, a war to win recognition of maritime rights by seizing a hostage could easily have escalated into a war for maritime rights *and* territorial conquest. It cannot be denied, furthermore, that certain members of Congress wanted both Canada and Florida, and it is possible that they voted for war hoping to get one or both.

A variety of factors, then, combined to induce a majority of Republicans to vote for war. More than anything else they had become convinced that every alternative had been tried and failed. One often reads in textbooks that the United States "blundered" into war. The declaration may have been a mistake, but certainly the decision was thoroughly debated and few governments have sought alternatives so eagerly and for such a long time. Beginning in 1807, diplomatic negotiation, economic coercion, and military preparations to deter war had all been tried without the slightest success so far as anyone could see at the time. In 1812 Jefferson summed up the views of many when he said: "Every hope from time, patience, and love of peace is exhausted and war or abject submission are the only alternatives left to us." Forced to abandon old policies, the Republicans naturally invoked those symbols that had wide appeal, phrases such as national character, honor, and the world's last and fairest hope of government by the people.

Though some Federalists professed to believe that the Republicans had never genuinely sought peace, others admitted that ample cause for war existed. The war hawks had convinced themselves that the state of the European world, far from being hopeless, presented an opportunity for the United States to advance its own interests. Since November, 1811, the war hawks had maintained that although England was one of the most powerful nations in the world, she was doubly vulnerable. Her first vulnerability was the province of Canada. Guarded by only a handful of British regulars, the thin settlements stretched along a single line of communications which for hundreds of miles ran adjacent to the border of the United States. Bending every resource to maintain an army on the Continent, Great Britain could spare little for the reinforcement of Canada and, if the United States acted with proper dispatch, that little would come too late.

Britain's second great vulnerability was her world-wide trade and especially her ships moving men and supplies to the Iberian Peninsula. This vast sea-borne traffic could be harried by privateers, armed merchant vessels, and the navy. To carry out commerce destruction most effectively the United States needed the use of friendly European ports. And here is another important reason why many Republicans opposed a triangular war. William Jones, who later became Secretary of the Navy, said that if the United States declared war on France, "we greatly impair our means of annoying G. Britain by excluding our flag and our prizes of commerce from the continent of Europe from whence we could more effectually annoy commerce & coasting trade than all the maratime [*sic*] forces of combined Europe." While the administration wished to use France to advantage, they had no wish to make common cause. Federalist charges that Madison and Monroe were sold to France were utterly without foundation. Considering herself morally superior not only to France but to all of Europe, the United States neither sought nor wanted an alliance. In his *Weekly Register* Hezekiah Niles expressed the hope that the war would finally separate the United States "from the strumpet governments of Europe."

The Jacksonian Era

Of the various forces that emerged after the War of 1812 to shape the Republic's destiny, none has commanded more attention than the advent of democracy. Historians still use almost unconsciously the expression "Jacksonian Democracy" or the "Age of Andrew Jackson" to summarize the nation's history from 1828–1848. But what does it mean? For most late 19th century historians, known as "the Turnerites", it meant the triumph of Western egalitarianism over Eastern conservatism. To them democracy was the result of the frontier's continuous effect on American society and with Jackson's election, the long process of democratization became reality. Arthur Schlesinger, Jr. argued quite the contrary in his *Age of Jackson* which won the Pulitzer Prize in 1945 and ignited an historical debate that engaged Jacksonian scholars for twenty years. Democracy triumphed with Old Hickory's election, but the democratic impulse, Schlesinger contended, came more from the urban masses than the frontier. It was linked closely with the Eastern workingmen's struggle against the privileged capitalist elite. Schlesinger's critics maintained, however, that the conflict was not between capitalists and laborers, but rather between one set of entrepreneurs and another; "men on the make," who rode to power on Jackson's shoulders and democratic dogma.

Regardless of the debate over which forces most directly shaped the era, historians agree that the democratic spirit acquired its supreme symbol with the election of Andrew Jackson. More than any other 19th century national leader, Jackson demonstrated that popular appeal could outweigh other advantages in the contest for political power. Jackson's image as the "perfect democrat" emanated principally from his frontier background. By the 1820's Americans tended to associate democracy with frontier characteristics, thus making the Western man democracy's "natural" champion and caretaker. Jackson, however, had a second and perhaps greater claim upon the people's affection—he was a military hero—the scourge of the Creeks and the victor of New Orleans. The young Republic, lacking an historical tradition that extended into a distant past, had to create its myths from contemporary events and individuals. Americans needed heroes as the basis for national legend, and heroic reputations were usually made on the battlefield.

Who were the "common folk" rallying to Old Hickory as their paladin? According to Edward Pessen, Jacksonian Americans were, on the whole, a deplorably backward and crude people in both their taste and manners. At least that was the impression chronicled by the army of European visitors who swarmed over this country during the Jacksonian era. In their travelers' accounts, the visitors covered almost every aspect of American civilization—its political, social, and economic institutions; its intellectual life; the striking features of its geography, as well as customs and habits. They found Americans to be basically anti-intellectual and anti-aesthetic. Artistic and scholarly pursuits were viewed with disdain as being effete, pretentious, and "aristocratic." Needless to say, refinement and sophistication were not the dominant traits of Jacksonian Americans. Their major concern seemed to be the acquisition of material wealth and its ostentatious display. The love of money and its accrual by any means possible superseded all endeavors. However, Jacksonian politicians shrewdly turned the people's coarseness and frenzied acquisitiveness and general lack of civility into the noble traits of the common man. The Jacksonians successfully made Americans believe that their bumptious, crass, and selfish attitudes were virtues, and flattered such inclinations in trade for votes.

Probably no other president embodied the characteristics of an American generation than did Andrew Jackson. As James C. Curtis observes in the second article of this section, Jackson personified the New West. He reflected its individualism, its Jack-of-all-trades versatility, its opportunism, its energy, its directness, and its prejudices. He was a genuine folk hero—an uncommon common man.

Afflicted with a violent temper, he was involved in numerous duels, stabbings, and other bloody fracases. But rough and outspoken as democracy itself, Old Hickory made things happen.

While President, Jackson demanded prompt and loyal support from subordinates. If one was not for him, one was against him. Obsessed with his Constitutional prerogatives, Jackson blatantly defied the Supreme Court on several occasions. He was equally contemptuous of Congress and was able to dominate that body as few Presidents have done. He often wielded his veto power on grounds of personal distaste rather than constitutional principle. Despite his irascibility, questionable motives, and intense partisanship, Andrew Jackson displayed a vigor and determination that captivated his contemporaries and the acclaim of future generations of Americans.

No sooner did Jackson become president than he was embroiled in controversy and engaged in bitter conflict with the forces of privilege and sectionalism. As Glydon G. Van Deusen discusses in the third essay of this chapter, Jackson's "war" on the Second Bank of the United States and his struggle with John C. Calhoun and the forces of Southern nationalism during the Nullification Crisis, proved to be the General's most serious and far-reaching challenges.

South Carolina's Ordinance of Nullification, challenging the legality of the 1828 and 1832 tariffs, reflected more than Southern economic discontent. By 1832 when the tariff issue reached a climax, it had become part of the larger, more ominous slavery issue. The new, aggressive tone of Northern abolitionists frightened the planter elite, who saw a serious threat to the stability and profitability of their slave society. Nullification seemed the appropriate weapon to defend the South's peculiar institution against the North's latest encroachments.

However, to a staunch Unionist like Andrew Jackson, South Carolina's declaration that the tariff was void in the Palmetto state, was perceived as overt treason. Old Hickory was enraged as he characteristically took South Carolina's actions as a personal affront. He called John C. Calhoun, the leader of the nullifiers, a madman, and threatened to burn Charleston to the ground if the ordinance was not rescinded. Fortunately, cooler minds prevailed and with the help of Henry Clay, a compromise tariff was adopted that placated both Jackson and South Carolinians.

Old Hickory hated banks—especially "The Bank"—even more than he hated Indians. Perhaps no bastion of privilege and special interest affected Jackson more than the Second Bank of the United States. The "monster bank" became Jackson's greatest obsession, consuming his executive attention more than any other single issue during his presidency. Jackson made the Bank's destruction a personal crusade, vowing to "kill it" before it "killed him." Though he won his private war with the Bank, his victory proved to be more personal than beneficial to the Republic's economic health. No sooner was the Bank destroyed than the consequences of victory proved to be disillusioning. Without the Bank's restraining hand, reckless speculation and inflation soon engulfed the economy, plunging the nation into one of its worst financial crises in 1837.

President and Defender

James Curtis

Andrew Jackson groped for the right words to explain his ambivalent feelings about the election results. "I am filled with gratitude, still my mind is depressed," he said shortly after receiving formal notification of his victory. At no time in the months ahead did he speak of party triumph or political mandate. His thoughts were intensely self-centered and almost entirely concerned with corruption and providential retribution. Thanks to "the great ruler of the universe" he had survived "the most bitter and wicked persecution, recorded in history." Jackson fully appreciated "the suffrages of a virtuous people," not because they anticipated a new era of politics, but because he felt they "pronounced a verdict of condemnation" against the "corrupt minions of a profligate administration" and "justified my character and course." How the candidate must have yearned to defend his character personally, instead of entrusting it to the care of his managers. Unable to speak out, Jackson was unable to find relief. With the luxury of time and further reflection, the president-elect might have taken a broader, less conspiratorial view of the election. But the "providence" that snatched him "from the snares of the fowler" suddenly plunged him into the dark abyss. On December 22, 1828, his wife died of a heart attack.

For weeks the distraught husband was immobilized; grief and guilt overwhelmed him. He knew that Rachel had been ill, that his constant absences had contributed to her growing despondency. Yet he could no more abandon his search for public vindication than she could cast aside her role as dutiful helpmate. They were prisoners of the ambition and social convention that troubled their last years together at the Hermitage. Throughout the campaign, Jackson kept the slanders from his wife; she did not even realize the whitewash committee had solicited depositions from old family friends attesting to her virtue and the regularity of the marriage. Rachel learned of her defense by accident, shortly after the completion of the canvass. The shock of seeing her character discussed in public pamphlets may well have hastened her final collapse. Even death did not still the debate. In memory of his beloved wife, Andrew Jackson commissioned a tombstone that assured the world that "a being so gentle and so virtuous slander might wound but could not dishonor."

Images of death constantly flitted before him. As a youth he had escaped them by wild indulgence; age, social prominence, and custom denied him that release now. Everywhere he turned there were reminders of his own mortality. The public expected him to remain in "deep mourning"; they sent tokens of their sympathy and respect. "Your invaluable present will aid me in my preparation to unite with her in the realms above," read one of Jackson's notes to a well-wisher. Public accolades bore the message: "Old Hickory," "Old Hero," "Old Chieftain," old, old, old. He was old, at sixty-one the oldest man ever elected to the prsidency and perhaps the most unhealthy. Although standing six-feet-one, he weighed barely 140 pounds. He suffered from stomach distress and fevers, legacies of his forays into the Alabama forests. To alleviate his cramps and pains, he took liberal doses of sugar of lead, adding more heavy metal to a system that already bore two leaden bullets. Periodic headaches, distorted vision, extreme shortness of breath, swelling of the legs—all suggest possible kidney and heart ailments. Frequent pulmonary abscesses caused internal hemorrhaging, violent coughs, and pleuritis, which sent sharp pains jabbing up his side. Jackson bore these afflictions, but always with the thought "that my time cannot be long here on earth." Such fatalism comforted the guilt-ridden husband who could not understand why the shafts aimed at him had killed his wife instead.

The suffering, the pain, the anguish might have incapacitated a man less bent on retribution. Indeed, there were times when Jackson wished "to spend my days in silent sorrow," "at the tomb of my wife," "in peace from the toils and strife of this world." A sense of duty kept him from this communion. "I cannot retire with propriety," he claimed. "My friends draged me before the public contrary to my wishes . . . to perpetuate the blessings of liberty to our country and to put down misrule." Tragedy thus magnified Jackson's fears of conspiracy and renewed his sense of self-righteous mission. But there was an added urgency now. "My enfeebled health and constitution . . . admonished me that it was time that I should place my earthly house in order and prepare for another."

Within weeks of his inauguration in March 1829, Jackson's earthly house stood in utter disarray as the result of a social scandal that the new president took far more seriously than have the guardians of his historical reputation. The "Eaton Affair" (Or "Eaton Malaria," as John Quincy Adams called it) involved the social ostracism of Mrs. John Eaton, wife of Jackson's confidant and new secretary of war. In rallying to Mrs. Eaton's defense, the president was not indulging some private quirk nor methodically preparing a political purge. He considered his own reputation at stake. By defending feminine virtue, he hoped to avenge the slanders of the campaign and put down the forces of corruption. No small task, the effort would shape his entire presidency.

The Eaton affair originated in conflicting views of social order and revealed the depths of Jackson's animosity for Washington politics. The new president had little respect for conventions and customs in the nation's capital. He did not understand the artificial society that had taken hold in this community of transients. The intrigues, the gossips, the social snubs, the incessant rankings and rerankings of respectability that were important diversions in this isolated outpost held little interest for him. Not that Jackson was antisocial; until Rachel's death the Hermitage literally thronged with visitors, sometimes nearly fifty a day. But the host understood his guests; they honored him by their presence. Jackson found little honor in Washington. "There is nothing done here but visiting and *carding each other*," he complained to Rachel during his brief term as senator in 1823. "You know how much I was disgusted with these scenes, when you and I were here." The disgust was fed by the frontiersman's fear that he was unwelcome in polite society and by the suspicion that social prejudices had played an important part in several running battles with his Washington enemies. Jackson saw a direct link between political corruption and social intrigue.

As president, Jackson fully intended to shield himself from these evils by "the council and society of my dear wife." When Rachel died, he surrounded himself with other relatives and Tennessee friends, who soon became the talk of the capital. Rachel's nephew Andrew Jackson Donelson came to Washington as the president's private secretary. Donelson's wife, Emily, a beautiful but somwhat naive woman, took over as social mistress of the new administration with considerably more enthusiasm than Rachel would have displayed. The president's closest Tennessee confidant was William B. Lewis, his former army quartermaster. Lewis's shady dealings in Indian lands had previously prompted considerable criticism, especially during the presidential campaign. Jackson never was a very good judge of character, especially of those who claimed his friendship. He not only brought Lewis to Washington; he gave him permanent lodging in the White House. Along with later arrivals Amos Kendall and Francis P. Blair, his coterie of Westerners enjoyed so much access to the president that critics soon invented a cabal of their own: the kitchen cabinet.

No presidential associate generated more controversy than the former senator from Tennessee, John Eaton. In part the animosity was pure jealousy. As Jackson's campaign manager, Eaton played a prominent role in the selection of the cabinet, a task that always enlivened the preinaugural atmosphere by stimulating appetites and expectations. Although he had sworn to oppose secrecy and intrigue, Jackson chose his cabinet without consulting key party leaders, not even those from his own state. Far from putting an end to political maneuvering, the selections furthered the ambitions of Martin Van Buren and John C. Calhoun. The New Yorker agreed to become secretary of state, the post traditionally held by the heir-apparent. The vice-president contented himself with the support of the second most powerful cabinet official, Pennsylvania's Samuel Ingham, the new secretary of the treasury. In appointing North Carolina's John P. Branch as secretary of the navy and Georgia's John M. Berrien as attorney general, Jackson sparked renewed criticism of a corrupt compact between the legislature and the executive. Actually, neither man had enjoyed much influence during his tenure in Congress.

Having made the customary bows to political fealty and sectional balance, Jackson reserved one cabinet position for a close personal friend. He offered the War Department to his Tennessee associates Hugh Lawson White and John Eaton with the understanding that the two men would decide between them who would be the president's confidant. Eaton desperately wanted the post. White was either too polite or disgusted with the selection procedure to stand in the way. Eaton had his cherished cabinet appointment, Jackson had his personal confidant, and the capital had a social tempest more powerful than the inaugural bacchanal. "It is heart-rending to reflect," wrote one injured participant two years later "that such may be the consequence of an incident that was at first too trifling to name; but it is now important enough to agitate the country and involve in its consequences the peace of families and the destiny of a great name and still greater public interests."

To the protectors of Washington's moral standards, John Eaton's appointment was no trifling matter. The middle-aged widower's marriage to the twenty-nine-year-old daughter of a local tavern keeper offended their sense of social order. Not that the new nation's social arbiters had a prejudice against tavern keepers; the son of one was about to become secretary of state. But for all his political machinations, Martin Van Buren was discreet. The new Mrs. Eaton was not.

Born at the turn of the century, Peggy O'Neale came to know the great and near great who frequented her father's inn. Her vivacious flirtations and uncommon beauty captivated lonely politicians, drove her first husband, a navy purser, to flee to the Mediterranean, and even sparked some gallant enthusiasm from Old Hickory himself, who at Eaton's urging stayed at the O'Neale establishment in 1823. Eaton was the most taken. He agreed to manage Peggy's business affairs. In the fall of 1828 her husband committed suicide in an obscure overseas port, and John Eaton volunteered to give Peggy his good name, a gift that mounting rumors of adultery would soon depreciate. Before his march to the altar, Eaton asked Jackson's blessing; the president-elect encouraged the alliance, claiming in a fit of romantic optimism that it would silence all the wagging tongues. Far from doing that, the wedding prompted snide remarks of "what a suitable lady in waiting Mrs. Eaton will make to Mrs. Jackson . . . birds of a feather will flock together." News of Rachel's death led many Washington socialites to assume that Mrs. Eaton would wait no longer in her quest for social power and prestige.

The first prominent member of the administration to confront the delicate problem of whether to socialize with the Eatons was Vice-President John C. Calhoun, whose presidential ambitions necessitated the awkward pose that he had long been Jackson's defender, even during the heated cabinet debates on the Seminole War. Calhoun's enemies, particularly William B. Lewis and the growing number of Van Buren adherents around the president, were all too eager to prove Calhoun faithless. Neither the vice-president nor his detractors controlled events. Had not Floride Calhoun turned on her heel, had not the cabinet wives joined in this "*noble* stand" by refusing to "visit one, who has left her strait and narrow path," the crisis might have been averted.

The stand was on grounds of high moral principle and soon drew support from the minister of the largest Washington congregation. The protest was not politically staged. No Machiavellian manipulator maneuvered astute, strong-willed women like Floride Calhoun, who fully realized the political chaos that would result from their decisions but considered social respectability more important than politics. Their husbands desperately wanted a return to domestic bliss. Protest against the president's social standards gave rise to the storm; Andrew Jackson's fury blew the protest to gale force. Only when at its height did it spawn the whirlwinds of ambition and collusion.

Had the president been able to summon a measure of detachment he might have realized what some of his good friends came to see—that involvement in the Eaton embroglio was beneath the dignity of his office. In the aftermath of Rachel's death, such objectivity was impossible. Andrew Jackson regarded the presidency, not as an institution with certain inherent customs and responsibilites, but as vindication of his injured reputation, a reward for his faithful service. As long as the slanders continued, he remained the candidate, courting public favor, seeking moral revenge. But this time he wold direct his own defense.

Jackson personalized the issue immediately. This was more than a contest over social etiquette; it was a clear case of intimidation, the work of "Clay and his minions" who had tried unsuccessfully to prevent his election and were now attempting to prevent Eaton from taking his rightful place in the cabinet. Jackson refused to cast Eaton aside, just as he refused to believe any of the stories circulated by these corrupt political gossip-mongers. Eaton was an honorable man; his wife was therefore above suspicion. "It was enough for his friends to know that he had married her to put down the slang of the gossips of the city." The wedding did not silence the defamers any more than Jackson's own marriage had spared Rachel nearly three decades of anguish. He would have to demonstrate Peggy's innocence just as conclusively as the whitewash committee had proved Rachel's purity. By doing so Jackson would complete the defense of feminine virtue begun during the campaign, remove any lingering doubts about his own commitment to social order, and absolve some of the awful guilt brought on by Rachel's death.

These deeply personal motives indicate that for Andrew Jackson, at least, the Eaton affair was no mere maneuver designed to oust Calhoun and other dissidents from the administration. Had he been bent on such a straightforward political mission, the president would no doubt have behaved differently during his first year in office. For one thing, he tried to silence all the gossip rather than exploit it for partisan advantage. For nearly six months Jackson played the moral inquisitor, privately investigating the charges against Peggy Eaton. Whether writing to obtain affidavits on the causes of her husband's suicide, sending agents to a New York hotel to check on rumors of Eaton's impropriety, or personally interrogating the Washington pastor who lent credence to the slanders, Jackson played the part denied him during the campaign. He wrote long letters in Peggy's defense, recorded a narrative of his investigations, and in the fall of 1829 held one of the most bizarre cabinet meetings in American history.

Having accumulated evidence to prove Peggy's innocence, the president summoned her accusers before the cabinet and tried to force them to recant, hoping that his councilors would then end their social boycott of the first family. The arraignment proceeded very badly. Two frightened ministers sat under Jackson's irate gaze, explaining that they had originally brought the rumors to the president's attention to save him embarrassment. Jackson wanted none of their good intentions; he demanded a recantation. During the course of these exceptional deliberations, the Reverend Ezra Styles Ely said that his own inquiries proved John Eaton innocent of any wrongdoing. "And Mrs. Eaton also!" the president broke in. "On that point I would rather not give an opinion," Ely replied. "She is chaste as a virgin," Jackson roared and soon disbanded the meeting in disgust.

After this abortive tribunal, the storm entered its most devastating phase. When Congress reassembled in December 1829, rumors circulated that Peggy Eaton was unwelcome at all social functions, including those given by the diplomatic corps. Additional stories told of deep rifts in the cabinet and hinted that Jackson had lost all control of his administration. In a sense all the gossip was true. When concerned congressmen questioned the president about the dissension, Jackson struck out blindly in all directions; he thought of banishing recalcitrant foreign diplomats and dismissing the cabinet in toto, thereby proving his mastery. Talked out of these desperate measures, he nevertheless began to judge officials by their social behavior. Those who accorded Mrs. Eaton the respect due her station fared well in his estimation. Those who supported the continuing social ostracism Jackson consigned to the vast conspiracy that grew daily. No one escaped scrutiny, not even his relatives. Jackson insisted that Emily Donelson call on Mrs. Eaton. "My duty is that my household should bestow equal comity to all," Jackson lectured, "and the nation expects me to controle my household to this rule." Emily refused to be badgered. In the fall of 1830, she and her husband reluctantly left the president's house. Jackson grieved at their departure, attributing it to "a want of experience and the corruption of the world." "I am thrown upon strangers," he moaned, "instead of those I took great pains in education that they might be a comfort & aid to me, in my declining years."

The president endured these defections as he endured physical torment, with a conviction of self-righteousness that at times bordered on obsession. Jackson was always prone to elevate private problems to the level of public issues, but as a result of Rachel's death and the attacks on Mrs. Eaton, he had even greater difficulty discriminating between personal duty and national honor, between family and country. "Was this proper treatment to me as President of the United States, and by those representing me as such in the place of my departed wife," he demanded to know after the Donelson's departure. "Was this proper as head of the family, & they in the place of my children?"

These doubts far more than any concern for ideology or party policy determined Andrew Jackson's behavior during his first term in office. Whether as spoilsman, government reformer, defender of strict construction, architect of Indian removal, or enemy of the Bank, the president acted more in self-defense than out of loyalty to the Democratic coalition.

In some respects, Andrew Jackson's quest for vindication served the party well. Without a positive platform, the Democratic alliance relied upon state political organizations like the Albany Regency and the Richmond Junto. These crude machines in turn derived their authority from controlling state legislatures and carefully dispensing patronage. Within each state, federal offices constituted a significant source of reward for the party faithful. Postmasters, district attorneys, collectors of customs, land agents—these were but a few of the important federal posts coveted by state partisans. Systematic catering might not satiate these appetites, but it could prevent the party from devouring itself.

Consumed by fears of intrigue, corrupt bargains, and conspiracy, Andrew Jackson entered office determined to achieve political reform by use of his patronage powers. He spoke often of appointments and removals but never as a source of party solidarity, never as the "spoils" of victory. Such realism ran counter to his belief that politics was dirty business. He thought of himself not as a methodical spoilsman but as the righteous avenger, whose task it was to "cleanse the Augean Stables." The classical imagery neatly conveys the sense of duty and distaste that he brought to the job. Furthermore, Jackson believed that his enemies had left the stables "in such a state" just "to embarrass me." He would not tolerate the contamination for long. "You know when I am excited all my energies come forth," he assured his friend John Coffee.

The transfer of power did bring forth his energies. In his first few months in office, Jackson gave every indication that he intended to sweep out all the "rats" that he believed had infested federal offices during the Adams administration. After observing these reforms Jackson's predecessor bitterly remarked, "To feed the cormorant appetite for place, and to reward the prostitution of canvassing defamers, are the only principles yet discernible in the conduct of the President." The sheer magnitude of this appetite soon drove Jackson to despair: "If I had a tit for every applicant to suck the Treasury pap, all would go away satisfied, but as there are not office for more than one out of five hundred who apply, many must go away dissatisfied." Despite his disenchantment with such maternal dispensation Jackson vowed to carry on. "All I can do is, select honest and competant men." At times Jackson selected men who were neither honest nor competent. Samuel Gwin, a land agent in the Southwest, openly speculated in government revenues; Samuel Swartwout, collector of customs in the Port of New York, absconded with $1,250,000. Ironically, at the time of his appointment Swartwout had urged the president to propose legislation that would relieve bankrupt merchants.

In view of these disastrous appointments, the Democratic coalition may have been fortunate that circumstances prevented the president from making a clean sweep. In his two terms in office, Jackson removed no more than a fifth of all federal office holders, including over a third of those requiring Senate confirmation. Although slightly higher than comparable figures for the Jefferson administrations, these statistics clearly indicate that Jackson did not originate the spoils system or carry it to extremes. During the first two years of the new coalition's rule, a time when the transfer of power stimulated the most heated patronage battles, the president was plagued by miserable health and concentrated his limited energies on the Eaton affair. Doubtless a vigorous, less preoccupied Jackson would have pushed reforms even further, for he was constantly referring to the need to purge the government of its accumulated wickedness. Doubtless, too, Jackson considered the defense of feminine virtue equally as important as the removal of federal officeholders. They were related tasks. By upholding the bonds of friendship, by raising the social standards of the Washington community, by putting down the vicious slanders against Petty Eaton, Jackson believed that he was serving the cause of reform just as surely as when he replaced a corrupt man with an honest one.

In December 1829, Jackson invited Congress to join the crusade by adopting the principle of rotation in office. Again his fears of corruption predominated. "There are, perhaps, few who can for any length of time enjoy office and power without being more or less under the influence of feelings unfavorable to the faithful discharge of their public duties." Jackson proposed

that the "length of time" be set at four years. Such a limitation would eliminate the experienced servant, but then the president believed that "the duties
of all public officials are so plain that men of intelligence may readily qualify
themselves . . . and . . . more is lost by the long continuation of men in office
than is generally to be gained by their experience." Jackson showed little sympathy for the individual distress that might accompany rotation; "he who is
removed has the same means of obtaining a living that are enjoyed by the
millions who never held office."

The political realist would interpret the president's suggestions as a thinly
disguised attempt to increase executive patronage. Indeed, many of Jackson's
contemporary critics raised this objection, enough so that Congress refused to
endorse rotation. Clearly, the president's distrust of political jobbery out-
weighed any thought of partisan advantage, as it did in his concurrent proposal that Congress alter the mode of presidential election. When Jackson
recommended that the House of Representatives have no role in the electoral
process, that the president be chosen by popular majority, that his term be
fixed by law at six years, and that, failing these modifications, all congressmen
be prohibited from "appointments in the gift of the President" they helped
select, Jackson was merely registering his disgust with the "corrupt bargain"
of 1825.

The president's preoccupation with corruption and his belief that he was
the target of congressional abuse had an equally telling impact on his handling
of internal improvements. Late in May 1830, Congress passed and sent to the
White House a bill authorizing government purchase of stock in a road to be
constructed between Maysville and Lexington, Kentucky. State-rights enthu-
siasts worried that Jackson might approve this measure and commit the federal government to support additional projects of purely local scope, especially
since he had taken no clear stand on the question of internal improvements.
Well aware of these apprehensions, Martin Van Buren advised the president
to veto the Maysville road bill. Van Buren hoped that disapproval would renew
the administration's pledge to curb the power of the central government.
Jackson accepted the advice. He had come to appreciate his secretary's political loyalty as well as his polite attentions to Mrs. Eaton.

Thanks to Van Buren's careful wording, the Maysville veto did appear to
be based on a strict construction of the Constitution. The message promised
to keep the national government "within its proper sphere," allowing "the states
to manage their own concerns in their own way." In his own personal draft,
Jackson appeared much less concerned with constitutional distinctions and
historical precedents, much more worried about endangered liberties and
"combinations in Congress." Grant the government the right to buy stock in
a state corporation, he argued, and it would soon become an engine of destruction, tampering with "state elections" and "destroying the morals of your
people." Encourage such appropriations and congressional standards would

further decay, clearing the way for more "flagitious Legislation arising from combinations if you will vote with me I will vote with you so disgraceful to our country." In Jackson's eyes, no one epitomized the pernacious legislative back-scratching more than Kentucky's Henry Clay, architect of the original "corrupt bargain" and the man who stood to gain most from construction of the Maysville Turnpike.

Having taken a symbolic stand against congressional logrolling and having gained revenge at the expense of his archrival from Kentucky, Jackson proceeded to approve more internal improvement bills during his two terms in office than all his predecessors combined. Not that Jackson suddenly overcame his fears of corruption or that he developed a more charitable view of human nature; most of the bills he approved were recommended by army engineers and were therefore acceptable. In addition, the president found in Indian affairs another outlet for his anxieties.

Few American presidents have taken such personal initiative in domestic affairs as Andrew Jackson took in Indian removal. "That great work was emphatically the fruit of his own exertions," Van Buren recalled sometime later. "It was his judgment, his experience, his indomitable vigor and unrelenting activity that secured success." Whereas other chief executives have been inclined to act as their own secretaries of state, Jackson intended to be his own secretary of war. He insisted that a personal friend, a Westerner, head the War Department. When Washington critics began their attacks on John Eaton, the president responded swiftly, in part because he took the criticism personally, but also because he wanted Eaton to press for Indian removal as quickly as possible. Eaton later resigned from the cabinet and Jackson was extremely reluctant to appoint a successor who was "unacquainted with Indian matters." He eventually settled on Michigan's governor Lewis Cass, an outspoken advocate of removal. Likewise, Jackson appointed Georgia's John Berrien as his first attorney general, knowing full well that the collision between that state and the Cherokee Indians would soon require the federal government to take a stand on the thorny question of Indian sovereignty. In addition to these critical appointments, Jackson maintained extensive personal correspondence on Indian affairs. He issued instructions to treaty negotiators, employed trusted advisers like John Coffee to treat with tribesmen, exchanged opinions with Indian agents, and even summoned Indian leaders to his summer residence for private negotiations.

It is tempting to dismiss Andrew Jackson's Indian policy as bigotry pure and simple. To do so is to miss its significance. In these matters, the president embodied contradictions that marred federal policy since the eighteenth century. Always a zealous warrior, Jackson was also something of a missionary at heart. Throughout his career as a military commander and treaty negotiator he had reiterated the hope first expressed on the smouldering Creek battlefields: that out of the ashes would arise a new, peaceful Indian society. This vision had intensely personal origins, but then so did the dreams of many an Indian missionary, for whom conversion of the heathen represented vicarious salvation. Jackson was less captivated by religious visions, more concerned with the secular transformation of warrior to peaceful agrarian. Neither the missionaries nor the president they so actively opposed demonstrated much appreciation for the integrity of Indian culture. In one respect, of course, they differed markedly. The last of the Jeffersonian philanthropists wanted to preserve the Indian tribal lands. By 1829, Jackson, along with a substantial number of American citizens and political leaders, had become thoroughly disenchanted with this traditional approach to the Indian problem. He readily accepted the suggestions of Lewis Cass and others that only a massive migration west of the Mississippi could remove the Indians from the degrading circumstances that had befallen them in the 1820s.

Once committed, Jackson pursued removal relentlessly. In December 1829, at a time when he was critically ill and under intense pressure from Peggy Eaton's detractors, the president formally proposed that Congress guarantee land west of the Mississippi to the Indians and appropriate funds to facilitate removal. "This emigration should be voluntary," Jackson assured Congress, "for it would be as cruel as unjust to compel the aborigines to abandon the graves of their fathers and seek a home in a distant land." With a dispatch rarely duplicated in subsequent deliberations, Congress approved an Indian removal bill in May 1830. The vote was extremely close, indicating the administration's tenuous position in the legislature. Nevertheless, this act was the only major legislative accomplishment of Jackson's first term. As such it demonstrated that support for Indian removal transcended party lines.

By appropriating the sum of $500,000, Congress empowered the president to begin direct negotiations with the southern Indians, offering them a home in the West in exchange for their tribal lands in the East. Jackson wasted little time in acting on this narrow mandate. In August 1830, he personally attended the council session at Franklin, Tennessee, where Eaton and Coffee negotiated a removal treaty with the Chickasaws. A month later these two trusted presidential aides met with the Choctaw Indians at Dancing Rabbit Creek and concluded a treaty that foreshadowed subsequent settlements with the Creeks and Cherokees. Despite the president's emphasis on voluntarism, the treaty commissioners resorted to bribery and intimidation to secure the Choctaw's consent. After the main body of the Choctaw delegation had abandoned the deliberations in disgust, Eaton dickered with a few remaining spokesmen, holding out "special reservations" of land in return for their support. Even the general allotments to heads of families were a form of bribery.

The Jackson administration was willing to confer generous grants on those tribesmen who decided to remain because it cynically calculated that few Choctaws would be able to retain their holdings in the face of white encirclement. Even to claim an allotment, an Indian had to rely upon strange legal codes; if successful in obtaining land, the claimant still had to live there five years before receiving title. Jackson reasoned that the speculators would persuade the Indians to sell long before the waiting period was over. Why else would he tell a prospective Indian agent: "The Government is endeavoring to concentrate the Indians west of the Mississippi and you just turn all your energy to this object—in the course of which, some more profitable business may present itself"? In urging the immediate acquisition and sale of Indian land, Jackson fancied that he was serving the cause of government economy. He hoped to pay for the entire cost of removal from the proceeds of these land sales and avoid increasing a national debt that he had pledged to extinguish. Characteristically, he saw no reason why his friends should not profit from these proceedings. "This will give you employment," Jackson told Coffee after sending one treaty to the Senate.

Previous presidents had sanctioned bribery at the treaty grounds; yet at Dancing Rabbit Creek, Jackson's representatives threatened the Choctaws with a frightening new form of pressure. In a fit of frustration Eaton confirmed what the president had already told Indian agents: either the tribes agreed to move, or they would be left totally at the mercy of state laws, without any legal form of self-government, without any federal protection whatever. From experience, Jackson knew that the nation's meager military establishment could hardly shield the Indians from white avarice and encroachment. As leader of a new coalition pledged to uphold state rights, the president also knew the politcal hazards of attempting to interfere with the decisions of a determined state regime. Jackson knew full well that the extension of state laws would destroy tribal government. "I was satisfied that the Indians could not possibly live under the laws of the states," he freely admitted in 1830. "If they now refuse to accept the liberal terms offered they can only be liable for whatever evils and difficulties may arise. I feel conscious of having done my duty to my red children," he concluded. In short, Jackson believed that his policy was benevolent. Since the states would force the Indians to move, since he felt powerless to resist such pressure, at least he could see that the Indian received token payment for his land.

Having offered what he considered to be liberal terms, Jackson could not understand Indian resistance. When the Creeks refused to meet their conqueror in 1830 and hired former Attorney General William Wirt to represent them, Jackson exploded: "The course of *Wirt* has been truly wicked. It has been wielded as an engine to prevent the Indians from moving across the Mississippi and will lead to the destruction of the poor ignorant Indians." The president resented Wirt's meddling but consoled himself that wickedness would soon find its own rewards. Meanwhile he was content to leave "the poor deluded Creeks and Cherokees to their fate, and their annihilation, which their wicked advisors has induced." Even when successful in overcoming Indian resistance, Jackson saw the "serpent" at work. In August 1830, after receiving news of the Treaty of Franklin, Jackson reported, "Thus far we have succeeded against the most corrupt and secret combination that ever did exist, and we have preserved my Chickasaw friends and red brethren."

In Jackson's view, the West offered the Indians a permanent home and Americans permanent relief from racial tensions. Like many of his contemporaries, the president regarded the vast trans-Mississippi region as a geographical nirvana. There a new Indian civilization would arise, secure in its right to the land, freed from the evils of alcohol, educated in the virtues of agrarian pursuits, and, above all, isolated from white society. Significantly, Jackson looked to the Army to keep peace and help maintain the new social order. This vision was no mere afterthought of the removal policy, but a clear expression of Jackson's disgust with the social decay he perceived affecting Indians and whites alike. "How many thousands of our own people would gladly embrace the opportunity of removing to the west on such conditions!" he asked in outlining federal support for removal.

Andrew Jackson took particular pride in "that great work," to use Van Buren's terms, because by removing the Indians, he believed he was exonerating "the national character from all imputation." In the success of his Indian removal policies, Jackson saw a measure of personal vindication as well. Unable to prove Peggy Eaton "chaste as a Virgin," nor able to "cleanse the Augean Stables," silence slander, preserve family harmony, or achieve other reforms he considered essential to his and the nation's well-being, he could at least take satisfaction from this act. He continued to perceive himself as a "slave to office." Surrounded by corruption, tormented by sickness, and deserted by family, he found rare release in asserting his authority over his "red children." But the president's satisfaction was short-lived. By the time his "friends and brothers" embarked on their "Trail of Tears," their "great father the President" found himself in a new war against corruption, this time on a strange, almost alien battlefield.

The Jacksonian Character: A Contemporary Portrait of American Personality, Traits, and Values

Edward Pessen

The pursuit of the essential Jacksonian continues. The elusive fellow has been interpreted as a child of the frontier, the democratic man, the product of equality, an entrepreneurial seeker after the main chance, and as a "venturous conservative" whose feet drew him irresistibly in the direction of speculative profit even as his mind held to "an ideal of a chaste republican order, resisting the seductions" of a dynamic capitalism. Nor do these explanations exhaust the list. These assessments have for the most part been arrived at through indirection, the nature of the man being inferred from the abundant evidence on his nation's behavior. The method is a sensible one and would in fact be the historian's only recourse were no other data available.

There does exist, however, a vast amount of evidence that throws a most direct light on the traits and values of Jacksonians. For not only did Americans themselves observe their fellow countrymen but an army of European, mainly English, visitors swarmed over this country during the Jacksonian era. They subsequently published hundreds of travelers' accounts in response to the great European interest in the young republic and an insatiable American curiosity about what the visitors thought of them. Covering almost every aspect of American civilization—its political, social and economic institutions and intellectual life.

Contemporary comments about Americans fall into four not always distinct categories: emotional traits or attributes of personality; mental or intellectual traits; manners, habits or customs; and values—themselves, of course, manifested in behavior. The notorious spitting done by males chewing tobacco is a nice example of a clear-cut *habit* which is distinct from personality and mind, and can be related to values only by the too imaginative. Shrewdness, on the other hand, is a trait that cuts across all lines, reflecting personality, intelligence, and one's appraisal of the scheme of things. In any case the categorization emerged naturally from the observations of contemporaries.

From Edward Pessen: JACKSONIAN AMERICA: SOCIETY, PERSONALITY AND POLITICS. Reprinted with permission of the author.

The natural or unspoiled part of his person—precisely that aspect of personality least touched by the artificial or institutional environment that gave distinctiveness to his society—was the most admired feature of the Jacksonian. Dickens found that "by nature [Americans were] frank, brave, cordial, hospitable and affectionate." Marryat took time out from his censure to remark that "at bottom [Americans] are a very good tempered people." Captain Hall was amazed at how even-tempered they were, despite his faultfinding. Harriet Martineau found that westerners were the most pleasant people in the world, a judgment that George Combe would expand to include Americans from the other sections. Charles Murray believed the American people unusually hospitable and cordial, while Peter Neilson was impressed by the small but significant fact that Americans went out of their way to give directions to the traveler. Sir Charles Lyell, the great geologist, was interested above all in the country's rock formations, Cincinnati's "alluvial terraces," for example, attracting more of his attention than did its society. When he did glance up from the fossil flora, however, he noted admiringly that the human fauna behaved with propriety and a wholesome openness.

American generosity was also applauded, if not always by the American people themselves. New Englanders, Miss Martineau was advised in the nation's capital, "do good by mania." She was herself most favorably impressed by "the generous nature of their mutual services." America was the land of assorted benevolent associations, the leaders of which clearly were not themselves suffering from the abuses they sought to correct. Sophisticated critics of a later time might explain their charitableness as only neurotic do-gooding, brought on by emotional discord of one kind or another. It might be due to a too strong or a too weak father, or to the crisis following the disappearance of the traditional opportunities for their privileged class to play its accustomed paternalistic part in society. Jacksonian travelers, less inclined to be psychoanalytical, noted the absence of economic or tangible self-interest in the charitable activities of Americans, and applauded.

If Miss Martineau experienced little impoliteness, a number of the visitors complained of rudeness shown by the Americans either to them or to others. Staring was characteristic and disconcerting. Requests that the plate be passed at hotel or boarding house table often went unheeded, as was true also of requests for removal of hats in theatres. A minister was dismayed to find a church service emptying before he "had scarcely named the text." He had not yet had time to be boring. Fanny Kemble, having been offended once too often by American women who unceremoniously interrupted a nap she was taking on a river boat for no better reason than to glance at the books lying by her side, exclaimed that "no person whatsoever, however ignorant, low or vulgar, in England, would have done such a thing." She attributed such conduct to "the mixture of the republican feeling of equality peculiar to this country and the usual want of refinement common to the lower classes;" together they formed "a singularly felicitous union of impudence and vulgarity, to be met nowhere but America." Miss Kemble's theorizing cannot be confused with Tocqueville's.

The American was curious, sometimes excessively so, according to visitors who felt themselves badgered by incessant questions they not only had no wish to answer but which they considered bad form even to ask. "They cannot bear anything like a secret," was the conclusion of Marryat, one of whose confidants had advised him that the Ursuline Convent had been stormed more because of curiosity about the life behind its sealed gates than out of bigotry.

Humorlessness was allied with dullness. Since the emotions of the people were too restrained, "there is little of what is called *fun* in America," mourned Francis Lieber. Admirable but not lovable, said Hamilton. The visitors were not sure whether Calvinism or other factors were to blame for this unattractive trait. Few blamed it on the weather, as did Beaumont, but many agreed with his verdict on the Americans: "cold as ice."

The cruelty displayed so often and by so many Americans was shocking. Whether tories or liberals, the visitors—with the exception of Lyell and a few others—were repelled at both the system of slavery and at white American attitudes towards Negroes, whether slaves or free. Joseph Pickering was horrified that a respectable crowd could watch, with feelings that ranged from indifference to enthusiasm, as a colored man was burned alive. In Hartford, according to Abdy, "to pelt [colored people] . . . with stones, and cry out nigger! nigger! as they pass, seems to be the pastime of the place." Europeans were dismayed not only by racism but at the cruelty shown unfortunates. Buckingham could understand neither newspapers nor their readers in treating flippantly poverty and misery "that ought to thrill the heart with horror or melt it with pity." Hangings or public executions of any kind attracted vast crowds of "respectable" or obviously well-to-do folk, as well as the other kind. William Dean Howells' father recollected that public hangings used to fill the taverns and grog shops, as thousands of people came from all over the countryside, most of them of "respectable appearance," drawn to the spectacle by "morbid curiosity." One visitor was appalled at the sight of young women cheerfully present at a hanging in New York City.

Violence was a much-observed trait, although it was reported mainly in the south and on the frontier. Personal quarrels occur everywhere but Americans seemed ready to mutilate one another for reasons that Europeans found incredible. In Kentucky one man came near to killing another for opening a coach window. As shocking as the ridiculous reasons for fighting were the extreme forms it took. Stabbing, shooting, gouging out of eyes, biting off of nose or ears were not uncommon. Frontier violence was not too surprising, but what amazed visitors was the proneness of "respectable men" of some standing to throw themselves savagely on someone who had inadvertently provoked them.

Less frightening if not more attractive was the selfishness of Americans. Tocqueville was aware that they could be public-spirited, but he found no one more dedicated to the gratification of his own physical wants than the American. (In his explanation, public-spiritedness was self-interest sensibly pursued.) The bad manners sometimes displayed at the dinner table were regarded by some as nothing more than the behavior of men so preoccupied with satisfying their own wants of the moment that they either ignored requests by others for food or else gave them inferior portions. Combe concluded that there was something in his training that led the American to the ignoble feeling that the purpose of life was nothing more than the satisfaction of "his own good pleasure."

Americans as individuals were wanting in self-confidence. The word "insecure" was not yet the vogue in those happy times but, if it were, it would have been applied to a people who, every day and in every kind of company, asked the visitor, "What do you think of us upon the whole?" Miss Martineau felt it was not a serious flaw but she admitted that like Captain Hall, she had suffered through innumerable variations on "the perennial question: 'How do you like America?' " Hamilton found this "restless and insatiable appetite for praise, which defies all restraint or common sense," one of the "most remarkable features" of the American character. Lieber, who came here to stay because he was so delighted with this country, reports being asked, "Do you think it as fine as the Rhine?"—"What, sir?"—"The Hudson." He describes his figurative gnashing of teeth, "when you enjoy on a hot day a glass of cool, sparkling cider of the best kind, and an officious acquaintance . . . seeing the praise of the liquid in the expression of your face, asks you: 'Now, tell me, is not it equal to any champagne?' The taste is gone at once." In Tocqueville's memorable words, the Americans "unceasingly harass you to extort praise, and if you resist their entreaties, they fall to praising themselves. It would seem as if, doubting their own merit, they wished to have it constantly exhibited before their own eyes." They were also insecure amongst one another, according to Abdy, whose explanation of their preoccupation with external appearance or conspicuous display anticipates the better known theories of Tocqueville and Veblen.

Marryat advised those who came after him: do not find fault with them if you seek their hospitality. Tudor referred to the "extraordinary sensibility to the slightest appearance of dispraise" as a "puerility" which had he "not witnessed on a thousand occasions (he) . . . should have believed utterly incredible." They *demanded* praise. "Such an unhappily sensitive community surely never existed in this world," wrote Fanny Kemble in her journal. An American woman had told her, "I hear you are going to abuse us dreadfully; of course, you'll wait till you go back to England and then shower it down upon us finely." The prediction was not inaccurate, for Miss Kemble did in fact "shower it down" upon them, finely. It was hard to insult Americans, however, for as Dickens noted, they quickly cited their newness as a country as the excuse for all faults. When the occasion demanded it, Americans could display a very thick skin, indeed, which made them immune to insults, let alone faint praise. "This man [the American]," wrote Tocqueville, "will never understand that he wearies me to death unless I tell him so, and the only way to get rid of him is to make him my enemy for life." There is no better proof that when it suited him an American could make himself impervious to criticism than in the friendly reception he gave the book that contains those devastating words.

"The most striking circumstance in the American character," wrote Captain Hall, "was the constant habit of praising themselves." Insecurity and thin skin seemed to go hand in hand with boastfulness. Only a few observers mistook the latter trait for arrogance but almost all of them found it unattractive. Lieber, like Miss Martineau, believed that this "national contentment" was an innocent blemish, in part a simple response to the criticisms of foreigners. She did feel, however, that much of this boasting was absurd, and that combined with the insatiable hunger for flattery, was "the most prominent of their bad habits." It was agreed that Americans, in view of their achievements, had much to be vain about but need they be so wearisome about it? Americans of every sort, in all sections and of every social order, praised to the heavens their weather, their rivers, the speed of their railroads, their political system, their orators, even their roads—which were notoriously bad or at the least discomfiting to a normal human anatomy—and, of course, themselves. Only America had anything worth seeing, according to Mr. Wenham, a typical villager in Cooper's *Home As Found*. An Englishman, to his consternation, read in an American geography text that "the English tongue is spoken in greater purity of idiom and intonation with us (in America) than in Great Britain."

Americans could make a virtue of necessity. That a slaughterhouse was situated in the midst of a residential district, was praised to Mrs. Trollope as an example of the antiaristocratic quality of American society. If Marryat was right, that "Americans are the happiest people in the world in their own delusions" Tocqueville had a logical explanation for it. "As the American participates in all that is done in his country, he thinks himself obliged to defend whatever may be censured in it; for it is not only his country that is then attacked, it is himself. The consequence is that his national pride resorts to a thousand artifices and descends to all the petty tricks of personal vanity."

The boasters were also inveterate complainers. Harriet Martineau was amazed to hear complaints even against "the confoundedly prosperous" state of the country, not to mention every other variety of phenomenon—with the exception of land, the only thing exempt from abuse. They were particularly enthusiastic in denouncing the people of sections other than their own, invariably describing them to foreigners as the *real* culprits, whatever the ascribed

fault. In Marryat's flamboyant description, easterners "pronounce the southerners to be choleric, reckless, regardless of law, and indifferent as to religion;
while the southerners designate the eastern states as a nursery of over-reaching
pedlars . . . ; Boston turns up her erudite nose at New York; Philadelphia
. . . looks down upon both, while New York . . . swears the Bostonians are
a parcel of puritanical prigs, and the Philadelphians a would-be aristocracy."
" 'Hatred' is not too strong a term for their sectional prejudice," concluded
Miss Martineau.

In matters of the mind, the American was above all practical. In Tocqueville's view, his spirit was "averse to general ideas; it does not seek theoretical discoveries." In politics Americans were interested in men more than
principles, immediate outcomes and success rather than long-range consequences or ethics. Anti-intellectualism was due in part to an aversion for the
nonutilitarian character of the speculative thinking that was done by the
learned. Americans therefore preferred newspapers to great literature and were
more capable of mechanical invention than of theoretical scientific innova-
tions. The New Englander only represented an exaggeration of a national
quality in being "content when he feels a grievance to apply a remedy," or in
dealing with "the business of common life [with] . . . practical good sense."
Their "fertility of resource," in Martineau's phrase, clearly stemmed from their
preoccupation with immediate and tangible problems.

Americans were clever but not profound. Their minds were quick enough
in dealing with a practical or a commercial issue, but ostensibly incapable of
appreciating or coping with intellectual problems of a fundamental sort. Nur-
ture triumphed over nature in this instance, since shrewdness was a characteristic of the American mind largely because it was so admired an ideal in
the American scheme of things. The most sympathetic observers conceded not
only that an unattractive cunning characterized their thinking, but that New
Englanders, believed to be its arch practitioners, were generally admired for
their gift. "Smart dealings" or a shrewdness which "gilds over many a swindle
and gross breach of trust," were extolled, as was "every fresh display of low
trickery." They smiled approvingly at a "clever villain's witty rogueries."
Commercial shrewdness or "commercial frauds" were "generally dignified by
the name of intelligence." Pickering expressed a typical judgment when he
said that "shrewdness was (one of) the . . . most striking features in the character of an American." If they were not profound, they pretended to be, according to Lieber. He was disturbed at the descent into "verbose and therefore
unfelt" cant indulged in by Americans who pretended to a depth of feeling
they did not truly have. Cooper and a number of the visitors felt they were
shallow. Their skewed sense of values testified to this. "Hint to them that they
eat peas with a knife, and they are highly enraged; tell them that their conduct
to the 'niggers' is inhuman and unmanly, and they laugh in your face," reported Abdy. Tocqueville's conclusion was that their paltry concerns and

preoccupations turned them ultimately into paltry men. "They strain their faculties to the utmost to achieve paltry results, and this cannot fail speedily to limit their range of view and to circumscribe their powers."

They were not gifted conversationalists. Urbane visitors and Americans alike were unhappy with a conversational style that was composed in part of bombast, swearing—if not in "the more polished circles"—a solemnity and dullness particularly ridiculous in view of the lightness of its content, and at the other extreme from their hyperbole, an incommunicativeness that was equally characteristic, particularly in the northeast. The laconic style was not a trait of the strong, silent man from the west but rather of a shrewd, selfish, opportunistic man of the city. Mrs. Trollope has given us a verbatim transcript of a marvelous conversation between two New Englanders she overheard while on a boat. It is a bravura example of an art of discourse in which the speaker reveals nothing of importance as he in turn darts questions, probing for weaknesses in his opponent's defenses:

Well, now, which way may you be traveling?
I expect this canal runs pretty nearly west.
Are you going far with it?
Well, now, I don't rightly know how many miles it may be.
I expect you'll be from New York?
Sure enough I have been at New York, often and often.
I calculate, then, 'tis not there as you stop?
Business must be minded, in stopping and in stirring.

"So they went on," she writes, "without advancing or giving an inch, 'till I was weary of listening." The harsh conclusion of a number of observers was that though Americans talked at great length they said nothing that was worth hearing.

Americans loved scandal and were quick to believe the worst. Hamilton was amazed that "no villainy is too gross or too improbable to be attributed to a statesman in this intelligent community." A distaste for aristocracy undoubtedly explained in part the delight in the exposure of foibles, actual or alleged. Hone's diary entry for September 22, 1837, reads "*Libels*. Everybody complains of the success which attends the publications of libels on private character; everybody condemns the depravity of the times in which, and the community by which they are encouraged. Everybody wonders how people can buy and read those receptacles of scandals, the penny papers, and yet everybody does encourage them."

A well-known modern theory postulates as the characteristic type of the early 19th century, an inner-directed American, marching to his own music, living his life according to his own and his family's notions as to how it should be lived. Observers during the Jacksonian era saw a very different American, indeed.

Whether the phrase "tyranny of the majority" was too strong, as some of Tocqueville's contemporaries thought it was, there was no doubt that in small things as in large, Americans guided their behavior by the anticipated reactions of their neighbors to it.

Combe was struck that in matters of great moral significance, men feared to affirm what they knew was the right, because of fear of majority opinion.

Mrs. Trollope's book had publicized certain uncouth American habits and customs. She was shortly to be immortalized, since subsequent visitors observed that the cry, "a trollope! a trollope!" went up from American audiences when one of their number happened to be caught in that public slouching that had so offended their critical visitor. Americans slouched in theatres, they slouched in church, they were even discovered slouching when attending sessions of the Supreme Court. At one theatrical performance, Mrs. Trollope had found "the bearing and attitudes of the men perfectly indescribable; the heels thrown higher than the head, the entire rear of the person presented to the audience, the whole length supported on the benches, are among the varieties that these exquisite posture-masters exhibit." Their subsequent attempts to police offenders indicate that Mrs. Trollope's description was not exaggerated. Like a famous statesman of more than a century later who used his shoe in part to show his scorn of the traditional diplomacy and the breeding associated with it, it seems fairly clear that some Americans slouched to political purpose, in their case to display indifference or contempt for the manners of an aristocratic society. Fortunately Mrs. Trollope's strictures had effect and Americans came to see ordinary civility as devoid of social implication.

Americans were great chewers of tobacco and, what was worse, notorious spitters. Poor Miss Kemble discovered that to her "profound disgust," gentlemen too did it. On board a boat, "it was a perfect shower of saliva all the time." Almost every user of public conveyances sounded variations on the theme. "Copious spitting" was the rule. In boarding houses and hotels after a meal, an orgy of spitting would commence—although less fastidious types did not wait for the meal to end. In homes, too, spitting "was incessant, the carpet serving as a receptacle . . . when boxes were not within immediate reach." Even among the upper classes, men of otherwise polished manners indulged themselves, although in all fairness, Boardman observed that the refined would not spit on living room floors. Dickens was amazed that even in the nation's Capitol, in law courts, and hospitals, "in all the public places of America this filthy custom is recognized." Senators and judges were adept in the art. Americans even spit in their sleep. The visitors must have exaggerated for their comments seemed to indicate that spitting threatened to drown the country.

There was some difference of opinion as to whether or not they were drunkards but there was agreement that Americans drank to excess. "Why do they get so confoundedly drunk?" asked Marryat. But Stuart denied that they did, claiming he saw only twelve drunkards during the course of three years. Mrs. Felton's explanation was that Americans drank so much from the time of infancy on, that "by the time they arrive at the years of maturity they become . . . habituated to the practice." She did believe, however, that the excessive number of fires in this country was due largely to the carelessness of people who had imbibed too heavily. To Buckingham as to many others, the love of liquor was one of the great evils ruining the country. Liquor was to be found everywhere, and as Tocqueville noted, at most reasonable rates. He agreed with Hall that its prevalence here was due to the inordinate influence of the common man. Senators were thus afraid to tax so popular a commodity. Jacksonian candidates plied their constituencies with quantities of fiery liquid. Vigne believed that the absence of a law of primogeniture was a major cause of the evil, elder sons burying their disappointments in brandy. Attending a meeting of the Worcester Temperance Society, Baldwin was dismayed to find that all members "drank very freely of cyder . . . of the very worst sort." What must they have drunk in the privacy of their homes?

Drinking went hand in hand with gambling. Oliver found incessant gambling on river boats. Southern boat trips featured all night bouts of drinking and gambling. The latter custom was also closely aligned to speculation. The Jacksonian era was characterized by what Miss Martineau called a "speculative mania." It would not have been, had the American people not been ready to gamble on the prospects of great future gains. "Everybody is speculating, and everything has become an object of speculation," wrote Chevalier. Shirreff, who liked to believe the best of the Americans, discovered in the west that "speculators have . . . brought up, at high prices, all the building ground in the neighborhood." Back in the east, in 1836, "if two persons were seen conversing in the street of New York . . . in nineteen instances out of twenty, you would have overheard 'lots' and 'thousands of dollars' as the sole topics of their discourse." In *Home As Found,* Cooper includes conversations that appear to be satirical exaggerations of the speed at which the price of a lot could appreciate and speculative fortunes be made. A Hone diary entry for January 14, 1835, when the bubble was still short of the bursting point, shows that truth was the source of Cooper's fiction. Unbelievable appreciation of the price of real estate did occur.

America the land of plenty was admired but American eating habits were not. Observers held that most Americans were gluttons or something close to it. They were accused of eating huge quantities of poorly prepared food with the manners and perhaps the charm of certain barnyard animals. In fairness to the critics, they did concede that their evidence was based not on what went on in American homes but outside of them. There seemed to be a touch of sour grapes in some of the envious comment of the visitors. This country had an unbelievable abundance of the most admired foods, particularly meats, fowl, and dairy products, easily available to ordinary persons. The visitors copied down menus with great relish; in fact they reported nothing so fully or so vividly. Since Horace was not above reporting in some detail the menu of heroic Roman feasts, perhaps a detailed report on Jacksonian delicacies, as contemporaries observed them, will be forgiven.

Visitors were disconcerted most by the American style at the dinner table. Speed and silence were the rule. Huge amounts were swallowed at breakneck speed; woe to the man who dawdled. The "extraordinary rapidity" with which food was gorged or "pitchforked down" fascinated some observers, although Miss Martineau was disquieted at the "celerity" of the American attack. Even more depressing was the absence of that pleasant talk that gave charm to a table or, in the words of the ancients, turned feeding into dining. The stillness of death was one common metaphor used to describe the atmosphere at the American table; another spoke of animal gratification. Marryat expressed the popular belief that the American "eats his meals with the rapidity of a wolf," in order to rush to his business or practical affairs. And yet it was also noted that on some occasions Americans rushed through a meal in order to do nothing better than to lounge, chew, and spit in another room.

The consensus was that the American was unrefined. Murray found middle-class Americans "deficient in those lighter accomplishments" which constitute charm, while Cooper bemoaned American ignorance of music— "which elevates and refines human tastes"—and in addition found his countrymen "wanting in most of the higher tastes."

High on the American's scale of values was his egalitarian belief that one man—particularly an American—was as good as any other, certainly that he should be treated like any other. White Americans simply would not be known as "servants." Those who worked in other people's homes would not be summoned by bells. The word "mister" was omitted from door plates. One visitor ran into a tailor who would not go to him to take the measure of a coat, insisting it was "not republican," and a carriage driver who complained that the travelers on his coach "had had private meals every day and not asked him to the table."

Many European visitors and, for that matter, Americans, were not particularly charmed by the American stress on egalitarianism, believing as did Cooper and Hone that it was responsible for the sordid manners and mean quality of American life, or like Tocqueville, that because of it liberty was downgraded. They took a dim view of the glorification of that same common man whose traits they found so depressing. Other visitors also agreed with Cooper, John Quincy Adams and other Americans that for all the lip service they paid to equality, Americans in fact practised the same forms of inequality as Europeans, the one great difference being that in this country money rather than blood divided men into rigidly separated worlds. In a word, Americans were hypocrites.

The transcendent American value according to most contemporaries was materialism. The distinguishing feature of the American was his love of money. "At the bottom of all that an American does," wrote Chevalier, "is money; beneath every word, money." His sacrifices, when made, "are systematic and calculated. It is neither enthusiasm nor passion that unties his purse strings, but motives of policy . . . in which he feels his own private interests to be involved." His motto is, "Victory or death! But to him, victory is to make money, to get the dollars, to make a fortune out of nothing. . . ."

The love of money had dismal side effects. It corrupted Americans, preoccupying them with vulgar displays of wealth or, in Miss Martineau's phrase, a "mean love of distinction." Tudor felt that it discouraged an appreciation of nature. Grund was startled to find theatre audiences who on the one hand counted the house at a performance of *Othello,* and on the other applauded Iago's admiration of a full purse. Hall blamed the love of money for all manner of American ills, including their indifference to women! How could there be time, interest or skill for pursuing the amenities in "a country where all men are engaged in one and the same engrossing pursuit—namely, that of making money (?)" DeRoos was present when "a young lady, talking of the most eligible class of life from which to choose a husband, declared that, for her part, she was all for the Commissions." His friend, a major, beamed happily until he found out that she meant commission merchants. Since the love of money was actually a love for the material things that money could buy, Dickens advised that "it would be well . . . for the American people as a whole if they loved the Real less, and the Ideal somewhat more." He agreed with Miss Martineau that nothing spoiled the American character more than their vulgar materialism.

Americans were snobs, though this trait and value was manifested mainly by the better sort or those who pretended to be, according to Miss Martineau. A New York female complained to Abdy that the marriage phrase should be, "wilt thou have this *lady,*" etc., while in Philadelphia, a sensible woman advised him that his "report on American manners and customs would be discredited or undervalued by his countrymen when it was known that [he] . . . had travelled with stage-drivers and conversed freely with working people." Great pains were taken by urban society circles to maintain the separation between them and lesser groups.

If those near the top were snobs, those below were social climbers. Vigne told a much-repeated tale: "The captain of a steamboat . . . happened to ask rather loudly, 'General, a little fish?' and was immediately answered in the affirmative by 25 of the 30 gentlemen that were present." Murray found "the tavern kept by a general, wagon wheels mended by a colonel, day laborers and mechanics are gentlemen." Lieber ridiculed the constant name changes that were designed to suggest a respectable origin. He believed that insanity was caused in America by "a diseased anxiety to be equal to the wealthiest, the craving for wealth and consequent disappointment which ruins the intellect of many."

Inevitably materialists and champions of equality had no respect for tradition. Americans "have no love for anything merely because it is old," observed Thomson. They were "so mutable, so much given to change . . . that [he] . . . had scarcely met with one who knew who his grandfather was." One visitor found something "cool and heartless," a sign of disrespect for the dead, in their funerals, performed in too great a hurry. Another was upset that the burial places of national heroes were so poorly kept. In Hall's indictment, "the unpleasant truth seems to be, that nothing whatsoever is venerated in America merely on account of its age, or, indeed on any other account. Neither historical associations, nor high public services, nor talents, nor knowledge, claim any peculiar reverence for the busy generation of the present hour."

Their disrespect for tradition merged into disrespect for law. Europeans were startled to observe a jury munching on food, the foreman announcing a verdict with his mouth full. Vigne blamed the spirit of equality for a courtroom informality in which lawyers sat casually on tables while judges spat. As a result of the growing feeling of self-importance on the part of the people, Chevalier believed, "the reverence for the laws (was) . . . wearing out with the Americans." In the case of so selfish a population, "the laws had no force when they jarred with interest."

Americans valued neither learning nor intellectual accomplishment. The attempt to limit medical practice to the trained, was resisted by Jacksonians. Tocqueville believed that "in no country in the civilized world [was] . . . less attention paid to philosophy than in the United States." Others expanded the charge to include literature and learning in general. Most visitors agreed with Mrs. Trollope that pure learning held little attraction to the American mind, the "pursuit of wealth" drawing it in other directions. Able sons were trained for business; a "poor boy who is a little hard of hearing, and rather slow of comprehension, shall go to college." Scholars were held in low repute because they commanded low incomes, the results of their intellectual efforts having little market value.

Americans seemed to have contempt for life. They blandly acquiesced in terrible steamboat accidents caused by faulty construction—"What are a few hundred persons more or less?" Hone wrote sarcastically in his diary, after a particularly terrible accident. The lust for profits overrode all other considerations, according to him. Americans were accused of manifesting an "utter want of . . . sympathy for the sufferings of others." They seemed ready on the slightest provocation to shoot or stab, particularly in the west and south. Murder was often lightly punished by the law, as was lynching. Duelists, often fighting over ridiculous alleged slights to their honor, in fact dueled not to satisfy honor but to kill. Marryat was surprised at the intensive practice by the involved parties prior to a duel. In this sense, certainly, Andrew Jackson captured very well the spirit of the times.

Some observers found glaring contradictions between American lip service and practice or between their professed and actual values, recording their judgments in a series of trenchant summaries. Americans were thus ambitious but lacking in lofty ambition. They talked up liberty but restricted its practice. They talked of lofty things in the absence of lofty feelings. Grund had been told, "in the absence of enthusiasm, which would inspire them with natural eloquence, they seek to maintain themselves at a certain elevation by pressing hard on lofty topics; having no wings, they endeavor to support themselves in the air by a *parachute*." Their principles were high but "their civilization and morals fall far below." They spoke glowingly of equality but strained to demonstrate their own exalted station. They loved change but dreaded revolution. Their bodies were in constant motion but their minds were inert. They loved to talk but had nothing to say. They were avid readers but preferred newspaper gossip to literature. They were in a constant "election fever" but cold to political principles. They had appetites but no passions. And finally, they knew how to make money but not how to spend it. This mournful catalog was dubious tribute to a people who were regarded as something less than they seemed.

The portrait of the Jacksonian drawn by his contemporary observers is of a good-natured but essentially shallow man: clever but not profound, self-important but uncertain, fond of deluding himself, living almost fanatically for the flesh (although not knowing too well how), straining every fibre to accumulate the things he covets and amoral about the methods to be used, a hypocrite who strains at gnats and swallows camels, an energetic and efficient fellow albeit a small one, who takes comfort in—as well as his standards of behavior from—numbers. It is not a very attractive picture.

What are we to make of him? There are several things he seems clearly not to be. This is no child of the frontier, neither his ways nor his values having much to do with Indian fighting. The people who lived in western towns imitated their eastern brethren, while the small minority living on the western outskirts of civilization, who were engaged in conversation by enterprising travelers, disclosed values very similar to those of their countrymen. This conformist was no inner-directed man. And there is little evidence that our Jacksonian, as he pursued the main chance, looked back longingly to a "chaste, republican" past. His thoughts were for today, while by a better, he meant a wealthier, tomorrow.

Possibly his materialism is his most significant characteristic, explaining as it does, not only his goals but so many of his ways and other values. What better explanation is there of his disinterest in the idealistic and reform movements which, while they proliferated during the era, commanded so little actual membership? What did it matter that some women felt unfulfilled or that colored persons were everywhere treated as less than human? What was it to him that his society might maldistribute status, so long as it promised to provide tangible comforts?

His values and intellectual traits appear to throw some light on his political and economic choices. Bigotry, supplemented by cruelty and cupidity, better explain atrocities against Indians and Negroes. Vanity and boastfulness made it easy for him to believe that his country—which was himself writ large—was superior to all others and could do no wrong. That much-admired pragmatic temper which rendered his mind indifferent to theories or fundamental principles, when combined with his lack of respect for learning, seemed to have a number of political consequences. For looked at one way, it was child's play for shrewd manipulators who sought his vote to convince this hardheaded, unlearned fellow that politics was a kind of simple morality play: good leaders v. bad, honest men v. dishonest, the people's friends v. their enemies. The unique American major party that was born during the era—which is many if not all things to most if not all men, which avoids or deflects crucial issues rather than meet them—is perfectly suited to the man who has neither interest in "fundamental principles" nor the wit to perceive them.

Our Jacksonian's lack of intellectual sophistication may account for his blissful unawareness of the central banking, or any other complex function, performed by the second Bank of the United States, and help explain the enthusiastic support he gave to those who would rid the nation of the monster of paper money by destroying the institution that best restrained its unlimited circulation. On the other hand, a combination of lust for gain, shrewdness and hypocrisy may have accounted for his zeal in overthrowing what he well understood to be the great obstacle to the speculative profits his dreams were made on. On a more general level, disinterest in the "principles" operating in his economy, would help explain his indifference to informed criticisms of its weaknesses, while his penchant for social climbing spurred him on to try to get what he could for himself. Finally, his conformity would explain his acquiescence even in policies he might secretly disapprove of or about which he might have qualms.

Jacksonians liked to think that Americans were different from—and of course better than—other people. Students of history, however, will have recognized many familiar traits, some of them manifested as long ago and far away as first-century Rome, whose gross new ways were so decried by spokesmen of the old patrician order. These were traits that sprang up where a booming commercial economy was emerging. It is by no means certain that there had been significant changes in this country from Washington's era to Jackson's, significant, that is, with regard to national character. Europeans, not having been here before, had no way of knowing whether change had occurred. They did, however, have that freshness of viewpoint that so often enables the foreigner to see things the native overlooks. Nothing was too commonplace for them, they took nothing for granted.

That the portrait they drew was not a very attractive one can be interpreted in ways flattering to the American psyche. (Of course such an interpretation runs the risk of itself being interpreted as a modern example of the American refusal to accept criticism.) In this country the mass of inhabitants, whether appealing or not, were at least *visible,* downright loquacious, inevitably unattractive to the urbane observers who wrote about them. My point is that the European counterpart of the Jacksonian common man was comparatively powerless and inarticulate, no object of fascination to an army of interested reporters. The American was sometimes admired, more often criticized, but in either case treated with a respect that was the more meaningful for being unspoken. Like him or not, he had to be reckoned with.

Politics, a Tariff, and a Bank

Glyndon Van Deusen

While the election of 1832 brought great joy to the Jacksonians, it also left them facing great responsibilities. The economic discontent of the South remained intense, and there had to be found some means of soothing the turbulent feelings of the plantation gentry. The Bank of the United States, though defeated in its effort to obtain a recharter, was still a power in the land, and many thought it a discordant element in a community where equal opportunity should be the rule of faith and practice. The Bank's influence, in the opinion of some of the most influential Jacksonians, should be restricted at once. It was evident also that the political opposition headed by Clay and orienting around his American system would lose no opportunity of harassing Jackson's administration and disrupting its attempts to formulate specific policies. This opposition must be thwarted.

The tariff, the Bank, and the maneuvering of the opposition party constituted grave problems. It was the South and its attitude toward the tariff, however, that demanded immediate attention. The tariff of 1832 was not a sign of peace, but of a period of crisis and tension that boded ill for the Union.

The tariff bill, which seemed so reasonable to the President, was deemed utterly unacceptable by many southerners, and after its passage resentment against the action of the federal government had steadily increased in South Carolina, the home of nullification. By voting for a man who had no earthly chance of election [John C. Calhoun], the state had scorned the candidates of the contending parties in 1832. Indeed, the election in South Carolina had centered not on the Presidency but on the question of nullification. The "Nullies," as they were called, wanted swift action. They were opposed by a Union party, led by Joel Poinsett, Adams's minister to Mexico but now a Jacksonian

Democrat. These Unionists had to face a rising storm of states' rights sentiment, and a lengthy disquisition by South Carolina's leading statesman "On the Subject of State Interposition."

Those who asserted that the Constitution of the United States was made by the people as a whole were wrong, Calhoun wrote to Governor Hamilton of South Carolina: "So far from the Constitution being the work of the American people collectively, no such political body either now or ever did exist . . . the Constitution is the work of the people of the States, considered as separate and independent political communities. . . . The Union, of which the Constitution is the bond, is a union of States, and not of individuals." Calhoun admitted that a state by ratifying the Constitution imposed obligations on its citizens, but he also asserted that it was the state's right to determine the extent of those obligations. When a state held an act of Congress unconstitutional, it could declare that act null and void, and such declaration was binding on the citizens of the state. Conversely, the national government had no authority to control or coerce a state.

Calhoun was arguing for nullification, not for secession. He was, he said, seeking to preserve the Union, a Union that was in essence a confederation, with each state the final judge as to the constitutionality of the acts of the national government. Such an argument was powerful justification for the nullifiers, but it left the form of national government without the substance. Despite Calhoun's intent, it blazed a path toward secession.

The nullifiers did their work swiftly. The convention passed an ordinance declaring that the tariffs of 1828 and 1832 were null and void, and that they would not be enforceable in South Carolina after February 1, 1833. The collection of duties by the federal government after that date was forbidden. Appeal of the validity of nullification to the Supreme Court of the United States was prohibited. The ordinance further declared that any forceful attempt by the federal government to coerce the state would dissolve the bonds of South Carolina's allegiance to the Union.

> And we, the People of South Carolina, to the end that it may be fully understood by the Government of the United States, and the people of the co-States, that we are determined to maintain this, our Ordinance and Declaration, at every hazard, *Do further Declare* that we will not submit to the application of force, on the part of the Federal Government, to reduce this State to obedience; but that we will consider the passage, by Congress, of any act . . . to coerce the State, shut up her ports, destroy or harass her commerce, or to enforce the acts hereby declared to be null and void, otherwise than through the civil tribunals of the country, as inconsistent with the longer continuance of South Carolina in the Union: and that the people of this State will thenceforth hold themselves absolved from all further obligation to maintain or preserve their political connexion with the people of the other states, and will forthwith proceed to organize a separate Government, and do all other acts and things which sovereign and independent States may of right do.

This ordinance was a fair representation of the spirit that prevailed among the leaders of the nullifiers. They were ready to fight. "All appear animated," wrote James H. Hammond, editor of the Columbia *Southern Times,* "by the most thorough conviction that we are unconquerable." When the legislature passed the laws necessary to implement the ordinance, it provided money for the purchase of arms and authorized the enlistment of volunteers.

The nullifiers called themselves "whigs" and scornfully applied the term "tory" to the Union men. Blood ran hot between the two factions. James Blair, member of Congress from South Carolina and a Unionist, was so enraged by the "tory" designation that he waylaid Duff Green on the Washington streets and assaulted him with a club.

Jackson's reply to South Carolina's defiance was the adoption of a carrot and stick policy, a blending of conciliation and threat. In his message to Congress, December 4, 1832, the President spoke soothingly of the tariff problem. The rapidly approaching extinction of the national debt, he said, was lessening the importance of the tariff as a source of revenue. Declaring that he was fully aware of the inequities in the existing tariff, he made it clear that he now stood for a substantial reduction of duties. It was his opinion that eventually protection should be limited to articles essential to the nation's safety in time of war. He noted with regret the excitement in South Carolina, but deemed federal laws sufficient for coping with the situation in that state.

Jackson's message was much calmer than the feelings that were stirring in his breast. As he read Poinsett's reports on the doings of the nullifiers, his eyes began to blaze. He wrote Poinsett that Calhoun showed signs of dementia, and that Hayne, McDuffie, and the rest were in a scarcely better condition of mind. South Carolina's attitude, he declared, was worse than rebellion. The raising of troops was "positive treason." Congressmen were assuring him that the legislative branch would sustain him in defending "this union, which alone secures our liberty, prosperity and happiness." He would meet nullification at the threshold "and have the leaders arrested and arraigned for treason. The wickedness, madness and folly of the leaders and the delusion of their followers in the attempt to destroy themselves and our union has not its parallel in the history of the world."

Deeply stirred though he was by the action of the nullifiers, the General moved cautiously. A warning to the people of South Carolina was drawn up, its drafting entrusted to the Secretary of State, Edward Livingston of Louisiana, a distinguished lawyer and politician who had stood shoulder to shoulder with Jackson at New Orleans and was in the President's confidence.

The "Proclamation to the People of South Carolina" was couched in the tones of a father admonishing his children. The South Carolina ordinance, said the President, prescribed a course of action that had as its object the destruction of the Union. The assumption that a state had power to annul a federal law was "incompatible with the existence of the Union, contradicted expressly by the letter of the Constitution, unauthorized by its spirit, inconsistent with every principle on which it was founded, and destructive of the great object for which it was formed." The arguments advanced by the state in justification of its action were inadequate, and he urged its citizens to recognize this inadequacy. Under the Constitution, a government had been formed which represented not the states but the people. No state, therefore, had the right to secede, "because such secession does not break a league, but destroys the unity of a nation. . . . To say that any state may at pleasure secede from the Union is to say that the United States is not a nation. . . ." Nullification, Jackson warned, could end only in failure and worse than failure:

> If your leaders could succeed in establishing a separation, what would be your situation? Are you united at home? Are you free from the apprehension of civil discord, with all of its fearful consequences? Do our neighboring republics, every day suffering some new revolution or contending with some new insurrection, do they excite your envy? But the dictates of a high duty oblige me solemnly to announce that you cannot succeed. The laws of the United States must be executed. I have no discretionary power on the subject; my duty is emphatically pronounced in the Constitution. Those who told you that you might peaceably prevent their execution deceived you; they could not have been deceived themselves. They know that a forcible opposition could alone prevent the execution of the laws, and they know that such opposition must be repelled. Their object is disunion. But be not deceived by names. Disunion by armed force is *treason*. Are you really ready to incur its guilt?

But even as this stick was being brandished, the carrot was again displayed. It took the form of the Verplanck bill, drawn up with the assistance of Secretary of the Treasury Louis McLane and other friends of the administration, and reported out by the Committee on Ways and Means of the House of Representatives on January 8, 1833. This bill proposed immediate and sweeping reductions in duties, with the tariff lowered 50 per cent by 1834.

Jackson and his whole administration supported the Verplanck bill. They were extremely anxious to see the tariff lowered, for the general expectation was that the whole South would go against the Force Bill unless a satisfactory tariff bill was passed. Indeed, Silas Wright wrote to Azariah Flagg from Washington that without such a bill the government would be virtually disbanded.

To make the situation even more difficult, Clay was pushing for the passage of his land bill. This was based on the principle of distribution of the land sales revenue to all the states and, it was estimated, would necessitate the raising of some $3 million in additional revenue each year to take the place of the land revenue that would go to the states instead of toward the expenses of the national government. Many members of Congress, including a number of Jacksonian Democrats, were planning to vote for this bill as a means of forcing higher duties than were provided in Verplanck's tariff measure. Greatly distressed by this situation, Wright declared that Clay's proposal was "the most mischievous bill, in my judgment, that ever originated in the Congress of the United States."

As ardent a nationalist as Jackson, Clay reluctantly supported the Force Bill, but the Verplanck measure was anathema to him. Nevertheless, it was obvious that the tariff was going to be lowered and that whoever was responsible for it would gain considerable credit, especially in the South. Clay wanted that credit. He was also moved by a complex of other motives. Dislike and distrust of Jackson, jealousy of Webster, a desire to recoup some of the prestige lost in his recent shattering defeat, all played a part in the thinking of the Kentucky statesman. There was also the possibility of a political alliance with Calhoun and, even more important, the enlisting of broad southern support for the land bill that he was attempting to push through Congress in the face of the administration's outspoken preference for cheap land.

Clay introduced his bill in the Senate on February 12, 1833. It provided for gradual reductions, at two-year intervals, of all tariff schedules in the 1832 tariff that were over 20 per cent. There were to be four of these reductions to 1840. Then, over a two-year period, there would be two relatively sharp reductions of the remaining duties above the 20 per cent level. By July 1, 1842, there would be a top-level duty rate of 20 per cent. The bill was amended, at the insistence of protectionist forces, by a salutary provision for the valuation of dutiable goods at the port of entry, thus striking a blow at the fraudulent invoices that had plagued the customs service for many years.

But despite its good features, the compromise tariff of 1833 was not a good bill from an economic viewpoint. It made no provision for specific duties as contrasted with ad valorem, though it was meant to apply to both; the duty reductions were irregular; the 20 per cent level of 1842 set a purely arbitrary and indiscriminate standard of duties. It was a bill framed primarily with an eye to political considerations.

The compromise tariff passed the House on February 26, 1833, by a vote of 119 to 85. There the South was almost solidly for the bill. New England was definitely against it, the Middle Atlantic states voted against it three to one, and the North Central states (Ohio, Indiana, and Illinois) split. The Senate vote, on March 1, was twenty-nine for to sixteen against.

The Force Bill passed at the same time as the tariff, and Jackson signed both measures on March 2, 1833. South Carolina promptly nullified the Force Bill but accepted the new tariff, and so, for the time being, the danger of civil war passed away.

The struggle which produced the compromise tariff of 1833 has a considerable significance in American history. The protectionists waxed melancholy over the act. Mathew Carey declared that "to remove the imaginary grievance of a portion of the states, real substantial grievances are inflicted on the remainder, whereby a large portion of their industry and happiness will be blasted and withered." Webster, now the great spokesman of New England's industrial interests, was embittered by the passage of the bill. Almost ten years after the event, he could still say that there was "no measure ever passed by Congress during my connection with that body that caused me so much grief and mortification. It was passed by a few friends joining the whole host of the enemy. . . . The principle was bad, the measure was bad, the consequences were bad." There can be no doubt that this tariff bill did much to widen the breach already opening between Webster and Clay.

The bill had other consequences besides emphasizing the cleavage between Webster and Clay, and between the pro- and antitariff men in the opposition. The industrialists were thrown into an unnecessary panic by the bill's passage. The reductions for which it provided down to 1840 were relatively slight, and there was every reason to anticipate, as Clay did, a revision of the act before its more drastic reductions went into effect. It is true that this revision did not appear, but the final 20 per cent duty for which the measure provided remained in effect only two months, July to September, 1842. Certainly the tariff of 1833 cannot be regarded as having had an injurious effect upon the national economy.

The conflict over the tariff was also significant for Clay's political future. Even though it sowed seeds of enmity between himself and Webster, it gave a new lease of life to his reputation as the "Great Pacificator." It gave him standing with such states' rights men as John Tyler and Littleton Tazewell of Virginia, men who either became politically neutral or moved into the ranks of the Kentuckian's supporters. And—an anticlimax as it proved—it rallied southern votes to his land bill, which passed Congress only to be pocket-vetoed by the indomitable Chieftain in the White House, who had now reversed himself on distribution as well as on the tariff.

Significant, too, was the emergence from the struggle over the tariff of a working agreement between Clay and Calhoun. The two men had worked together on the compromise, and their *rapprochement* was made all the more evident by the way in which Congress handled the appointments to the lucrative offices of printers to the House and Senate. The House rejected Blair (member of the Kitchen Cabinet and editor of the Washington *Globe*), choosing instead Duff Green, whose daughter had married Calhoun's son and who was a stout supporter of the South Carolinian. Gales and Seaton, the editors of Clay's organ, the *National Intelligencer,* were made printers to the Senate.

The understanding between Calhoun and Clay was to last for the remainder of Jackson's term of office and was to provide formidable opposition, particularly in the Senate, to "King Andrew." Ambition, and hatred of the Hero, had made the great nationalist and the great nullifier lie down together on an uneasy bed of political alliance. It was a combination as opposed to nature as the lion and the lamb of Holy Writ, but while it lasted the opposition to "Jacksonism" could, through astute leadership, challenge the Jacksonians' control of the legislative branch.

While the passage of the compromise tariff was a triumph for nationalism and majority rule, the controversy had been full of sad omens for the future. South Carolina had gone beyond the Virginia and Kentucky resolutions of 1798. The possibility and even the desirability of secession had been openly discussed, and men wore the blue cockade which the nullifiers had adopted as their emblem long after the tempest over the tariff had died down. To all sections the conflict between the free, diversified economy of the North, with its rapidly developing industrial capitalism, and the agrarian, slave-labor economy of the South, with its need for foreign markets, was becoming fearfully apparent.

But despite gloomy portents, the doctrine of "interposition," so stoutly upheld by Calhoun, had been answered with crushing force by Webster and the Unionists. The Constitution is a compact. It must be interpreted in accordance with its provisions for interpretation, that is, by the courts. If it does not properly protect the rights of the states, the remedy is not interposition by them for the purpose of rendering nugatory the decisions of the Supreme Court, or the constitutional acts of any other branch of the federal government. The remedy is amendment of the federal Constitution itself. All other expedients weaken and, if persisted in, destroy both the compact and the Union.

Important as was the conflict over the tariff, it was not the only battle royal in which the administration became engaged during the winter of 1832–33. Jackson was determined to continue his assaults upon the Bank of the United States. Its charter had four more years to run, but this made no difference. The General was moved by dislike and distrust of an institution, which he did not understand and which had sought to thwart his will, and the arguments of Taney and Kendall fortified his determination to deprive it of its remaining power in the financial and political community. Taney opposed the Bank on the ground that it had made excessive loans, some of which had been for political support. He also believed it to be unconstitutional—a definitely strict constructionist point of view. Kendall regarded the Bank as a corrupt and dangerously powerful institution which was still plotting for a renewal of its charter. Its destruction, he held, was essential to the preservation of a purely republican government.

Jackson told a Cabinet meeting in November, 1832, that he was convinced the Bank was insolvent, and suggested withdrawing the deposits in it which had been made by the government. Attorney General Taney supported this suggestion. Then the President asked Congress for an investigation to discover whether or not the government deposits in the Bank were safe. The House investigated and replied that they were safe, but the President cared not one whit for this opinion. He next sent Amos Kendall on a mission to bankers in Baltimore, Philadelphia, New York, and Boston to find out if they would take the government deposits. Kendall reported that the bankers would be more than glad to have the funds. It became more and more apparent that removal of the deposits was to be the next step. Such a move, Biddle told Webster, would be "a declaration of war."

The President had Taney and Kendall at his back in removing the deposits, but the Secretary of the Treasury was of another mind altogether. Louis McLane could see no good reason for this step, especially since Congress was opposed, and he said so. It had already been decided to shift McLane from the Treasury to the State Department so that Livingston could become Minister to France. This was now done, and William J. Duane, a Philadelphia lawyer and anti-Bank man was made Secretary of the Treasury.

Jackson took it for granted that Duane would remove the deposits, but he soon discovered that he had caught a tartar. Duane had no more love for state banks than he had for the Bank of the United States and he, too, refused to do the President's bidding. He told the President that the House had voted the public money safe in the Bank (so it had, 110 to 46); that a change to local banks as depositories would shake public confidence; that local banks already had an overinflated currency of better than six dollars in paper to one in silver (the implication being that deposit in local banks would inevitably result in further inflation of the currency).

Duane's arguments, sound though they were, fell upon deaf ears. He was summarily dismissed, and now the President shifted Taney from the Attorney General's office over into the Treasury. At last he had the right man in he right place, so far as his policy was concerned.

The Treasury continued drawing on its balance in the Bank for the current expenses, but it now made its deposits in a number of state banks, the "Pets," located in the principal cities in the country. Its balance in the Bank of the United States grew steadily smaller.

Biddle, meantime, had determined to do the sensible thing—contract the Bank's obligations as the funds at its disposal diminished, and at the same time make the institution ready to repel any other assaults that might be made upon it. He also cherished the hope that, by utilizing the power the Bank still had left, he might yet be able to effect a recharter. During the winter and spring of 1834, the cultured banker and the fiery, iron-willed President confronted one another like two armed and implacable enemies.

The effects of the contraction of credit are not easily determined. There was some credit stringency, some tightness in the money market. The administration at first denied that there was anything the matter with the financial situation, then pointed to the Bank as the cause of all the trouble. The pro-Bank forces claimed that the financial status of the country was precarious, that it was growing worse, and that it was all Jacksons' fault. Hundreds of petitions for relief flooded Congress and deputations of businessmen waited on Jackson to beg for relief.

They found the President adamant. Trembling with rage and with the intensity of his convictions, he told the suppliant businessmen to "go to the Monster, go to Nicholas Biddle," if they wanted relief. "I never will restore the deposits," he stormed at the New York committee. "I never will recharter the United States Bank, or sign a charter for any other bank, so long as my name is Andrew Jackson." He told the Baltimore committee that "the failures that are now taking place are amongst the stock-jobbers, brokers, and gamblers, and would to God, they were all swept from the land! It would be a happy thing for the country." The Hero wrote to Van Buren that he was "fixed in my course as firm as the Rocky Mountain . . . Providence has a power over me, but frail mortals who worship Bale [sic] and the golden calf, can have none."

Actually, the crisis in financial affairs seems to have been exaggerated by both sides for the purposes of political war. There was some unemployment, and some decline in stock values in the winter of 1833–34, but imports, commodity exports, and internal commerce all increased during that period. John A. Dix wrote to Wright and Van Buren from Albany in February, 1834, that times were better than they had been in the previous year, and that the only people being hurt by the contraction were gamblers in stocks and commodities. Isaac Hill believed that the Bank's contraction policy would, at most, create only a temporary distress. So thought Robert Rantoul in Boston. Even the New York *Evening Post,* which was disposed to cry havoc about the Bank's policy, admitted that the decline in cotton prices abroad, the exaction of cash duties on imported goods, and the failure of the sugar crops at the South were in part to blame for the tight money market in the winter of 1834.

The chief result of the pressure exerted by Biddle was a marked lessening of the Bank's popularity. The contraction, as the Richmond *Enquirer* put it, had given the Jacksonians an opportunity to view with alarm. This they had done, calling upon the people to "tremble at the enormous power of this mammoth institution," and the people's response had been that anticipated by the Democratic politicians.

The government now deposited its money in the "Pets." Some of these were well chosen, others not. They all promptly expanded their loans, and in this way fostered the speculative craze that characterized the eighteen-thirties and terminated in the depression of 1837.

In 1836 the Bank received a new charter as the United States Bank of Pennsylvania. This charter committed it to pay a bonus of $2 million to the state, to make loans to the state for internal improvements, and to purchase the state's public utility stocks. Biddle estimated that the cost of the charter to the Bank was $5,775,000, a price that he did not regard as high but that proved to be a heavy financial burden.

The United States Bank of Pennsylvania soon found itself in other difficulties than those imposed by its charter. While times were yet good, it began borrowing heavily abroad, a debt that proved embarrassing in the depression years. It also became involved in a disastrous cotton corner, this being the result of Biddle's effort to support the price of United States cotton in the face of a falling world market. As cotton prices continued to sag and the Bank found itself more and more heavily involved, it sought salvation by raiding the New York, Boston, and Baltimore money markets. Its credit became more and more shaky. Wise investors disposed of their holdings in its stock. Early in 1841 it closed its doors forever, a bankrupt institution.

On March 29, 1839, Nicholas Biddle resigned as president of the United States Bank of Pennsylvania, but nevertheless he was closely associated with the last disastrous phases of the Bank's career. He continued to advise his successors in the Bank after his retirement and was heavily involved in the cotton corner. As this corner failed and the Bank's financial situation deteriorated, stockholders in the institution sued Biddle for $240,000, and he and four other former officers of the Bank were arrested on charges of criminal conspiracy. They were exonerated in court proceedings. Other court actions ensued, but Biddle was not long involved. He died February 27, 1844, at the age of fifty-eight.

The career of the United States Bank of Pennsylvania has often been used to support the argument that the Jacksonians were justified in destroying the Second Bank of the United States. Certain it is that the same management developed the policies of both institutions. The Bank of the United States, however, had been a central bank, operating under a federal charter and vested with great responsibility for the public welfare. This was not the case with the United States Bank of Pennsylvania. There the public responsibility was gone and with it the restraint upon daring speculative enterprise. Biddle, as head of the Bank of the United States, had been a conservative and conscientious banker. When he became head of a state bank, he made errors of judgment that were disastrous to the institution he served. Such capacity for error was, perhaps, inherent in his character, but it had not been apparent before the Jacksonians leagued to destroy him and the Bank of the United States together.

Such was the story of the Second Bank of the United States and its tragic aftermath. The Bank had been given too much power by the charter granted it in 1816. Had it been rechartered, this power could have been curbed by regulatory provisions; indeed, some attempt at this had been made by the Bank's friends. The idea of charter modification was much in the air during the early eighteen-thirties. Hezekiah Niles, Nathan Appleton, Daniel Webster, Horace Greeley, even Jackson himself, projected such plans. The modifications in the Bank's charter provided by the recharter bill of 1832 were constructive. They would have made for a better institution. But when the Bank became a political football, the issue was no longer susceptible to rational analysis. Its destruction as a federal bank fostered speculation, was a blow to the development of a sound credit policy, and contributed materially to the currency chaos that characterized the succeeding decades. The economic development of the United States along sound and constructive lines was clearly hindered by the destruction of the Bank.

Politically, the Jacksonians profited by the Bank war. Clay, Webster, and their followers generally had rallied to the Bank's support, and this gave the Jacksonians an opportunity to pillory their political opponents as the lackeys of a "mammoth corporation," friends of the wealthy and powerful, exploiters of the masses. Whig leaders, such as Thurlow Weed and William Henry Seward, sought to dissociate themselves from the "Monster," but it was uphill work. The Jacksonians knew a good thing when they saw it. Isaac Hill told Gideon Welles that the Bank issue between the parties was "primarily the question that democrats should most desire," and Van Buren wrote gleefully to Jackson in July, 1834, "The Opposition labor hard to shake off the Bank, but we are determined to hold them to it. A fitter union was never formed."

The struggle over the deposits was only one aspect of the political conflict that raged during Jackson's second term. The Twenty-third Congress had a House of Representatives that could generally be counted safe by the administration, but the Clay-Webster-Calhoun group could muster a majority in the Senate. This opposition took away from the Senate's presiding officer the power of appointing committees which he had exercised since 1828, restoring it to the body of the Senate, that is, to the anti-Jackson coalition. The President's opponents were out to embarrass the administration in every possible way, as was soon to be shown by their assaults upon the Cabinet and upon Old Hickory himself.

The opposition knew what it wanted, but its great handicap was a lack of discipline. It held together only through its detestation of the Old Hero. Clay commanded great loyalty among the lesser lights, but Webster could not always be counted upon to support him. Calhoun was but a recent convert, and both the rival chieftains found the Kentuckian's imperious manner difficult to bear. There could always be defection, too, where economic or other sectional interests were at stake. Clay counted himself, rightly, as the leader, but he never knew from day to day whether his shaky coalition would hold firm.

The country, Harry of the West charged, was in the midst of a revolution, "hitherto bloodless," that was rapidly changing the government from a republic to a dictatorship. Jackson's use of the veto, his frequent and arbitrary appointments and removals of government functionaries, his contemptuous disregard of the judiciary, his attitude toward the American system, and the union of the purse and the sword that was being effected by the subjection of the Treasury to the Executive will constituted Clay's evidence in the case. If the trend continued until March 4, 1837, said Clay, the government would become an elective monarchy—"the worst of all forms of government." Lengthily, Clay argued that the Constitution and the Fathers had lodged the power of the purse in the hands of Congress; that the Secretary of the Treasury was responsible to Congress, not to the President. The function of the Chief Executive was to execute the laws, not to interpret or override them. His office was one "of observation and superintendence," not of dictation to other officials of the government. The Western Hotspur closed his speech with a darkly shadowed verbal picture of the contemporary scene:

> We behold the usual incidents of approaching tyranny. The land is filled with spies and informers; and detraction and denunciation are the orders of the day. People, especially official incumbents in this place, no longer dare speak in the fearless tones of manly freedom, but in the cautious whispers of trembling slaves. The premonitory symptoms of despotism are upon us; and if Congress do not apply an instantaneous and effective remedy, the fatal collapse will soon come on, and we shall die—ignobly die! base, mean, and abject slaves—the scorn and contempt of mankind—unpitied, unwept, unmourned!

A running debate of three months' duration followed Clay's onslaught. Benton, Wright, and Forsyth bore the brunt for the administration. Webster and Calhoun supported Clay. The latter reiterated his concern over "the rapid strides of Executive power." Webster declared that the country's welfare, its Constitution, and its laws were at stake. Calhoun, proclaiming himself independent of both the major parties and an impartial judge, asserted that the removal of the deposits was an unconstitutional act and an alarming portent of "the approach of despotic power." What was it, asked the South Carolinian, but a distribution through the pet banks "in the shape of discounts and loans to corrupt partisans as a means of increasing political influence?" The crisis was a fearful one, he said, and there was danger of both dissolution and despotism.

The Jacksonians vigorously fought back. Wright defended removal of the deposits as both constitutional and wise, and made an impassioned plea for the Hero of New Orleans, the Indian fighter, the people's choice, who was now being condemned without trial. Benton declared that all the pother trumped up by the opposition was for the purpose of obtaining a recharter of the Bank of the United States. The Bank was the head of the American system. If rechartered, it would re-establish that system—tariffs, local internal improvements, and all—in greater power and glory than ever before. Forsyth pooh-poohed the dire predictions of calamity and despotism that accompanied the removal of the deposits. For years such predictions had been the stock in trade of congressmen, but the crisis predicted had always vanished and the pictures exhibited had always turned out to be "fancy sketches."

The administration forces fought a losing battle against Clay's resolutions. On March 28, 1834, the resolutions, their phraseology slightly softened, passed the Senate by votes of twenty-six to twenty and twenty-eight to eighteen.

The debate had centered around the powers and prerogatives of the President. Here the opposition was on dangerous ground, particularly in regard to the Treasury, for the Chief Executive had always appointed the Secretary of the Treasury, and had been expressly given the right to remove him from office. It was only when the President's critics assailed his destruction of the Bank and the removal of the deposits that they were on safe ground. It was better to question the wisdom of Jackson's acts than their constitutionality.

Clay's impassioned description of the effect of Jacksonism was, of course, exaggerated. It took no account of the interest in preserving equality of opportunity which was at least one basis of the Jacksonian war on the Bank. It ignored that devotion to the rights of the common man which the Jacksonians proclaimed, and which in part underlay rotation in office, their inclination toward a cheap land policy, and their ready acceptance of white manhood suffrage. But in the realm of finance Jacksonian influence had been destructive, while the introduction of the spoils system had had a deteriorating influence on the public administration.

And in still another way Jacksonism had meant to retrograde movement. This was in science and scientific discovery. The first Presidents of the United States had been men of broad culture, interested in the advancement of science and learning. Washington and Madison and John Quincy Adams had advocated a national university. John Adams had been an intellectual and a scholar. Jefferson was one of America's early scientists, interested in Virginia's flora and fauna and in the scientific possibilities of the Lewis and Clark expedition. From 1797 to 1815 he was president of the American Philosophical Society, and his correspondence with foreign scientists was voluminous. John Quincy Adams, in his first message to Congress, urged contributions to geographical and astronomical science, the outfitting of scientific expeditions, the establishment of an astronomical observatory (he mentioned these "lighthouses of the skies" in flattering terms), and an examination of the patent laws with a view of stimulating scientific invention. These men gave a tone to the national administration which, had it been continuous, would have given a constant stimulus to the development of scientific research.

Jackson's administration ushered in a change of view at Washington in connection with science, to say nothing of the other aspects of intellectual life. The triumph of an administration whose principal organ declared that the world is governed too much, the devotion to governmental economy, the lack of intellectual interest characteristic of the Old Hero and many of those who surrounded him, diminished the likelihood of assistance for scientific learning from the national government. Jackson did sign a bill for exploration of the Pacific that eventually resulted in the despatch of the Wilkes expedition of

1838, but aside from this the record was mainly negative. The federal government refused to take any practical steps to safeguard public health, this at a time when local government was becoming increasingly concerned with health problems. Jacksonians such as Benton and Silas Wright were fearful of another centralizing agency like the Bank that they had just destroyed. Consequently, they defeated a proposal by Whig Senator Asher Robbins that Englishman James Smithson's $500,000 bequest to the United States should be used to create a scientific and literary institution in Washington, and it was not until 1846 that the efforts of men like John Quincy Adams and Joel Poinsett established the Smithsonian Institution. The idea of a national university was abandoned. A national observatory went by the board. The conclusion is inescapable that the advent of Jacksonian Democracy delayed the advance of scientific thought and experimental research in the United States.

Reform and Antebellum America

W ithin the last decade social historians have been revising their interpretations concerning the history of social reform in antebellum
America. They are searching for a clearer, more tenable explanation of the
reform impulse that swept the country from 1820–1860. Primarily concerned
with the motivation of the reformers, the revisionists assert that the impetus
for reform was much more than the infusion of an "activist" evangelical
Christianity into a spiritually and morally exhausted middle class.

Of central importance to these historians is the theme of reform as a means
of social control. Thus they focus on the sentiments, activities, and programs
of the reformers as they attempted to deal with the unprecedented problems
of crime, poverty, insanity, and vices unleashed on a society in transition. For
many reformers it was an uneasiness with the socioeconomic transformation
taking place that prompted them to join the reform crusade. They were distressed by their own inabilities to cope with a nation that was no longer a
simple rural and agrarian society secure from the excesses of modern capitalism. In their time America was fast becoming an urban, industrial, and
impersonal society—a society that could no longer guarantee its inhabitants
protection from the passions and vagaries of change.

One of the articles in this section by David Rothman shows that the Jacksonian reformer's response to the deviant and dependent was first and foremost
a vigorous attempt to promote the stability of society at a time when traditional ideas and practices appeared obsolete, constricted, and ineffective. According to Rothman, the reformers were convinced that as the nation became
more urban and left the nurturing confines of the rural community for the
corruption of the cities, the Republic faced unprecedented dangers that could
destroy the moral fiber of the country and end the democratic experiment. As
Rothman points out, incarceration in an "asylum" became the favorite means
by which antebellum reformers hoped to rehabilitate the delinquent and
homeless. Reformers shared an intense faith in the redemptive powers of a
carefully designed environment. They were certain that only the removal of

the depraved from their homes and the temptations of the streets, and their placement in an orderly and properly structured institution could bring about their desired redemption.

Jacksonian crusaders were not only determined to resurrect the Republic's moral decline, but were equally devoted to the abolition of slavery which became for many the most consuming of all their reform efforts. Black slavery was perceived by many to be the worst of the nation's "sins". It was a horrible blight upon a people who believed themselves to be the most righteous and just on earth—a people devoted to equality and freedom. Yet, reformers asked, how can we purport to be such a noble people when all around us there exists the stigma of human bondage? As Merton Dillon observes in the second article of this chapter, the abolitionists were determined to rid the land of what they believed to be its most serious flaw—slavery. To many of these individuals the manumission of the black race became an obsession, turning many a young crusader into an unattractive, self-righteous, and bellicose fanatic. Yet their agitation, regardless of its quality, is alleged to have generated a unique American spirit of moral responsibility unparalleled in the Western world.

Perhaps one of the most significant repercussions of the reform impulse was its impact upon American women. Few, if any, male crusaders realized that their demands for freedom and justice for black Americans would arouse the desire for equality from another oppressed group—American women.

The Reform Movement provided American women with their first "outlet" into the larger society. Once allowed to leave the home and her traditional roles as its caretaker, the Jacksonian woman displayed a "natural" solicitude for the downtrodden and oppressed. Thus her presence in the various crusades was grudgingly accepted as a logical and innate extension of her domestic responsibilities. As Gerda Lerner observes in the third monograph of this section, the abolition movement was particularly receptive to women, allowing them the greatest degree of visibility and recognition. Antebellum women not only participated in the movement to help save and liberate others, but also saw the cause as the opportunity to demand their own parity. Often confronted with open hostility, prejudice, and even violence, feminists were determined to prove by their thoughts and actions that they were entitled to full equality. Led by such advocates as the Grimke sisters, many Jacksonian women were resolved to defeat the chauvinism and assuage the insecurity of their male counterparts and win their rightful place in American society.

Goading the Monster

Merton Dillon

While vague disapproval of slavery became commonplace in the North by 1830, willingness to take strong stands against it remained rare. Thus it was not surprising that when in November 1831 fifteen men—the earliest and most earnest of Garrison's white friends—met with him in Samuel E. Sewall's law office at Boston to consider founding an antislavery society, only nine admitted that they were ready to join a society based on immediatism. Since immediate abolition was the principle Garrison considered essential, formation of the New England Anti-Slavery Society waited several weeks until the twelve adherents that Garrison decreed to be the required number had declared themselves. This feeble outward appearance sharply contrasted with the dynamism and intensity of purpose of the movement whose leadership Garrison had assumed.

Garrison's crusading zeal was reflected in his rhetoric. An imperiousness not unlike that of the revivalists' sermons characterized his writings. He condemned slavery and slaveholders as relentlessly as revivalists condemned sin and sinners. The revivalists called for total commitment to Christ; Garrison demanded total commitment to the abolitionist cause. For Garrison, there was no middle ground. In effect he held that those who did not join him in the abolitionist camp were against him and thereby supported slavery.

An antislavery advocate who did not accept the abolitionist doctrine in its totality, and exactly as Garrison defined it, was likely to see himself condemned in the *Liberator* as a minion of slaveholders. So doctrinaire a position inevitably antagonized moderates and lost some potential support. But for the most part, the loss was of lukewarm adherents of the sort Garrison believed might profitably be sacrificed. As a consequence of this winnowing process, Garrison soon surrounded himself with a tightly knit circle of men and women as intense and as single-mindedly devoted to abolition as he himself was. Dozens

203

of abolitionist reformers recalled in later years Garrison's influence in awakening them to the failings of American society and in giving meaning and direction to their lives. "I remember very distinctly the first time I ever saw Garrison," wrote Lydia Maria Child, one of the most self-analytical of his converts.

> I little thought then that the whole pattern of my life-web would be changed by that introduction. I was then all absorbed in poetry. . . . He got hold of the strings of my conscience and pulled me into reforms. It is of no use to imagine what might have been, if I had never met him. Old dreams vanished, old associates departed, and all things became new.

Young men and women ardently seeking a cause commensurate with their capacity for passion found it in abolitionism, as Garrison opened their eyes to the hideousness of slavery. Persons who, for whatever reason, were not content with existing practice and values were likely to seize upon his program as the means for renovating the nation.

Garrison's call for immediate emancipation met especially eager response from free Negroes, from certain young people caught up in the widespread religious revivals of the late 1820s, and from a number of older persons, many of them Quakers, who already had established for themselves a record of antislavery persuasion. Such kindred spirits might be found anywhere, but they appeared earliest and most plentifully in parts of New England and western New York, where revivalism was common; in Ohio, particularly on the New England-dominated Western Reserve; among established antislavery groups of Southern origin in Ohio and Illinois; and among Quakers, especially in Pennsylvania, Ohio, southern Michigan, and Indiana.

Important and influential though the converts to abolitionism came to be, their numbers remained relatively few, simply because the number of persons capable of sustained moral commitment at the level of intensity demanded by that stage of the antislavery movement is always limited. Not many members of any generation are likely to see themselves as a saved remnant set apart to rescue a lost society from the consequences of its own folly, and not many will wish to subject themselves to the hostility and ridicule such a position ordinarily calls forth.

The abolitionists' appeal was religious, moral, and intellectual. It therefore was self-limiting in scope, except perhaps among free Blacks, who, whatever their attitudes on other matters might be, were likely to share the white abolitionists' determination that slavery and racial oppression must end.

The converts to abolitionism never expected to pursue their activities as solitary reformers. Even before the New England Anti-Slavery Society was formed, Garrison and other abolitionists, especially those in New York and Philadelphia, made plans to coordinate antislavery action on a nation-wide scale. "The guilt of slavery is national, its danger is national, and the obligation to remove it is national."

Antislavery men from the beginning disagreed among themselves on some of the goals of the movement, particularly on the future they envisaged for the Negro. William Jay, the New York lawyer, for instance, worried that certain abolitionists accepted Negroes on terms of equality—Garrison's New England Anti-Slavery Society had even admitted black members—and that they went very far in advocating Negro rights. Was it true, Jay asked, that some abolitionists intended to call for black suffrage? Justice and humanity required emancipation, he agreed, but those principles did not also require abolitionists to endorse the explosive proposal of extending political privileges to Blacks. Jay later moved considerably to the left of his early position on these matters, but for the moment he agreed with other conservatives that insistence on full implementation of the principles of racial equality would arouse unmanageable hostility to the abolitionists' entire program. It was such solicitude for public opinion and such readiness to accommodate to popular prejudices that most clearly distinguished moderates within the antislavery ranks from such radicals as Garrison.

Not until December 1833, after the British Parliament had emancipated the West Indian slaves to the accompaniment of much favorable publicity throughout the North, did the three most active antislavery groups—Philadelphia Quakers, New England Garrisonians, and New York reformers—finally join with representatives of the free Blacks to call a convention at Philadelphia for the purpose of organizing the American Anti-Slavery Society. Garrison had long urged such action, only to be rebuffed by the New York group. Only after Evan Lewis, a respected Quaker philanthropist from Philadelphia, journeyed to New York in support of the project, did the New Yorkers agree that the time for organization had come and should not be further postponed.

Of the sixty-two persons who assembled at Philadelphia in an atmosphere heavy with local suspicion and hostility, twenty-one (including four women) were Quakers. Three of the signers of the new society's constitution were black: James G. Barbadoes, Robert Purvis, and James McCrummell. Although the best known person at the convention was Garrison, the proceedings were dominated by the New York associates of the Tappan brothers, a group that outnumbered the delegates from New England.

After several better known men had shied away from the assignment, the delegates selected one of Garrison's early converts, the Reverend Beriah Green, president of Oneida Institute in western New York, as presiding officer. They chose Garrison along with two of his circle—Samuel J. May, a Unitarian clergyman who had helped found the New England Anti-Slavery Society, and John Greenleaf Whittier, the young Quaker poet—to draw up a Declaration of Sentiments, which would serve as a platform for the new Society. As is characteristic of committees, one man did most of the work: the document presented to the convention was essentially Garrison's.

The declaration breathed a spirit at once militant and pacific. The abolitionists, Garrison wrote, were uniting in order to complete the unfinished work of the American Revolution. Their ancestors had "waged war against their oppressors" and spilled human blood "like water in order to be free." Yet the colonists' grievances against England "were trifling in comparison with those of the slaves." This statement, which seemed to promise advocacy of violence, might well have caused apprehension among those convention members who were pacifists and nonresistant Quakers. But Garrison went on to assure them that abolitionists renounced "all carnal weapons for deliverance from bondage." Unlike Americans of the Revolutionary era who took up arms against oppression, abolitionists would seek "the destruction of error by the potency of truth—the overthrow of prejudice by the power of love—and the abolition of slavery by the spirit of repentance."

The abolitionists would take their stand, Garrison continued, on a platform demanding immediate, uncompensated emancipation without colonization. He then added, in defiance of moderates within the movement and of all but universal prejudice, that they also would seek "to secure to the colored population of the United States, all the rights and privileges which belong to them as men and as Americans. . . ."

The declaration pronounced all laws supporting slavery to be "before God utterly null and void," but at the same time, in an apparently contradictory statement, it recognized the right of each state to legislate on slavery within its own borders. It conceded that Congress "under the present compact" had no power to interfere with slavery in any state. Such a restrictive view of national power and of constitutional limits was to be expected in the early 1830s; but by the late 1840s, it would be recognized as an obstacle to antislavery accomplishment and therefore rejected by an important group of abolitionists.

Then, after establishing such general principles, the declaration went on to describe the mode of operations abolitionists planned to use in their proclaimed crusade. They intended to persuade residents of the free states to endorse the abolition of slavery "by moral and political action." To accomplish this goal, they would organize antislavery societies "in every city, town, and village in our land." They would send out antislavery agents and circulate antislavery tracts and periodicals. They would try especially to convert preachers and editors to the abolitionist cause, since these were the men thought to be the effective molders of public opinion. In particular abolitionists would "aim at a purification of the churches from all participation in the guilt of slavery." As a practical device to weaken slavery and also to end their own involvement with it, they would urge all abolitionists to adopt the old Quaker tactic of abstaining from the use of goods produced by slave labor.

The American Anti-Slavery Society would focus its efforts on groups thought to be particularly receptive to the abolitionist message. In practice, this meant that it intended especially to work among the evangelicals, who presumably would be sympathetic to abolitionism. Given the close ties the antislavery movement had long had with religion, such a policy probably would have been followed in any event, but it was encouraged by the fact that the headquarters of the new Society was established in New York City. There the antislavery movement was dominated by the Tappan reformers, most of whom were themselves profoundly religious men and whose connections with nationally prominent evangelical churchmen were close.

If clergymen and church members could be persuaded to accept the Society's program, the evangelical churches would be transformed into powerful agencies of abolitionism. Except for the political parties and government itself, the Protestant denominations were practically the only institutions that functioned in every part of the nation. Their power, though not yet thoroughly tested, presumably was enormous. Their endorsement of the abolitionist program would virtually assure its success because, it was thought, slavery could not long withstand such a concentration of moral power arrayed against it. Churches thus would become the institutions by which American society would be renovated.

It was the policy of addressing its efforts primarily to clergymen and to church members, as well as the fact that so many prominent abolitionist leaders were themselves evangelicals, that accounted for some of the chief characteristics of the antislavery movement throughout the 1830s. The abolitionists' message typically was presented as a religious appeal. Slavery was shown to be a sin. Rarely was it any longer analyzed as an economic, social, or political liability. The rhetoric and the arguments used against slavery were familiar to persons accustomed to listening to sermons and to thinking in theological terms. Church members and clergymen made up the majority of the abolitionists' converts during the early and middle 1830s. But even such people did not always find acceptance of abolitionist doctrine easy.

The revivalists' plea for the immediate abandonment of sin strikingly resembled the abolitionists' demand for the immediate end of slavery. Immediate emancipation generally was presented as a religious imperative. But the strength of the obligation to accept the doctrine ignored the difficulty of doing so. Religious persons, when confronted with the abolitionist call to commit themselves to immediatism, often went through an observable agony of spirit. Just as the process of religious conversion involved dramatic readjustment of values that might be accompanied by inner torment, so desperate soul-searching and spiritual anguish might accompany conversion to immediatism. For many, acceptance of the doctrine was itself a climactic spiritual act resembling baptism into a new faith. For such persons the decision to identify themselves with the abolitionist cause came only after tortured self-examination. Those who successfully completed the ordeal felt themselves dedicated soul and body to a holy crusade. Their commitment then knew no limit.

A number of abolitionists who took part in the most tumultuous phase of the movement, the 1830s, reported the profound spiritual effect such participation had on them. They felt themselves altered; as a consequence their values changed. Abby Kelley, one of Garrison's Quaker converts and a strong exponent of women's rights, remarked in 1838 that abolitionists had "good cause to be grateful to the Slave for the benefit we have received to *ourselves,* in working for *him.* In striving to strike *his* chains off, we found most surely, that *we* were manacled ourselves."

For such persons participation in the antislavery movement seemed a duty quite apart from the objective benefits it might render the slave and society. The Garrisonian view of the imperious demands of individual conscience was perhaps more widely shared than has sometimes been supposed. Even James G. Birney, sometimes considered the epitome of the practical abolitionist on account of his commitment to antislavery politics, once remarked that "God has, at no time, told us . . . that we are responsible for the country; but he has told us . . . that we must *individually* give a good example. He has given us only our *own selves* to be responsible for."

There can be no doubt that many opponents of slavery underwent emotional upheaval in the early 1830s as they struggled to achieve total commitment to the abolitionist creed and then went on to attempt to win others to similar conviction. Their turmoil at such moments was thoroughly justified, for in accepting abolitionism they were setting out on the hazardous path of opposition to entrenched institutions and prevailing values. They proposed to defy the course of American development which seemed to be moving the nation toward ends that denied the ideals upon which it had been founded. In such a setting a man who joined the abolitionist crusade was likely to do so in a spirit of resignation, consciously facing the prospect of tragedy and sacrifice, but undertaking a holy obligation that could not be shirked. "I am the one," an abolitionist may be imagined as saying, "And there is no way not/ To be me[.]"

Despite their crusading efforts and considerable success in gaining converts, abolitionists failed to win the churches to their cause. In 1837, the Presbyterian General Assembly "excised" from the church its most thoroughly antislavery synods. No major denomination endorsed abolitionism. This reluctance on the part of clergymen and church bodies was to have profound consequences for the course of the antislavery movement. It helped push Garrison and others into taking militant anti-clerical stands, and it caused the movement in the later 1830s and 1840s to adopt increasingly secular policies.

While the abolitionists were attempting to secure converts, they also engaged in a war against certain of their rivals who had once been thought to form part of the antislavery alliance. Essential to their success, abolitionists believed, was the discrediting of the rival programs of gradual emancipation and colonization. The older notion that slavery could be ended in easy, gradual stages and that free Negroes must be transported out of the country still exercised a stubborn hold on many philanthropists. Until reformers were made to understand that such ideas were erroneous and harmful to the antislavery cause, the doctrine of immediatism would seem radical, dangerous, and wholly impracticable.

Thus one of Garrison's first undertakings after launching the *Liberator* in 1831 was a campaign to destroy support for the American Colonization Society. In doing this, he found himself in opposition to a highly respected project which enjoyed the support of powerful and prestigious men. It seems likely that this campaign, rather than the doctrine of immediatism itself, was the source of much of the hostility directed against him. Colonization had nearly achieved the status of being a national goal. The fact that free Blacks and abolitionists had long opposed it did little to lessen its esteem in the public mind. But Garrison was never deterred from his attacks merely by the respectability of his target.

Soon after the New England Anti-Slavery Society was founded in 1832, its agents began speaking against colonization to audiences in southern New England. Garrison delivered a series of anti-colonization addresses and in May 1832 published *Thoughts on Colonization,* a long and heavily documented work exposing the American Colonization Society as a pro-slavery, anti-Negro organization.

The American Colonization Society recognized Garrison and the new American Anti-Slavery Society as enemies. War between the two societies was soon underway. The most conspicuous and significant incident in the long battle occurred at Lane Seminary in Cincinnati in the spring of 1834.

The New York reformers had recently established Lane as a training school for evangelists. Its graduates were expected to convert the West, whose unchurched population, Easterners feared, risked falling into unbelief. It was a measure of the project's importance that Lyman Beecher, perhaps New England's most distinguished clergyman at that time, was willing to resign his pastorate in Boston to become president of the new Western institution.

The reformers expected much from Lane; they received more than they anticipated. Gathered at Lane from many parts of the country, including the South, was a student body composed of pious and highly competent young men who had committed themselves to something more than books and lectures. Their evangelical ideals did not allow them to retreat from secular concerns; rather, evangelicalism thrust them directly into the tumult of their time. The students took for granted their duty to participate actively in helping decide the great issues of the day. They would use their talents to shape the course of American development. Shortly, under the leadership of Theodore Weld, perhaps the most able member of the seminary, the students began a public discussion of immediate emancipation.

Having accepted immediatism with its implied requirement to abandon racial prejudice, the students began to work among the local black population. Shocked Cincinnatians soon saw that the students were advocates and practitioners of racial equality. They had begun associating with Negroes as partners, friends, and fellow workers. Two students, Augustus Wattles and Marius Robinson, dropped out of the seminary to spend all their time conducting a school for free Blacks. Others organized black churches and in various other ways tried to aid members of Cincinnati's black community. They established a lending library and conducted lyceums, an evening class in reading, Sunday schools, and Bible classes.

The Negroes of Cincinnati, many recently arrived from the slave states, were generally poor and oppressed and eager for all the help they could get. But however great the social needs may have been, the students' interracial activities could only arouse old antipathies in the city, where scarcely five years earlier white citizens had rioted against the black population, forcing many of them to flee to Canada.

Their goal, like Garrison's, was to win Americans—slaveholders and non-slaveholders, Southerners and Northerners—to the principle of immediate emancipation. As might have been anticipated, they made little headway in changing Southern views. It was no doubt naive for them to expect slaveholders to surrender some three billion dollars worth of property and the institution upon which their political and social power depended simply because abolitionists declared that slavery was rooted in sin; yet as evangelicals these men considered the power of the gospel irresistible, a universal solvent of earthly obstacles. Their expectation of mass Southern conversions, however unrealistic a later generation may consider it, was nonetheless consistent with evangelical faith. But of course they were disappointed. As early as 1835, James G. Birney, himself a native of the South, concluded that the South's conversion to immediatism was unlikely—"repentance is far off," he wrote, "if at all likely to be expected."

With a fair amount of success, slaveholders sealed off their section from exposure to antislavery argument. Southern legislatures made it illegal to circulate or possess antislavery publications. It became most hazardous for abolitionist agents to venture into the South, and almost none did. When Lundy passed through the Southern states in 1832 on his first trip to Texas, he thought it prudent to travel under an assumed name. Officials in Charleston warned Angelina Grimké not to visit her old home after she became identified with abolitionism, and she never tried to do so. Birney's father informed him that to return to Kentucky would cost him his life. William T. Allan, one of Weld's converts at Lane, was told that his former neighbor at Huntsville, Alabama, had threatened to cut his throat should he reappear there. During the summer of 1835 Amos Dresser, another of the Lane Rebels, journeyed into Tennessee to sell Bibles and probably also to do some private antislavery work. He was arrested by city authorities in Nashville, charged with being an antislavery agent, tried by a vigilance committee, publicly whipped, and ordered out of the city.

Such Southern reaction was predictable. After all, as Garrison observed, no oligarchy willingly gives up power or unprotestingly allows the subversion of its institutions. Less readily understandable was the fierce hostility that met abolitionist efforts nearly everywhere in the North. The anti-abolition mobs and the riots that occurred in the North with such frequency during the 1830s become comprehensible only if one remembers that while slavery was practiced only in the South, it nonetheless was sustained as a national institution. Abolitionists demanded the destruction of a system that had become interwoven with the very structure of American society.

The aspect of the abolitionists' program that particularly antagonized persons in the North, who otherwise quite readily conceded that slavery was evil and destructive, was the demand that the Blacks, when freed, remain in the United States, be elevated in status and condition, and be allowed to participate as equals in society.

It is true that many abolitionists, especially those in New York and the West, attempted to reassure the timid by explaining that they expected the Negro's freedom to be hedged with restrictive laws—that "immediate emancipation" did not really mean what it seemed to mean. But the explanations were never very persuasive, for it was obvious to anyone who thought seriously about the matter that even abolitionists who supplied such assurances (and these became less numerous as years passed) did not intend restrictions on the free Black to be more than a temporary expedient. Equality of status, abolitionists insisted, rightfully was his. He was to be prepared for it, and eventually it would be granted. Soon most abolitionists abandoned the effort to explain away the immediatist slogan.

Similarly disturbing to white Northerners was the abolitionists' inability to give satisfactory assurance that emancipation would not cause one of their strongest apprehensions to be realized—the emancipated slaves would be free to move into the North. There they would settle in vast numbers among the Whites, compete with them for jobs, and marry their daughters. For many Northerners a more frightful prospect could scarcely be imagined, and they recoiled at the thought of it. Economic fears and racial prejudice warred in Northern minds with religious and political principle. More often than not principle was the loser.

Abolitionists did not modify their program in order to accommodate the prevailing racial bias. Instead they confronted it squarely. The ending of prejudice, they insisted, was prerequisite to the abolition of slavery. As soon as the Negro is "felt to be in *fact* and in *right* our own countryman, the benevolence of the country will be emancipated from its bondage," predicted an early abolitionist. "It will flow out to meet the colored man . . . it will proclaim his rights—and the fetters of the slave will fall asunder."

Abolitionists in the 1830s became convinced that belief in the Negro's inferiority more than anything else caused Northerners who otherwise accepted the abolitionists' view of slavery to hesitate to endorse their program to end slavery. Prudence Crandall, whose integrated school for girls in Canterbury, Connecticut, was closed by public pressure in 1833, concluded that racial prejudice was "the strongest, if not the only chain that bound those heavy burdens on the wretched slaves." Birney agreed: "Whilst the poor black is treated so contemptuously in, what are called, the free states . . . it is not to be wondered that the cause of negro-emancipation moves so slowly." Unless racial prejudice could in some way be destroyed, the antislavery crusade was not likely to succeed, for adherence to the idea of the Negro's inferiority, abolitionists discovered, had the effect of producing not ardent crusaders but, as one of them said, half-hearted antislavery men "who would abolish slavery only in the abstract, and somewhere about the middle of the future."

In their effort to counteract such prejudice, abolitionists used varied appeals. Naturally, they cited Scripture to prove the brotherhood of all men. But they put forward other arguments as well. As early environmentalists, they pointed out that the blighting effects of slavery and prejudice explained the free Black's apparent shortcomings. They cited the numerous instances of accomplishment by Blacks to disprove allegations of their innate inferiority. They especially dwelt on the genius of Frederick Douglass, the outstanding fugitive-slave orator and editor, whose talents outshone those of many other Americans of his time, whatever their color. They continued the efforts begun by their predecessors to help free Blacks improve themselves. Any evidence of progress in this area, they believed, would help eliminate bias.

In its first years the American Anti-Slavery Society concentrated more on spreading information about slavery and on winning white converts than on work among black people. But in 1836, Weld proposed to the Society that it reconsider its priorities and "turn more of its attention to the education and elevation of the *free colored* population." Besides helping to relieve prejudice, such activity, he believed, also would have the important result of convincing Southerners, who delighted in accusing abolitionists of hypocrisy, that "*real* benevolence," and "not politics, sectional feeling, *party*ism," or any similar motive was at the bottom of the antislavery movement.

By 1837, the American Anti-Slavery Society had followed Weld's advice in part, if not in every detail. Yet its success in solving so vast a problem was slight. Individual abolitionists seem not to have given free Blacks much economic aid. Numerous instances can be found of antislavery farmers who furnished them jobs. Occasionally, as in the instance of Gerrit Smith, a wealthy and eccentric antislavery landowner in New York, such aid was given on an extensive scale, but in Northern cities less was accomplished. Business establishments run by abolitionists often employed no black workers, except perhaps in menial positions, a fact that came to be greatly resented by certain black spokesmen. Many leading abolitionists, however, were clergymen, writers, and professional reformers who commanded no labor force and thus had no jobs to give. Their efforts to help Blacks necessarily were confined to education and moral uplift.

As it turned out, abolitionists in the 1830s worked less intently than their predecessors had done in the 1820s to aid free Blacks and thus to demonstrate the truth of their assumptions of racial equality. They tirelessly proclaimed such equality, but for most of them projects directly aimed at improving black people became only a side issue, if they were interested in them at all. This relative neglect did not result from wavering determination or from abandonment of principle, but only from their conclusion that demonstration of Negro abilities no longer was either essential or effectual. Ample evidence already was at hand to prove the capacity of the Negro for achievement. Helping him to make still more progress would be a commendable act of benevolence, but it would not solve the problem of prejudice. What was needed was not further improvement of Blacks in the hope of thereby making them more acceptable to Whites. Instead, the requirement was to improve Whites so that they would renounce their racial prejudice and anti-Negro practices.

For that reason, abolitionists after 1830 more often worked with Whites than they did with Blacks. The key point in their program was their call for a change of heart—the shedding of racial pride—and this was an event more likely to come through faith than through reason. White Americans already had observed abundant demonstrations of the Negro's capacity, but more often than not they remained blind to their import. Abolitionists in the 1830s were content to rely on the evidence of things *not* seen. But this made their program in no way more acceptable to the white majority.

No doubt a significant number of white abolitionists possessed their share of the prejudice that afflicted most Americans of that day. Sarah Grimké in 1838 commented to the English abolitionist Elizabeth Pease on "the horrible prejudice which prevails against colored persons, and the equally awful prejudice against the poor." Probably even the most enlightened of the abolitionists occasionally behaved as paternalistically toward Blacks as they sometimes did toward white persons who were poorer and less culturally advantaged than themselves. Some of them were unable to surmount the limitations of the culture to which they belonged and within which they worked. It would be difficult, however, to demonstrate any conspicuous degree of either paternalism or prejudice in such leading abolitionists as Lundy, Garrison, or Weld. They succeeded, so far as we can tell, in shedding their sense of racial pride and their desire for racial exclusiveness. Even those who failed in these respects were far ahead of the rest of their society in insisting that these things ought to be done. There should be no surprise to discover examples of abolitionists who retained notions of white superiority and sometimes behaved condescendingly toward the objects of their philanthropy. But it should be noted that such lapses on the part of certain abolitionists did nothing at all to endear them to the defenders of slavery or to the opponents of equality for Blacks. Whatever their personal failings may have been, the aim of the abolitionists was freedom and equality for black people. Their enemies at that time never misunderstood their purpose and generally enlightened point of view, even though some of their later critics may have done so.

So far as we can now tell, however, abolitionists had little appreciation for what a later age would call "black culture." They did not find anything precious or vital or especially worth cherishing in the black man's peculiar way of life—if indeed they thought it at all peculiar. They took for granted that Blacks would share the common American culture. Their observation led them to believe that Blacks held similar expectations. They expected them to be sober and thrifty, to work hard, to be law-abiding, to educate their children, to attend church faithfully. The model they held up to Negroes was not fashioned for their exclusive use. They thought many poorer Whites as much in need of instructions in these respects as Blacks.

The great tragedy of the abolitionists was not that they themselves were blinded by prejudice but that however successfully they purged themselves of prejudice they could not overcome this flaw in the majority of their countrymen. Racial bias was not limited to poorer Whites, who understandably feared the eventual economic consequence to themselves of a rising black population. Persons of high standing in nearly every community likewise exhibited similar attitudes. Years of antislavery activity failed to do more than mitigate racial prejudice. Anti-Negro attitudes perhaps softened somewhat throughout the North as a consequence of the abolitionists' efforts, but those attitudes remained strong enough even during the Civil War to allow the Democratic party to capitalize on them in organizing opposition to Abraham Lincoln's war policies.

This does not mean that Northerners were generally intent on debasing free Blacks and treating them cruelly. The contrary is true. Many persons in the North aided Negroes in their efforts to obtain education and extended help to them in other important ways. Quakers especially were noted for this kind of benevolent activity. Yet, while increasing numbers of Northerners were willing to aid Negroes and to cease being flagrantly oppressive toward them, few welcomed them into society as equals or believed that they might achieve as much as other men. Most Northerners still preferred that Blacks remain in the South and not attempt to settle in Northern white communities. In 1845—after more than a decade of intense abolitionist agitation—an Illinois state legislative committee asserted that "by nature, education, and association, it is believed that the negro is inferior to the white man, physically, morally, and intellectually; whether this be true to the fullest extent, matters not, when we take into consideration the fact that such is the opinion of the vast majority of our citizens." Little evidence exists to prove that the Illinois committee was unjust in its charge.

Abolitionists of the 1830s thus discovered for themselves the same formidable obstacles that had stood in the way of all their predecessors' campaigns against slalvery. Racial prejudice remained the strongest of these obstacles, but to it were added in still greater force other sources of opposition that had more recently become apparent: Increased Southern influence in the North exercised through the national political parties; strengthened economic ties between Northern business interests and the plantation South; and growing fears that antislavery agitation imperiled the Union and drove the sections toward civil war.

Southerners had long considered the Constitution of 1787, and the Union it created, as guarantors for their peculiar institution. Not long after the Constitution went into effect, Thomas Coke, an English clergyman visiting in the South, reported finding that "defenders of slavery began to link that defense to loyalty to the new federal constitution which recognized slavery. . . . They now begin to take the position that attacks on slavery were attacks on the Constitution" and hence on the Union itself. The threat of Southern secession, explicit at least as early as the debates over the admission of Missouri, became commonplace as abolitionist agitation grew during the 1830s. By that time leading Southerners, who regarded slavery as essential, repeatedly threatened to take their states out of a Union in which their fundamental institution was menaced.

Patriots—a term that encompassed the great majority of nineteenth-century Americans—who viewed the nation with pride and optimism and believed it had a mission to perform, could only deplore an agitation, however well intentioned it might be, which imperiled the Union. If the Union were destroyed, all else, they believed, would be lost. There could be no denying that sectional discord grew after 1830 and that abolitionist agitation contributed heavily to it. Some opposition to the antislavery movement derived from that fact.

Abolitionists were resented too on account of the religious zeal so many of them manifested and because of the uncompromising rigor of their ethic. Many a person of only ordinary virtue must have felt uncomfortable when in the presence of such awsomely intense spirits as Theodore Weld and his evangelical associates. The anticlericalism that became common in the Jacksonian era militated against the success of religious abolitionism. The abolitionists' critique of slavery could not be separated from their religious intensity or from the ecclesiastical organizations most of them represented. Westerners in particular resented the reform efforts of Easterners, whom they were likely to regard at best as pious meddlers and at worst as religious fanatics. Their ultimate aim, some suspected, was to extend New England's cultural and political hegemony throughout the land. It was no doubt easy for contemporaries to view them as hostilely as Judge Luke E. Lawless of St. Louis did in 1836, when he commented that abolitionists labored "under a sort of religious hallucination. They seem to consider themselves as special agents . . . in fact, of Divine Providence. They seem to have their eyes fixed on some mystic vision—some Zion . . . within whose holy walls they would impound us all, or condemn us to perish on the outside."

For the many ordinary persons to whom such visions were not granted, who feared the impositions of organization, and who had no access to the evangelical spirit, abolitionists appeared to be mad. As purveyors of an impossibly austere ethic, they were sometimes thought objectionable on that account alone.

In view of all this, it was hardly surprising that opposition, frequently reaching to the pitch of mob violence, met the abolitionists' efforts to speak and to organize. When anti-abolitionist riots broke out in cities, they often shifted their focus from white abolitionists to the free black population, as in the New York City riots of July 1834, when a mob plundered Lewis Tappan's house and then moved on to destroy Negro churches, schools, businesses, and homes. A month after the outbreak in New York, mobs roamed the streets of Philadelphia destroying forty-five houses owned by Negroes.

The violent reaction to abolitionists, so frequently expressed throughout the North in the mid-1830s, demonstrated deep-seated popular hostility toward them and their goals, but however general the hostility in a community may have been, some impulse always was needed to trigger the opposition into action. The anti-abolitionist mobs were generally made up of Negro-hating persons of very low social standing and by certain others who wished to be identified with the status quo and to win the favor of powerful men. With but few exceptions, however, mobs were either led or encouraged by "gentlemen of property and standing," who let it be known that they would do nothing to protect the rights and the persons of abolitionists.

Abolitionists based their arguments on familiar religious teachings and on American principles as embodied in the Declaration of Independence; yet despite their association with those revered ideals, no special powers of discernment were needed to recognize them as disturbers of the existing order. They insisted on agitating issues that most persons preferred to ignore. In denouncing slavery as sin, they condemned a whole social system as illegitimate. In calling for the acceptance of Blacks as equals, they appeared to threaten the economic well-being of poorer Whites and to shake the foundations upon which the status and self-esteem of countless Americans were based. In working for abolition, they pledged themselves to the destruction of the plantation South and even of American society and government as it was then constituted. It would indeed have been strange had their activities not encountered violent resistance.

Slavery as an institution so patently contradicted the religious and political principles held by most Americans that it found few open defenders outside the South. Hence, part of the abolitionist argument gained general acceptance—slavery was wrong. Indeed, if everyone who agreed in theory with that statement had joined the organized antislavery movement, it could easily have overwhelmed the opposition. But it was one thing to condemn slavery as an evil; it was quite another to agree that slavery must be done away with at once. Such a policy, it was thought, would destroy the Union, lead to community discord, endanger property rights, and worst of all, require painful social adjustments. When abolitionists called for the acceptance of the Negro as an equal and for his elevation in America, great wrath fell upon them.

Abolitionists in the 1830s and afterward succeeded in persuading many Americans to agree with their assessment of the evils of slavery and of slaveholders, but they did not convince them that slavery should be ended immediately. Still less did they persuade them to discard their ingrained cultural notions of race.

The Well-Ordered Asylum

David J. Rothman

No reformers were more confident of the advantage and success of their program than the philanthropists who founded childsaving institutions. For proponents, the movement to incarcerate the orphan, the abandoned child, the youngster living in dire poverty, the juvenile vagrant, and the delinquent promised enormous benefits while entailing few risks. Like their colleagues sponsoring insane asylums and penitentiaries and almshouses, they shared an intense faith in the rehabilitative powers of a carefully designed environment and were certain that properly structured institutions would not only comfort the homeless but reform the delinquent.

Child-care institutions, new to Americans, fundamentally altered traditional practices. In the colonial period, overseers of the poor, in the absence of responsible relatives and friends, typically had apprenticed the orphan to a local householder. In unusual circumstances, when the child suffered from a major disability, they might have recourse in one of the larger towns to the almshouse. The orphan asylum was all but unknown in the eighteenth century. There was one notable exception. George Whitefield in 1740 almost single-handedly organized an orphan house in Savannah, Georgia. This was the work of an Englishman primarily concerned with bringing young souls to Christ; moreover, he established the house in a colony whose peculiar origin and mission had weakened the stable ties of community and strengthened experimental philanthropic impulses.

After the Revolution, local officials perpetuated colonial precedents. In some of the larger cities, overseers had to dispatch a number of children to new and growing almshouses; this step was, however, an ad hoc solution to an immediate problem and not considered of special benefit to the child or the community. So, too, the fifteen privately sponsored orphan asylums that opened between 1800 and 1830 were not part of a systematic program but the work

From David J. Rothman, *The Discovery of the Asylum: Social Order and Disorder in the New Republic.* Copyright © 1971 by David J. Rothman. Reprinted by permission of the publisher, Little, Brown and Company.

of dedicated yet idiosyncratic philanthropists, or of a religious minority, usually Catholic, eager to keep coreligionists within the faith and out of Protestant households. The dominant treatment of the orphan in the first years of the new republic remained noninstitutional.

In the 1830's a basic transformation occurred as child-care institutions spread rapidly through the country. In this decade alone, twenty-three private orphan asylums began operating in various towns and cities, and the movement continued to grow in the 1840's with the founding of thirty more of them. They opened not only in New York, Boston, and Philadelphia—as usual, among the leaders in building institutions—but also in Bangor, Maine; Richmond, Virginia; Mobile, Alabama; Avondale and Cincinnati, Ohio; and Chicago, Illinois. By 1850, New York State alone had twenty-seven public and private child-care institutions. Within two decades they had become common structures, widespread and popular, with their own unique and important attributes, not just a last resort when apprenticeship was impossible. Indeed, their promise seemed so great that trustees quickly spread their nets to catch a wide variety of dependent children. They admitted the abandoned as well as the orphaned child, and those whose widowed or deserted mothers, hard pressed to make ends meet, had little time for supervision. They accepted minors whose parents were quite alive but very poor, and those from families that seemed to them morally, if not financially, inadequate to their tasks. From an administrator's perspective, there was no reason to penalize the unfortunate child for the fact of his parents' survival.

During these decades another type of caretaker institution became popular—the reformatory for disobedient children, the house of refuge. It took in several types of minors—the juvenile offender, convicted by a court for a petty crime, the wandering street arab, picked up by a town constable, and the willfully disobedient child, turned over by distraught parents. The reformatory, like the orphan asylum, maintained a flexible admissions policy, prepared to accept the commitment decisions of a judicial body, the less formal recommendations of overseers of the poor, or the personal inclinations of the head of a household. Its administrators expressed no fears about a possible miscarriage of justice and were disinclined to bring the protections of due process to these minors. A good dose of institutionalization could only work to the child's benefit.

The founders of orphan asylums and houses of refuge shared fully with the proponents of other caretaker institutions a fear that anyone not carefully and diligently trained to cope with the open, free-wheeling, and disordered life of the community would fall victim to vice and crime. The orphan, robbed of his natural guardians, desperately needed protection against these dangers. Many children of the poor were in no better position, since their parents—at best too busy trying to eke out a living and at worst intemperate—provided no defense against corruption. The vagrant, by definition lacking in supervision, would certainly come under the sway of taverns, gambling halls, and theaters, the crowd of drunks, gamblers, thieves, and prostitutes. The nightmare come true, of course, was the juvenile delinquent, his behavior ample testimony to the speed and predictability of moral decline.

To counter these conditions, the asylum was shelter and sanctuary. Supporters pleaded vigorously and passionately for funds in order to snatch the child from the contagion of vice. The directors of the Orphan Society of Philadelphia asked patrons to endow a place where children of misfortune "are sheltered from the perils of want and the contamination of evil example." The Boston Children's Friend Society assumed the task of removing the sons and daughters of intemperate, depraved, and pauper parents as rapidly as possible "from those baleful influences which inevitably tend to make them pests to society, and ultimately the tenants of our prisons." A state reformatory in New Hampshire also defined its function in terms of "the separation of the young convict from society; his seclusion from vicious associates." And the managers of the Philadelphia House of Refuge, appealing for funds, boasted that visitors would find "the orphan, deserted or misguided child, shielded from the temptations of a sinful world."

But the asylum program had another, more important component—to train and rehabilitate its charges. It would not only shelter the orphan and delinquent, but discipline and reform them. Some philanthropic societies, it is true, limited their activities to rescuing the child from his poverty and giving him over to others, to a sea captain going on a lengthy whaling voyage, or to a country farmer needing another hand. For them, removal was a sufficient program. Many organizations, however, assumed a broader function, eager to carry out the tasks of childrearing. Starting afresh, they would organize a model routine, design and administer an upbringing that embodied the highest standards. In a manner clearly reminiscent of the mental hospital and the penitentiary, and to some degree of the almshouse as well, they expected to demonstrate the validity of general principles through the specific treatment of deviants and dependents. The experiment would rehabilitate the particular inmate and by exemplification spark the reform of the whole society.

This perspective dominated the asylum movement. Proponents insisted that the discipline at the Philadelphia House of Refuge would provide delinquents with "a healthy moral constitution, capable of resisting *the assaults of temptations,* and strong enough to keep the line of rectitude through *the stormy and disturbing influences by which we are continually assailed.*" This siege mentality united those attending the first national convention of house of refuge officials. They quickly formed a consensus around the sentiments expressed by Orlando Hastings, the delegate from the Rochester reformatory. Defining the fundamental purpose of the program, Hastings declared: "The object is not alone to make the boys behave well while in our charge; that is not difficult. . . . [But] any discipline . . . which does not enable the boy to *resist temptation* wherever and whenever he finds it, is ineffectual, and the whole object of houses of refuge is a failure." An even more elaborate rationale emerged in the reports of the Boston asylum. "There are," its managers explained, "two ways to aid in the redemption of society—one is to remove the sources of corruption, and the other is to remove the young from the temptations that exist." While some reformers chose to follow the first strategy, they were determined to adopt the second, "to enlighten their [inmates] minds, and aid them in forming virtuous habits, that they may finally go forth, *clothed as in invincible armour.*" Let others try to weaken the force of vice in the society. They would gird the young to withstand temptation.

Once again, the analysis which diagnosed an ostensibly desperate state of things also promised a sure remedy. Since the root of the problem lay in a faulty environment, the means for improvement were ready at hand, and asylum proponents were even more confident than their counterparts in other caretaker institutions of the prospects for success. Although all reformers assumed a plasticity of human nature that gave a logic to their efforts, asylum supporters felt themselves singularly fortunate: their clientele was young, especially impressionable, and not fixed in deviant or dependent behavior. "Youth," happily reported the governors of the Philadelphia House of Refuge, "is particularly susceptible of reform. . . . It has not yet felt the long continued pressure, which distorts its natural growth. . . . No habit can then be rooted so firmly as to refuse a cure." In the same spirit, the Boston Children's Friend Society looked forward to rehabilitating those "whose plastic natures may be molded into images of perfect beauty, or as perfect repulsiveness." And managers of the New York House of Refuge assumed that "the minds of children, naturally pliant, can, by early instruction, be formed and molded to our wishes." If the young were highly vulnerable to corruption, they were also eminently teachable.

Asylum proponents were not apprehensive about promoting the very vices they planned to eradicate. Overseers of the poor in this period anxiously wondered whether too comfortable an almshouse might inadvertently attract the lower classes, thereby promoting idleness; wardens also feared that a short sentence in a lax prison which coddled the criminal would increase recidivism. But child-care institutions were free of these concerns. Managers were confident that incarceration would not rob orphans of initiative—they were simply too young for that—or encourage their parents to avoid responsibility through commitment. And an indeterminate sentence to a house of refuge, for a term as long as the young offender's minority, could hardly be considered too lenient. Thus, without hesitation or qualification, they urged the new program.

At the core of the child-reformers' optimism was a faith completely shared by colleagues promoting other caretaker institutions: that a daily routine of strict and steady discipline would transform inmates' character. The asylum's primary task was to teach an absolute respect for authority through the establishment and enforcement of a rigorous and orderly routine. Obedience would bring reform. The function of the orphan asylum, according to Charleston, South Carolina, officials, was to train boys to a proper place in a community where "*systematic labor* of *order* and *regularity* established, and *discipline* enforced, are the social obligations." A strict training in accord with these virtues "disciplines them for . . . various walks of life," enabling them to become "practical men of business and good citizens, in the middle classes of society." The Boston Asylum and Farm School for destitute and vagrant children was dedicated to the same means and ends. These classes, managers told would-be donors, "have been received within the walls of a Christian asylum, where they have listened to good counsel, and acquired habits of *order, industry* and *usefulness*. . . . We know not how anyone interested in the preservation of order or stability of government . . . can withhold his sympathy." Its annual reports regularly replayed this theme, noting that "it is almost astonishing how readily boys, hitherto accustomed to have their own way, and to dispute supremacy with inefficient or indulgent parents, are brought into habits of respect and order by a system of *uniformly firm discipline*." The Boston asylum directors recognized fully the affinity between their program and that of other contemporary caretaker institutions. "A hospital for the insane," they announced, "has hardly greater superiority over the private family in regulating its inmates, in this respect, than the Farm School over the misgovernment or no-government of the weak and careless parent."

The primacy of obedience and respect for authority in the process of rehabilitation was even more apparent in the institutions treating delinquents and vagrants. The New York Juvenile Asylum, serving these groups, put the matter aggressively. "We do not believe," announced its superintendent, "in the mawkish, sentimental and infidel philosophy of modern days, which discards the Bible method of disciplining the child into obedience. . . . It is manifest that but little good can be effected with all our appliances, unless order and obedience to established rules are vigilantly maintained. . . . What is needed for the children whom the law entrusts to us is the government of a well-ordered Christian household." Their neighbors at the New York House of Refuge agreed. Let inmates, officials declared, "be made tractable and obedient . . . [through] a vigorous course of moral and corporal discipline." With fidelity to this principle, the refuge superintendent argued that "the most benevolent and humane method for the management of children, is, to require prompt and implicit obedience." And to support his point he presented some sample cases. For one typical delinquent, the "discipline of the House was all that was requisite to make him obedient." For another, an especially refractory youngster bent on escaping, "it was found necessary to apply severe and continued punishments, in order to break the obstinacy of his spirit." Ultimately success came: "The discipline enforced had a most happy effect. He became submissive and obedient."

The prescriptions for the well-ordered asylum embodied and reflected contemporary opinion on proper child-rearing techniques. The guidelines that superintendents established for institutional procedures fit closely with the advice that appeared in the new spate of child-guidance books. Indeed, the popularity of the asylum coincided with the proliferation of domestic tracts. The volumes first appeared in significant numbers in the United States in the 1830's, growing increasingly popular in the 1840's and 1850's. The best sellers, such as Lydia Child's *The Mother's Book,* Mrs. Sigourney's *Letters to Mothers,* Jacob Abbott's *The Rollo Code of Morals,* and Catherine Beecher's *A Treatise on Domestic Economy for the Young Ladies at Home,* went through many editions, becoming fixtures in American homes. To be sure, there had always been some kind of literature giving advice to parents. In the colonial period, ministers' pamphlets had served the task—Benjamin Wadsworth's *A Well-Ordered Family* was an outstanding one—and there were reprints of English classics. In the pre-Civil War era, however, the tracts not only greatly increased in number, but were now almost all American in origin and were the work of laymen. Their style was a relaxed and homey one, and cautionary tales replaced biblical references. A new genre had appeared.

The guidebooks conveyed a clear sense of crisis, an image of the American community, and especially the family, confronting unprecedented challenges. The authors were a nervous group, one after another lamenting the "unhappy tendency of our age and country," the "alarming feature of this age," the need to ward off "the fearful crisis," to combat the "many influences which are in vigorous operation to corrupt the family." Their analysis of the causes of the dangers was highly general, without delineation, and not as intricate as the critique of asylum reformers. But it repeated, albeit in briefer and somewhat more clichéd form, the same points. Some writers complained about the whirl of commercial activity and the concomitant lack of fixed social positions: others worried that political democracy bred a social libertarianism which often degenerated into license. Still others took alarm at the complex and artificial character of civilization. All of them agreed that antebellum America acutely suffered from a lack of order and stability. All feared for the cohesion of the community, finding in the swelling number of deviants and dependents dreadful confirmation of the dimensions of the crisis. Here was dramatic evidence that the very foundations of the republic were in imminent danger of collapse.

Nevertheless, these authors were confident that the public crisis had a private remedy. Together with medical superintendents, penologists, and proponents of child-care institutions, they hoped to secure social stability through individual rehabilitation. They traced the origins of the problem to the decline of the community life and the weakness of family government, and found in their diagnosis a solution. If they could teach parents their correct role and encourage them to follow it, if they could define the components of proper family government and persuade readers to adopt them, then they would insure the nation's stability. In this sense, the child-rearing tracts were ventures in reform. Institutions treated those already in trouble; these authors would move back one step and try to eliminate the first cause of the problem. They wished to bring the rules of the asylum into the home, confident that as soon as parents became surrogate superintendents, the refuge, the penitentiary, and the rest could be eliminated. The well-ordered family would replace the well-ordered asylum.

The ideal mother in child-rearing literature was strict but loving, ever affectionate with her blood, but always successful in commanding their absolute obedience. The prototype runs through the pages of Lydia Child's *The Mother's Book:* the woman who combined firmness with gentleness, whose children cheerfully acted from the conviction that she knew best. John Abbott's *The Mother at Home* cautioned her not to depend exclusively upon the father to enforce discipline. It was "the efficient government of a judicious mother," that kept children from deception and disobedience. "The *mother* of Washington," he contended, "is entitled to a nation's gratitude. *She* taught her boy the principles of obedience, and moral courage, and virtue. She, in a great measure, formed the character of the hero, and the statesman." The ideal father in this scheme reinforced maternal authority, intervening whenever a stronger or more consistent discipline was necessary. As one author explained, young boys often grew restive under a mother's rule; at such times, "a father's counsels, wisdom and firmness, and a father's authority, are demanded." Much of the child-rearing literature instructed fathers to keep somewhat aloof from their children, lest they compromise their ultimate authority.

The guidebooks, to be sure, did maintain that the best way to achieve obedience was through the child's affections. In a model family the youngsters offered "cheerful submission," obeying their parents out of love. But again, there was no confusing priorities. For all the discussion, affection was never more than a means to a higher end—obedience—and by no stretch of the imagination, the goal itself. Without the slightest misgivings, therefore, every author urged parents to use the rod when all else failed: far better to punish the child than allow him to grow up disobedient. "Secure this great end," declared one of Miss Porter's open letters, "by love and gentle means if you can—try it long and patiently—but if that fail, do not hesitate to use the rod." In a later period, in the beginning of the twentieth century, love and affection would move to the center of the childrearing literature, to become important virtues in themselves and not just useful means for accomplishing other, more important ends. At that time, the cautionary tales would reveal a new twist; rather than kill off the child for disobedience, the mother would die for her sin, for not having recognized and returned the full love of the child. But in the Jacksonian period, the moral was very different. Counselors worried that too much affection would breed disobedience, not that the child might suffer from an excess of discipline.

At the root of this popular insistence on the primacy of obedience was a conception of individual respect for authority as the cornerstone of an orderly society. Like almost all others in this period who thought about deviancy and dependency, the authors of these tracts remained convinced that only a rigorous training in obedience could stabilize individual behavior and the social order. In their view, the community seemed to be in such a state of crisis that this message took on unprecedented significance. They saw change as declension, believing that the insularity of the community was now broken, its integrative functions having all but disappeared. Under these circumstances the family became the chief—really the last—barrier between the citizen and a life of vice and crime, between the nation and rampant disorder. The good order of the family had to promote the good order of the society. Hence this formula, basic to every eighteenth-century sermon on the family, appeared with special intensity in the nineteenth-century child-rearing volumes. The youngster had to learn obedience within the family or would all too predictably move from the candy store to the tavern and brothel, and then to a prison cell. The message of the tracts was clear, unqualified, and in accord with the dictums of asylum proponents. The well-ordered family, like the well-ordered institution, could not be too absolute in its discipline.

If fidelity to a doctrine could have guaranteed success, the antebellum orphan asylums and houses of refuge would have enjoyed remarkable achievements. Like the other caretaker institutions of the era, they too made isolation and order central to the design. Trustees and managers systematically attempted to remove and protect inmates from the corrupting influences of the community, to impose an exact and demanding schedule, and to enforce rules and regulations with strict and certain discipline. To these ends, they arranged admission policies and visiting rights, established daily activities, and meted out punishments. They translated a good part of prevailing theory into institutional reality.

The first element in the asylum superintendents' program was to abrogate parental authority and substitute their own. To bring the inmate under as absolute a control as possible, trustees characteristically insisted that the parent transfer to them all legal rights upon the child's admission. The requirement was a new one; the occasional colonial benevolent society that had housed dependent children did not attempt to erect legal barriers against parental intervention. Should a family's fortune improve, eighteenth-century officials willingly returned the youngster, at most asking for repayment for past expenses. But nineteenth-century institutions typically would brook no actual or potential interference.

Reversing the natural order of things, they established regulations whereby the closer a person was to an inmate, the less he was permitted to come. Foreign tourists had no trouble gaining admission; they could inspect the premises anytime with a ticket from the managers, the mayor, the ladies' committee, or a local judge. Interested citizens were slightly more restricted, entitled to admission on the first and third Wednesday of the month. But parents, guardians, and friends of the inmates, could visit only once in every three months. As a further safeguard, no one was permitted to converse with the children without special permission. Having rescued their charges from a foul environment, officials had no intention of bringing corruption to them.

At least not until the institution had the opportunity to do its work. Asylum and refuge managers did not envision long periods of incarceration for inmates, and had no desire to isolate dependent or delinquent children from the community for the length of their minority. For one thing, they lacked the facilities; if the original group admitted stayed on till age twenty-one, the buildings would be too crowded to admit anyone else. For another, proponents expected asylum discipline to take effect relatively quickly. House of refuge trustees believed that confinement for one to two years would usually be sufficient for rehabilitation. "The inhabitants," declared the organizers of the Philadelphia refuge, "instead of being outcasts from society, with scarcely a possibility of return, will be withdrawn only for a season"; after proper training they could reenter the community and even "hope for its rewards." Others treating less depraved children were still more optimistic. "A month's stay in company with boys accustomed to systematic discipline and obedience," estimated officials of the Boston Asylum and Farm School, "with a sense that there is no escape from order and regularity, generally converts the most wayward into good pupils." The institution would sow the seeds, declared the New York Juvenile Asylum, and leave their cultivation to others.

After short periods of incarceration, asylums dispatched inmates to an apprenticeship with respectable families in the country, where ostensibly vice was less prevalent than in the cities, or returned them to relatives or friends who, in the managers' opinion, were not totally depraved. Delinquents demonstrating no improvement were sent on a whaling voyage that at least would keep them out of the community if not out of trouble. But for all this, officials devoted a minimum of attention and energy to the problems of release. They did not diligently investigate the households to which they apprenticed inmates, or make a sustained effort to facilitate adjustment back into the society. They, like their contemporaries, focused almost exclusively on the organization of the institution, locating within it the hope for correction and reform. Asylum care, and not aftercare, monopolized their interest.

The daily routine at the New York House of Refuge represented in slightly exaggerated form the kind of discipline and control that managers everywhere wished to exercise. Officials carefully organized a schedule for the 160 inmates, divided segments of time precisely, and used the house bells to announce each period. The first bells rang at sunrise to wake the youngsters, the second came fifteen minutes later to signal the guards to unlock the individual cells. The inmates stepped into the hallways and then, according to the managers' description, "marched in order to the washroom. . . . From the washroom they are called to parade in the open air (the weather permitting), where they are arranged in ranks, and undergo a close and critical inspection as to cleanliness and dress." Inmates next went in formation to chapel for prayer (it was the Sunday variant on this that so impressed the visitors from the Philadelphia refuge), and afterwards spent one hour in school. At seven o'clock the bells announced breakfast and then, a half hour later, the time to begin work. The boys spent till noon in the shops, usually making brass nails or cane seats, while the girls washed, cooked, made and mended the clothes. "At twelve o'clock," officials reported, "a bell rings to call all from work, and one hour is allowed for washing . . . and dinner. . . . At one o'clock, a signal is given for recommencing work, which continues till five in the afternoon, when the bell rings for the termination of the labor of the day." There followed thirty minutes to wash and to eat, two and one half hours of evening classes and, finally, to end the day, evening prayers. "The children," concluded the refuge account, "ranged in order, are then marched to the Sleeping Halls, where each takes possession of his separate apartment, and the cells are locked, and silence is enforced for the night."

The institution's architecture was as monotonous as its time-table. Boys and girls occupied separate buildings, each structure of bare brick and unvarying design; as the refuge expanded, adding more wings, the repetition and uniformity increased. The buildings were usually four stories high, with two long hallways running along either side of a row of cells. The rooms, following one after another, were all five by eight feet wide, seven feet high, windowless, with an iron-lattice slab for a door and flues for ventilation near the ceiling. Each group of eleven cells could be locked or unlocked simultaneously with one master key; every aperture within an inmate's reach was guarded by iron sashes, every exit door from the asylum was made of iron. On the first floor of each wing was a huge tub for bathing, sizable enough to hold fifteen to twenty boys; on the fourth floor were ten special punishment cells. In keeping with the external design, all inmates wore uniforms of coarse and solid-colored material. No sooner did they enter the institution than they were stripped, washed, their hair cut to a standard length, and put into common dress. Managers appropriately claimed that the refuge's "main object, that of reformation, is never lost sight of, in any of its regulations, in all its discipline. From the entrance of the child, he becomes subject to a routine of duties. . . . *Order* and *method* it is the effect of this system practically to enforce."

Precision and regularity dominated other aspects of asylum life. Many institutions habitually drilled their inmates, organizing them in parade ranks and marching them up and down the field. "In one place," noted Lydia Child after a visit to the Long Island asylum, "I saw a stack of small wooden guns, and was informed that the boys were daily drilled to military exercises, as a useful means of forming habits of order." She discovered that this drill-like quality had infected other parts of the institution, the infant school, and even the chapel. "I was informed," wrote Child, "that it was 'beautiful to see them pray; for at the first tip of the whistle, they all dropped on their knees.' " Her verdict on this asylum may well stand for the others: "Everything moves by machinery, as it always must with masses of children never subdivided into families."

The extraordinary emphasis of child-care institutions on obedience and authority was most apparent in their systems of classification and punishment. Houses of refuge in particular went to great lengths to enforce discipline, conceiving and administering elaborate programs. They depended first upon a highly intricate pattern of grading. Some institutions established four classes, others used seven—but the principle was constant. Superintendents assigned a new inmate to the bottom category and then, depending upon his subsequent behavior, promoted him. Every teacher, dormitory guard, and work supervisor had to file reports on each child's performance as a basis for rank, and the inmate wore a numbered badge on his arm to signify his standing. An obedient child at the Philadelphia refuge could move from class four to class one in seven months and win his tricolor badge. At Pittsburgh those who were well-behaved advanced one grade a month, and after spending three months in Class I were promoted to the Class of Honor. The Chicago Reform School put degrees within each of the four ranks, five levels for class IV, four for class III, seven for Class I; the perfect candidate would take fifteen weeks to pass each class and take his place in the Red Book of Honor. The higher grades carried their own privileges, the lower ones, their penalties. At the Providence refuge, those in the bottom category were, by the rules, "excluded almost entirely from the others [in the house]; not being permitted to join them in sports, or hold any conversation with them."

Fundamental to the institutions' discipline was habitual and prompt punishment, so that inmates' infractions not only brought a mark in the grading system, but an immediate penalty as well. Corrections ranged from a deprivation of a usual privilege to corporal punishment, with various alternatives along the way. There was the loss of a play period, increased work load, a diet of bread and water, Coventry—with no one permitted to talk with the offender—solitary confinement in a special prison cell, wearing a ball and chain, the whip—and any one or two of these penalties could be combined with yet another and inflicted for varying lengths of time.

Given their perspective on discipline and order, managers openly admitted and vigorously defended strict punitive tactics. They quoted with predictable regularity Solomon's warnings on spoiling the child, insisting that although the rod should be saved for a last resort, it still had to be used. A resolution of the convention of refuge superintendents set out the creed most succinctly: "The first requisite from all inmates should be a strict obedience to the rules of the institution; and where moral suasion fails to produce the desired result, the more severe punishments of deprivation of meals, in part, and of recreation, and the infliction of corporal punishment should be resorted to: the latter only, however, in extreme cases." The superintendent of the Western House of Refuge at Pittsburgh made the matter a precondition for remaining in his post. "I advocate the judicious use of the rod," he announced. "So well am I convinced of its efficacy . . . that I could not think of retaining my connection with such institutions, were the power of using it denied to me. . . . I never yet have seen the time when I thought the rod could be dispensed with."

Refuge records do not often reveal precisely how superintendents exercised their authority, although there is little reason to expect that public statements were harsher than institutional practice. An occasional well-kept journal of daily decisions, however, does indicate the close correspondence between ideas and action. The first manager of the New York House of Refuge, Joseph Curtis, at a time when the institution was new, experimental, and a frequent stopping place for tourists and philanthropists, diligently recorded his decisions—and the result testifies to the frequency and severity of punishment. Few inmates in the course of their incarceration escaped the whip, the ball and chain, or solitary confinement. Some typical incidents from 1825 and 1826 case histories convey the tone and quality of the discipline:

> Ann M.: Refractory, does not bend to punishment, put in solitary.
> William C.: Questioned guard's authority, whipped.
> John B.: A few strokes of the cat to help him remember that he must not speak when confined to a prison cell.
> Joseph R.: Disregarded order to stop speaking, given a bit of the cat.
> William O.: Escaped. Returned, put in prison with irons.
> Simon B.: Escaped. Returned, in handcuffs for 66 days.
> John M.: No respect for rules of the Refuge; ball and chain for fifty-two days.
> Edmund E.: Quarrelsome, in leg irons.
> Samuel S.: Denied talking, given a little of the cat to assist his memory.

Curtis's daily journal also pointed to the regularity of punishments. The notes for the month of March, 1825, for example, read:

March 1: Whipped J. T. for bed wetting.

March 3: J. P. whipped for talking last night; E. D. paddled, with his feet tied to one side of a barrel, his hands to the other.

March 6: M. Y. whipped for continuous disobedience.

March 8: D. S. never practiced obedience, boxed his ears; W. C. shamefully disobedient, put in the prison cell.

March 13: J. M. does not obey the orders for coming when called and neglects her work for play in the yard, leg iron and confined to House.

March 15: M. S. artfully sly, ball and chain and confined to House.

March 17: E. E. continually disobedient, locked in prison 1 day.

March 18: J. T. again wet his bed; certain he does it when awake, whipped.

March 19: J. P. released from prison, but keeps on ball and chain until he learns to be obedient.

March 20: M. S. still not obedient, despite ball and chain, so put in prison.

Superintendents of orphan asylums undoubtedly exercised a more restrained authority than their colleagues in houses of refuge, dispensing fewer and less severe punishments. Their charges were younger and without records of delinquency, and therefore more easily prevented from breaking the rules, and the asylum placed lighter demands on inmates, reducing the need to coerce behavior and prevent escapes. The orphan did not have to suffer an eight-hour workday, and even the strictest classroom routine was considerably less onerous than that of the shop. Yet, here too one probably found little tolerance for disobedience and a predisposition to keep a steady and heavy hand over the inmates. The surviving records are too sparse to allow any firm conclusions, but managers' outlook and rhetoric not only sanctioned punishments but required them. Since every infraction, important as well as trivial, was a portent of a future crisis, since violating a rule of the institution was tantamount to breaking the most basic codes of society, superintendents had to respond quickly and punitively. There was simply too much at stake to do otherwise. Strokes of the whip or days of solitary confinement, no matter how painful to administer, were preferable to allowing the child to grow up in license. The asylum could not risk being a permissive place.

To follow the metaphors of superintendents of asylums and refuges, the family was the model for institutional organization. Whether serving the poor or the orphan or the delinquent, they repeatedly described their operations in household terms. The Baltimore Home of the Friendless, for example, announced a determination to "see that the order and decorum of a well regulated Christian family be strictly observed." The tougher the clientele, the more elaborate the family metaphor. The New York Juvenile Asylum insisted that "the government of the Institution has been strictly parental. The prominent object has been to give a home feeling and home interest to the children—to create and cultivate a family feeling . . . to clothe the Institution as far as possible with those hallowed associations which usually cluster about home." The manager of the St. Louis Reform School was just as committed to this language. The refuge, he insisted, would succeed "by assimilating the government in Reformatories, as nearly as possible, to that of the *time-honored* institution which guided the infancy of nearly all the truly great and good men and women—that model, and often humble institution—the *family* . . . 'God's University' . . . the well-ordered Christian family."

But as is readily apparent, rhetoric and reality had little correspondence. Except for these public declarations, one would not have considered the family to be the model for the asylum. Rather, from all appearances, a military tone seems to have pervaded these institutions. Managers imposed on their charges a routine that was to resemble an army camp. They grouped inmates into large companies under a central administration, rather than establishing small familylike units under the individual care of surrogate parents. Inmates slept in separate cells or in cots in large dormitories, all neatly spaced and arranged in ways more reminiscent of orderly military barracks than of households. They ate silently in large refectories, using hand signals to communicate their needs, in a style that was much closer to an army mess than a family meal. They marched about the institution, stood in formation for head counts and public quizzes, and carried wooden guns in parades for recreation. They followed an exact schedule, responding to bells like recruits to a bugler's call. They wore uniforms with badges for insignias and grades for ranks. They learned to drop to one knee at the sound of a whistle, even making prayer into a military exercise. They obeyed rules of silence or suffered punishment. They took the whip like disobedient soldiers being flogged. If anyone escaped, or went AWOL, the ball and chain awaited him upon his return.

As surprising as it may seem, the superintendents saw no contradiction between their language and actions, no opposition between parading children in ranks while paying homage to the family. For they believed that they were offering a critique of the conduct of the antebellum family, and an alternative to it. In their view the family had to emulate the asylum as constituted—that is, put a greater premium on order, discipline, and obedience, not on domestic affections, pampering the child, or indulging his every whim. The family did not need to march its members from bedroom to kitchen or keep children silent throughout a meal (although the adage did call for children to be seen and not heard), but parents were to exercise a firm and consistent authority and brook no willfulness. Thus, managers found no real divergence between the well-ordered asylum and the well-ordered family. The quasi-military quality of the institution was a rebuke and an example to the lax family. The problem was that parents were too lenient, not that the refuge or asylum were too strict.

As long as the desideratum was order and discipline, as long as the virtues most in demand in child rearing were regularity and respect for authority, then the asylum was at least as effective a training center as the home. To the extent that the family neglected or overindulged or corrupted its members, the institution was a distinctly preferable setting.

The Grimké Sisters
from South Carolina

Gerda Lerner

We Abolition Women are turning the world upside down.
Angelina E. Grimké,
February 25, 1838

On Wednesday, February 21, 1838, starting about noon, people from all over Boston began arriving at the State House in carriages, by horseback and on foot. By one o'clock the crowd was so great that guards were posted inside the Hall of Representatives to reserve seats for the members of the Legislative Committee scheduled to meet at two. It was what the newspapers then called a "mixed" audience, which meant mostly men with a sprinkling of ladies who in their ruffled skirts, their frothy bonnets and gaily colored shawls brightened the galleries. One could recognize many of the more prominent citizens in the hall, while the inevitable ruffian element clustered around the entrance, undecided whether the coming spectacle merited giving up a few hours in the tavern. Here and there, a few respectable colored people could be seen in the crowd. The attendance of so many people at a legislative hearing was quite out of the ordinary, especially since no advance public notice had been given, but news of this kind could be trusted to travel speedily by word of mouth. Today, a *woman* would address a Committee of the Legislature of the State of Massachusetts.

Groups of abolitionists had come early from Lynn, Lowell, Worcester, Shrewsbury and several other of the surrounding townships. A good many of them had previously heard the speaker on her recent tour through New England. They could testify to the scoffers and doubters that she was perfectly capable of sustaining oratory and refuting objections by logical argument. However, they had to admit that for a woman to speak before a friendly small-town crowd was quite a different matter from speaking before a legislative body. Questions from the legislators in the presence of such a large crowd might well overawe the young woman, despite her customary eloquence.

By two o'clock the members of the legislature had to fight their way to the seats reserved for them. The gallery, the staircase, even the platform, were crowded. Every seat was taken; the aisles and lobby were filled with standees. Men clustered around the windows and doors and many, after waiting patiently for an hour to be admitted, had to leave disappointed. No one, apparently, wanted to miss this unprecedented event. Until this day, no American woman had ever spoken to a legislative body. Women did not vote nor stand for office and had no influence in political affairs. They received inferior elementary schooling and were, with the exception of recently opened Oberlin College, excluded from all institutions of higher learning. No church, except the Quakers, permitted women any voice in church affairs or in the ministry. The belief that a woman's name should properly appear in print only twice in her life, on her wedding day and in her obituary, described accurately the popular dread of female "notoriety." Woman's sphere was the home. There, she was the "grace, the ornament, the bliss of life." With an education which provided her with just enough "skill in household matters and a certain degree of cunning in culinary disposition" she might rule supreme over children and servants and expend what energies she had left after the care of her large family on the care of the community's indigent and poor. This gospel of woman's "proper role" was preached from pulpit and press and enshrined in the law, which classified women with slaves and imbeciles regarding property and voting rights. Married women had no legal rights over their inherited property or their earnings, could not make contracts, could not sue or be sued. While American practice, especially that of premarital contracts, tended to mitigate the generality and severity of these restrictions, the concept of woman's inferior position remained firmly entrenched in the law and in the popular mind. Children were under the sole guardianship of the father; mothers had no rights over them even in cases of legal separation. Few occupations were open to women and in those her wages were often less than half of those of men. As a result unmarried and widowed women were dependent on their nearest male relatives, and spinsterhood was considered a tragic fate. Prescribed in scriptures and fixed by tradition, woman's secondary role in society was taken for granted by most men and women. "A woman is a nobody," declared *The Public Ledger* of Philadelphia as late as 1850 in an article ridiculing the advocates of equal rights for women: "A wife is everything. A pretty girl is equal to 10,000 men and a mother is, next to God, all powerful. The ladies of Philadelphia therefore . . . are resolved to maintain their rights as wives, belles, virgins and mothers and not as women."

One daring woman had attempted to break through this web of restrictions, but she had been a foreigner, a radical and an infidel. In 1828 Frances Wright had lectured to large audiences in several American cities, but had been hooted and jeered as a freak. Her name had become an epithet across the land. It was considered unthinkable that any American woman would follow the example of this "female monster."

Several years later a Negro woman, Mrs. Maria W. Stewart, gave four lectures in Boston, speaking to her own people in favor of abolition and education for girls. But she soon gave up and admitted failure. "I find it is no use for me, as an individual, to try to make myself useful among my color in this city. . . . I have made myself contemptible in the eyes of many."

But the woman who would address the legislators today was not only American-born, white and Southern, but the offspring of wealth, refinement and the highest social standing. Angelina Grimké and her sister, notorious as the first female antislavery agents, were ladies whose piety and respectability had been their shield against all attacks during their recent precedent-shattering nine months' speaking tour.

Angelina Grimké was well aware that people regarded her as a curiosity and came not so much to listen to her as to stare and scoff. Now, as she approached the hall and noticed the large number of people who could not find room inside, she felt her courage waning.

> I never was so near fainting under the tremendous pressure of feeling. My heart almost died within me. The novelty of the scene, the weight of responsibility, the ceaseless exercise of mind thro' which I had passed for more than a week—all together sunk me to the earth. I well nigh despaired.

She knew that a great many in this crowd were at best unsympathetic, at worst openly hostile. They had read derogatory accounts of the Grimké sisters' brazen defiance of public opinion, of their unwomanliness in appearing on public platforms, of their radical and inflammatory speeches against slavery. A Pastoral Letter of the Council of Congregationalist Ministers had warned all the churches of Massachusetts against these dangerous females. Outrageous caricatures of Angelina Grimké and William Lloyd Garrison had daily been hawked in the streets. She was experienced enough in judging audiences to know that a crowd such as this might easily become a mob. Somewhat anxiously, she turned toward the woman walking with her, a beautiful Bostonian of unequalled poise. Maria Weston Chapman was a veteran of the antislavery movement and had an unusually thorough acquaintance with mobs. The intrepid courage of the Boston antislavery women, who had walked through the mob attacking their meeting, their hands folded in white cotton gloves, their eyes fixed sternly on each threatening face had become almost a legend. Now, Mrs. Chapman cast an experienced eye over the waiting crowd and for an instant placed her hand on Angelina Grimké's shoulder. "God strengthen you, my sister," she said quietly and smiled her radiant smile. Angelina relaxed; the faintness left her. She was surrounded by friends, by women who had felt the shame of slavery deep in their hearts as she had. Twenty thousand of them had signed the antislavery petitions she was about to present to the legislators. It was for them she was speaking, for them she must do what no American woman had done before her. If only her sister Sarah could have been beside her to support and sustain her as she had all during their speaking tour. But

Sarah, who had been the scheduled speaker today, was suffering from a violent cold and could not leave her room. In a last-minute change of plans, Angelina, who had originally intended speaking at the next session, had to substitute for her.

Once inside the hall, Angelina recognized many familiar faces: Reverend Samuel May with his kindly smile, the Samuel Philbricks, whose houseguests she and Sarah had recently been, Brother Allen from Shrewsbury, nodding encouragement. The delicate features of Lydia Maria Child expressed her affection and sympathy. The presence of these friends gave Angelina courage. And, as always, in moments of tension, her religious faith sustained her. ". . . our Lord and Master gave me his arm to lean upon and in great weakness, my limbs trembling under me, I stood up and spoke. . . ."

In this first moment of hushed attention Angelina Grimké impressed her audience most of all by her dignity. Slight of build, often described as frail, she stood before them in her simply gray Quaker dress, her delicate features framed by a white neckerchief. Beneath her dark curls deep blue eyes dominated a thoughtful, serious face. Her earnestness and concentration transmitted itself to the crowd even before she began to speak. "For a moment a sense of the immense responsibility resting on her seemed almost to overwhelm her," Lydia Maria Child later wrote to a friend. "She trembled and grew pale. But this passed quickly, and she went on to speak gloriously, strong in utter forgetfulness of herself." Angelina was not beautiful in the conventional sense, but when she spoke in her clear, well-modulated voice her personality and deep convictions captivated her audiences and transformed her in their eyes. She was often described as beautiful, powerful, a magnetic, gifted speaker.

Now she reached far back in time for a precedent to her appearance before the legislature. Like her, Queen Esther of Persia had pleaded before the King for the life of her people.

> Mr. Chairman, it is my privilege to stand before you on a similar mission of life and love. . . . I stand before you as a citizen, on behalf of the 20,000 women of Massachusetts whose names are enrolled on petitions which have been submitted to the Legislature. . . . These petitions relate to the great and solemn subject of slavery. . . . And because it is a political subject, it has often tauntingly been said, that women had nothing to do with it. Are we aliens, because we are women? Are we bereft of citizenship because we are mothers, wives and daughters of a mighty people? Have women *no* country— *no* interests staked in public weal—no liabilities in common peril—no partnership in a nation's guilt and shame?

The bold words rang out in the hall. Woman's influence on the nations, the speaker asserted, had been largely as courtesans and mistresses through their influence over men.

If so, then may we well hide our faces in the dust, and cover ourselves with sackcloth and ashes. This dominion of woman must be resigned—the sooner the better; in the age which is approaching she should be something more— she should be a citizen. . . . I hold, Mr. Chairman, that American women have to do with this subject, not only because it is moral and religious, but because it is *political,* inasmuch as we are citizens of this republic and as such our honor, happiness and well-being are bound up in its politics, government and laws.

Here the speaker paused, and a stirring, like a sigh, went through the audience. Not only the event itself, but the words here spoken were so daring and novel, it staggered the imagination. The women in the audience listened in rapt fascination as one of their own sex dared to speak out what many had thought in silence. Some of the ministers present nodded sagely; they were hearing blasphemy, just as they had expected. Not for nothing had this woman been called "Devil-ina" in the daily press. The devil did indeed work through her attractive form, her poised and ladylike manner. But the abolitionists in the audience, even those who had previously expressed their disagreement with the speaker's approach, now were clearly won over. It had seemed to many that it would be best for Angelina Grimké simply to speak about the anti-slavery petitions and avoid offending the sensibilities of the audience by bringing up the extraneous subject of woman's place in society. But it was obvious that she had the audience spellbound and even those most critical could not help but admire her accomplishment. Angelina felt their sympathetic support, like "a body guard of hearts faithful and true" and drew strength from it. Her voice, previously calm, now took on a passion that gripped her listeners' emotions.

I stand before you as a southerner, exiled from the land of my birth by the sound of the lash and the piteous cry of the slave. I stand before you as a repentent slaveholder. I stand before you as a moral being and as a moral being I feel that I owe it to the suffering slave and to the deluded master, to my country and to the world to do all that I can to overturn a system of complicated crimes, built upon the broken hearts and prostrate bodies of my countrymen in chains and cemented by the blood, sweat and tears of my sisters in bonds.

The audience was deeply moved and eagerly looked forward to her next appearance, which was scheduled for Friday, February 23, two days later. The arrangements caused some dissension among the legislators. A Boston representative claimed that the crowds she attracted were so great that the galleries were in danger of collapsing. This caused a witty legislator from Salem to propose that "a committee be appointed to examine the foundations of the State House of Massachusetts to see whether it will bear another lecture from Miss Grimké." This, apparently, ended the discussion.

Angelina described the scene on her arrival for the second session:

> . . . the hall was jambed to such excess that it was with great difficulty we were squeezed in, and then were compelled to walk over the seats in order to reach the place assigned us. As soon as we entered we were received by clapping. . . . After the bustle was over I rose to speak and was greeted by *hisses* from the doorway, tho' profound silence reigned thro' the crowd within. The noise in that direction increased and I was requested by the Chairman to suspend my remarks until at last order could be restored. Three times was I thus interrupted, until at last one of the Committee came to me and requested I would stand near the Speaker's desk. I crossed the Hall and stood on the platform in front of it, but was immediately requested to occupy the Secretaries desk on one side. I had just fixed my papers on two gentlemen's hats when at last I was invited to stand *in* the Speaker's desk. This was in the middle, more elevated and far more convenient in every respect.

It was a bad beginning and might have upset the most seasoned speaker. But Angelina now felt "perfectly calm"; her "self possession was unmoved." This time, her sister Sarah had been able to accompany her. In fact, she, whose timidity was proverbial among her friends, had been invited to sit in the chair of the Speaker of the Massachusetts Assembly. "We Abolition Women are turning the world upside down," thought Angelina.

She was better satisfied with her speech on this occasion than she had been earlier. She spoke on "The Dangers of Slavery, the Safety of Emancipation, Gradualism, and Character of the Free people of Color, the cruel treatment they were subjected to thro' the influence of prejudice—this prejudice always accompanied *gradual* emancipation." It was a speech she had frequently given during her New England tour and represented, essentially, her theoretical contributions to antislavery thought. The attention she gave to prejudice, especially in the North, was characteristic of her and distinguished her from other antislavery speakers. Again, the audience was deeply moved. "The Chairman was in tears almost the whole time that I was speaking," Angelina reported. "What affected him so much I do not know but I never saw a greater struggle of feeling than he manifested." By request of the committee, she was invited to complete her remarks to them on another occasion, the following week.

Abolitionists were jubilant and conscious of a triumph. And the press, as it had done and would continue to do, sneered:

Miss Grimké

She exhibited considerable talent for a female, as an orator; appeared not at all abashed in exhibiting herself in a position so unsuitable to her sex, totally disregarding the doctrine of St. Paul, who says "Is it not a shame for a woman to speak in public?" She belabored the slaveholders, and beat the air like all possessed. Her address occupied about 2 hours and a half in delivery, when she gave out, stating that she had a sister who was desirous to speak upon the same subject but was prevented by ill health. She, however, intimated, that after taking a breath for a day, she would like to continue the subject and the meeting was accordingly adjourned to Friday afternoon, at 3 o'clock, when she will conclude her speech.

The reporter from *The Olive Branch* concluded an article in which he ridiculed Sarah Grimké's speech, never realizing that it was Angelina Grimké he had heard, with the following cutting remarks: "It is rather doubtful whether any of the South Carolina lords of creation will ever seek the heart and hand of their great orator in marriage. . . ."

And from as far west as Pittsburgh came an attack in a similar vein: "Miss Grimké, a North Carolinian [!], we believe, is delivering abolition lectures to the members of the Massachusetts Legislature. Miss Grimké is very likely in search of a *lawful* protector, who will take her for better or worse for life, and she has thus made a bold dash among the Yankee lawmakers."

But there were other voices: "It was a noble day when for the first time in civilized America, a Woman stood up in a Legislative Hall, vindicating the rights of women. . . . This noble woman gave our legislators . . . one of those beautiful appeals for which she alone, as an American female, has been so justly distinguished." And from distant Detroit the reporter of the Detroit *Morning Post* declared, "Miss Grimké, a pretty Quakeress . . . is a woman of splendid eloquence and has made me 19/20 of an abolitionist."

It is obvious that contemporaries had some appreciation of the meaning of this event. The Grimké sisters' pioneering speaking tour, which culminated in Angelina's appearance before the Legislature, took place a full ten years before the Seneca Falls convention. It was at this convention that for the first time in history women organized to demand their rights as citizens. Many of the key figures in the coming struggle for woman's rights, Elizabeth Cady Stanton, Lucy Stone, Susan Anthony, Abby Kelley, were personally inspired by the Grimké sisters. The woman who, in February 1838, stood up and spoke for her sex before a legislative assembly of men, was an emancipated, a "new woman," half a century before the phrase had been coined. In working for the liberation of the slave, Sarah and Angelina Grimké found the key to their own liberation. And the consciousness of the significance of their actions was clearly before them. "We Abolition Women are turning the world upside down."

The Grimké sisters knew they were ushering in a new era.

The World of the Slaves

Chattel slavery was not deliberately imported to the New World by England's early settlers. As Winthrop Jordan observes in the following article, "Unthinking Decision: The Enslavement of Negroes in America in 1700", "At the start of English settlement in America, no one had in mind to establish the institution of Negro slavery." Nevertheless, while there remains some doubt about when the institution of slavery was actually established, it is clear that by 1660 black people had become chattel slaves and the inexorable, ensuing process of black debasement was underway. Throughout most of the eighteenth century declining tobacco profits, soil erosion, and the embarrassing contradiction between human bondage and revolutionary proclamations of liberty and equality allowed prominent Americans to believe that Southern slavery would soon disappear "naturally" as it had in the North. However, when Eli Whitney's invention of the cotton gin in 1793, combined with burgeoning demand from England, made cotton growing commercially feasible, nineteenth century Southern planters found more economic justification than ever for their slave system, and the continued subjugation of America's blacks was assured for another three generations. Eventually, only executive fiat, the Emancipation Proclamation of 1863, removed the chains of chattel slavery from black Americans.

Essential to understanding the history of black Americans is a grasp of how the "unthinking decision" developed. Winthrop Jordan provides the best analysis of this historical process. Jordan demonstrates that slavery occurred as a means of combating idleness; as an antidote for heathenism; as accepted treatment of prisoners of "just wars"; and as a result of labor shortages. But how could *racial* slavery be justified? Were there not idle heathen Englishmen, or Scottish and Irish prisoners of "just wars"? Jordan's answer lies in the exaggerated sense of differentness between native Indians and African blacks and England's white men. Race prejudice alone cannot explain slavery, claims

Jordan, but the overwhelming differentness of the Africans—ritual and religious practices, manners, behavior, languages, color, physical characteristics—made them "special candidates for degradation." Unfortunately, the early Americans interpreted what was strange and different as inferior and in doing so laid the foundations for one of America's most vexing social problems.

The second article in this section is Sterling Stuckey's "Through the Prism of Folklore: The Black Ethos in Slavery" which is concerned with how slaves came to terms with their condition. The crucial question of what it meant to be a slave has occupied the attention of many historians. In the nineteenth and early twentieth centuries slavery scholarship tended to reflect the narrow social prejudices of the Jim Crow years, seeing slavery as a benign institution, blacks as socially inferior, incompetent and lacking ambition, childlike, shiftless, and ultimately satisfied as slaves. After all, writers such as Ulrich B. Philips asked, how else can the relative paucity of slave rebellions in America be explained? Then, in the mid-1950's, broadly paralleling the nascent civil rights movement, a new approach to slavery studies began. Personified by Kenneth Stampp's The Peculiar Institution (1956), modern scholarship insisted that historians should judge slavery and slave ambitions by the same moral and political criteria as white American history. Next came Stanley Elkin's *Slavery* claiming that in the American South the slave was subject to a profound dehumanizing process which robbed the individual of any semblance of physical and intellectual freedom. Plantations, to Elkins, were brutal, enervating, degrading camps which contorted the slave psyche into the cruel paradies of personal free-will known as "Uncle Tom" and "Sambo". Provocative as the Elkins view is, it has proved unsatisfactory as a generalization of the slave experience. In the flood of social history of the 1960's came yet another revision of the slave debate. Lawrence Levine, Eugene Genovese, Sterling Stuckey, and John Blassingame, among others, argued that within the confines of the slave system, spiritually and intellectually, the slave was able to maintain a remarkable degree of cultural independence and community cohesion. Stuckey's 1968 article is based on an examination of folk songs, slave oral traditions, spirituals, and poetry—*i.e.,* slave art. The author's contention is that an independent slave ethos, a "slave lifestyle and set of values which was an amalgam of Africanisms and New World elements" developed during the ante-bellum era which helped blacks to endure slavery. The black ethos, in part, allowed slaves to make sense of their world, rationalize it, and ultimately cope with it without either losing identity or resorting to violence. Here, says Stuckey, are the roots of Afro-American culture, ignored by white America until the politics and popular culture of the 1960's made America's "invisible man" visible for good.

The final article in this section is Peter Kolchin's "Reevaluating the Slave Community: A Comparative Perspective." Here the author's goal is to restore balance to the ongoing slavery debate. Specifically, Kolchin is concerned to redress the tendency of 1970's scholarship to exaggerate the cohesive aspects of the "slave community" and forget that black slaves were victims of white oppression before they were anything else. Employing the comparative approach, slave systems in pre-revolutionary Russia, the Caribbean, and Latin America are analyzed. Slave-owner residence patterns, size and distribution of Southern slaveholdings, slave-owner paternalism, and the peculiar American origins of Southern slaves, were all corrosive agents that weakened slave community solidarity. Moreover, Kolchin asserts, in comparison to other slave systems, America's blacks had little opportunity to develop independent economic activity, as well as an undeveloped sense of communal, institutional autonomy. Finally, individualistic, non-collaborative patterns of protest and resistance demonstrate not slave community cohesion, but fragmentation, discord, and atomization.

From the illiterate field hands of back country Mississippi to the skilled craftsmen of downtown Savannah and New Orleans the "condition of the slave" in ante-bellum America varied enormously. However, until 1863 the great majority of black Americans shared the slave experience in all its manifestations, and the combined total of the millions of individual responses add up to "the American slave experience." Nowadays the slavery debate is no longer concerned with facile generalizations such as whether the slave was passive or belligerent, content or dissatisfied, independent or intellectually dispossessed. Instead, modern scholarship searches for sophisticated insight into the origins, development, and meaning of Afro-American culture, and for continuity in the black American experience during slavery and since. In so doing, the debate has progressed immeasurably since Kennth Stampp's trail-blazing work for some thirty years ago.

Enslavement of Africans in America to 1700

Winthrop Jordan

At the start of English settlement in America, no one had in mind to establish the institution of Negro slavery. Yet in less than a century the foundations of a peculiar institution had been laid. The first Africans landed in Virginia in 1619, though very little is known about their precise status during the next twenty years. Between 1640 and 1660 there is evidence of enslavement, and after 1660 slavery crystallized on the statute books of Maryland, Virginia, and other colonies. By 1700, when Africans began flooding into English America, they were treated as somehow deserving a life and status radically different from English and other European settlers. Englishmen in America had created a new legal status which ran counter to English law.

Unfortunately the details of this process can never be completely reconstructed; there is simply not enough evidence to show precisely when and how and why Negroes came to be treated so differently from white men. Concerning the first years of contact especially we have very little information as to what impression Negroes made upon English settlers: accordingly, we are left knowing less about the formative years than about later periods of American slavery. That those early years were crucial is obvious, for it was then that the cycle of Negro debasement began; once the African became fully the slave it is not hard to see why Englishmen looked down upon him. Yet precisely because understanding the dynamics of these early years is so important to understanding the centuries which followed, it is necessary to bear with the less than satisfactory data and to attempt to reconstruct the course of debasement undergone by Africans in seventeenth-century America.

The Necessities of a New World

When Englishmen crossed the Atlantic to settle in America, they were immediately subject to novel strains. A large proportion of migrants were dead within a year. The survivors were isolated from the world as they had known it, cut off from friends and family and the familiar sights and sounds and smells which have always told men who and where they are. A similar sense of isolation and disorientation was inevitable even in the settlements that did not suffer through a starving time. English settlers had undergone the shock of detachment from home in order to set forth upon a dangerous voyage of from ten to thirteen weeks that ranged from unpleasant to fatal and that seared into every passenger's memory the ceaselessly tossing distance that separated him from his old way of life.

Life in America put great pressure upon the traditional social and economic controls that Englishmen assumed were to be exercised by civil and often ecclesiastical authority. Somehow the empty woods seemed to lead much more toward license than restraint. At the same time, by reaction, this unfettering resulted in an almost pathetic social conservatism, a yearning for the forms and symbols of the old familiar social order. When in 1618, for example, the Virginia Company wangled a knighthood for a newly appointed governor of the colony the objection from the settlers was not that this artificial elevation was inappropriate to wilderness conditions but that it did not go far enough to meet them. English social forms were transplanted to America not simply because they were nice to have around but because without them the new settlements would have fallen apart and English settlers would have become men of the forest, savage men devoid of civilization.

For the same reason, the communal goals and values that animated the settlement of the colonies acquired great functional importance in the wilderness; they served as antidotes to social and individual disintegration. For Englishmen planting in America, it was of the utmost importance to know that they were Englishmen, which was to say that they were educated (to a degree suitable to their station), Christian (of an appropriate Protestant variety), civilized, and (again to an appropriate degree) free men.

It was with personal freedom, of course, that wilderness conditions most suddenly reshaped English laws, assumptions, and practices. In America land was plentiful, labor scarce, and, as in all new colonies, a cash crop desperately needed. These economic conditions were to remain crucial for many years; in general they tended to encourage greater geographical mobility, less specialization, higher rewards, and fewer restraints on the processes and products of labor. In general men who invested capital in agriculture in America came under fewer customary and legal restraints than in England concerning what they did with their land and with the people who worked on it. On the other hand their activities were restricted by the economic necessity of producing cash crops for export. Men without capital could obtain land relatively easily: hence the shortage of labor and the notably blurred line between men who had capital and men who did not.

Three major systems of labor emerged amid the interplay of these social and economic conditions in America. One, which was present from the beginning, was free wage labor. Another, which was the last to appear, was chattel slavery. The third, which virtually coincided with first settlement in America, was temporary servitude, in which contractual arrangements gave shape to the entire system. It was this third system, indentured servitude, which permitted so many English settlers to cross the Atlantic barrier. Indentured servitude was linked to the development of chattel slavery in America, and its operation deserves closer examination.

A very sizable proportion of settlers in the English colonies came as indentured servants bound by contract to serve a master for a specified number of years, usually from four to seven or until age twenty-one, as repayment for their ocean passage. The time of service to which the servant bound himself was negotiable property, and he might be sold or conveyed from one master to another at any time up to the expiration of his indenture, at which point he became a free man. (Actually it was his *labor* which was owned and sold, not his *person,* though this distinction was neither important nor obvious at the time.) Custom and statute law regulated the relationship between servant and master. Obligation was reciprocal: the master undertook to feed and clothe and sometimes to educate his servant and to refrain from abusing him, while the servant was obliged to perform such work as his master set him and to obey his master in all things.

Freedom and Bondage in the English Tradition

While in retrospect we can readily see these three distinct categories, thinking about freedom and bondage in Tudor England was in fact confused and self-contradictory. In a period of social dislocation there was considerable disagreement among contemporary observers as to what actually was going on and even as to what ought to be. *Ideas* about personal freedom tended to run both ahead of and behind actual social conditions. Both statute and common law were sometimes considerably more than a century out of phase with actual practice and with commonly held notions about servitude. Finally, both ideas and practices were changing rapidly. It is possible, however, to identify certain important tenets of social thought that served as anchor points amid this chaos.

Englishmen lacked accurate methods of ascertaining what actually was happening to their social institutions, but they were not wrong in supposing that villenage, or "bondage" as they more often called it, had virtually disappeared in England. In the middle ages, being a villein had meant dependence upon the will of a feudal lord but by no means deprivation of all social and legal rights. By the fourteenth century villenage had decayed markedly, and it no longer existed as a viable social institution in the second half of the sixteenth century. Personal freedom had become the normal status of Englishmen. Most contemporaries welcomed this fact; indeed it was after about 1550 that there began to develop in England that preening consciousness of the peculiar glories of English liberties. This consciousness was to flower in America as well.

How had it all happened? Among those observers who tried to explain, there was agreement that Christianity was primarily responsible. They thought of villenage as a mitigation of ancient bond slavery and that the continuing trend to liberty was animated, as Sir Thomas Smith said in a famous passage, by the "perswasion . . . of Christians not to make nor keepe his brother in Christ, servile, bond and underling for ever unto him, as a beast rather than as a man." They agreed also that the trend had been forwarded by the common law, in which the disposition was always, as the phrase went, "in favor of liberty."

At the same time there were in English society people who seemed badly out of control. From at least the 1530's the countryside swarmed with vagrants, sturdy beggars, rogues, and vagabonds, with men who *could* (it was thought) but *would not* work. They committed all manner of crimes, the worst of which was remaining idle. It was an article of faith among Tudor commentators that idleness was the mother of all vice and the chief danger to a well-ordered state. Tudor statesmen valiantly attempted to suppress idleness by means of the famous vagrancy laws which provided for houses of correction and (finally) for whipping the vagrant from constable to constable until he reached his home parish. They assumed that everyone belonged in a specific niche and that anyone failing to labor in the niche assigned to him by Providence must be compelled to do so by authority.

In response, Tudor authorities gradually hammered out the legal framework of a labor system which permitted compulsion but which did *not* permit so total a loss of freedom as lifetime hereditary slavery. And as things turned out, it was indentured servitude which best met the requirements for settling in America. Of course there were other forms of bound labor which contributed to the process of settlement: many convicts were sent and many children abducted. Yet among all the numerous varieties and degrees of non-freedom which existed in England, there was none which could have served as a well-formed model for the chattel slavery which developed in America. This is not to say, though, that slavery was an unheard-of-novelty in Tudor England. On the contrary, "bond slavery" was a memory trace of long standing. Vague and confused as the concept of slavery was in the minds of Englishmen, it possessed certain fairly consistent connotations which were to help shape English perceptions of the way Europeans should properly treat the newly discovered peoples overseas.

The Concept of Slavery

At first glance, one is likely to see merely a fog of inconsistency and vagueness enveloping the terms *servant* and *slave* as they were used both in England and in seventeenth-century America. When Hamlet declaims "O what a rogue and peasant slave am I," the term seems to have a certain elasticity. When Peter Heylyn defines it in 1627 as "that ignominious word, *Slave;* whereby we use to call ignoble fellowes, and the more base sort of people," the term seems useless as a key to a specific social status.

In one sense it was, since the concept embodied in the terms *servitude, service,* and *servant* was widely embracive. *Servant* was more a generic term than *slave.* Slaves could be "servants," but servants *should not* be "slaves." This principle, which was common in England, suggests a mesaure of precision in the concept of slavery. In fact there was a large measure which merits closer inspection.

First of all, the "slave's" loss of freedom was complete. "Of all men which be destitute of libertie or freedome," explained one commentator in 1590, "the slave is in greatest subjection, for a slave is that person which is in servitude or bondage to an other, even against nature." "Even his children," moreover, ". . . are infected with the Leprosie of his father's bondage." At law, much more closely than in literary usage, "bond slavery" implied utter deprivation of liberty.

Slavery was also thought of as a perpetual condition. While it had not yet come invariably to mean lifetime labor, it was frequently thought of in those terms. Except sometimes in instances of punishment for crime, slavery was open ended; in contrast to servitude, it did not involve a definite term of years. Slavery was perpetual also in the sense that it was often thought of as hereditary servitude, no matter how long, brutal, and involuntary, was not the same thing as perpetual slavery. Servitude comprehended alike the young apprentice, the orphan, the indentured servant, the convicted debtor or criminal, the political prisoner, and, even, the Scottish and Irish captive of war who was sold as a "slave" to New England or Barbados. None of these persons, no matter how miserably treated, served for life in the colonies, though of course many died before their term ended. Hereditary lifetime service was restricted to Indians and Africans. Among the various English colonies in the New World, this service known as "slavery" seems first to have developed in the international cockpit known as the Caribbean.

Enslavement: The West Indies

The Englishmen who settled the Caribbean colonies were not very different from those who went to Virginia, Bermuda, Maryland, or even New England. Their experience in the islands, however, was very different indeed. By 1640 there were roughly as many English (and Irish and Scots) in the little islands as on the American continent. A half-century after the first settlements were established in the 1620's, many of the major islands—Barbados, and the Leeward Islands—were overcrowded. Thousands of whites who had been squeezed off the land by sugar plantations migrated to other English colonies, including much larger Jamaica which had been captured from the Spanish in 1655. Their places were taken by African slaves who had been shipped to the islands, particularly after 1640, to meet an insatiable demand for labor which was cheap to maintain, easy to dragoon, and simple to replace when worked to death. Negroes outnumbered whites in Barbados as early as 1660.

In that colony, at least, this helpful idea that Negroes served for life seems to have existed even before they were purchased in large numbers. Any doubt which may have existed as to the appropriate status of Africans was dispelled in 1636 when the Governor and Council resolved "that *Negroes* and *Indians,* that came here to be sold, should serve for life, unless a Contract was before made to the contrary." Europeans were not treated in this manner. In the 1650's several observers referred to the lifetime slavery of Negroes as if it were a matter of common knowledge. "It's the Custome for a Christian servant to serve foure yeares," one wrote at the beginning of the decade, "and then enjoy his freedome . . . the Negroes and Indians (of which latter there are but few here) they and the generation are Slaves to their owners to perpetuity." As another visitor described the people of the island in 1655:

> The genterey heare doth live far better than ours doue in England: they have most of them 100 or 2 or 3 of slaves apes whou they command as they pleas. . . . This Island is inhabited with all sortes: with English, french, Duch, Scotes, Irish, Spaniards they being Jues: with Ingones and miserabell Negors borne to perpetuall slavery thay and thayer seed . . . some planters will have 30 more or les about 4 or 5 years ould: they sele them from one to the other as we doue shepe. This Illand is the Dunghill wharone England doth cast forth its rubidg: Rodgs and hors and such like peopel are those which are gennerally Broght heare.

Dunghill or no dunghill, Barbados was treating its Negroes as slaves for life.

Enslavement: New England

It was ironic that slavery in the West Indies should have influenced, of all places, New England. The question with slavery in New England is not why it was weakly rooted, but why it existed at all. No staple crop demanded regiments of raw labor. That there was no compelling economic demand for Negroes is evident in the numbers actually imported: there could have been no need for a distinct status for only 3 per cent of the labor force. Indentured servitude was completely adequate to New England's needs. Why, then, did New Englanders enslave Negroes, probably as early as 1638? Why was it that the Puritans rather mindlessly (which was not their way) accepted slavery for blacks and Indians but not for whites?

The early appearance of slavery in New England may in part be explained by the fact that the first Negroes were imported in the ship *Desire* in 1638 from an island colony where Negroes were already being held perpetually. After 1640 a brisk trade got under way between New England and the English Caribbean islands. These strange Negroes from the West Indies must surely have brought with them to New England prevailing notions about their usual status. Ship masters who purchased perpetual service in Barbados would not have been likely to sell service for term in Boston.

No amount of contact with the West Indies could have by itself created Negro slavery in New England; settlers there had to be willing to accept the proposition. Because they were Englishmen, they were so prepared—and at the same time they were not. Characteristically, as Puritans, they officially codified this ambivalence in 1641 as follows: ". . . there shall never be any bond-slavery, villenage or captivitie amongst us; unlesse it be lawfull captives taken in just warrs, and such strangers as willingly sell themselves, or are solde to us. . . ." Thus as early as 1641 the Puritan settlers were seeking to guarantee their own liberty without closing off the opportunity of taking it from others whom they identified with the Biblical term, "strangers."

It would be wrong to suppose, though, that all the Puritans' preconceived ideas about freedom and bondage worked in the same direction. While the concepts of difference in religion and of captivity worked against Indians and Negroes, certain Scriptural injunctions and English pride in liberty told in the opposite direction. In Massachusetts the magistrates demonstrated that they were not about to tolerate glaring breaches of "the Law of God established in Israel" even when the victims were Africans. In 1646 the authorities arrested two mariners who had carried two Negroes directly from Africa and sold them in Massachusetts. What distressed the General Court was that the Negroes had been obtained during a raid on an African village and that this "haynos and crying sinn of man stealing" had taken place on the Lord's Day. The General Court decided to free the unfortunate victims and ship them back to Africa, though the death penalty for the crime (clearly mandatory in Scripture) was not imposed. More quietly than in this dramatic incident, Puritan authorities extended the same protections against maltreatment to Negroes and Indians as to white servants.

From the first, however, there were scattered signs in New England that Negroes were regarded as different from English people not merely in their status as slaves. In 1652, for example, the Massachusetts General Court ordered that Scotsmen, Indians, and Negroes should train with the English in the militia, but four years later abruptly excluded Negroes, as did Connecticut in 1660. Evidently Negroes, even free Negroes, were regarded as distinct from the English. They were, in New England where economic necessities were not sufficiently pressing to determine the decision, treated differently from other men.

Enslavement: Virginia and Maryland

In Virginia and Maryland the development of Negro slavery followed a very different course, for several reasons. Most obviously, geographic conditions and the intentions of the settlers quickly combined to produce a successful agricultural staple. Ten years after settlers first landed at Jamestown they were on the way to proving, in the face of assertions to the contrary, that it was possible "to found an empire upon smoke." More than the miscellaneous productions of New England, tobacco required labor which was cheap but not temporary, mobile but not independent, and tireless rather than skilled. In the Chesapeake area more than anywhere to the northward, the shortage of labor and the abundance of land—the "frontier"—placed a premium on involuntary labor.

This need for labor played more directly upon these settlers' ideas about freedom and bondage than it did either in the West Indies or in New England. Perhaps it would be more accurate to say that settlers in Virginia (and in Maryland after settlement in 1634) made their decisions concerning Negroes while relatively virginal, relatively free from external influences and from firm preconceptions. Of all the important early English settlements, Virginia had the least contact with the Spanish, Portuguese, Dutch, and other English colonies. At the same time, the settlers of Virginia did not possess either the legal or Scriptural learning of the New England Puritans whose conception of the just war had opened the way to the enslavement of Indians. Slavery in the tobacco colonies did not begin as an adjunct of captivity; in marked contrast to the Puritan response to the Pequot War, the settlers of Virginia did not react to the Indian massacre of 1622 with propositions for taking captives and selling them as "slaves."

In the absence, then, of these influences in other English colonies, slavery as it developed in Virginia and Maryland assumes a special interest and importance over and above the fact that Negro slavery was to become a vitally important institution there and, later, to the southwards. In the tobacco colonies it is possible to watch Negro slavery *develop,* not pop up full-grown overnight, and it is therefore possible to trace, very imperfectly, the development of the shadowy, unexamined rationale which supported it. The concept of Negro slavery there was neither borrowed from foreigners, nor extracted from books, nor invented out of whole cloth, nor extrapolated from servitude, nor generated by English reaction to Negroes as such, nor necessitated by the exigencies of the New World. Not any one of these made the Negro a slave, but all.

In rough outline, slavery's development in the tobacco colonies seems to have undergone three stages. Africans first arrived in 1619, an event Captain John Smith referred to with the utmost unconcern: "About the last of August came in a dutch man of warre that sold us twenty Negars." Africans trickled in slowly for the next half-century; one report in 1649 estimated that there were three hundred among Virginia's population of fifteen thousand—about 2 per cent. Long before there were more appreciable numbers, the development of slavlery had, so far as we can tell, shifted gears. Prior to about 1640 there is very little evidence to show how Negroes were treated. After 1640 there is mounting evidence that some Negroes were in fact being treated as slaves. This is to say that the twin essences of slavery—lifetime service and inherited status—first became evident during the twenty years prior to the beginning of legal formulation. After 1660 slavery was written into statute law.

Concerning the first of these stages, there is only one major historical certainty. There simply is not enough evidence to indicate whether Negroes were treated like white servants or not. At least we can be confident, therefore, that the two most common assertions about the first Negroes—that they were slaves and that they were servants—are *unfounded,* though not necessarily incorrect. And what of the positive evidence?

Some of the first group bore Spanish names and presumably had been baptized, which would mean they were at least nominally Christian, though of the Papist sort. They had been "sold" to the English; so had other Englishmen but not by the Dutch. Probably these Negroes were not fully free, but many Englishmen were not. It can be said, though, that from the first in Virginia Negroes were set apart from white men by the word *Negroes.* The earliest Virginia census reports plainly distinguished Negroes from white men; often Negroes were listed as such with no personal names—a critical distinction. It seems logical to suppose that this perception of the Negro as being distinct from the Englishman must have operated to debase his status rather than to raise it, for in the absence of countervailing social factors the need for labor in the colonies usually told in the direction of non-freedom. There were few countervailing factors present, surely, in such instances as in 1629 when a group of Negroes were brought to Virginia freshly captured from a Portuguese ship which had snatched them from Angola a few weeks earlier. Given the context of English thought and experience sketched in this chapter, it seems probable that the Negro's status was not the same as that accorded the white servant. But we do not know for sure.

When the first fragmentary evidence appears about 1640 it becomes clear that *some* Negroes in both Virginia and Maryland were serving for life and some Negro children inheriting the same obligation. Not all blacks, certainly, for after the mid-1640's the court records show that some Negroes were incontestably free and were accumulating property of their own. At least one black freeman, Anthony Johnson, himself owned a slave. Some blacks served only terms of usual length, but others were held for terms far longer than custom and statute permitted with white servants. The first fairly clear indication that slavery was practiced in the tobacco colonies appears in 1639, when a Maryland statute declared that "all the Inhabitants of this Province being

Christians (Slaves excepted) Shall have and enjoy all such rights liberties immunities priviledges and free customs within this Province as any naturall born subject of England." Another Maryland law passed the same year provided that "all persons being Christians (Slaves excepted)" over eighteen who were imported without indentures would serve for four years. These laws make very little sense unless the term *slaves* meant Negroes and perhaps Indians.

The next year, 1640, the first definite indication of outright enslavement appears in Virginia. The General Court pronounced sentence on three servants who had been retaken after absconding to Maryland. Two of them, both white, were ordered to serve their masters for one additional year and then the colony for three more, but "the third being a negro named John Punch shall serve his said master or his assigns for the time of his natural life here or else where." No white servant in any English colony, so far as is known, ever received a like sentence.

After 1640, when surviving Virginia county court records began to mention Negroes, sales for life, often including any future progeny, were recorded an unmistakable language. In 1646 Francis Pott sold a Negro woman and boy to Stephen Charlton "to the use of him . . . forever." Similarly, six years later William Whittington sold to John Pott "one Negro girle named Jowan; aged about Ten yeares and with her Issue and produce duringe her (or either of them) for their Life tyme. And their Successors forever"; and a Maryland man in 1649 deeded two Negro men and a woman "and all their issue both male and Female." The executors of a York County estate in 1647 disposed of eight Negroes—four men, two women, and two children—to Captain John Chisman "to have hold occupy posesse and injoy and every one of the afforementioned Negroes forever."

Further evidence that some Negroes were serving for life in this period lies in the prices paid for them. In many instances the valuations placed on Negroes (in estate inventories and bills of sale) were far higher than for white servant, even those servants with full terms yet to serve. Higher prices must have meant that Negroes were more highly valued because of their greater length of service. The labor owned by James Stone in 1648, for example, was evaluated as follows:

	lb tobo
Thomas Groves, 4 years to serve	1300
Francis Bomley for 6 years	1600
John Thackstone for 3 years	1300
Susan Davis for 3 yeares	1000
Emaniell a Negro man	2000
Roger Stone 3 yeares	1300
Mingo a Negro man	2000

Besides setting a higher value on Negroes, these inventories failed to indicate a last name and the number of years they had still to serve, presumably because their service was for an unlimited time.

Where Negro women were involved, higher valuations probably reflected the facts that their issue were valuable and that they could be used for field work while white women generally were not. This latter discrimination between black and white women did not necessarily involve perpetual service, but it meant that blacks were set apart in a way clearly not to their advantage. This was not the only instance in which Negroes were subjected to degrading distinctions not immediately and necessarily attached to the concept of slavery. Blacks were singled out for special treatment in several ways which suggest a generalized debasement of blacks as a group. Significantly, the first indications of this debasement appeared at about the same time as the first indications of actual enslavement.

The distinction concerning field work is a case in point. A law of 1643 provided that *all* adult men were taxable and, in addition, *Negro* women. The same distinction was made twice again before 1660. Maryland adopted a similar policy beginning in 1654. This official discrimination between black women and other women was made by white men who were accustomed to thinking of field work as being ordinarily the work of men exclusively. The essentially racial character of this discrimination stood out clearly in a law passed in 1668 at the time slavery was taking shape in the statute books:

> Whereas some doubts, have arisen whether negro women set free were still to be accompted tithable according to a former act, *It is declared by this grand assembly* that negro women, though permitted to enjoy their Freedome yet ought not in all respects to be admitted to a full fruition of the exemptions and impunities of the English, and are still lyable to payment of taxes.

Virginia law set blacks apart from all other groups in a second way by denying them the important right and obligation to bear arms. Few restraints could indicate more clearly the denial to Africans of membership in the English community. This first foreshadowing of the slave codes came in 1640, at just the time when other indications first appeared that blacks were subject to special treatment.

Finally, an even more compelling sense of the separateness of Negroes was revealed in early reactions to sexual union between the races. Prior to 1660 the evidence concerning these reactions is equivocal, and it is not possible to tell whether repugnance for intermixture preceded legislative enactment of slavery. In the early 1660's, however, when slavery was gaining statutory recognition, the assemblies acted with full-throated indignation against miscegenation. These acts aimed at more than merely avoiding confusion of status. In 1662 Virginia declared that "if any christian shall committ Fornication with a negro man or woman, hee or shee soe offending" should pay double the usual fine. Two years later Maryland regulated interracial marriages: "forasmuch as divers freeborne English women forgettfull of their free Condicion and to the disgrace of our Nation doe intermarry with Negro Slaves by which alsoe divers suites may arise touching the issue of such woemen and a great damage doth befall the Masters of such Negros for prevention whereof for deterring such freeborne women from such shameful Matches," strong language indeed if "divers suites" had been the only problem. A Maryland act of 1681 described marriages of white women with Negroes as, among other things, "always to the Satisfaccion of theire Lascivious and Lustfull desires, and to the disgrace not only of the English butt allso of many other Christian Nations." When Virginia finally prohibited all interracial liaisons in 1691, the Assembly vigorously denounced miscegenation and its fruits as "that abominable mixture and spurious issue."

From the surviving evidence it appears that outright enslavement and these other forms of debasement appeared at about the same time in Maryland and Virginia. Indications of perpetual service, the very nub of slavery, coincided with indications that English settlers discriminated against Negro women, withheld arms from Negroes, and—though the timing is far less certain—reacted unfavorably to interracial sexual union. The coincidence suggests a mutual relationship between slavery and unfavorable assessment of blacks. Rather than slavery causing "prejudice," or vice versa, they seem rather to have generated each other. Both were, after all, twin aspects of a general debasement of the Negro. Slavery and "prejudice" may have been equally cause and effect, continuously reacting upon each other, dynamically joining hands to hustle the Negro down the road to complete degradation. Much more than with the other English colonies, where the enslavement of Africans was to some extent a borrowed practice, the available evidence for Maryland and Virginia points to less borrowing and to this kind of process: a mutually interactive growth of slavery and unfavorable assessment, with no cause for either which did not cause the other as well. If slavery caused prejudice, then invidious distinctions concerning working in the fields, bearing arms, and sexual union should have appeared *after* slavery's firm establishment. If prejudice caused slavery, then one would expect to find these lesser discriminations preceding the greater discrimination of outright enslavement. Taken as a whole, the evidence reveals a process of debasement of which hereditary lifetime service, while important, was not the only part.

Certainly it was the case in Maryland and Virginia that the legal enactment of Negro slavery followed social practice, rather than vice versa. In 1661 the Virginia Assembly indirectly provided statutory recognition that some Negroes served for life: "That in case any English servant shall run away in company with any negroes who are incapable of makeing satisfaction by addition of time," he must serve for the Negroes' lost time as well as his own. Maryland enacted a similar law in 1663, and in the following year came out with the categorical declaration that Negroes were to serve "Durante Vita"—for life. During the next twenty-odd years a succession of acts in both colonies defined with increasing precision what sorts of persons might be treated as slaves.

By about 1700 the slave ships began spilling forth their black cargoes in greater and greater numbers. By that time racial slavery and the necessary police powers had been written into law. By that time, too, slavery had lost all resemblance to a perpetual and hereditary version of English servitude, though service for life still seemed to contemporaries its most essential feature. In the last quarter of the seventeenth century the trend was to treat Negroes more like property and less like people, to send them to the fields at younger ages, to deny them automatic existence as inherent members of the community, to tighten the bonds on their personal and civil freedom, and correspondingly to loosen the traditional restraints on the master's freedom to deal with his human property as he saw fit. In 1705 Virginia gathered up the random statutes of a whole generation and baled them into a "slave code" which would not have been out of place in the nineteenth century.

Racial Slavery: From Reasons to Rationale

And *difference,* surely, was the indispensable key to the degradation of Africans in English America. In scanning the problem of *why* Negroes were enslaved in America, certain constant elements in a complex situation can be readily, if roughly, identified. *It may be taken as given* that there would have been no enslavement without economic need, that is, without persistent demand for labor in underpopulated colonies. Of crucial importance, too, was the fact that Africans in America were relatively powerless. In themselves, however, these two elements will not explain the enslavement of Indians and Negroes. The pressing need in America was labor, and Irish, Scottish, and English servants were available. Most of them would have been helpless to ward off outright enslavement if their masters had thought themselves privileged to enslave them. As a group, though, masters did not think themselves so empowered. Only with Indians and Africans did Englishmen attempt so radical a deprivation of liberty—which brings the matter abruptly to the most difficult and imponderable question of all: what was it about Indians and Negroes which set them apart from Englishmen, which rendered them *different,* which made them special candidates for degradation?

To ask such questions is to inquire into the *content* of English attitudes, and unfortunately there is little evidence with which to build an answer. It may be said, however, that the heathen condition of Negroes seemed of considerable importance to English settlers in America—more so than to English voyagers upon the coasts of Africa—and that heathenism was associated in some settlers' minds with the condition of slavery. Clearly, though, this is not to say that English colonists enslaved Africans merely because of religious difference. In the early years, the English settlers most frequently contrasted themselves with Negroes by the term *Christian,* though they also sometimes described themselves as *English.* Yet the concept embodied by the term *Christian* embraced so much more meaning than was contained in specific doctrinal affirmations that it is scarcely possible to assume on this basis that Englishmen set Negroes apart because they were heathen. The historical experience of the English people in the sixteenth century had made for fusion of religion and nationality; the qualities of being English and Christian had become so inseparably blended that it seemed perfectly consistent to the Virginia Assembly in 1670 to declare that "noe negroe or Indian though baptised and enjoyned their owne Freedome shall be capable of any such purchase of christians, but yet not debarred from buying any of their owne nation."

From the first, then, the concept embedded in the term *Christian* seems to have conveyed much of the idea and feeling of *we* as against *they:* to be Christian was to be civilized rather than barbarous, English rather than African, white rather than black. The term *Christian* itself proved to have remarkable elasticity, for by the end of the seventeenth century it was being used to define a kind of slavery which had altogether lost any connection with explicit religious difference. In the Virginia code of 1705, for example, the term sounded much more like a definition of race than of religion: "And for a further christian care and usage of all christian servants, *Be it also enacted* . . . That no negroes, mulattos, or Indians, although christians, or Jews, Moors, Mahometans, or other infidels, shall, at any time, purchase any christian servant, nor any other, except of their own complexion, or such as are declared slaves by this act." By this time "Christianity" had somehow become intimately and explicitly linked with "complexion." The 1705 statute declared "That all servants imported and brought into this country, by sea or land, who were not christians in their native country . . . shall be accounted and be slaves, and as such be here bought and sold notwithstanding a conversion to christianity afterwards." As late as 1753 the Virginia slave code anachronistically defined slavery in terms of religion when everyone knew that slavery had for generations been based on the racial and not the religious difference.

It is worth making still closer scrutiny of the terminology which Englishmen employed when referring both to themselves and to the two peoples they enslaved, for this terminology affords the best single means of probing the content of their sense of difference. The terms *Indian* and *Negro* were both borrowed from the Hispanic languages, the one originally deriving from (mistaken) geographical locality and the other from human complexion. When referring to the Indians the English colonists either used that proper name or called them *savages,* a term which reflected primarily their view of Indians as uncivilized. In significant contrast, the colonists referred to *negroes,* and by the eighteenth century to *blacks* and to *Africans,* but almost never to African *heathens* or *pagans* or *savages.* Most suggestive of all, there seems to have been something of a shift during the seventeenth century in the terminology which Englishmen in the colonies applied to themselves. From the initially most common term *Christian,* at mid-century there was a marked shift toward the terms *English* and *free.* After about 1680, taking the colonies as a whole, a new term of self-identification appeared—*white.*

So far as the weight of analysis may be imposed upon such terms, diminishing reliance upon *Christian* suggests a gradual muting of the specifically religious elements in the Christian-Negro distinction in favor of secular nationality: Negroes were, in 1667, "not in all respects to be admitted to a full fruition of the exemptions and impunities of the English." As time went on, as some Negroes became assimilated to the English colonial culture, as more "raw Africans" arrived, and as increasing numbers of non-English Europeans were attracted to the colonies, English colonists turned increasingly to what they saw as the striking physiognomic difference. In Maryland a revised law prohibiting miscegenation (1692) retained *white* and *English* but dropped the term *Christian*—a symptomatic modification. By the end of the seventeenth century dark complexion had become an independent rationale for enslavement: in 1709 Samuel Sewall noted in his diary that a "Spaniard" had petitioned the Massachusetts Council for freedom but that "Capt. Teat alledg'd that all of that Color were Slaves." Here was a barrier between "we" and "they" which was visible and permanent: the black man could not become a white man. Not, at least, as yet.

What had occurred was not a change in the justification of slavery from religion to race. No such justifications were made. There seems to have been, within the unarticulated concept of the Negro as a different sort of person, a subtle but highly significant shift in emphasis. A perception of Negro heathenism remained through the eighteenth and into the nineteenth and even the twentieth century, and an awareness, at very least, of the African's different appearance was present from the beginning. The shift was an alteration in emphasis within a single concept of difference rather than a development of a novel conceptualization. Throughout the colonies the terms *Christian, free, English,* and *white* were for many years employed indiscriminately as synonyms. A Maryland law of 1681 used all four terms in one short paragraph.

Whatever the limitations of terminology as an index to thought and feeling, it seems likely that the English colonists' initial sense of difference from Africans was founded not on a single characteristic but on a cluster of qualities which, taken as a whole, seemed to set the Negro apart. Virtually every quality in "the Negro" invited pejorative feelings. What may have been his two most striking characteristics, his heathenism and his appearance, were probably prerequisite to his complete debasement. His heathenism alone could not have led to permanent enslavement since conversion easily wiped out that failing. If his appearance, his racial characteristics, meant nothing to the English settler, it is difficult to see how slavery based on race ever emerged, how the concept of complexion as the mark of slavery ever entered the colonists' minds. Even if the English colonists were most unfavorably struck by the Negro's color, though, blackness itself did not urge the complete debasement of slavery. Other cultural qualities—the strangeness of his language, gestures, eating habits, and so on—certainly must have contributed to the English colonists' sense that he was very different, perhaps disturbingly so. In Africa these qualities had for Englishmen added up to *savagery;* they were major components in that sense of *difference* which provided the mental margin absolutely requisite for placing the European on the deck of the slave ship and the African in the hold.

The available evidence (what little there is) suggests that for Englishmen settling in America, the specific religious difference was initially of greater importance than color, certainly of much greater relative importance than for the Englishmen who confronted Negroes in their African homeland. Perhaps Englishmen in Virginia, tanning seasonally under a hot sun and in almost daily contact with tawny Indians, found the Negro's color less arresting than they might have in other circumstances. Perhaps, too, these first Virginians sensed how inadequately they had reconstructed the institutions and practices of Christian piety in the wilderness; they would perhaps appear less as failures to themselves in this respect if compared to persons who as Christians were *totally* defective. Perhaps, though, the Jamestown settlers were told in 1619 by the Dutch shipmaster that these "negars" were heathens and could be treated as such. We do not know. The available data will not bear all the weight that the really crucial questions impose.

Of course once the cycle of degradation was fully under way, once slavery and racial discrimination were completely linked together, once the engine of oppression was in full operation, then there is no need to plead lack of knowledge. By the end of the seventeenth century in all the colonies of the English empire there was chattel racial slavery of a kind which would have seemed familiar to men living in the nineteenth century. No Elizabethan Englishman would have found it familiar, though certain strands of thought and feeling in Elizabethan England had intertwined with reports about the Spanish and Portuguese to engender a willingness on the part of English settlers in the New World to treat some men as suitable for private exploitation. During the seventeenth century New World conditions had enlarged this predisposition, so much so that English colonials of the eighteenth century were faced with full-blown slavery—something they thought of not as an institution but as a host of ever present problems, dangers, and opportunities.

Through the Prism of Folklore:
The Black Ethos in Slavery

Sterling Stuckey

It is not excessive to advance the view that some historians, because they have been so preoccupied with demonstrating the absence of significant slave revolts, conspiracies, and "day to day" resistance among slaves, have presented information on slave behavior and thought which is incomplete indeed. They have, devoted very little attention to trying to get "inside" slaves to discover what bondsmen thought about their condition. Small wonder we have been saddled with so many stereotypical treatments of slave thought and behavior.

Though we do not know enough about the institution of slavery or the slave experience to state with great precision how slaves felt about their condition, it is reasonably clear that slavery, however draconic and well supervised, was not the hermetically sealed monolith—destructive to the majority of slave personalities—that some historians would have us believe. The works of Herbert Aptheker, Kenneth Stampp, Richard Wade, and the Bauers, indicate that slavery, despite its brutality, was not so "closed" that it robbed most of the slaves of their humanity.

It should, nevertheless, be asserted at the outset that blacks could not have survived the grim experience of slavery unscathed. Those historians who, for example, point to the dependency complex which slavery engendered in many Afro-Americans, offer us an important insight into one of the most harmful effects of that institution upon its victims. That slavery caused not a few bondsmen to question their worth as human beings—this much, I believe, we can posit with certitude. What is at issue is not whether American slavery was harmful to slaves but whether, in their struggle to control self-lacerating tendencies, the scales were tipped toward a despair so consuming that most slaves, in time, became reduced to the level of "Sambos."

My thesis, which rests on an examination of folk songs and tales, is that slaves were able to fashion a life style and set of values—an ethos—which prevented them from being imprisoned altogether by the definitions which the

Reprinted from The Massachusetts Review, © 1968 The Massachusetts Review, Inc.

larger society sought to impose. This ethos was an amalgam of Africanisms and New World elements which helped slaves, in Guy Johnson's words, "feel their way along the course of American slavery, enabling them to endure. . . ." In short, I shall contend that the process of dehumanization was not nearly as pervasive as Stanley Elkins would have us believe; that a very large number of slaves, guided by this ethos, were able to maintain their essential humanity.

II

Frederick Douglass, commenting on slave songs, remarked his utter astonishment, on coming to the North, "to find persons who could speak of the singing among slaves as evidence of their contentment and happiness."

> They (spirituals) are the music of an unhappy people, of the children of disappointment; they tell of death and suffering and unvoiced longing toward a truer world, of misty wanderings and hidden ways.

Though few historians have been interested in such wanderings and ways, Frederick Douglass, probably referring to the spirituals, said the songs of slaves represented the sorrows of the slave's heart, serving to relieve the slave "only as an aching heart is relieved by its tears."

Sterling Brown, has observed: "As the best expression of the slave's deepest thoughts and yearnings, they (the spirituals) speak with convincing finality against the legend of contented slavery." Rejecting the formulation that the spirituals are mainly otherworldly, Brown states that though the creators of the spirituals looked toward heaven and "found their triumphs there, they did not blink their eyes to trouble here." . . . these songs, in Brown's opinion, "tell of this life, of 'rollin'' through an unfriendly world!" To substantiate this view, he points to numerous lines from spirituals: "Oh, bye and bye, bye and bye, I'm going to lay down this heavy load"; "My way is cloudy"; "Oh, stand the storm, it won't be long, we'll anchor by and by". To those scholars who "would have us believe that when the Negro sang of freedom, he meant only what the whites meant, namely freedom from sin," Brown rejoins:

> Free individualistic whites on the make in a prospering civilization, nursing the American dream, could well have felt their only bondage to be that of sin, and freedom to be religious salvation. But with the drudgery, the hardships, the auction block, the slave-mart, the shackles, and the lash so literally present in the Negro's experience, it is hard to imagine why for the Negro they would remain figurative. The scholars certainly did not make this clear, but rather take refuge in such dicta as: "the slave never contemplated his low condition."

"Are we to believe," asks Brown, "that the slave singing 'I been rebuked, I been scorned, done had a hard time sho's you bawn,' referred to his being outside the true religion?" Sometimes, in these songs, we hear slaves relating to divinities on terms more West African than American. The easy intimacy and argumentation, which come out of a West African frame of reference, can be heard in "Hold the Wind."

> When I get heaven, gwine be at ease,
> Me and my God *gonna do as we please.*
>
> Gonna chatter with the Father, argue with the Son,
> *Tell um 'bout the world I just come from.* (Italics added.)

If there is a tie with heaven in those lines from "Hold the Wind," there is also a clear indication of dislike for the restrictions imposed by slavery.

If slaves could argue with the son of God, then surely, when on their knees in prayer, they would not hesitate to speak to God of the treatment being received at the hands of their oppressors.

> Talk about me much as you please, (2)
> Chillun, talk about me much as you please,
> Gonna talk about you when I get on my knees.

To be sure, there is a certain ambiguity in the use of the word "chillun" in this context. The reference appears to apply to slaveholders.

The spiritual, *Samson,* as Vincent Harding has pointed out, probably contained much more (for some slaves) than mere Biblical implications. Some who sang these lines from *Samson,* Harding suggests, might well have meant tearing down the ediface of slavery. If so, it was the ante-bellum equivalent of today's "burn baby burn."

> He said, "An' if I had-'n my way,"
> He said, "An' if I had-'n my way,"
> He said, "An' if I had-'n my way, I'd tear the build-in' down!"
>
> He said, "And now I got my way, (3)
> And I'll tear this buildin' down."

Both Harriet Tubman and Frederick Douglass have reported that some of the spirituals carried double meanings. Whether most of the slaves who sang those spirituals could decode them is another matter. It seems to me that slaves, as their folktales make eminently clear, used irony repeatedly, especially with animal stories. Their symbolic world was rich. Indeed, the various masks which many put on were not unrelated to this symbolic process. It seems logical to infer that it would occur to more than a few to seize upon some songs, even though created originally for religious purposes, assign another meaning to certain words, and use these songs for a variety of purposes and situations.

At times slave bards created great poetry as well as great music. One genius among the slaves couched his (and their) desire for freedom in a magnificent line of verse. After God's powerful voice had "Rung through Heaven and down in Hell," he sang, "My dungeon shook and my chains, they fell."

In some spirituals, Alan Lomax has written, Afro-Americans turned sharp irony and "healing laughter" toward heaven, again like their West African ancestors, relating on terms of intimacy with God. In one, the slaves have God engaged in a dialogue with Adam:

"Stole my apples, I believe."
"No, marse Lord, I spec it was Eve."
Of this tale there is no mo'
Eve et the apple and Adam de co'.

Douglass informs us that slaves also sang ironic seculars about the institution of slavery. He reports having heard them sing: "We raise de wheat, dey gib us de corn; We sift de meal, dey gib us de huss; We peel de meat, dey gib us de skin; An dat's de way dey take us in." Slaves would often stand back and see the tragicomic aspects of their situation, sometimes admiring the swiftness of blacks:

Run, nigger, run, de patrollers will ketch you,
Run, nigger run, it's almost day.
Dat nigger run, dat nigger flew;
Dat nigger tore his shirt in two.

In the ante-bellum days, work songs were of crucial import to slaves. As they cleared and cultivated land, piled levees along rivers, piled loads on steamboats, screwed cotton bales into the holds of ships, and cut roads and railroads through forest, mountain, and flat, slaves sang while the white man, armed and standing in the shade, shouted his orders. Through the sense of timing and coordination which characterized work songs well sung, slaves sometimes literally created works of art. These songs not only militated against injuries but enabled the bondsmen to get difficult jobs done more easily by not having to concentrate on the dead level of their work. "In a very real sense the chants of Negro labor," writes Alan Lomax, "may be considered the most profoundly American of all our folk songs, for they were created by our people as they tore at American rock and earth and reshaped it with their bare hands, while rivers of sweat ran down and darkened the dust."

Ol' massa an' ol' missis,
Sittin' in the parlour,
Jus' fig'in' an' a-plannin'
How to work a nigger harder.

Missus in the big house,
Mammy in the yard,
Missus holdin' her white hands,
Mammy workin' hard (3)
Missus holdin' her white hands,
Mammy workin' hard.

Old Marse ridin' all time,
Niggers workin' round,
Marse sleepin' day time,
Niggers diggin' in the ground, (3)
Marse sleepin' day time,
Niggers diggin' in the ground.

Courlander tells us that the substance of the work songs "ranges from the humorous to the sad, from the gentle to the biting, and from the tolerant to the unforgiving." The statement in a given song can be metaphoric, tangent or direct, the meaning personal or impersonal. Pride on their strength rang with the downward thrust of axe—

When I was young and in my prime, (hah!)
Sunk my axe deep every time, (hah!)

Blacks later found their greatest symbol of manhood in John Henry, descendant of Trickster John of slave folk tales:

A man ain't nothing but a man,
But before I'll let that steam driver beat me down
I'll die with my hammer in my hand.

Though Frances Kemble, an appreciative and sensitive listener to work songs, felt that "one or two barbaric chants would make the fortune of an opera," she was on one occasion "displeased not a little" by a self-deprecating song, one which "embodied the opinion that 'twenty-six black girls not make mulatto yellow girl,' and as I told them I did not like it, they have since omitted it." What is pivotal here is not the presence of self-laceration in folklore, but its extent and meaning. While folklore contained some self-hatred, on balance it gives no indication whatever that blacks, as a group, liked or were indifferent to slavery, which is the issue.

To be sure, only the most fugitive of songs sung by slaves contained direct attacks upon the system. Two of these were associated with slave rebellions. The first, possibly written by ex-slave Denmark Vesey himself, was sung by slaves on at least one island off the coast of Charleston, South Carolina, and at meetings convened by Vesey in Charleston. Though obviously not a folk-song, it was sung by the folk.

Hail! all hail! ye Afric clan,
Hail! ye oppressed, ye Afric band,
Who toil and sweat in slavery bound
And when your health and strength are gone
Are left to hunger and to mourn,
Let independence be your aim,
Ever mindful what 'tis worth.
Pledge your bodies for the prize,
Pile them even to the skies!

The second, a popular song derived from a concrete reality, bears the marks of a conscious authority:

> You mought be rich as cream
> And drive you coach and four-horse team,
> But you can't keep de world from moverin' round
> Nor Nat Turner from gainin' ground.
>
> And your name it mought be Caesar sure,
> And got you cannon can shoot a mile or more,
> But you can't keep de world from moverin' round
> Nor Nat Turner from gainin' ground.

The introduction of Denmark Vesey, class leader in the A.M.E. Church, and Nat Turner, slave preacher, serves to remind us that some slaves and ex-slaves were violent as well as humble.

It is also well to recall that the religious David Walker, who had lived close to slavery in North Carolina, and Henry Highland Garnett, ex-slave and Presbyterian minister, produced two of the most inflammatory, and vitriolic, polemics America has yet seen. There was theological tension here, loudly proclaimed, a tension which emanated from and was perpetuated by American slavery and race prejudice. This dimension of ambiguity must be kept in mind, if for no other reason than to place in bolder relief the possibility that a great many slaves and free Afro-Americans could have interpreted Christianity in a way quite different from white Christians.

Even those songs which seemed most otherworldly, those which expressed profound weariness of spirit and even faith in death, through their unmistakable sadness, were accusatory, and God was not their object. If one accepts as a given that some of these appear to be almost wholly escapist, the indictment is no less real. Thomas Wentworth Higginson came across one—". . . a flower of poetry in that dark soil," he called it.

> I'll walk in de graveyard, I'll walk through de graveyard,
> To lay dis body down.
> I'll lie in de grave and stretch out my arms,
> Lay dis body down.

There seems to be small doubt that Christianity contributed in large measure to a spirit of patience which militated against open rebellion among the bondsmen. Yet to overemphasize this point leads one to obscure a no less important reality: Christianity, after being reinterpreted and recast by slave bards, also contributed to that spirit of endurance which powered generations of bondsmen, bringing them to that decisive moment when for the first time a real choice was available to scores of thousands of them.

When that moment came, some slaves who were in a position to decide for themselves did so. W. E. B. DuBois re-created their mood and the atmosphere in which they lived.

There came the slow looming of emancipation. Crowds and armies of the unknown, inscrutable, unfathomable Yankees; cruelty behind and before; rumors of a new slave trade, but slowly, continuously, the wild truth, the bitter truth, the magic truth, came surging through. There was to be a new freedom! And a black nation went tramping after the armies no matter what it suffered; no matter how it was treated, no matter how it died.

The gifted bards, by creating songs with an unmistakable freedom ring, songs which would have been met with swift, brutal repression in the antebellum days, probably voiced the sentiments of all but the most degraded and dehumanized. Perhaps not even the incredulous slavemaster could deny the intent of the new lyrics. "In the wake of the Union Army and in the contraband camps," remarked Sterling Brown, "spirituals of freedom sprang up suddenly. . . . Some celebrated the days of Jubilo: 'O Freedom; O Freedom!' and 'Before I'll be a slave, I'll be buried in my grave!', and 'Go home to my lord and be free.' " And there was: " 'No more driver's lash for me. . . . Many thousand go.' "

DuBois brought together the insights of the poet and historian to get inside the slaves:

There was joy in the South. It rose like perfume—like a prayer. Men stood quivering. Slim dark girls, wild and beautiful with wrinkled hair, wept silently; young women, black, tawny, white, and golden, lifted shivering hands, and old and broken mothers, black and gray, raised great voices and shouted to God across the fields, and up to the rocks and the mountains.

Some sang:

Slavery chain done broke at last, broke at last, broke at last,
Slavery chain done broke at last,
Going to praise God till I die.

I did tell him how I suffer,
In de dungeon and de chain,
And de days I went with head bowed down,
And my broken flesh and pain,
Slavery chain done broke at last, broke at last, broke at last.

Whatever the nature of the shocks generated by the war, among those vibrations felt were some that had come from Afro-American singing ever since the first Africans were forcibly brought to these shores. DuBois was correct when he said that the new freedom song had not come from Africa, but that "the dark throb and beat of that Ancient of Days was in and through it." Thus, the psyches of those who gave rise to and provided widespread support for folk songs had not been reduced to *tabulae rasae* on which a slave-holding society could at pleasure sketch out its wish-fulfillment fantasies.

We have already seen the acute degree to which some slaves realized they were being exploited. Their sense of the injustice of slavery made it so much easier for them to act out their aggression against whites (by engaging in various forms of "day to day" resistance) without being overcome by a sense of guilt, or a feeling of being ill-mannered. To call this nihilistic thrashing about would be as erroneous as to refer to their use of folk lore as esthetic thrashing about. For if they did not regard themselves as the equals of whites in many ways, their folklore indicates that the generality of slaves must have at least felt superior to whites morally. And that, in the context of oppression, could make the difference between a viable human spirit and one crippled by the belief that the interests of the master are those of the slave.

When it is borne in mind that slaves created a large number of extraordinary songs and greatly improved a considerable proportion of the songs of others, it is not at all difficult to believe that they were conscious of the fact that they were leaders in the vital area of art—giving protagonists rather than receiving pawns. And there is some evidence that slaves were aware of the special talent which they brought to music. Higginson has described how reluctantly they sang from hymnals—"even on Sunday"—and how "gladly" they yielded "to the more potent excitement of their own 'spirituals.' " "They soon found," commented Alan Lomax, "that when they sang, the whites recognized their superiority as singers, and listened with respect." He might have added that those antebellum whites who listened probably seldom understood.

What is of pivotal import, however, is that the esthetic realm was the one area in which slaves knew they were not inferior to whites. Small wonder that they borrowed many songs from the larger community, then quickly invested them with their own economy of statement and power of imagery rather than yield to the temptation of merely repeating what they had heard. Since they were essentially group rather than solo performances, the values inherent in and given affirmation by the music served to strengthen bondsmen in a way that solo music could not have done. In a word, slave singing often provided a form of group therapy, a way in which a slave, in concert with others, could fend off some of the debilitating effects of slavery.

The field of inquiry would hardly be complete without some mention of the slave tales. Rich in quantity and often subtle in conception, these tales further illumine the inner world of the bondsmen, disclosing moods and interests almost as various as those found in folksongs. That folk tales, like the songs, indicate an African presence, should not astonish; for the telling of tales, closely related to the African griot's vocation of providing oral histories of families and dynasties, was deeply rooted in West African tradition. Hughes and Bontemps have written that the slaves brought to America the "habit of storytelling as pastime, together with a rich bestiary." Moreover, they point out that the folk tales of slaves "were actually projections of personal experiences and hopes and defeats, in terms of symbols," and that this important dimension of the tales "appears to have gone unnoticed."

Possessing a repertoire which ranged over a great many areas, perhaps the most memorable tales are those of Br'er Rabbit and John. Br'er Rabbit, now trickster, ladies' man and braggart, now wit, joker and glutton, possessed the resourcefulness, despite his size and lack of strength, to outsmart stronger, larger animals. "To the slave in his condition," according to Hughes and Bontemps, "the theme of weakness overcoming strength through cunning proved endlessly fascinating." John, characterized by a spiritual resilience born of an ironic sense of life, was a secular high priest of mischief and guile who delighted in matching wits with Ole Marster, the "patterollers," Ole Missy, and the devil himself. He was clever enough to sense the absurdity of his predicament and that of white people, smart enough to know the limits of his powers and the boundaries of those of the master class. While not always victorious, even on the spacious plane of the imagination, he could hardly be described as a slave with an inferiority complex. And in this regard it is important to note that his varieties of triumphs, though they sometimes included winning freedom, often realistically cluster about ways of coping with evryday negatives of the system.

Slaves were adept in the art of storytelling, as at home in this area as they were in the field of music. But further discussion of the scope of folklore would be uneconomical, for we have already seen a depth and variety of thought among bondsmen which embarrasses stereotypical theories of slave personality. Moreover, it should be clear by now that there are no secure grounds on which to erect the old, painfully constricted "Sambo" structure. For the personalities which lay beneath the plastic exteriors which slaves turned on and off for white people were too manifold to be contained by cheerful, childlike images. Slave folklore, on balance, decisively repudiates the thesis that Negroes *as a group* had internalized "Sambo" traits, committing them, as it were, to psychological marriage.

III

It is one of the curiosities of American historiography that a people who were as productive esthetically as American slaves could be studied as if they had moved in a cultural cyclotron, continually bombarded by devasting, atomizing forces which denuded them of meaningful Africanisms while destroying any and all impulses toward creativity. One historian, for example, has been tempted to wonder how it was ever possible that "*all* this (West African) native resourcefulness and vitality have been brought to such a point of *utter* stultification in America." (Italics added.) This sadly misguided view is, of course, not grounded in any recognition or understanding of the Afro-American dimension of American culture. In any event, there is a great need for students of American slavery to attempt what Gilberto Freyre tried to do for Brazilian civilization—an effort at discovering the contributions of slaves toward the shaping of the Brazilian national character. When such a study has been made of the American slave we shall probably discover that, though he did not rival his Brazilian brother in staging bloody revolutions, the quality and place of art in his life compared favorably. Now this suggests that the humanity of people can be asserted through means other than open and widespread rebellion, a consideration that has not been appreciated in violence-prone America. We would do well to recall the words of F. S. C. Northrop who has observed:

> During the pre-Civil War period shipowners and southern landowners brought to the United States a considerable body of people with a color of skin and cultural values different from those of its other inhabitants. . . . Their values are more emotive, esthetic and intuitive. . . . (These) characteristics can become an asset for our culture. For these are values with respect to which Anglo-American culture is weak.

These values were expressed on the highest level in the folklore of slaves. Through their folklore, black slaves affirmed their humanity and left a lasting imprint on American culture. No study of the institutional aspects of American slavery can be complete, nor can the larger dimensions of slave personality and style be adequately explored, as long as historians continue to avoid that realm in which, as DuBois has said, "the soul of the black slave spoke to man."

In its nearly two and one half centuries of existence, the grim system of American slavery doubtless broke the spirits of uncounted numbers of slaves. Nevertheless, if we look through the prism of folklore, we can see others transcending their plight, appreciating the tragic irony of their condition, then seizing upon and putting to use those aspects of their experience which sustain in the present and renew in the future. We can see them opposing their own angle of vision to that of their oppressor, fashioning their own techniques of defense and aggression in accordance with their own reading of reality and doing those things well enough to avoid having their sense of humanity destroyed.

Slave folklore, then, affirms the existence of a large number of vital, tough-minded human beings who, though severely limited and abused by slavery, had found a way both to endure and preserve their humanity in the face of insuperable odds. What they learned about handling misfortune was not only a major factor in their survival as a people, but many of the lessons learned and esthetic standards established would be used by future generations of Afro-Americans in coping with a hostile world. What a splendid affirmation of the hopes and dreams of their slave ancestors that some of the songs being sung in antebellum days are the ones Afro-Americans are singing in the freedom movement today: "Michael, row the boat ashore"; "Just like a tree planted by the water, I shall not be moved."

Reevaluating the Antebellum Slave Community: A Comparative Perspective

Peter Kolchin

During the 1970s a huge outpouring of revisionist works drastically altered our understanding of antebellum slavery in the Unites States South. Despite differences in approach and emphasis, most of these works shared a common thrust: the accentuation of slave culture and community. Beginning at least in part as an effort to refute Stanley M. Elkin's thesis that southern slavery left its victims depersonalized, docile "Samboes," slavery revisionism soon widened its focus to deal with the slaves' folklore, religion, family lives, community organization, and resistance. Relying heavily on previously little-used black sources such as slave autobiographies, interviews, folktales, and songs, historians came to see southern blacks as subjects in their own right rather than simply as objects of white oppression. A common recognition spread that the slaves' lives were by no means entirely prescribed by their masters. As George P. Rawick puts it, "While from sunup to sundown the American slave worked for another and was harshly exploited, from sundown to sunup he lived for himself and created the behavioral and institutional basis which prevented him from becoming the absolute victim."

A second, subsidiary theme of recent studies has been a comparative approach to slavery and race relations. Beginning in 1946 with Frank Tannenbaum's pathbreaking *Slave and Citizen* and stimulated by Elkin's controversial *Slavery,* an increasing number of scholars realized that slavery was not an institution peculiar to the United States South and turned to compare southern slavery and race relations with those of Latin America and with those of other regions. Through comparison, historians could show developments to have a significance that in isolation might not appear—for example, the unique natural growth of the United States slave population—and could distinguish particular features of specific slave societies from elements common to slavery in

Kolchin, Peter, "Reevaluating the Antebellum Slave Community: A Comparative Perspective," JOURNAL OF AMERICAN HISTORY, 70 (December 1983), 579–601.

general. In the process, they helped rid the study of antebellum slavery of the parochialism that had for so long engulfed it.

Despite its promise, however, the comparative approach to slavery has been less productive than has been the focus on the slave community. The number of comparative studies peaked in the late 1960s and very early 1970s, and diminished sharply thereafter, precisely when community studies were burgeoning. While there are a number of possible explanations for this decline, one of the most striking is the curious difference between the subject matter of most of the comparative works and that of other recent research on slavery: whereas the main focus of slavery research in the 1970s was on the lives of the slaves themselves, the comparative studies dealt largely with the slaveowners, owner ideology, and race relations. With the exception of some attention to demography, little comparative work on the slave experience has appeared. It is almost as if two distinct groups of historians have been working on slavery, largely in isolation from each other; indeed, Eugene D. Genovese is the only major figure with a foot in each camp.

Although comparative historians of slavery have paid relatively little attention to slave culture and community, comparative analysis has much to tell us about the slaves as well as about the masters, and a broader perspective modifies significantly our view of antebellum slave life. What follows is a preliminary effort to show how comparison can shed light on the nature of the antebellum slave community.

Even without the insights offered by comparative analysis, there are grounds for believing that some of the recent studies of antebellum slavery present an exaggerated picture of the strength and cohesion of the slave community. Historians during the 1970s performed an extremely valuable service in destroying the myth that slaves were depersonalized Samboes and in focusing on slaves as actors who helped shape their own world. In doing so, however, they tended increasingly toward celebration and even mystification of slave life. There consequently appears to be a real danger that in rejecting old myths we are in the process of embracing a new one: that of the utopian slave community.

Even the best of the revisionist studies from the 1970s exhibit this celebratory tone. If once it was common to portray slavery as undermining black family ties and as leading to rampant promiscuity, now historians argue that slaves were "not promiscuous but prudish," insist that their sexual morality was healthier than that of straitlaced Victorian whites, and describe families as "a towering source of strength for the slaves." If once historians lamented the psychological damage wrought upon the victims of bondage, now they praise black cultural institutions—religion, family, community, quarters—for protecting blacks from the worst rigors of slavery and for enabling them to lead fulfilling lives apart from and usually unbeknown to their owners. Often this position leads scholars to play down the socioeconomic setting of slavery and, indeed, the work experience of the slaves, as if the slave community somehow flourished outside the institution of slavery. "The social organization of the quarters was the slave's primary environment which gave him his ethical rules and fostered cooperation, mutual assistance, and black solidarity," insists John W. Blassingame, while "the work experiences which most often brought the slave in contact with whites represented his secondary environment and was far less important." Slavery, in short, hardly touched the slave community.

Many of the new works are studded with evocative terms—"solidarity," "community," "kinship ties," "communal consciousness," "culture"—that seem to suggest life as a slave must have been an enviable experience. Thus Thomas L. Webber concludes in a recent study:

> To understand the nature of education in the slave quarter community is to come to grips with the paradox of the "free slave.". . . By passing their unique set of cultural themes from generation to generation, the members of the quarter community were able to resist most of white teaching, set themselves apart from white society, and mold their own cultural norms and group identity. While still legally slaves, the black men, women, and children of the quarter community successfully protected their psychological freedom and celebrated their human dignity.

On the face of it, the revisionist portrait of the slave community seems distorted if not implausible. In reading about it one rarely comes across child abuse, wife beating, and unhappy, or even squalid and mundane, families; one encounters little black cruelty or meanness, few bullies, thieves, and rapists, or just dull, plodding, uninteresting people. Instead, historians trained to be highly skeptical of their sources often accept uncritically the assertions of ex-slaves concerning their previous attitudes and behavior. For example, Paul D. Escott's interesting book *Slavery Remembered* explores slave life on the basis of the Federal Writers' Project interviews conducted during the 1930s. "Many former slaves spoke respectfully of the love that had held their parents close together throughout life," Escott notes, "and indicated that as children they had tried to replicate that devotion and give it to their parents." Given what we know of the world, it is hard to believe that the slave quarters were peopled by men and women quite so loving, cheerful, cooperative, and resourceful as we are told.

Denying or playing down the injury slavery caused its victims is equally questionable. A central feature of virtually every slave autobiography and of many of the slave interviews, for example, is the trauma caused slaves by forced family separations. "No white man ever been in my house," declared an old black women from Virginia in 1937. "Don't 'low it. Dey sole my sister Kate. I saw it wid dese here eyes. Sole her in 1860, and I ain't seed nor heard of her since. Folks say white folks is all right dese days. Maybe dey is, maybe dey isn't. But I can't stand to see 'em. Not on my place." Any treatment of slavery that focuses only on the resilience and successful adaptation of the slaves, rather than also on the pain, brutality, and disruption they suffered, is bound to be one-sided.

Viewing southern slavery from a comparative perspective puts into question an exaggerated emphasis on communal solidarity and felicity. Demographic reality severely limited the potential for autonomous slave life. To begin with, unlike Caribbean slaveholding lands such as Jamaica and St. Domingue, where blacks constituted over 90 percent of the population, and serfholding Russia, where peasants made up about 90 percent of the population, the antebellum South as a whole had a minority of blacks, and even in the Deep South blacks constituted only about half the population. Southern slaves lived, by international standards, on small holdings dispersed among many whites. Three-quarters of all southern slaves were held by owners with fewer than 50 slaves; by contrast, three-quarters of all Jamaican slaves were held in units of over 50, and more than one-third were held in units of over 200. Concentration of serfholding in Russia was even greater: over four-fifths of the serfs had owners with more than 200 serfs. (See table 1.) A wealthy southern planter might own 50 slaves, a wealthy Jamaican several hundred, and a wealthy Russian nobleman several thousand.

Relatively little communal autonomy was possible for slaves on small farms with five or ten slaves, or even on plantations with twenty or thirty. Finding a marriage partner on such a holding, for example, was highly problematical,

Table 1. Distribution of Slaves and Serfs

	Number per Holding	1–49	50–199	200+
American Slaves (1860)				
	Percentage of Total	75.1	22.5	2.4
	Number per Holding	1–50	51–200	201+
Jamaican Slaves (1832)				
	Percentage of Total	24.3	39.6	36.1
	Number per Holding	1–40	41–200	201+
Russian Serfs[a] (1858)				
	Percentage of Total	3.2	15.9	80.9

[a]Data based on estimates of total number of serfs derived from figures on male serfs only.

SOURCES: Lewis Cecil Gray, *History of Agriculture in the Southern United States to 1860* (2 vols., Washington, 1933), I, 530; B. W. Higman, *Slave Population and Economy in Jamaica, 1807–1834* (Cambridge, Eng., 1976), 70; A. Troinitskii, *Krepostnoe naselenie v Rossii, po 10-i narodnoi perepisi [The Serf Population in Russia, according to the 10th National Census]* (St. Petersburg, 1861), 45.

and throughout the South the practice of slaves' marrying others belonging to different owners, although bemoaned by whites, was widespread.

Because they were held in small units, the great majority of American slaves, unlike those in many other countries, were in constant contact with whites. As a consequence they were unable to develop their social institutions in the kind of isolation possible in Russia or in the Caribbean. Southern blacks lived in a largely white world to which in varying degrees they adjusted, accommodated, or protested; Jamaican slaves and Russian serfs lived in overwhelmingly black and peasant worlds in which their owners were the intruders.

This pattern was reinforced by that of slaveowners' residence. Masters in the Caribbean and in Russia frequently lived far from their estates, which were typically run by a hierarchy of administrators. In Russia the tradition of state service, whereby noblemen were expected to spend much of their lives serving the government in either civil or military capacity rendered absenteeism the norm. In Jamaica the masters' cultural predilections had the same effect. Planters typically regarded themselves as Englishmen, not Jamaicans, and yearned to return "home" after even the briefest stint in "the islands."

In the southern United States—and to a lesser extent in northeastern Brazil—the situation was far different. Slaveowners generally resided on their farms and plantations, and they took a personal hand in managing their slaves. Of course, there were exceptions. Most southern slaveowners, large as well as small, lived on their holdings. Equally important was their resident mentality. If Russian and West Indian lords longed for the cosmopolitan life provided by St. Petersburg and London, most southern planters felt torn from their roots when forced to be away from home. When Thomas Jefferson referred to Virginia as "my country," he was expressing a sentiment foreign to a Russian nobleman or a West Indian planter.

As a result of their resident character, southern slaveowners impinged far more than most others on the daily lives of their slaves and showed what some historians have described as "paternalistic" tendencies. The small size of southern holdings enabled masters to know their slaves personally, and, they routinely intervened in their slaves' lives on a daily basis. Such interference was by no means always desirable from the point of view of the slaves. True, southern slaveowners read the Bible to their slaves, gave parties for them, personally nursed the sick, and bombarded the reading public with admonitions to feed, clothe, and house their "people" well. At the same time, however, they meddled constantly in the slaves' lives, scolding, nagging, chiding, punishing, and insisting that blacks were incapable of managing without the loving care and direction of their superiors.

Finally, the antebellum southern slave population was set off from that of most other New World slave societies by its almost totally creole, or native-born, composition. In Brazil and Cuba continuation of the slave trade until the mid-nineteenth century combined with an absence of natural population growth to create a slave body in which African-born blacks predominated. In Jamaica the majority of slaves—and the vast majority of adult slaves—were African-born until after the abolition of the slave trade in 1808, only twenty-five years before emancipation; the same was true in St. Domingue at the time of Toussaint L'Ouverture's revolution. In the United States, however, unique natural population growth resulted in a slave population that was already about four-fifths American-born by the late eighteenth century; after the end of the slave trade in 1808 the number of African-born slaves in the South faded to statistical insignificance. There is no need here to reopen the long-standing debate over "African survivals"; the point is that during the antebellum period southern slaves lacked the large-scale infusions from Africa that might have served to foster separate black cultural forms by reinforcing a cultural continuity with the traditions of their ancestors. (Among Russian serfs, of course, such cultural continuity was made possible by geographic continuity: the serfs were held on their home turf.)

In short, a variety of factors that facilitated the development of autonomous slave life elsewhere were either totally absent or greatly diminished among southern slaves. These factors include slaves' constituting a substantial majority of the population, large plantations, absentee owners, and a high degree of cultural continuity resulting from a preponderance of African-born slaves (or in the case of Russia an even higher degree of cultural continuity resulting from geographic continuity).

Antebellum United States South and other slave societies was not absolute: some of the others lacked one or more of these attributes as well. But only the United States South lacked all of them. The various slave societies can thus be placed on a continuum, with the United States at one end, as a society where conditions severely limited slave autonomy, Russia at the opposite end, as a society whose environment fostered such autonomy, and other slave societies in between. (See table 2.)

The peculiar conditions faced by antebellum slaves affected many aspects of their existence, from family life to material well-being. For present purposes, however, the most important impact was on the independence of the slave community. Compared with bondsmen elsewhere, southern slaves found it difficult to develop an autonomous life and exhibited markedly fewer examples of collective behavior. The relative lack of independence of the antebellum slave community is evident in many areas, but three of the most obvious are economic activities, communal organization, and resistance.

Slaves in many other countries, unlike those in the United States, were economically self-supporting: they raised their own food and sometimes engaged in substantial commercial activity. While many factors helped determine the degree to which slaves could engage in their own economic activity,

Table 2. Conditions Faced by Slaves

	Large Non-white or Peasant Majority	Large Holdings Prevail	Absenteeism Prevails	Cultural Continuity[a]	Score[b]
United States	no	no	no	no	0
Brazil	somewhat	no	somewhat	somewhat	1½
Cuba	no	somewhat	yes	somewhat	2
St. Domingue	yes	yes	yes	somewhat	3½
Jamaica	yes	yes	yes	somewhat	3½
Russia	yes	yes	yes	yes	4

Note: The time frame for each country is the century preceding emancipation.

[a] Resulting either from predominance of African-born slaves (somewhat) or from geographical continuity (yes).
[b] Yes = 1, somewhat = ½, no = 0.

the most basic was their masters' residence: absentee owners found it more convenient to allow their laborers a substantial amount of economic independence than to care for them themselves.

Economic self-sufficiency, wherever it existed, inevitably brought with it considerable communal autonomy. Nowhere was this more the case than among serfs of eighteenth- and nineteenth-century Russia. Although serfs could not legally own any property, by tradition most received from their owners allotments of land that they used to support themselves and increasingly to raise goods for market. Some serfowners, prompted by the nuisance of directing servile labor abandoned seigneurial cultivation entirely, dividing their landholdings among their serfs and, in exchange, requiring payments in cash or kind. A large proportion of their serfs specialized in such handicrafts as woodworking or tailoring, and others received their owners' permission to leave their estates altogether in search of work in nearby towns or on the rivers. More often, noblemen kept some of their land for direct cultivation and distributed the remainder to the serfs for their own support. Thus a dual economy existed in the Russian countryside: ther serfs cultivated their owners' seigneurial land, but they also cultivated their allotted land and were free to use its product as they saw fit.

Many serfowners disliked the independence that this system provided their serfs and insisted that peasants, considered naturally lazy, improvident, and disinclined to work well, needed the supervision provided by steady seigneurial labor. They were powerless to curtail the independence, however, because they were unwilling to commit the only resources that would have enabled them to do so: their own time and effort. Absentee landlords simply could not exercise the kind of supervision necessary to enforce total dependence among their peasants; hence they had little choice but to allow the serfs a substantial degree of local autonomy.

Serfs made their own decisions concerning what to grow on their allotted land, how to cultivate it, and how and where to market it. They played a major—and increasing—role in the development of the rural commercial economy by selling surplus agricultural goods and handicraft items in local fairs and markets throughout the country. An independent serf economy thus inevitably led to independence in many other areas of the bondsmen's life.

Many New World slaves were similarly self-supporting. Although historians of slavery have paid insufficient attention to the slaves' economic activities, enough evidence exists to make clear that self-sufficiency was not a phenomenon that separated serfdom from slavery but, rather, one that distinguished some slave societies from others. As in Russia, both absentee slaveowners and resident owners with an absentee mentality frequently found it easiest to let their laborers fend for themselves. In St. Domingue slaves not only raised their own food on their own time but also produced a surplus for sale at weekly Sunday markets; according to one source, in the years before the Haitian revolution as many as 15,000 slaves brought their produce to Sunday market in the capital city of Cap François.

It was in Jamaica, however, that the economic independence of New World slaves most closely approached that of Russian serfs. Jamaican slaves received from their masters "provision grounds" on which they not only raised their own food without planter supervision but also produced a surplus for market. These provision grounds, which were entirely separate from the house or yard plots immediately adjoining the slaves' huts, were usually located some distance away, frequently in hilly land not needed for sugar production. By custom the slaves enjoyed one-half day on Saturdays in addition to Sundays to work on their crops, which usually included yams, bananas, and plantains. As in Russia, the practice led to the emergence of small-scale slave capitalism: on Sundays slaves sold surplus goods in local markets, which came to play an important role both for the island's economy and for their own well-being. Sometimes they were able to earn a good deal of money. In short, a wide variety of slave societies allowed for the emergence among the slaves of a protopeasantry that enjoyed partial economic independence.

Slaves in the United States came closest to enjoying this kind of economic autonomy on the rice estates of coastal South Carolina and Georgia where, under widespread owner absenteeism and the "task" system of labor, a real although limited "internal" slave economy developed as slaves raised and sold their "own" provisions on their "own" time. Even this limited autonomy, however, was highly atypical in the South as a whole. Away from coastal South Carolina and Georgia, few southern slaves worked under the task system; most had resident owners who strove to keep them in positions of utter dependence.

More significant for most antebellum slaves was the practice followed by many slaveowners of allowing their slaves to have small garden plots, which they could use to supplement the basic allotment of food they received from their masters and even sometimes to produce goods to sell or trade for small luxuries such as tobacco and coffee. Such plots, while important, did not provide the basis for any substantial economic independence, primarily because of their extremely limited scope. Garden plots virtually never provided the entire slave diet or even its core; slaves got their basic rations from their owners and used garden plots, when allowed, in a supplementary capacity. Even so, some owners were convinced that giving slaves patches to cultivate produced in them an excessively independent spirit and flatly refused to do so.

Unlike many slaves elsewhere, therefore, southern slaves were severely limited in their own economic activity and were largely dependent on their masters for their daily sustenance. Planters went to extraordinary lengths to maximize this dependence. James Henry Hammond ordered food on his South Carolina plantation to be distributed weekly; he explained that "because Negroes are improvident with a longer interval between allowances many will consume, waste or barter their provisions before it closes." Many planters, however, felt that even weekly intervals were too long. As one remarked, some slaves would "steal the meat from others" and, like children, some would eat their weekly rations all at once; his solution was to dole out provisions daily and to have a plantation cook prepare everyone's meals properly. Not all planters used cooks to prepare slaves' meals, but many agreed that such a system was preferable to allowing families to cook on their own. As one author explained in an essay entitled "The Health of Negroes," although the slaves "prefer to cook for themselves . . . there are always some negroes on every place who are too careless and indolent to cook their food in a proper manner." Of course, Russian noblemen, too, insisted that their serfs were childlike and irresponsible, but it would not have occurred to them to suggest that they were incapable of preparing their own food, much less to offer to provide it for them.

If southern slaves lacked the economic independence of slaves in many other countries, they also lacked much of the institutional autonomy that this independence was capable of sustaining. The rudimentary nature of communal organization among southern slaves is highlighted by a brief examination of the commune (*obshchina, mir*) that existed among Russian peasants throughout the era of serfdom. A formal organization whose legitimacy was recognized by serfowners and governmental authorities, the commune constituted the local political representation of the peasantry, "the organizing basis of all village life," through which serfs ordered their lives and expressed their needs. While the role and influence of the commune varied considerably everywhere it performed certain essential functions that changed little over the course of the eighteenth century and the first half of the nineteenth. Among the most important of these functions was regulating the serfs' internal economic activity, the independence of the serf commune was thus integrally related to the independence of the serf economy.

Perhaps the most immediately apparent function of the commune was to serve as the lowest level of estate administration. Elected communal officials, headed by the *starosta,* helped maintain order, supervised labor, and handled minor infractions of estate discipline.

In addition to exercising broad authority in village affairs—settling minor disputes among peasants, enforcing family morality, maintaining a reserve of grain and money to help the needy in time of crisis, and selecting recruits to meet government-imposed military levies—the most important regular function of the *mir* was to apportion obligations and land among the serfs. Because absentee owners typically cared little about the internal distribution of work and resources so long as their estates produced the requisite income, they usually assigned labor and money dues, as well as the land for the peasants' plots, to villages or estates collectively and allowed the commune to allocate these on the basis of local conditions. Typically, the commune reallocated land and obligations every few years, applying as a guiding principle the relative ability to pay or to perform labor as determined by family size, income, and any unusual circumstances (such as illness, weddings, or fires). Periodic redistribution of land both prevented extreme pauperization of families and maximized productive use of the land by assigning plots to families on the basis of their ability to cultivate them.

The practice of communal repartition also both reflected and fortified the peasants' collective mentality. "Their" land was held by the whole community rather than by individual families. Not only did periodic redistribution result in most serfs' having widely scattered strips of land; it also meant that any individual parcel might well be assigned to someone else in the future. Critics of the communal system argued that it undermined individual initiative and inhibited development of the concept of private property among the peasantry, but collective landholding, like communal responsibility in general, also reinforced the serfs' sense of solidarity with each other, their recognition that their fate was bound up with that of their fellow villagers.

In the light of the peasant *obshchina,* the absence of any similar communal organization among American slaves is striking. Of course, some slaves did play managerial roles on southern plantations. More numerous were planters with black drivers who were given considerable administrative authority, in some cases serving as virtual overseers.

Nevertheless . . . drivers hardly constituted the equivalent of serf officials. Except in isolated localities or on unusual, experimental plantations, drivers worked under the close supervision of owners and overseers, and lacked the authority to serve the interests of the slaves. Many slaves looked upon drivers not as protectors but as ruthless oppressors. "Ol miss had a nigger o'seer an' dat wuz de meanest debil dat ebber libed," recalled an ex-slave from Alabama, who went on to describe inhuman tortures imposed on his mother and aunt. "I promised mahse'f when I growed up I wuz goin' tuh kill dat nigger."

The slave community, in short, lacked both economic autonomy and an institutional expression. The absence of communal organization did not, of course, preclude the existence of communal sentiment among slaves. It did, however, severely restrict the ability of slaves to express their communal feelings, in the process limiting the collective nature of their life and ultimately of their world view.

No better illustration of the restrictive nature of the antebellum slave community can be found than in the methods slaves used to resist their oppressors. It has been widely noted that slave rebellions within the United States were small-scale affairs compared with those in Haiti, Jamaica, Brazil, and Russia. Although Herbert Aptheker, in the most complete study of the subject to date, asserts that there were at least 250 "revolts and conspiracies in the history of American Negro slavery" involving at least ten slaves, even the biggest of these constituted relatively minor incidents of unrest. Several of the most famous, such as those led by Gabriel Prosser in Virginia in 1800 and Denmark Vesey in South Carolina in 1822, never reached the rebellion stage and were nipped in the bud before any slave violence occurred. Those revolts that did occur were uniformly small, local in scope, and short in duration. Nat Turner's insurrection of 1831, the bloodiest uprising, involved only about seventy slaves and was easily put down by local forces in less than two days.

Organized rebellions in other slave societies sometimes reached massive proportions. In St. Domingue slave insurgents under the leadership of Toussaint L'Ouverture succeeded, after a protracted armed struggle, in defeating their French masters and in establishing the first independent black republic. As the only successful black slave rebellion, the Haitian revolution was admittedly exceptional, but organized armed resistance on a substantial scale was widespread elsewhere. In Russia during the seventeenth and eighteenth centuries, hundreds of thousands of serfs took part in four great "peasant wars," each of which seriously threatened the survival of the tsarist government. In Jamaica substantial rebellions occurred throughout the seventeenth and eighteenth centuries and culminated in the Christmas rising in 1831, just two years before the beginning of emancipation. In Brazil slave rebellions, although less massive than those in Russia and in the Caribbean, were both more frequent and larger than those in the United States South and caused considerably more disruption.

The reasons for the relative weakness of slave rebellions in the antebellum South are not hard to fathom. As Genovese and others point out, "the military and political balance of power" was stacked far more heavily against southern slaves than against those of other major slaveholding powers. Many of the conditions that tipped the balance of power against southern slaves—their numerical disadvantage, their creole composition, their dispersal in relatively small units among resident whites—were precisely the same conditions that limited their communal potential. Whereas Genovese stresses the strength of southern whites as the crucial factor in forestalling slave rebellions, one might equally well consider the relative lack of slave autonomy and the relative weakness of the slaves' collective mentality. Their significance becomes clear if one examines in comparative perspective two forms of resistance that indeed were common among southern slaves: small-scale confrontations with owners or overseers and flight. Such an analysis underlines the fact that the absence of major rebellions in the South indicated not docility on the part of the slaves so much as a largely noncollective pattern of resistance.

The most characteristic form of active protest by Russian serfs might best be labeled a strike. Aggrieved serfs on a given estate would call a communal meeting and decide on some type of collective action designed to remedy the situation. This action might include sending petitions to their owner or to government officials, refusing to recognize the authority of a hated steward, refusing to work for their owner for more than what they regarded as an appropriate amount of time, and in extreme cases refusing to work for their owner at all or to accept his ownership of them. The course of such strikes varied considerably.

Important for present purposes is . . . strikes' collective form. They invariably began with a *mir* gathering in which the assembled serfs voted to pursue a particular course of action. The commune's leaders were expected actively to support the strike—when they did not they sometimes found themselves replaced by new leaders—and to negotiate with representatives of the "other side" in a kind of primitive collective bargaining.

The strike's strength was sustained by the common efforts of the peasants involved, who often showed extraordinary solidarity in defying owners and officials. Authorities attempting to talk the strikers into submission frequently reported to their superiors that the serfs "all in one voice announced that they would not obey" or "all in one voice shouted that they . . . would not submit." Often the peasants collectively interceded to prevent the arrest of strike leaders. In a typical case, when a government official tried to record the names of two strike leaders, "the whole crowd in one voice repeated, 'write us all down, we all speak as one'." To the serfs the legitimacy of their protest stemmed from its origin in the communal gathering.

Similar, though less extensive, strikes occurred among Brazilian slaves. In Ilhéus in 1789, for example, a group of fifty slaves killed their overseer, fled into the surrounding forest, and set up a *mocambo,* or fugitive community, whose representatives negotiated with their former master on the terms under which they would return to his authority.

Antebellum slaves, too, often resisted what they regarded as unfair demands by owners, overseers, and hirers, but their actions were typically those of individuals or of very small groups. Occasionally, it is true, a number of slaves surprised in some forbidden act combined to resist capture or punishment as in the case described by Austin Steward, when twenty-five slaves caught by patrollers in an illicit dance attacked their unfortunate discoverers, killing three and wounding two, while themselves suffering six killed and two wounded. Such acts, however, were almost invariably spontaneous responses to particular circumstances rather than planned and coordinated undertakings. I am not aware of any instance in the entire antebellum South when all the slaves on a plantation got together and decided collectively to defy their owner.

Confrontation in the Old South characteristically took the form of an individual slave's open resistance to plantation authorities. Sometimes such resistance came from one of the "bad niggers" who plagued most large holdings, making trouble for owners, overseers, and even other slaves; many plantations had at least one slave who was widely regarded as unpunishable because of the resistance he would offer to physical chastisement. More often, however, slaves who had previously complied meekly with everything demanded of them suddenly refused when pushed too far to submit to unjust treatment and physically challenged their would-be correctors. Such actions met with varying consequences. Josiah Henson's father, who fought with an overseer assaulting the slave's mother, received one hundred lashes, had his "right ear nailed to the whipping-post, and then severed from the body"; when he became moody he was sold; But terrible retribution was by no means certain; some slaves were able to get away with physically confronting authorities, primarily because taming them was not worth the effort. As Frederick Douglass, who himself had engaged in a prolonged fight with an oppressive hirer, generalized, "he is whipped oftenest, who is whipped easiest." Whatever the consequences of the confrontation, however, the form was almost always that of an individual slave's resisting an individual white authority.

Also typically carried out on an individual basis was the most prevalent single form of slave resistance—flight. Unlike Russian serfs, who often fled in large groups, fugitive southern slaves usually traveled alone or in pairs. With relatively minor exceptions, the most notable of which occurred along the border between Georgia and Spanish Florida in the late eighteenth and early nineteenth centuries, the South saw nothing like the Jamaican maroons or Brazilian *quilombos,* in which hundreds and sometimes thousands of fugitives banded together to form long-lasting exile communities.

The point is not, of course, that American slaves were passive or docile, they certainly were not. But in their resistance to slavery they showed substantially less collective spirit than was evident elsewhere. In this respect, too, the South appears at one end of a spectrum, with Russia at the other end, and with major Latin American slave societies scattered in between. That this is the case should come as no surprise, for as we have seen the same sort of spectrum exists in regard to the conditions faced by the slaves in those countries. These conditions were such as to encourage collective action in Russia, and to a lesser extent in the Caribbean and in Brazil, but to restrict it in the United States South . . . clearly, we cannot deny the existence of communal behavior among southern slaves; to do so would be foolish. Slaves' family ties, religious activities, festivals, dances, and folklore testify to the existence of a vital slave subculture, and revisionist historians have performed yeoman service both in probing this subculture and in demolishing the view of slaves as little more than depersonalized victims. Recently, however, many have tended to push the argument too far by replacing the Sambo myth with one equally untenable—that of the idyllic slave community. It is time to begin the inevitable process of reevaluating the nature and role of the antebellum slave community, both in the light of what we have recently learned about slavery in the United States and through comparison with slavery elsewhere.

Crisis of the 1850s

In 1846 the United States attacked a weak neighbor, Mexico, won an easy military victory, and stripped her of her northern provinces. Fifteen years later, largely as a result of political conflicts aggravated by those acquisitions, the nation went to war again. Only this time it was American against American, Confederate against Unionist, Rebel against Yankee.

The American people have the oldest written Constitution in the world, and for generations displayed an almost uncanny ability to "compromise" away their differences. However, there was one question that proved too vexing for the politicians to dispose of in this customary fashion: slavery. The passions it aroused shattered the second party system and consensus politics, inflamed sectional fears and hates, and climaxed in a violent struggle that destroyed slavery and killed 600,000 men.

As Otis Singletary discusses in the first reading of this section, the early 1840's saw the Republic experience its first surge of imperialist energy known as "Manifest Destiny." The term has since become a label for the whole complex of attitudes, concepts and actions that swept American dominion to the shores of the Pacific Ocean. At the heart of manifest destiny was an exuberant faith in the democratic creed: Americans were a chosen race and their appointed mission was to extend the area of freedom. Thus, in 1846, Americans, animated by feelings of Anglo-Saxon superiority and righteousness were prepared to relieve Mexico of a large measure of her national domain.

Few wars in the nation's brief history have been provoked as ignominiously as the Mexican War. President James K. Polk, caught up in the fervor of national expansionism and the turgid rhetoric of manifest destiny, was determined to establish American hegemony over the entire Southwest. Yet to accomplish this objective, he either had to negotiate for the territory or take it by force from its Mexican rulers. Though Polk, with only a modicum of saber-rattling had been willing to compromise with England on the Oregon question, he showed no such inclinations in his dealings with Mexico. Using the United States annexation of Texas and its claim of the Rio Grande as its southern border, Polk knew that such an assertion would only further insult an already anxious Mexico for having lost Texas in 1836. The President knew that Mexican pride would not allow the humiliating surrender of more territory to the Americans. Believing that might makes right, Polk ordered the United States Army to march to the Rio Grande to reaffirm America's claim to that frontier. When news of a skirmish between Mexican and United States' forces reached the White House, Polk immediately asked Congress for a declaration of war on the grounds that "Mexico has passed the boundary of the United States and shed American blood on American soil."

The conflict that ensued became a major turning point in American history. It was the first foreign war in which American forces triumphed in every engagement, even when overwhelmingly outnumbered. Despite the nation's resounding military victory, it was a morally dubious war—clearly a war of conquest despite excuses to the contrary. Polk shamelessly misrepresented the facts of the situation in order to win Congressional approval for a war of subjugation. Ironically however, the Republic's spectacular victory proved to be the Pandora's Box from which poured the issue that would tear the nation apart—slavery.

In the second article of this section, David Potter explores the dynamics of Southern society shaping the South's attitude toward the Union and eventually leading Southerners to secession and rebellion. Professor Potter raises a most significant question regarding the South's growing sense of alienation in the 1850s. Few Southern leaders had perceived the Union to be anything more than a legal arrangement in which North and South shared little fellow-feeling for one another. If such was the relationship Southerners then asked, why should the South stay in the Union? Indeed, was it safe for the South to remain part of the Union? Southerners had argued for more than a generation that the Union was originally an association of sovereign states, each of which had joined the Confederation voluntarily by ratifying the Constitution. Each state however retained ultimate sovereignty and could thus withdraw from the compact if it felt that their autonomy was being violated. By the 1850s Southern nationalists claimed that the original Union had been subverted and a "consolidated nation" under Northern auspices had been created. Southerners were correct that a more coherent nation was replacing a federation of states. But they were unrealistic in failing to recognize that nations are created not by written agreements and legal contracts but by organic growth.

Southern spokesmen further warned that the North was becoming abolitionized and thus it threatened the slavery system which was not merely a labor system but also a social system basic to the whole of Southern life.

The ideals of Southern life—plantation life, rural society, and bountiful hospitality—the "moonlight and magnolia" myth with its idyllic relationship between master and slave—were all said to be threatened by antithetical

Northern attitudes. The North had begun its defilement of Southern life in 1846 by cheating Southerners of their rights in the territories which they had done more than their share to win. By 1857 the North was refusing to obey a Supreme Court decision; by 1859 it was applauding an attempted slave insurrection; by 1860 it was electing a strictly sectional president who pledged to eliminate slavery. The South must defend itself, said these prophets, now or never.

As Kenneth Stampp observes in the third reading, for three months after Lincoln's election, as the prospects of compromise diminished, it appeared to many Northerners that they had only two alternatives left: to either allow the dissolution of the Union or to go to war to keep it intact. The Northern public, which had grown accustomed to occasional threats of Southern secession, was slow to realize that the crisis had come at last. The victorious Republicans themselves were divided on the issue of secession. Horace Greeley, as staunch an opponent of slavery as any, advised letting "the erring sisters go in peace." Ecstatic at the prospect of at last seeing the nation free of the stigma of slavery, Garrisonian abolitionists seconded Greeley. But Republicans led by Henry Seward and other antislavery factions generally were determined to prevent secession. As strong Unionists they could not contemplate the nation's breakup. Yet what was to prevent it from happening? Could anything stop national dissolution once it began? These were questions Northerners asked themselves during "secession winter" as they searched for remedies that would hopefully prevent not only the Republic's collapse but also the plunging of the nation into a horrible conflict.

The Coming of the War

Otis Singletary

Among the urgent problems demanding the attention of James Knox Polk when he was sworn in as President of the United States on March 4, 1845, was the rapidly deteriorating relationship between his country and the Republic of Mexico over the issue of Texas' annexation. This was altogether fitting, since the new President had had a direct hand in creating the problem. In the recently concluded campaign of 1844, Polk, the Democratic nominee, had placed himself on record as an ardent annexationist and had defeated his Whig opponent, Henry Clay, who unsuccessfully attempted to avoid this controversial issue. The election of Polk, whatever else it might have signified, seemed to the embattled Tyler administration a vindication of its own unhappy attempts to secure Texas by treaty. The discredited Tyler now moved to accomplish as a "lame duck" what had heretofore been denied him, and in the closing hours of his administration his supporters pushed through Congress a joint resolution offering annexation to the Texans. On the eve of Mr. Polk's inauguration, the outgoing President officially transmitted the offer.

Mexican reaction to this move was instantaneous. The long-smoldering resentment of the Mexicans was fanned into open flames, and talk of war with the United States was heard on all sides. In the meantime, official protests were lodged by the Mexican government questioning both the propriety and the legality of the act. To these protests the United States government repeatedly answered that, aside from all questions of national interest, the right to annex the Republic of Texas, which had won its freedom, maintained its independence, and been officially recognized as a member of the family of nations, was a matter solely between the United States and Texas and that the United States therefore felt no obligation to consult with any other power. Such a reply was in no way satisfactory to Mexico, and toward the end of March, 1845, her minister to the United States demanded his passport and

From THE MEXICAN WAR by Otis Singletary, The University of Chicago Press, 1960. Reprinted by permission.

left the country. With the subsequent withdrawal of the American minister to Mexico, the rupture was complete—all diplomatic intercourse between the two nations officially ceased.

As relations between the two countries grew worse, President Polk issued warnings to his military commanders to be prepared for any eventuality. In May, 1845, General Zachary Taylor, the sixty-year-old Indian fighter in command of United States troops in the Southwest, was ordered to hold his forces in readiness, and shortly thereafter the commander of the naval flotilla in Pacific waters, Commodore J. D. Sloat, was instructed to seize ports along the California coast if war should break out. A few weeks later, in response to the angry reaction in Mexico to the annexation of Texas, Polk moved Taylor and his men to Corpus Christi and ordered the navy to assemble the Home Squadron off Mexico ports in the Gulf. Then, in an effort to forestall impending hostilities, the President again resorted to diplomacy. Acting upon the intimated willingness of the Mexican government to receive a representative from this country, Polk dispatched John Slidell as "envoy extraordinary and minister plenipotentiary" to settle outstanding grievances. The mission proved a bootless enterprise, for even as Slidell journeyed southward, pressures within Mexico were brought to bear against the insecure Herrera regime to prevent acceptance of the envoy. Desperately hoping to prevent the fall of his tottering government, José Herrera yielded to the popular clamor and refused to receive Slidell not only on the technical grounds that he had agreed to receive only a "commissioner" but also because acceptance would, in his view, imply the existence of friendly relations between the two countries, which, in turn, could conceivably be misinterpreted as condoning the annexation of Texas. Slidell withdrew to Jalapa to await developments and in March, 1846, was handed his passport.

When on January 12, 1846, word reached Washington of the rejection of Slidell and the refusal of Mexico to negotiate, Polk issued the fateful order that set General Taylor in motion. Secretary of War William L. Marcy instructed Taylor to advance to the Rio Grande and take up a defensive position on the east bank of that stream. The General was expressly cautioned not to treat the Mexicans as an "enemy," but he was also authorized to take "appropriate action" should hostilities occur. On the basis of this order Taylor moved out of Corpus Christi and with his little army of less than four thousand men headed southward, preceded by a proclamation written in Spanish and signed by the General, guaranteeing that all civil and religious rights of the inhabitants would be respected and emphasizing his "friendly intentions."

Taylor's movements created great excitement in Mexico City, and Paredes instantly retaliated by ordering Mexican troops northward with instructions to concentrate at Matamoros. This action did nothing to impede the progress of Taylor, and, although Mexican troops were frequently seen in the distance, the American force marched to within fifty miles of Matamoros before being challenged. As Taylor drew up before the Arroyo Colorado, a shallow stream north of the Rio Grande, Mexican troops in his front made preparations to dispute his crossing. A messenger was sent to the American General informing him that any further advance would be considered an act of "open hostility" and that the Mexicans would open fire upon any American attempting to cross that line. Taylor's reply was simply that he intended to cross the stream and that he would open fire if any interference or opposition was offered.

In the city across the river, Mexican troops were commanded by General Francisco Mejia, an officer who busied himself in constructing batteries when not engaged in exchanging angry words with Taylor. On the eleventh of April, General Pedro Ampudia, veteran of the Alamo and San Jacinto, bringing three thousand reinforcements with him, assumed command in Matamoros and immediately reversed Mejia's essentially passive policy. In a peremptory message to Taylor, Ampudia ordered him to return to Corpus Christi and gave him twenty-four hours in which to break camp, threatening to begin hostilities if his order was not complied with. Taylor answered by stating that he had been ordered to his present position and there he intended to stay and that while he "regretted" the possibility of war, he would not "avoid" it.

At this point, Ampudia was superseded in command by General Mariano Arista, who brought with him additional troops raising the total Mexican forces to approximately eight thousand. Arista assumed command on April 24, 1846, and on the following day sent a sizable cavalry force under Torrejón across the river. Taylor, upon learning of this movement, dispatched a small squadron of dragoons under the command of Captain S. B. Thornton in their direction. Early next morning, the dragoons were surrounded by the Mexicans, and after an unsuccessful attempt to cut their way out they surrendered with the loss of several lives. Here, then, was an overt act of war. No longer could the adversaries pretend that only "irregular forces" were engaged, for Torrejón's attack was carried out by Mexican regulars. As a result of this encounter, General Taylor immediately informed his government that "hostilities may now be considered as commenced" and General Arista was later able to boast: "I had the pleasure of being the first to start the war."

Not until two weeks later did news of the Mexican attack reach Washington. On May 9, after a cabinet meeting in which the issue of war with Mexico had been inconclusively discussed, news of the attack shattered the calm of the capital city. Two days later, the President's war message was read to a tense Congress. The Mexicans, Polk charged, had "shed American blood upon the American soil!" "War exists," he declared, "by the act of Mexico herself." Within two days, both houses of Congress had approved the war bill authorizing the President to accepty fifty thousand volunteers and appropriating ten million dollars for national defense. The war was now official.

Among the claims made and opinions held about the causes of the Mexican War, none has shown more persistence than the glib assertion that the event resulted from the annexation of Texas. This is, of course, gross oversimplification. Annexation was merely the immediate cause of hostilities, the spark that touched off the explosion. Deeper, older, more fundamental causes can be seen in the Mexican resentment which had been created by an aggressive American expansionism, in the hatred engendered in the American heart as a result of Mexican atrocities committed in the barbarous border warfare that had been waged intermittently since the revolt of the Texans, in the almost incredible political instability of the Mexican government, and in the utter failure of diplomacy. All these in one way or another helped set the stage for conflict; annexation was merely the lancing of a festered sore in which a ravaging infection had already done its deadly work.

It would have been hoping for too much to expect Mexico to accept with docility the despoiling of her territory by her land-hungry neighbor. "Manifest Destiny," a euphemism coined by a New York newspaperman for this bumptious expansionism, was a dynamic force in American society, and the penchant of the Yankee for acquiring contiguous territory far antedated the annexation of Texas. Jefferson's purchase of Louisiana, Burr's tangled schemes and impenetrable intrigues, the acquisition of Florida—all were symptoms of the same disease, and long after the guns of the Mexican War were silenced, a rash of filibustering expeditions into Latin America offered irrefutable evidence that the movement had not even then spent its force. By virtue of her geographic proximity to the United States, Mexico was an inevitable target for her acquisitive northern neighbor, and it was only natural that her nationals should be deeply offended by this tendency to absorb her territory. In such a devious way did geography and history conspire to bring on disaster.

This Mexican resentment was, however, a pale thing compared to the hostility many Americans felt toward Mexico, a feeling particularly strong among Texans and their relatives but by no means confined to them. A series of excesses and cruelties running like a red thread through the history of the 1830's and 40's gave rise to this hostility against Mexicans, the intensity of which would be difficult to describe.

Yet another factor which contributed to the necessity of war was the political instability of the Mexican government. The position of any leader was at best precarious because of a pronounced predilection for revolt, a Spanish inheritance highly refined in Mexican experience. While Spain was engaged in a life-or-death struggle with Napoleon, her grip on the Spanish-American colonies loosened. Mexican political history, beginning with the Hidalgo revolt of 1810, was largely the story of a struggle for independence, culminating in the Iturbide revolt of 1821. The result was the establishment of an independent Mexican empire—an unwieldy creation lasting barely three years.

With the overthrow of that empire in 1824, a republic was proclaimed, but this change in form did nothing to increase stability. There followed a kaleidoscopic rise and fall of governments. The first president, Victoria, was overthrown by his subordinate Guerrero, who was, in turn, overthrown within a year by Bustamante. Thus, within the first half-dozen years of its existence, the republic witnessed the overthrow of its first two executives by the very men who had been elected their vice-presidents. Nor did it end here. This fixed pattern continued through the thirties, into the forties, and, indeed, all during the war. Bustamante was duly deposed in 1832 by Santa Anna, who then dominated the political scene until driven from public office in 1837 by his countrymen for concessions made to the Texans following his disastrous defeat in San Jacinto. Into the resulting political vacuum moved several competing factions. Bustamante enjoyed a temporary revival of power which was ended by a revolt led by Paredes in 1841. The ubiquitous Santa Anna, in a dazzling display of political footwork, took advantage of the turmoil again to seize power which he held until his exile in 1844. The vacillating Herrera administration retained office during most of 1845, but in the last month of that year was forced out by Paredes, who thereupon assumed personal direction of the affairs of state which he held until after the outbreak of war. In so fluid a situation, it was, perhaps, inevitable that mere survival would become the paramount concern of every regime.

This political instability explains in part why the twenty years of diplomatic intercourse between the United States and Mexico preceding the annexation of Texas were filled with frustration and failure. In 1825, shortly after the republic was proclaimed, the United States sent its first minister, Joel R. Poinsett, to Mexico. His mission was the extremely delicate one of affirming the boundary which had been agreed upon with Spain in the Adams-Onis Treaty of 1819, an assignment which made him *ipso facto* unpopular with the Mexican people. After Bustamante overturned the Guerrero government in 1829, he demanded, as a token gesture to Mexican nationalism, the recall of Poinsett, who thereupon left the country and was eventually replaced by Anthony Butler. Butler's primary achievements were the negotiation in 1832 of a Treaty of Amity and Commerce and a Treaty of Limits, accomplishments which were unfortunately neutralized by his clumsy maneuvers to obtain Texas through what he described as "the influence of money." His blunders led to his recall in 1835, when Powhatan Ellis was named chargé d'affaires.

It was over the question of Texas, however, that the deepest bitterness was stirred, and so keen was Mexican feeling on this particular issue that by the middle of 1843 the Mexican Minister of Foreign Relations flatly warned our resident minister that war would be inevitable if Texas were annexed, a threat that was reiterated in Washington by the Mexican representative to the United States. Polk's election on an annexation platform in 1844 was looked upon with unconcealed disfavor in Mexico, and, when annexation was finally consummated, all diplomatic relations with the United States were broken off.

Annexation, then, was one, but by no means the sole, cause of war. The bad feelings that had slowly but surely grown out of the encroachments of one power and the brutalities of the other set the stage for war; political instability increased its probability; the failure of diplomacy made it inevitable.

War, even as it was waged in the middle of the last century, is a vast and complicated enterprise severely taxing the energy and the imagination of those engaged in it. Any nation that hopes to prosecute a war successfully, as indeed warring nations generally do, must face and somehow find solutions for such diverse problems as maintaining unity in support of the war, making correct assumptions about its own power and the relative power of the opposition, organizing and training the necessary military forces, and providing the means, ultimately, for delivering a crushing blow to the enemy. War makes great demands upon a nation, and its eventual outcome is in large measure dependent upon the vision and industry that has gone into the making of basic plans and preparations. Seldom in history have two nations gone to war with such cavalier disregard for realities as did the United States and Mexico in 1846. Indifferent to the staggering problems that faced them, innocent of having conceived even the most elementary plan of campaign, wholly unprepared, each country entered the conflict with an enormously exaggerated view of its own strength and with a feeling of contempt for the other.

In Mexico, there was widespread belief, even as war moved closer, that the United States would not willingly fight. This consoling view, long and lovingly held by many important Mexicans, was supported by an imposing array of arguments, chief among them being the well-known military weakness of the United States, the vulnerability of American shipping, the immorality and injustice of such a war, and the internal dissensions over slavery and tariff which made any kind of unity seemingly impossible. And even should an awareness of these handicaps fail to restrain the United States, there were reassuring indications that in any war between the two nations, Mexico would enjoy tremendous advantages. For one thing, her armed forces appeared to be in superb condition. Her artillerymen and European-trained engineers were highly regarded in military circles and her numerous infantry units were officered by the flower of Mexican society. The cavalry, most popular of all Mexican military forces, numbered in its ranks horsemen who yielded to none in skill and grace. These impressive forces were further blessed by the advantages which always accrue to the defensive power: interior lines, the use of fortifications, thorough knowledge of the terrain, and general control of time and place of battle.

The international situation, as interpreted by the Mexicans, also buttressed their faith in Mexico's superiority should war come. It was commonly

believed in Mexico that European intervention and support would be immediately forthcoming in case of war. This belief was based upon the assumption
that the fear and jealousy which European powers, especially England and
France, felt toward the United States would leave them no alternative. These
various beliefs combined to produce in the Mexican mind a feeling of security,
even of smugness, as the threat of war grew daily more serious.

It soon became obvious, however, that the Mexicans greatly overrated their
advantages. Disunited, torn with factionalism, rotten with corruption and
nearly bankrupt, the government of Mexico proved unequal to the huge tasks
imposed by war. Her vaunted military machine was vastly overrated. The in-
effectiveness of the artillery was appalling, and the cavalry proved too light
to absorb the bruising shock of the charges hurled against it. Indeed, the entire
army was vitiated by the flaws inherent in the Mexican military system, a
system properly belonging to the eighteenth century, when aristocratic officers
commanded soldiers from the depressed classes. The infantry, recruited from
the offscourings of society, was commanded by men who frequently were ignorant of the military profession, incompetents who held their positions through
favor or intrigue or both. Everywhere there was a shortage of arms and equipment, and there was no industrial plant in Mexico capable of producing them.
Mexican seapower, furthermore, was a fiction.

Equally serious were the misconceptions being circulated north of the Rio
Grande. The American people have historically been overconfident of victory,
and the Mexican War was no exception to this tradition. The careless contempt of the Anglo-Saxon for "inferiors," sharpened by revulsion against
Mexican brutalities and reinforced by an unfaltering belief in the superiority
of his own military prowess, made it easy for the average American to accept
the popular assertion that one great thrust was all that would be required to
end the war. There was, of course, little basis for such easy optimism. Though
few Americans were willing to face them, the problems of waging offensive
war against Mexico were staggering. The great distances involved, the rugged
and forbidding mountain ranges, the problem of subsisting an army on arid
desert terrain, and the ever present danger of attack by that most deadly and
dependable of Mexican allies, yellow fever, presented difficulties of no small
dimensions. Then, too, the obvious lack of national unity was bound to have
an adverse effect on the war effort. The most determined opposition came from
New England abolitionists who saw in the war a gigantic and devious plot to
insure the spread of slavery, but there was also a noticeable lack of enthusiasm
on the part of influential members of the Whig party who disliked Mr. Tyler
and distrusted his successor. After an initial wave of enthusiasm, opposition
to the administration began to coalesce, and the charge was frequently repeated that there had, in reality, not been sufficient provocation for such extreme action. This opposition, further disgruntled by the onerous taxes that
were levied, began openly and unreservedly to condemn the causes, conduct,
and consequences of what was fashionably referred to as "Mr. Polk's War."

Another obstacle to successful prosecution of the war was the lack of co-ordination between foreign policy and military policy. Few nations have equaled the United States in so recklessly inviting destruction by ignoring the need for some semblance of balance in this important area. In the 1830's and 40's we were pursuing a most aggressive foreign policy with regard to both Texas and Oregon. Such a course by its very nature entailed great risks. Yet at the same time, when our foreign policy threatened to embroil us not in one but quite possibly in two wars, we were pursuing a casual, weak, even negligent military policy. At a moment when war with England and/or Mexico was imminent, the United States had less than seven thousand men under arms. When war finally came, Congress was busily engaged in a debate over whether or not the military academy at West Point should be abolished! This schism in national policy could have but one result. Consequently, in spite of United States superiority in naval power and industrial capacity, our military prospects were far from encouraging. The small regular force, in which over a third of the soldiers were foreign-born, was wholly inadequate. Except for Indian campaigns, there had been no war since 1812, and the troops, having served most of their time in scattered frontier garrisons, were unacquainted with the intricacies of military maneuver.

Thus, the two nations drifted into war. Mexico, for her part, entered the struggle heavily laden with burdens of her own creation. Even before her troops crossed the Rio Grande, she had been made vulnerable by virtue of having underestimated the power of her adversary, of having seriously miscalculated her own strength and having completely misread the international scene. The United States, on the other hand, apparently oblivious to the inadequacy of her military force, unperturbed by the serious threat of internal division and indifferent to the calamitous effects of a disjointed policy, entered lightly into the war with scarcely a thought of the monumental problems involved.

Washington in the spring of 1846 was the scene of feverish activity as the Polk administration hastily and belatedly, began to make plans for the war which had just been officially declared. If American military history taught no other lesson, it would still be worth studying because it so clearly underscores the fact that we are a people upon whom the gods have smiled. How else can the remarkable fact be explained that we have so often escaped the destruction which our own blunders and stupidities seemed to invite? Fully half a dozen times in our history we have gone into a war for which we were totally unprepared—each time managing to survive while hastily forging a military machine and, miraculously enough, each time attaining victory. The Mexican War was yet another example of the national preference for a policy of "hurry up and catch up."

During the week following receipt of the news of the outbreak of hostilities, the administration in Washington was steeped in planning. Faced suddenly with the ugly reality of war, the President and his cabinet members were forced to give immediate consideration to such urgent needs as selecting a strategic plan, raising the necessary manpower, and performing the other countless chores essential to victory.

With the aid of General Winfield Scott, Polk and his advisers speedily decided upon a plan of operation involving both invasion and blockade. Two overland routes were selected: one toward Monterrey, Saltillo, San Luis Potosí, and central Mexico and the other westward into New Mexico, Chihuahua, and California. Both movements were hastily conceived, and very little thought was given to such important matters as the condition of roads, the availability of water, or transportation and supplies for the army. Simultaneously, orders were issued by the Navy Department to blockade Veracruz and other ports in the Gulf of Mexico.

Having made these basic decisions, attention was next focused on the problem of raising troops. Based on an estimation that, in addition to the regular army, 25,000 men were needed immediately, steps were taken to fill these billets by means of federal requisitions on the states. Because of their proximity to the enemy, the states in the south and southwest were called upon to provide the 25,000 urgently needed troops. A quota of 40,000 troops was levied among the rest of the states with the understanding that these would be made available for duty when the government should require their services. The twelve-month enlistment of volunteers was in keeping with the widespread optimism that the war would be over in a relatively short time.

Perhaps the most far-fetched and certainly the most ridiculous scheme hatched by the planners in Washington was their attempt to secure peace with Mexico by conniving to restore Santa Anna to power. The General's erratic political career had once again been interrupted when in 1844 he was deposed and subsequently banished. His exile was spent in Havana, where for eighteen months he divided his time betwen two favorite Latin pastimes, cockfighting and political intrigue. President Polk had several reasons for thinking that Santa Anna's restoration might mean the return of peace—not the least among them being the assurances of a confidant of the General to that effect. At any rate, in an effort to facilitate Santa Anna's return, Polk asked his Secretary of the Navy, George Bancroft, to notify the American naval commander in the Gulf that if the General made any attempt to enter a Mexican port, he was to be allowed to "pass freely." Shortly thereafter, an emissary, Alexander Slidell Mackenzie, a naval officer who had attained notoriety in 1842 for having hanged the son of the Secretary of War for an attempted mutiny aboard Mackenzie's ship, the "Somers," was dispatched from Washington. Mackenzie, who spoke Spanish fluently, journeyed to Cuba ostensibly to investigate a report that privateers were being outfitted there. Nevertheless, he conveniently found time for a lengthy visit with the exiled Mexican leader.

Santa Anna evidently played his cards extremely well, for Polk remained unshaken in his faith in the soundness of this plan. The overthrow of Paredes early in August, 1846, was the signal Santa Anna had been awaiting, and on the sixteenth he made a triumphant entry into Mexico, landing at Veracruz without hindrance from United States naval forces. Within a month Santa Anna was once again given command of the Mexican army, a position from which he moved with energy to organize and train a force to defeat the advancing North Americans. Whatever results President Polk might have been expecting, there is no escaping the ironic fact that his ultimate achievement was to have aided in placing in command of the enemy's army the most competent soldier in their service. The price for this amateurish dabbling was soon paid in American lives on the battlefield at Buena Vista and in numerous bloody encounters fought along the road to Mexico City.

The Nature of Southern Separatism

David Potter

Ten days after the election of Lincoln, the Augusta, Georgia, *Daily Constitutionalist* published an editorial reflecting on what had happened to American nationalism:

> The most inveterate and sanguine Unionist in Georgia, if he is an observant man, must read, in the signs of the times, the hopelessness of the Union cause, and the feebleness of the Union sentiment in this State. The differences between North and South have been growing more marked for years, and the mutual repulsion more radical, until not a single sympathy is left between the dominant influences in each section. Not even the banner of the stars and stripes excites the same thrill of patriotic emotion, alike in the heart of the northern Republican and the southern Secessionist. The former looks upon that flag as blurred by the stain of African slavery, for which he feels responsible as long as that flag waves over it, and that it is his duty to humanity and religion to obliterate the stigma. The latter looks upon it as the emblem of a gigantic power, soon to pass into the hands of that sworn enemy, and knows that African slavery, though panoplied by the Federal Constitution, is doomed to a war of extermination. All the powers of a Government which has so long sheltered it will be turned to its destruction. The only hope for its preservation, therefore, is out of the Union. A few more years of unquiet peace may be spared to it, because Black Republicans cannot yet get full possession of every department of the Government. But this affords to the South no reason for a moment's delay in seeking new guards for its future safety.

When the *Constitutionalist* declared that not a single sympathy was left between the two sections, it exaggerated the degree to which Unionism had been eroded. The tenacity with which Maryland, Virginia, North Carolina, Kentucky, Tennessee, Missouri, and Arkansas clung to the Union during the next five months proved that Unionism retained much vigor. The great body

Abridgement of "The Nature of Southern Separatism" from THE IMPENDING CRISIS 1848–1861 by David M. Potter. Compiled and Edited by Don E. Fehrenbacher. Copyright © 1976 by Estate of David M. Potter. Reprinted by permission of Harper & Row, Publishers, Inc.

of Americans, in both the North and the South, still cherished their images of a republic to which they could respond with patriotic devotion, and in this sense American nationalism remained very much alive—so much alive, in fact, that it was able to revitalize itself speedily after four years of devastating war. But though they cherished the image, the sectional conflict had neutralized their many affinities, causing antislavery men to depreciate the value of a Union which was flawed by slavery, and causing men in the slaveholding states to give the defense of the slave system such a high priority that they could no longer offer loyalty to a Union which seemed to threaten that system. As these forces of repulsion between North and South came into play, the southern states were, at the same time, drawn closer together by their common commitment to the slave system and their sense of need for mutual defense against a hostile antislavery majority. Southern separatism had been developing for several decades, and now it was about to end in the formation of the Confederate States of America. Historians have spoken of this separatism as "southern nationalism," and of the Confederacy as a "nation." Yet it is clear that much of the old devotion to the Union still survived among many citizens throughout the South and even dominated the action of some southern states until they found themselves forced to fight on one side or the other. Therefore, one must ask: What was the nature of southern separatism? What was the degree of cohesion within the South on the eve of the Civil War? Had the cultural homogeneity of the southern people, their awareness of shared values, and their regional loyalty reached the point of resembling the characteristics of nationalism? Were they drawn together by a sense of separate destiny which required separate nationhood, or were they rather impelled to united action by their common fears of forces that seemed to threaten the foundations of their society?

The problem of the South in 1860 was not a simple one of southern nationalism versus American nationalism, but rather one of two loyalties coexisting at the same time—loyalty to the South and loyalty to the Union. Because these loyalties were soon to be brought into conflict, they have often been categorized as "conflicting loyalties," with the implication that if a person has two political loyalties they are bound to conflict, that one of the two must be illegitimate, and that a right-minded person would no more maintain two loyalties then he would commit bigamy. But in fact, strong regional loyalties exist within many nations, and they existed in the United States in other areas besides the South. There was nothing inherently incompatible between regional loyalties and national loyalties as long as they could both be aligned in a pattern in which they remained congruent with one another instead of being at cross-purposes with one another. Any region which had enough power in the federal government could always prevent federal policy and regional policy from coming into any sort of major collision. But the South, by 1860, no longer had such power, or at least no longer had confidence of maintaining such power.

Thus the loyalties of southerners became "conflicting loyalties," not necessarily because they loved the Union less but because they had lost the crucial
power to keep them from conflicting.

But what were the factors of affinity making for cohesion within the South
in 1860, and what were the factors of repulsion between the South and the
rest of the Union which gave negative reinforcement to southern unity?

The vast and varied region extending from the Mason-Dixon line to the
Rio Grande and from the Ozarks to the Florida Keys certainly did not constitute a unity, either physiographic or cultural. But the whole area lay within
what may be called the gravitational field of an agricultural economy spe-
cializing in staple crops for which plantations had proved to be effective units
of production and for which Negro slaves had become the most important
source of labor. This, of course, did not mean that all white southerners engaged in plantation agriculture and owned slaves—indeed only a small but
very influential minority did so. It did not even mean that all of the states were
heavy producers of staple crops, for the cotton states were only in the lower
South. But it did mean that the economy of all of these states was tied, sometimes in secondary or tertiary ways, to a system of plantation agriculture.

Agricultural societies tend to be conservative and orthodox, with strong
emphasis on kinship ties and on the observance of established customs. If land
is held in great estates, such societies tend to be hierarchical and deferential.
Thus, even without slavery, the southern states would have shared certain attributes to a high degree. But the presence of slavery had dictated conditions
of its own, and these too were shared very widely throughout the South. Indeed
they became the criteria for determining what constituted the South.

A slave system, since it means the involuntary subordination of a significant part of the population, requires a social apparatus distinctively adapted
in all its parts to imposing and to maintaining such subordination. In the South,
this subordination was also racial, involving not only the control of slaves by
their masters but also the control of a population of 4 million blacks by 8
million whites. Such a system cannot be maintained simply by putting laws
on the statute books and making formal records that one individual has acquired legal ownership of another. It is axiomatic that the enslaved will tend
to resist their servitude and that the slaveowners must devise effective, practical means of control. The first requisite is that the system shall be able to
deal with the contigency of insurrection. This alters the priorities, for though
the system of subordination may have originated as a means to an end—to
assure a permanent labor supply for the cultivation of the staple crops—the
immediacy of the hazard of insurrection soon makes the subordination of the
slaves an end in itself. This was what Thomas Jefferson meant when he said,
"We have a wolf by the ears."

From the time of Spartacus, all slaveholding societies had lived with the danger of slave revolt. But for the South, no reminders from antiquity were needed. On the island of Santo Domingo, between 1791 and 1804, black insurrectionists under a series of leaders including Toussaint L'Ouverture and Jean Jacques Dessalines had risen in revolt, virtually exterminating the entire white population of the island and committing frightful atrocities, such as burying people alive and sawing them in two. Survivors had fled to New Orleans, Norfolk, and other places in the United States, and southerners could hear from their own lips the stories of their ordeal. Santo Domingo lived as a nightmare in the mind of the South. Within the South itself, of course, there were also revolts or attempted revolts. Gabriel Prosser led one at Richmond in 1800. Some sort of conspiracy under the leadership of Denmark Vesey apparently came near to hatching at Charleston in 1822. Nat Turner led his famous insurrection in Southhampton County, Virginia, in 1831. All of these were negligible compared with Santo Domingo or even with revolts in Brazil, but, each one hit an exposed nerve in the southern psyche. Also there were local disturbances. Altogether, one historian has collected more than two hundred instances of "revolts," and while there is reason to believe that some of these were wholly imaginary and that many others did not amount to much, still every one is a proof of the reality of southern apprehensions if not of the actual prevalence of the danger. On isolated plantations, and in districts where blacks heavily outnumbered whites, the peril seemed a constant one. Every sign of restlessness in the slave quarters, every stranger seen along a lonely road, every withdrawn or cryptic look on a slave face, even the omission of some customary gesture of deference, might be the forewarning of nameless horrors lurking just beneath the placid surface of life.

The concern about antislavery propaganda as a potential cause of slave unrest explains in part why white southerners seemed so oblivious to the great difference between the moderate attitude of an "ultimate extinctionist" like Lincoln and the flaming abolitionism of an "immediatist" like Garrison. When southerners thought of extinction it was in terms of Santo Domingo and not in terms of a gradualist reform to be completed, maybe, in the twentieth century. From their standpoint, the election to the presidency of a man who stated flatly that slavery was morally wrong might have a more inciting effect upon the slaves than denunciatory rhetoric from the editor of an abolitionist weekly in Boston.

Since the determination to keep blacks in subordination took priority over other goals of southern society, the entire socio-economic system had to be conducted in a way that would maximize the effectiveness of racial control. This went far beyond the adoption of slave codes and the establishment of night patrols in times of alarm. It meant also that the entire structure of society must be congruent with the objective, and no institutional arrangements should be countenanced which would weaken control. The blacks should live on plantations not only because plantations were efficient units for cotton production, but because in an era prior to electronic and bureaucratic surveillance, the plantation was a notably effective unit of supervision and control. Also, it provided maximum isolation from potentially subversive strangers. Slaves should be illiterate, unskilled, rural workers not only because the cotton economy needed unskilled rural workers for tasks in which literacy would not increase their usefulness, but also because unskilled rural workers were limited in their access to unsupervised contacts with strangers, and because the illiterate could neither read seditious literature nor exchange surreptitious written communication. In fact, the conditions of employment in the cotton culture seemed to fit the needs of a slave system as neatly as the conditions of slavery fitted the needs of employment in the cotton culture, and if cotton fastened slavery upon the South, it is also true that slavery fastened cotton upon the South.

By 1860, southern society had arrived at the full development of a plantation-oriented, slaveholding system with conservative values, hierarchical relationships, and authoritarian controls. No society is complete, of course, without an ethos appropriate to its social arrangements, and the South had developed one, beginning with a conviction of the superior virtues of rural life. At one level, this conviction embodied a Jeffersonian agrarianism which regarded landowning cultivators of the soil as the best kind of citizens, because their landownership and their production for use gave them self-sufficiency and independence, uncorrupted by commercial avarice—and also because their labor had dignity and diversity suitable to well-rounded men. But at another level, the commitment to rural values had led to a glorification of plantation life, in which even slavery was idealized by the argument that the dependence of the slave developed in the master a sense of responsibility for the welfare of the slaves and in the slaves a sense of loyalty and attachment to the master. This relationship, southerners argued, was far better than the impersonal, dehumanized irresponsibility of "wage slavery," which treated labor as a commodity.

From an idyllic image of slavery and plantation conditions, it was but a short step to the creation of a similar image of the planter as a man of distinctive qualities. Thus, the plantation virtues of magnanimity, hospitality, personal courage, and loyalty to men rather than to ideas held a social premium, and even the plantation vices of arrogance, quick temper, and self-indulgence were regarded with tolerance. From materials such as these, in an era of uninhibited romanticism and sentimentality, the southern upper class built a fully elaborated cult of chivalry, inspired by the novels of Sir Walter Scott and including tournaments, castellated architecture, a code of honor, and the enshrinement of women. Thus, with a mixture of self-deception and idealism, the South adopted an image of itself which some men used as a fiction to avoid confronting sordid reality, while others used it as a standard toward which to strive in order to develop, as far as they were able, the better aspects of human behavior that were latent even in a slaveholding society.

One other belief shared by the men of the South in 1860 was especially important because they felt just uncertain and insecure enough about it to be almost obsessively insistent and aggressive in asserting it. This was the doctrine of the inherent superiority of whites over Negroes. The idea was not distinctively southern, but it did have a distinctive significance in the South, for it served to rationalize slavery and also to unite slaveholders and nonslaveholders in defense of the institution as a system, primarily, of racial subordination, in which all members of the dominant race had the same stake.

This racial prejudice against Negroes cannot, of course, be dismissed as nothing but a rationalization to justify their subordination of the blacks, for in fact it was in part just such prejudice which had originally made blacks and Indians subject to enslavement, while servants of other races were not. Initially, the prejudice may have stemmed from the superiority which technologically advanced societies feel over less advanced societies; it may have reflected something of the attitude of Christians toward the "heathen"; it may have reflected the universal antagonism of in-groups and out-groups or the universal distrust of the unfamiliar. In these aspects, prejudice may even be regarded as a relatively innocent form of ethnocentrism, uncorrupted by consideration of self-interest. But once it became firmly tied to slavery, prejudice began to have certain functional uses which added immeasurably both to the strength of slavery and also to its brutalizing quality. Racial prejudice and slavery together created a vicious circle in which the assumed inferiority of the blacks was used as justification for their enslavement, and then their subordination as slaves was used to justify the belief that they were inferior. The stigma of race increased the degradation of slavery, and servile status, in turn, reinforced the stigma of race.

Doctrines of race not only served to minimize the potentially serious economic divisions between slaveholders and nonslaveholders, but also furnished southerners with a way to avoid confronting an intolerable paradox: that they were committed to human equality in principle but to human servitude in practice. The paradox was a genuine one, not a case of hypocrisy, for though southerners were more prone to accept social hierarchy than men of other regions, still they responded very positively to the ideal of equality as exemplified by Jefferson of Virginia and Jackson of Tennessee. In their politics, they had moved steadily toward democratic practices for whites, and in fact it was argued, with a certain plausibility, that the system of slavery made for a greater degree of democracy within that part of the society which was free, just as it had made for democracy among the freemen of ancient, slaveholding Athens. Still, this only made the paradox more glaringly evident, and no doubt it was partly because of the psychological stress arising from their awareness of the paradox that southern leaders of the late eighteenth and early nineteenth centuries had played with the idea of some day eliminating slavery. That was, in part, why the South had acceded to the exclusion of slavery from the Northwest Territory in 1787 and to the abolition of the African slave trade in 1808. It was why a limited number of southerners had emancipated their slaves, especially during the half-century after the Declaration of Independence, and why a greater number had indulged themselves in a rhetoric which deplored slavery without exactly condemning it. Some had even joined antislavery societies, and southerners had taken the lead in emancipating slaves and colonizing them in Liberia. Thus, for a generation, the great paradox had been masked by the vague and pious notion that at some remote future, in the fullness of time and God's infinite wisdom, slavery would pass away.

With the theory of race thus firmly linked to the theory of slavery, the belief in Negro inferiority was as functional and advantageous psychologically as slavery itself was economically. The belief could be used to justify a certain amount of ill treatment of the blacks and even hostility toward them, since, lacking full humanity, they did not deserve fully human treatment and might justifiably be despised for their inherent deficiencies. By maintaining slavery, the South had violated its own ideal of equality, but by adopting racist doctrine it had both perverted and rejected the ideal, as the only way, other than emancipation, to escape from their dilemma.

All these shared institutions, practices, attitudes, values, and beliefs gave to southern society a degree of homogeneity and to southerners a sense of kinship. But a sense of kinship is one thing, and an impulse toward political unity is another. If one searches for explicit evidence of efforts to unify the South politically because of cultural homogeneity, common values, and other positive influences, rather than as a common negative response to the North, one finds relatively little of it.

Yet any separatist movement in the middle of the nineteenth century could scarcely fail to absorb some of the romantic nationalism that pervaded the Western world. At the Nashville convention in 1850, Langdon Cheves of South Carolina had appealed to all the slaveholding staes, "Unite, and you shall form one of the most splendid empires in which the sun ever shone, one of the most homogeneous populations, all of the same blood and lineage [note that to Cheves the black population was invisible], a soil the most fruitful and a climate the most lovely." At about the same time, another South Carolinian had declared that as long as the South was in the Union, it occupied a false and dangerous position as "a nation within a nation."

Even when men in the southern states saw their political destiny as being outside the American union, they did not necessarily visualize a southern republic as the alternative. In 1832, John Pendleton Kennedy declared, "Virginia has the sentiments and opinions of an independent nation," but he meant independence of the Gulf Coast states as well as the Yankees. Twenty-eight years later, Kennedy denounced South Carolina's secession as "a great act of supreme folly and injustice passed by a set of men who have inflamed the passions of the people."

The "set of men" whom Kennedy denounced as inflaming the passions of the people might have included at least four well-known southern figures. Two of these, Edmund Ruffin of Virginia and William Lowndes Yancey, might well be labeled southern nationalists, for they both had the vision of a South united by shared distinctive qualities, and both seemed to care more for the South as a whole than for their own states. The other two, Robert Barnwell Rhett of South Carolina and James D. B. De Bow of Lousiana, were also major actors in the secession movement, but for them a united South was primarily an alliance against the North. If nationalism means something more than bitterness against another country, it would be difficult to show that Rhett and De Bow were southern nationalists.

The southern commercial conventions provided perhaps the best opportunities to coordinate the impulses of southern nationalism. At first, they had carefully disavowed any spirit of sectional antagonism, even toasting the North and proclaiming a purpose to emulate the enterprise of their northern brothers. But at Charleston in 1854, Albert Pike of Arkansas advocated a program of southern joint action in the form of a corporation, chartered and financed by the fifteen slave states collectively, to build a Pacific railroad by the southern route. Pike also introduced overtly, perhaps for the first time at any of these conventions, the theme of disunion. The South, he said, should seek equality with the North within the Union, but if the South "were forced into an inferior status, she would be better out of the Union than in it." The following year at New Orleans, one delegate proposed the reopening of the African slave trade, another complained that the monopoly of northern textbooks in southern schools made for an education that was "unsouthern," and the St. Louis *Democrat* denounced the convention as disunionist. At Richmond in 1856, a toast was offered which for the first time defined the boundaries of a prospective southern republic: "on the North by the Mason-Dixon line, and on the South by the Isthmus of Tehuantepec, including Cuba and all other lands on our Southern shore which threaten Africanization."

Since nationalism is frequently as much a negative phenomenon as a positive one, it does not disprove the reality of southern nationalism to say that the southern movement arose primarily from antagonism to the North. Yet one is left with a feeling that the South did not want a separate destiny so much as it wanted recognition of the merits of southern society and security for the slave system, and that all the cultural ingredients of southern nationalism would have had very little weight if that recognition and that security had been forthcoming. Southern nationalism was born of resentment and not of a sense of separate cultural identity. But the cultural dissimilarities of North and South were significant enough to turn a campaign for the protection of southern interests into a movement with a strong color of nationalism. This does not mean that there was *never* a deeply felt southern nationalism. There was. But it resulted from the shared sacrifices, the shared efforts, and the shared defeat (which is often more unifying than victory) of the Civil War. The Civil War did far more to produce a southern nationalism which flourished in the cult of the Lost Cause than southern nationalism did to produce the war.

Even the manifestoes of the self-appointed custodians of southernism do not reflect the impulse to fulfill the unique potentialities of a unique society. Their complaint was not that the Union inhibited a robust but repressed culture struggling to be born, but rather that their cultural dependence upon the Yankees was humiliating. Why must southern children study textbooks written and published in the North, and incompatible with southern values? Why must southern readers subscribe to northern magazines instead of supporting southern journals which published southern authors? The frequency and the plaintiveness of this question is evidence of the rather self-conscious literary irredentism of a very small number of southern writers, but it also affords striking proof of the lack of cultural self-consciousness on the part of a large number of southern readers who ignored these pleas and continued to get their reading matter from the North. What the South's struggling authors wanted was not separation from the North but recognition by the North. Why must northern critics insist, they wanted to know, on lauding the doggerel of John Greenleaf Whittier while ignoring the genius of William Gilmore Simms? It was intolerable to have the *Atlantic Monthly* characterizing the South as a coarse and sordid oligarchy unhallowed by antiquity and unadorned by culture. But instead of separation, what they wanted was to escape the condescension of the metropolis toward the provinces, to attain some literary triumph which would force the North to acknowledge southern merit. Meanwhile, they retorted in kind, disparaging northern society as mercenary, materialistic, hypocritical, Godless, ill-mannered, and lacking in any class of gentlemen. In 1858 a prominent Tennessee historian declared, "The high-toned New England spirit has degenerated into a clannish feeling of profound Yankeeism. . . . The masses of the North are venal, corrupt, covetous, mean, and selfish." But "the proud Cavalier spirit of the South," he added, not only remained but had become "intensified." Early in 1860, Robert Toombs remarked in the Senate, "The feeling of a common interest and a common destiny, upon which foundations alone society can securely and permanently rest, is . . . rapidly passing away."

During the secession winter, the South produced a ceaseless flow of statements such as these—all affirmed with such intensity that they suggest the rise of southern nationalism to a fully matured, triumphant, and unchallenged fulfillment. If antipathy toward the Yankees and antipathy toward the American Union could be equated, this inference might be valid. But feelings of anger and fear which part of a society may feel toward another part are not the same as the cultural differences between two distinct civilizations. Nor did hostility toward other elements in the Union necessarily imply hostility toward the Union itself. There was still a vigorous Union nationalism remaining in the South, and in spite of all the emotional fury, there was probably more cultural homogeneity in American society on the eve of secession than there had been when the Union was formed, or than there would be a century later. Most northerners and most southerners were farmer folk who cultivated their own land and cherished a fierce devotion to the principles of personal independence and social equalitarianism. They shared a great pride in the Revolutionary heritage, the Constitution and "republican institutions," and an ignorance about Europe, which they regarded as decadent and infinitely inferior to the United States. They also shared a somewhat intolerant, orthodox Protestantism, a faith in rural virtues, and a commitment to the gospel of hard work, acquisition, and success. Southern aristocrats might disdain these latter attributes, but the cotton economy was itself prime evidence of southern possession of them. The development of steamboats and railroads and the telegraph had generated an internal trade which bound the sections increasingly closer economically and had generated a nationwide faith in American progress and in the greatness of America's destiny. The South participated in all of these experiences, and the crisis of 1860 resulted from a transfer of power, far more than from what some writers have called the divergence of two civilizations.

The degree to which southern nationalism still fell short of a culmination was evident from the continued devotion to the Union of a large part of the population of the South. In the election of 1860, southern voters had had a choice between two stout defenders of the Union—Douglas and Bell—and one candidate who denied that he favored disunion. The Unionist candidates carried 49 percent of the vote in the seven states of the original Confederacy. Even after Lincoln's election, Unionism survived in those states and maintained dominance in the upper South. A high proportion of former Whigs, who had supported Bell in the election, boldly reaffirmed their Unionism. The Vicksburg *Whig* declared, "It is treason to secede." It also predicted the consequences of secession: "strife, discord, bloodshed, war, if not anarchy." Disunion would be a "blind and suicidal course." The Unionists also castigated the secessionists for their irresponsibility. The governor of Louisiana said regretfully that the dissolution of the Union was spoken of, "if not with absolute levity, yet with positive indifference"; and Alexander H. Stephens complained that the secessionists really did not want redress for their grievances; they were "for breaking up" merely because they were "tired of the govnt." In the upper South, the Unionists reminded one another of the importance of their material ties with the North. Senator Crittenden of Kentucky had pointed out in 1858 that "the very diversity of . . . resources" of the two sections led to interdependence and was "a cause of natural union between us." In 1860 a Tennessee newspaper declared "We can't do without their [the North's] productions, and they can't do without our Rice, Sugar, and Cotton."

Southern nationalism had arrived, but Union nationalism had by no means departed. Sometimes, indeed, a man might declare his allegiance to both, in the same breath. Thus, Alexander H. Stephens as early as 1845 had said, "I have a patriotism that embraces, I trust, all parts of the Union, . . . yet I must confess that my feelings of attachments are most ardent towards that with which all my interests and associations are identified. . . . The South is my home—my fatherland."

To one who thinks of nationalism as a unique and exclusive form of loyalty, the divisions of the South between Union nationalism and southern nationalism, and the movement of individuals from one camp to the other, will look like some sort of political schizophrenia. But if one thinks of nationalism instead as but one form of group loyalty, it becomes easier to see that the choice between Union nationalism and southern nationalism was basically a question of means—a question of whether the slaveholding society would be safer in the Union or in a southern Confederacy. The South had fared extremely well in the Union of 1787, with its bisectional balance, its lack of centralized power, and most of all, its indulgent attitude toward slavery. As these advantaes dwindled, men began to speak of the Union of 1787 as the "Old Union," and the South cherished its memory with nostalgia and reverence, as "the Union of our Fathers." In 1861 the New Orleans *Picayune* opposed secession and called instead for "the reconstruction of the old Union."

Not only did southerners think fondly of a nation within which the southern social system had been secure. They also said quite directly that the security of their system was the criterion by which they should choose between the existing nation and the incipient one. Many recognized that even if a southern confederacy were successfully formed, its existence would not prevent slaves from fleeing north to freedom, would not silence abolitionist attacks on slavery, and would probably mean an abandonment of the rights which slavery, under the Dred Scott decision, enjoyed in the territories. The South would have to resist antislavery in any case, and so perhaps it could fight more effectively inside the Union than outside. Abolitionists might be more dangerous as foreign neighbors than as fellow citizens.

As long as the North and the South had remained fairly equal in economic and political power, and as long as slavery had been immune to serious attack, the two sections had coexisted in a reasonably harmonious way. They could differ and even quarrel fiercely over various political questions without placing the Union in great danger. But as time passed, the sections ceased to be evenly balanced, and slavery lost its immunity. These simultaneous developments had an overpowering effect in the South. They generated a feeling of being on the defensive, the psychology of a garrison under siege.

At the beginning of the century, the population of the slave states had been equal to that of the North, and the South had had 40 percent of the total white population. But by 1860, northerners outnumbered southerners in a ratio of 6:4 in total population and 7:3 in white population. At the beginning of the century, Virginia and Kentucky might talk about the power of individual states to prevent enforcement of the Alien and Sedition Acts, but they really did not need to resort to such minority devices, for they still had enough political muscle to put a Virginian into the White House in 1801 and to keep the presidency in the hands of southerners for forty-two of the next fifty years. But by 1860, a man might win the presidency without even being on the ticket in most of the southern states. The increasing discrepancies in wealth, productive capacity, and technological advancement were equally apparent. William L. Yancey told a New York audience in 1860, "You have power in all the branches of the government to pass such laws as you like. If you are actuated by power, or prejudice, or by the desire of self-aggrandizement, it is within your power . . . to outnumber us and commit aggression upon us." The South was not only in a minority but, more ominously, in a permanent and dwindling minority.

Its power was dwindling, moreover, at the very time when the South found itself exposed to increasingly sharp attack by antislavery spokesmen. During the first forty years of the republic, slavery had certainly been criticized, but it had virtually never been threatened. Antislavery men had been gradualists, who proposed no sudden action; emancipationists, who relied on reasoned appeals to the slaveholders to practice voluntary manumission; colonizationists, whose program looked to the removal of the blacks along with the removal of slavery. Slavery had been respectable, and eight of the first twelve men who reached the presidency were slaveholders. Until 1856, no major political party had ever, at the national level, made a public prnouncement against slavery, and in northern cities, mobs that included "gentlemen of property and standing" had hounded and harassed the abolitionists. But in the 1830s, the abolitionists had captured the antislavery movement, demanding immediate, involuntary emancipation enforced by law, denouncing all slaveholders with unmeasured invective, and even sometimes proclaiming the equality of the blacks. Antislavery parties had appeared for the first time in the 1840s, and a major antislavery party in the mid-fifties. In 1856 the Republicans had branded slavery as a relic of barbarism, and in 1860 they had elected to the presidency a man who said that slavery must be put on a course toward ultimate extinction. In 1859 many northerners had mourned the hanging of a would-be leader of slave insurrection. Meanwhile, slavery had been disappearing from the Western world and remained significant only in Brazil, Cuba, and the southern United States.

If the government of the United States should pass into the control of opponents of slavery, as it seemed about to do in 1860, the South had realistic reason to fear the consequences, not so much because of legislation which the dominant party might adopt, but because the monolithic, closed system of social and intellectual arrangements upon which the South relied for the perpetuation of slavery might be disrupted. Once Lincoln was in office, he could appoint Republican judges, marshals, customs collectors, and postmasters in the South. This would strike a heavy blow at the mystique of planter control which had been vital to the maintenance of the southern system. With their political domination challenged, the planter class might lose some of their social ascendancy also. More explicitly, Lincoln might appoint abolitionists or even free Negroes to public office in the South. And even if he did not do this, the new Republican postmasters would refuse to censor the mails or to burn abolitionist papers. The temptation of postmasterships might attract some nonslaveholding southerners and make them the nucleus of an antislavery force in the South. For a slave system vitally dependent upon the solidarity of the whites, this loomed as a frightful menace. It was irrelevant to say that the Republicans did not constitute a threat because they still lacked the majorities which would enable them to enact legislation in Congress. They did not need to enact legislation.

By 1860, southerners were acutely conscious of their minority status and their vulnerability to abolitionist agitation. After Harpers Ferry, a wave of fear swept through the South, subsiding somewhat in the spring and then rising again during the presidential campaign. There were reports and more reports of dark conspiracies for slave revolts, engineered by abolitionist incendiaries infiltrating the South in guises such as peddlers and itinerant piano tuners. Though seldom verified, the rumors were usually rich in details of plots uncovered; murder, rape, and arson prevented; and malefactors punished. For a time, the atmosphere was such that any fire of unknown origin or any white southerner's death of obscure causes might set off a report of arson or poisoning. And editors, no more immune than their readers, transformed into "news items" the fantasies of a society obsessed with fears of slave insurrection and with apocalyptic visions of terrible retaliation.

When Lincoln's election came at last, the people of the slaveholding states were not united in any commitment to southern nationalism, nor to a southern republic, nor even to political separatism. But they *were* united by a sense of terrible danger. They were united, also, in a determination to defend slavery, to resist abolitionism, and to force the Yankees to recognize not only their rights but also their status as perfectly decent, respectable human beings. "I am a Southern man," a Missouri delegate had asserted in the Baltimore convention, "born and raised beneath the sunny sky of the South. Not a drop of blood in my veins ever flowed in veins north of Mason's and Dixon's line. My ancestors for 300 years sleep beneath the turf that shelters the bones of Washington, and I thank God that they rest in the graves of honest slaveholders."

Motivated by this deeply defensive feeling, the people of the South also tended to accept an interpretation of the Constitution maximizing the autonomy of the separate states. According to this view, each state, when ratifying the Constitution, had retained its full sovereignty. The states had authorized the federal government, as their agent, to administer for them collectively certain of the functions which derive from sovereignty, but they had never transferred the sovereignty itself, and they could resume the exercise of all sovereign functions at any time by an act of secession, adopted in the same kind of state convention that had ratified the Constitution. However arid, and antiquarian it may now seem, the acceptance of this doctrine by a majority of the citizens of the Old South gave to it a historical importance independent of its validity as a constitutional theory. It is impossible to understand the rift between North and South without recognizing that one factor in this rift was a fundamental disagreement between the sections as to whether the American republic was a unitary nation in which the states had fused their sovereign identities or a pluralistic league of sovereign political units, federated for certain joint but limited purposes. Perhaps the United States is the only nation in history which for seven decades acted politically and culturally as a nation, and grew steadily stronger in its nationhood, before decisively answering the question of whether it was a nation at all. The framers of the Constitution had purposely left this question in a state of benign ambiguity. They did so for the best possible reason, namely that the states in 1787 were in hopeless disagreement about it, and some would have refused to ratify an explicitly national Constitution. Thus, the phrase *"E pluribus unum"* was a riddle as well as a motto. The utmost which the nationalists of 1787 could accomplish was to create the framework within which a nation might grow, and to hope it would grow there. But the legal question of the nature of the Union had been left in doubt and became a subject of controversy. The leading spokesmen on both sides were lawyers who confined themselves largely to drawing refined inferences from the exact wording of the Constitution and following every clue as to the intentions of the framers. In this kind of deductive reasoning, as it turned out, the defenders of state sovereignty had quite a strong case, made up essentially of five arguments:

First, at the time of the Articles of Confederation, proposed in 1777 and ratified in 1781, the states had explicitly included a statement that "each state retains its sovereignty, freedom and independence," and the treaty by which Britain recognized independence in 1783 named each of the thirteen states individually and acknowledged them to be "free, sovereign and independent states."

Second, when the Constitution was framed in 1787, it was ratified by each state, acting separately and for itself only, so that the ratification of the requisite number of states (nine) would not have made any other state a member of the "more perfect union" under the Constitution unless that other state ratified. It was true that the preamble said, "We the people of the United States . . . do ordain and establish this Constitution," and Daniel Webster, the Great Expounder of the Constitution and the great oracle of nationalism, had rung the changes on "We the people" as a proof that the citizens of all the states were merged into a consolidated Union. But the term "people" was not used to indicate that one people instead of thirteen peoples were ratifying, but rather to distinguish between action by state governments and action by citizens exercising their ultimate power. Under the Articles, the central government had derived its power from the state governments and they in turn had derived their power from the people. Hence the central government could act only upon the state governments and not upon any citizens directly. But under the state constitutions *and* the Constitution of 1787, the people of each state (or the peoples of the thirteen states), by two separate acts, established for themselves two separate governments—a state government, operating locally for that state only, and a central government, operating collectively for the states together. Neither government had created the other; neither was subordinate to the other; they were coordinate governments, both sanctioned directly by the action of citizens, both operating directly on citizens without having to mediate through the machinery of the other government, and both subject to the ultimate authority, not of one or the other, but of the constituencies which had established them. It was a truly dualistic system. This was the real implication of the term "We the people," and in the Convention the framers had originally planned a phrasing which would have avoided the confusion that later arose. They had agreed to list by name, one after another, "the people" of each of the thirteen states, severally, as the ordaining and establishing parties. But recognizing the awkwardness that would result if the Constitution should name as a member of the Union a state whose people later refused to ratify, they substituted the term "We the people of the United States," using it as a plural and not as a singular term.

Third, the proceedings of the Convention showed clearly that its members had deliberately taken up the question of whether the federal government could coerce a state government, and had positively refused to confer any such power.

Fourth, at the time of ratification, three states had specifically reserved their right to resume the powers which they were granting by their acts of ratification.

Fifth, the continued integrity of the states was reflected in the structural features of the new government which provided that the states should be represented equally in the Senate, that the states alone could cast electoral votes for president, that the states alone could ratify amendments to the Constitution, and that, under the Tenth Amendment in the Bill of Rights, "The powers not delegated to the United States by the Constitution nor prohibited by it to the States are reserved to the states respectively, or to the people."

From these arguments, the political theorists of the South had developed the doctrine of state sovereignty and, from it, of the right of secession. The Virginia and Kentucky Resolutions of 1798, written by Jefferson and Madison, had asserted state sovereignty and had declared each state to be "the judge . . . of the mode and measure of redress" in cases in which the federal government might violate the Constitution.

There were, to be sure, a good many southerners who preferred to claim instead a right of revolution, as asserted in the Declaration of Independence. But the southern majority had committed itself to the right of secession during the crisis of 1846–1850, and James M. Mason, in 1860, was able to say, "Fortunately for the occasion and its consequences, this is not an open question in Virginia. Our honored state has ever maintained that our Federal system was a confederation of sovereign powers, not a consolidation of states into one people. . . . Whenever a state considered the compact broken, and in a manner to endanger her safety, such state stood remitted, as in sovereign right, to determine for herself . . . both the mode and measure of redress."

Against the defenders of this doctrine, the defenders of nationalism did not come off as well as they might have, partly because they accepted the assumption that the nature of the Union should be determined by legal means, somewhat as if it were a case in the law of contracts. Yet in fact, the nature of the Union had been changing constantly, as the states increased in number until those which had created the Union were outnumbered by those which the Union had created. Between 1804 and 1865, the Constitution was not once amended, the longest such interval in American history. But while the text of the charter remained the same, the republic itself was transformed.

A thousand forms of economic and cultural interdependence had developed. Such changes do not occur without corresponding changes in the attitude of the people, and in a century of rampant nationalism throughout the Western world, there were probably no people who carried national patriotism and self-congratulation to greater lengths than the Americans, and this included the South. Regardless of arrangements made in 1787, nationalism changed the nature of the Union and began to answer the riddle of *pluribus* or *unum*. But nationalism grew at different rates and in different ways in North and South, and by 1860, the sections found themselves separated by a common nationalism. Each was devoted to its own image of the Union, and each section was indistinctly aware that its image was not shared by the other. The South had no idea how ruthlessly its northern Democratic allies were prepared to deal with anyone who tried to tamper with the Union. The North had no idea how fiercely southern Unionists who valued the Union for themselves would defend the right of other southerners to reject it for *them*selves and to break it up without being molested.

The dual focus of southern loyalties, even as late as 1860, has led one author to say very aptly that the South by then had become a kingdom, but that it did not become a nation until thrust into the crucible of the Civil War. Within this kingdom there was sharp disagreement between the advocates of a southern Confederacy and those who favored remaining in the Union. Yet underneath the disagreement was consensus on two important points. Most southern Unionists shared with secessionists the conviction that no state should be forced to remain in the Union, and most of them also believed in secession as a theoretical right. Whether it was justified or opportune could still be debated. But for southerners generally, the *right* of a state to secede, if it chose to do so, had become an article of faith given the social institutions and political standards which generated and shaped the forces making for war. The five months following Lincoln's election were to show that, once released, these forces became too powerful for human resistance.

The Search for Remedies

Kenneth Stampp

In November 1860 the Republicans won but a narrow and limited victory at the polls. They failed to get control of either branch of Congress. Their presidential candidate, Lincoln, while gaining a clear majority in the free states, received in the country as a whole almost a million fewer votes than his three opponents. In this dubious triumph the Chicago *Tribune* saw "only another incentive for continuing the revolution which has begun." Another Republican organ found some consolation in the fact that the country had been spared the transfer of the presidential contest to the House of Representatives, "which might have threatened the stability of the government." Now, presumably, the people could settle down for a quadrennium of relative quiet.

Politicians in the Deep South, however, thought otherwise. In response to Lincoln's election they quickly prepared to carry their states out of the Union. Within a few weeks South Carolina's senators had resigned, seven states had called conventions to consider secession, specially appointed commissioners had begun to advance and co-ordinate the general withdrawal, and such prominent Southerners as Howell Cobb, Secretary of the Treasury, and Robert Toombs, Senator from Georgia, had publicly declared for immediate southern action. Fire-eaters sketched vivid pictures of coming northern aggressions upon southern rights. Newspapers predicted the early formation of a new Confederacy. These activities in the South made interesting copy, and the northern press gave them much space.

But the majority of Yankees who read these reports in November were little more impressed than they had been by southern bluster during the recent campaign. "As to disunion," wrote William Cullen Bryant, "nobody but silly people expect it will happen." A friend of Charles Sumner's rejoiced that "the gasconading Slave drivers" would "find it necessary to eat their own words."

Reprinted with permission of Louisiana State University Press from AND THE WAR CAME: THE NORTH AND THE SECESSION CRISIS, 1860–1861 by Kenneth M. Stampp. Copyright © 1950, 1970.

Senator Wade knew that Southerners would "howl and rave, like so many devils, tormented before their time," but believed it was "all a humbug" and meant nothing. Other Republican leaders such as Seward, Sumner, Charles Francis Adams, and Edward Bates found no reason to disagree. In Springfield, Illinois, the President-elect received the news from the South with "equanimity," for "he could not in his heart believe that the South designed the overthrow of the Government." Neither could the Republican press; as late as December 13 the New York *Evening Post* still doubted that "the secession of a single state—even of South Carolina" would actually be accomplished.

Some Democrats showed no greater perspicacity in their initial reactions to the southern movement. A pro-Douglas paper in New York declared, "The Disunion furor will have blown pretty well over, long before the 4th day of next March. It will be a fizzle on a grand scale. . . ." The pro-Breckinridge Boston *Post* thought the South was talking much but would do little. Even President Buchanan was at first inclined to doubt that the South was in earnest. Well might the Springfield *Republican* tell the secessionists that they "would feel mortified" if they knew how indifferent the masses of the people of the free states were. "All the startling reports that come from the South fail to waken a conviction that there is anything real or permanent in the whole thing."

The majority of Democratic spokesmen professed to believe that Southerners meant what they said. But the Republicans tried to make it appear that the Democrats, too, really had their doubts. Secession, said the Republicans, was only a rumor, a Democratic effort to frighten the northern people and discredit and disorganize the Republicans by forcing them to abandon their principles. Only for that purpose did Democrats wail dismally about impending national ruin and beg Lincoln to arrest the crisis by renouncing his party's platform. How, indeed, could Republicans give assurances to the South when their newspapers were not read there? Rather, it was for those who had misrepresented the Republicans to retract their lies, to "acknowledge their slanders . . . , assuring their southern friends that these were but electioneering falsehoods manufactured to frighten voters."

These skeptics were equally cavalier in dismissing the business panic which grew in intensity after the election. There was no denying that stocks were falling, that wheat prices were dropping sharply, that a bank crisis was taking shape, or that factories were curtailing operations and discharging mechanics. Nor could they ignore the increasing number of bankrupt merchants. The New York *Times* had to confess that the panic feeling "appeared to run as wild as in some of the blackest days of 1857." Nevertheless, it was still possible to describe the disturbance as temporary, or explain it as the result of an effort of political panic makers to wreck the Republican party. At least it was comforting to know that the chief sufferers were those tricksters who had engineered the crisis in the first place.

But suppose there was substance to the disunion reports; suppose an effort would actually be made to separate the slave states from the free. Many in the minority who had expected such a move from the start, and others who gradually came around to that opinion, still could see no cause for serious concern. Was it not true that Douglas and Bell had polled more southern votes than Breckinridge, that important newspapers were favoring the Union, and that influential politicians like Alexander H. Stephens were fighting the disunionists at home? Was it not logical to assume that, given sufficient time, the excitement would subside and the Unionists gain control? Certainly the Republican press found abundant evidence that separation was not popular with the southern masses. A typical conclusion was that, while secession might be attempted, "sane men of the South" would soon "take care of the thing, and prevent the Hotspurs from absolutely ruining that section." The New York *Times* thought it likely that the whole movement would "resolve itself into a convention of the Southern States," and in such a gathering the Union would be "safe." That, it was recalled, had been the outcome of another crisis a decade before.

From this smug and comforting diagnosis of the malady there emerged a simple remedy. It was particularly popular during the first six weeks after the election, although some had faith in it almost to the end. According to this prescription there was nothing for the North to do but remain calm, avoid any word or act that would produce further irritation, wait for the South to regain its senses, and encourage the growth of the inevitable Unionist reaction.

Accordingly, great numbers of Northerners started out to save the Union by sitting tight, regarding the South with cool indifference, and letting the "Heathen" rage. Moderate Republican papers sniffed auspicious omens in the winds from the South. Correspondents of Salmon P. Chase assured him that the secessionists would "be put down by the sober second thought of the people of that region without any help from the North." "If we give the disunionists . . . rope enough to hang themselves," wrote Carl Schurz, "they will perform that necessary and praiseworthy task with their own hands."

That Lincoln also shared this early hope for the triumph of the southern Unionists was evident from the few lines he wrote for insertion in Senator Lyman Trumbull's speech at Springfield on November 20. The secessionists, thought Lincoln, were in "hot haste" to leave the Union at once, for they saw that they would be unable to misrepresent the Republican party to their people much longer. Fortunately the current military preparations in the south would "enable the people the more easily to suppress any [secessionist] uprising there. . . ." President Buchanan, too, looked expectantly to this solution. "Time is a great conservative answer," he reminded Congress. "Let us pause at this momentous point and afford the people, both North and South, an opportunity for reflection."

Of all the northern politicians who put their faith in this remedy, no one adhered to it with more persistence or administered it with greater shrewdness than Senator Seward of New York. His peculiar genius was perfectly suited to the intricate maneuvering that such a formula involved. While many others had spontaneously opted this strategy, it was Seward's great influence in party councils that gave it significance, and his political adroitness that kept this hope alive so long. Aided by Thurlow Weed, his crafty political manager, he gathered key men about him and secured their endorsements of his nostrum.

To some it came as a shock to hear the apostle of the "higher law," the prophet of the "irrepressible conflict," speak so serenely and address the South with such tolerance and affection. But there need have been no shock. In actual fact Seward was never an abolitionist as was Sumner nor a political radical as was Chase. His occasional flings at the South had been sufficient to hold the support of antislavery Whigs but never went far enough to alienate completely the conservative business interests of New York. He never supported the Free-Soil party and was slow to desert the Whigs for the Republicans. Always he managed to maintain cordial relations with numerous southern Whigs, some of whom he now found useful in the development of his crisis strategy. With all his hostility to slavery, the Boston *Post* now shrewdly observed, "it is far from his purpose to prosecute the 'irrepressible conflict' to the extremity of breaking up the government which he aims to control, and producing a revolution which would annihilate the Union and his party together."

So Seward moved among the politicians, puffing cheerfully at his cigar and breathing confidence and kindly sentiments. Arriving in Washington for the opening of Congress, he freely stated that there was nothing which need cause great alarm. He was "chipper as a lark," swearing "by yea and by nay that everything was going on admirably," as Henry Adams said after dining with him. He jovially assured the solid men of the New England Society of New York that secession was growing weaker. "I believe," he said, "that . . . if you only give it time, sixty days more suns will given you a more cheerful atmosphere." To the very last, almost alone, Seward kept his hopes bright, while state after stae seceded and the seceders set up a government of their own. Only the guns of Sumter were able to silence the optimism in his voice.

Though his program was destined to failure, Seward played a glorious role until the tragic end. He vindicated his claim to the Republican presidential nomination in 1860. Recovering slowly from his bitter disappointment, he found himself again in the months of crisis. While the President-elect sat silently in Springfield, Seward assumed the task of saving his party and the country from ruin. He got public attention with every movement he made; he, it was generally conceded, was the real party leader, the "premier" of the incoming administration. "It seems to me that if I am absent only three days," he wrote his wife with disarming sincerity, "this Administration, the Congress, and the District would fall into consternation and despair." All parties "cast themselves upon me."

Early in March young Henry Adams titillated the Seward ego with a tribute to his masterful performance. Adams told how Republicans had gone to him "in despair to say that something must be done. . . . And he did save us. For two months he has swayed the whole nation." But it was only a respite, not salvation, that Seward had achieved. At best he deserved a large measure of credit for preserving the peace until the inauguration of Lincoln.

In retrospect there is no escaping the fact that the disingenuous device of saving the country by doing essentially nothing—by waiting for a pro-Union reaction—was doomed from the start. Underlying it were two fatal misconceptions: first, an overestimation of the southern-Unionist strength, and second, a failure to understand that in the South Unionism meant one thing, in the North another. Southern Unionism did not mean unconditional opposition to secession, for that was a negligible quantity in the majority of slave states. Among Northerners these errors were widespread in the first days of the crisis. Seward and some others continued to harbor them to the end, but growing numbers began as early as December to doubt whether disunion would be suppressed by Southerners alone. A few occasionally returned to this idea; the majority sought other and more positive remedies.

On December 11, Hamilton Fish of New York, man of property, conservative Whig-Republican, and intimate associate of wealthy business interests, observed the change in attitudes that was occurring. He was impressed by the prevailing anxiety which resulted from the disarrangement of business and the depreciation of values. Republican politicians, he believed, were simply "whistling to keep their courage up." Fish noted an increasing desire among Republican merchants to grant further concessions to the South. "It cannot be doubted that a great change has taken place," he said. "It cannot be denied that these men are now turning to, (if now upon,) their friends & calling upon them to save them." Democrats and Constitutional Unionists had already come out overwhelmingly for compromise, and now an effort was being made to unite conservative Republicans with these groups.

Here was an early sign of a widening realization that the secession movement had reached serious proportions. With another Union crisis taking shape, a vast element in the North grasped almost automatically for the time-tested remedy of compromise. Perhaps the issue could be evaded once again by "reasonable and honorable" concessions. By December a great variety of schemes for sectional adjustment had found sponsors among politicians and editors. Generally they were focused around proposals to give additional guarantees to slavery in the form of a constitutional amendment, to repeal personal-liberty laws, to compensate Southerners for the loss of fugitive slaves, to admit New Mexico as a slave state, or to extend the Missouri Compromise line to

California. While Democrats assumed the prime role of "Union-savers," a minority of Republicans was ready ultimately to support moderate concessions— "adjustment without dishonor."

A smaller faction of Republicans, however, appeared to favor a more drastic remedy. Whether or not there was a legal right of secession, they argued, it would be best for the national health to remove the infected part, to let the disloyal slave states secede in peace. Horace Greeley's New York *Tribune* was unquestionably the most influential exponent of this course. But it was by no means the only important Republican paper that seemed to look upon it with favor. The Philadelphia *Public Ledger,* Boston *Traveller,* Springfield *Republican, Ohio State Journal,* Indianapolis *Journal,* Cincinnati *Commercial,* Chicago *Tribune,* and a score of others at one time or another echoed Greeley's sentiments. "If she [South Carolina] will," said the Chicago *Tribune,* "let her go, and like a limb lopped from a healthy trunk, wilt and rot where she falls." Northern Democrats howled that these quacks would kill the patient with their radical cure.

But Greeley's solution was a fraud from the start. He was ready to let the South depart in peace only so long as some doubt remained of its desire to go, and so long as there was danger of Republicans abandoning their principles. Moreover, from the very beginning he placed so many qualifications on the process as to render it absolutely meaningless. And almost every other advocate of this course was guilty of the same deception.

Peaceful secession as envisioned by these northern nationalists hardly fitted the pattern of the state-rights concept. It was not a matter to be initiated and consummated by a single state upon its own terms. "I have no appetite for blood," wrote a correspondent of Senator Wade's, "& will not say that in a proper way, I will not consent to let the South go, provided it shall appear that in the Cotton States there is a very general determination to break up the Union." But, this writer hastened to add, "I do not think that feeling exists outside of South Carolina, to the extent of unanimity that I would require." In other words, the seceders must first satisfy northern skeptics that the secession movement had sufficient popular support.

Next, Southerners must make formal application for permission to secede. The request could be submitted to Congress, which in turn could refer it directly to the people, or to a national convention for approval. Until such consent had been granted, "the Government must maintain its authority even in South Carolina, and punish if assailed." Finally, should separation ultimately be approved, a constitutional amendment would still be required to make it legal.

Meanwhile the South must wait quietly until the Federal government and the northern people had time for careful deliberation. A constituent of Representative E. B. Washburne of Illinois explained the proper procedure: "Hold still, entirely still, . . . neither threaten or coax, and 'let 'em wiggle' and if secession has sense and discretion enough (which I doubt) to avoid overt act of treason, and rebellion, and can get their case fairly before the nation by proper means, and in a proper spirit, and wish to form a separate government, if the thing should be found practible [*sic*] and mutualy [*sic*] benificial [*sic*] let them go." Or, as another advocate of peaceful secession put it, *"The first thing* to be done is to execute the laws. *The second* to decide whether the States shall be allowed to secede—& if so, on what terms."

Secession, then, must be slow and painless, a product of negotiation which would respect the authority of the Federal government and protect the interests of the nonseceding states. Accordingly, the Philadelphia *Public Ledger* would have demanded that the seceders "make such terms as shall render those States which do not secede no worse off in point of security by the separation." This would require that all guns on the shores of the Mississippi be dismantled, that New Orleans be made a free city under joint protectorate, and that the Federal government retain possession of such vital positions as Key West and Pensacola. Others believed that strategic considerations would probably make it impossible to permit Florida and Louisiana to secede.

It was but a short step from this position to the next. Peaceful separation was impossible because Southerners themselves were attempting to illegally through violence. "The rebellious states . . . insist upon treating the Constitution as a nullity," indignantly complained the *World*. "The great law-abiding North will not give way to it." Representative Charles H. Van Wyck of New York raised the same objection: "I desire not to preserve this Union at the point of the bayonet; but we do not mean to be driven from it by force. If you desire a peaceful secession, why do you not seek it? . . . But when you forcibly seize the federal property, and then fire upon its flag, you should not sit down and picture the horrors of civil war." The New York *Tribune* finally escaped through the same wide opening: "That we no longer advocate acquiescence in the demands of the seceding States is because the nature and tone of these demands have altogether changed. Instead of asking for a peaceable and legal separation, the seceding States . . . have resorted to violence; . . . and now stand defiantly in the attitude of traitors and rebels."

Thus the circle was complete. Peaceful secession was desirable, but it must be on northern terms and in accordance with a rigid formula. Since the South rejected both the terms and the formula, there could be no peaceful secession. Greeley's deception seemed to be motivated chiefly by his implacable hostility to any form of compromise. A few adopted his position in good faith but added the nullifying qualifications as they slowly appreciated the serious complications which would result from disunion.

In any event, except for a handful of Garrisonian abolitionists and extreme prosouthern Democrats, the scheme of peaceful separation had nearly evaporated by the end of December. Greeley's *Tribune* ultimately confessed: "The right of secession has been almost universally denied at the North, . . . and but a very small proportion of the Northern people have been willing to acknowledge that the bonds of our Union were utterly broken. . . ." In December, Greeley wrote in a private letter to Lincoln that Southerners would "have to be made to behave themselves." Thereafter the *Tribune's* columns contained a confusing mixture of empty talk about qualified peaceful disunion and increasingly violent demands for the enforcement of the laws and the suppression of rebellion. By a devious route Greeley, like so many others, finally arrived in the camp of the proponents of force.

Military coercion, as a remedy for disunion, had its advocates from the start. At first some of those who spoke belligerently may have had suspicions—perhaps, more accurately, hopes—that the crisis would blow over. Whether or not their warlike tone was conceived merely as a counterbluff, the important fact was that ultimately the bluff (if such it was) was called.

Even before the election of 1860 some in the minority who believed the South in earnest had warned that the North would resist secession. Now, as the weeks passed and the illusions began to fall away, those who had originally talked of force were finding new recruits. As early as November the New York *Herald* noted deploringly that numerous Republican journals were "using violent, defiant and exasperating language toward the Southern States, as if they were anxious to precipitate disunion and civil war upon the country."

One of the editors the *Herald* doubtless had in mind was James Watson Webb, whose New York *Courier and Enquirer* was reputedly Seward's "Wall Street organ." But "Chevalier" Webb, long famous for his contentiousness and for his vitriolic pen, had no faith in the Senator's gentle moderation toward the South. He began at once to boast of the North's military power and vowed that "no disruption of . . . this nation . . . could be accomplished without . . . terrible penalties upon the rebellious population engaged in the effort."

Scores of newspapers quickly agreed with the Boston *Transcript's* pronouncement, "Secession, when it is manifested in act, must be met at once by the full power of the government. . . ." The Indianapolis *American,* while admitting that it expressed a minority view for the present, boldly said, *"Our voice is for war!* If it be bloody, fierce and devastating, be it so." But few surpassed in violence the radical "Long John" Wentworth's Chicago *Democrat:* "You [Southerners] have sworn that if we dared to elect such a man [as Lincoln] you would dissolve the Union. We have elected him, and now we want you to try your little game of secession. Do it, if you dare! . . . But every man of you who attempts to subvert this Union, which we prize so dearly, will be hung as high as Haman. We will have no fooling about this matter. By the eternal! the Union must be preserved."

Many of these journals did not speak consistently and exclusively for military coercion. Editorial consistency was never one of the virtues of the northern press during the secession crisis. A Greeley could advocate qualified peaceful secession and force, a Webb compromise and force, simultaneously, often in different columns of the same issue. Others fluctuated from one remedy to another as conditions changed.

There is abundant evidence that the war press had a substantial popular following even in the days immediately succeeding the election. A Syracuse correspondent reported many of the farmers and townspeople of upstate New York "ready and willing for a fight" if the South desired one. On November 14 the Republican Central Committee of New York City resolved: "There is the power and the will to defend the Constitution with forbearance but without faltering." At a victory celebration in Boston's Music Hall, Charles W. Slack told the Lincoln Wide-Awakes that they might have a further duty to discharge. It might be necessary to go to the aid of the new commander in chief and carry him "triumphantly . . . to the head of the government." Senator Henry Wilson added his vow, "We intend to stand by the Constitution—(Applause.) by the Union at any and every hazzard [*sic*] come what may. (Great applause.)" And Carl Schurz assured a Republican gathering in Milwaukee that if Southerners tried to prevent the inauguration of Lincoln "the traitors would find justice swift, and the indignation of an outraged people inexorable." If need be, "we can rally hundreds of thousands of armed men at the tap of the drum. . . ."

The correspondence of Republican politicians was peppered with similar sentiments from colleagues and constituents. "Tell Mr. Lincoln that little Boone [county] can be relied on for 500 Wide Awakes, well armed and equipped," wrote an Illinois man to Senator Trumbull. A correspondent reminded Chase: Lincoln "must *enforce the laws of the U. States against all rebellion;*—no matter what are the consequences." A friend advised Representative John Sherman, "If five or six of the Petted Slave States does Secede we may spend a few millions [*sic*] to whip them into their propper [*sic*] place. . . ." Congressman Oris S. Ferry of Connecticut advised Gideon Welles that ten years of civil war would be preferable to a division of the Union. And Edward Bates recorded in his diary a fear that the "dangerous game" of the secessionists might lead to open rebellion. "If they *will* push it to that dread extremity, the Government . . . will no doubt, find it wise policy to make the war as sharp and prompt as possible. . . ."

With some, as Bates's opinion indicated, it was less a matter of *advocating* the use of force than of entertaining the fatalistic conviction that disunion, if it actually came, placed an inescapable duty upon the government to coerce the secessionists into submission. The President-elect gave early evidence of belonging to this group. Even while he still doubted that Southerners would actually secede, Lincoln was saying, "I must run the machine as I find it." In December he became more explicit: "The very existence of a general and national government implies the legal power, right and duty of maintaining its own integrity. . . . It is the duty of a President to execute the laws and maintain the existing government." The New York *Times* presented one of the best reflections of this state of mind: "If South Carolina is determined upon secession, she should make the plunge with her eyes open. She must face all the consequences,—and *among them all, the most unquestionable is War.* Not that we wish it,—not that thousands and tens of thousands of good men among us would not weep the bitterest tears they ever shed in their lives, over so dismal, so dreadful a prospect. But there is no possibility of escaping it. We cannot permit secession if we would."

A demand for "preparedness" was still another variation of the force doctrine. The secession crisis produced its share of innocents who spoke of national mobilization as the road to peace and safety. The way to avoid civil war was to prepare for it, to provide overwhelming military and naval power so that secession would cease to be a holiday affair. "You have only to put the Government in a position to make itself respected," affirmed Senator Trumbull, "and it will command respect." The Chicago *Tribune* reminded Northerners that secessionists were, after all, only men. As long as they believed that they could plot against the government with impunity, they would go on with their conspiracy. But if they perceived the danger of punishment for treason, "thousands of the rampant bullies . . . would become as mild as so many sucking doves. . . ."

With the government adequately prepared, if worst came to worst "a little show of force" entailing a minimum of bloodshed would suffice to crush the southern rebellion. This was a common belief: "The national government may have to *show* its teeth, but it is not at all likely that it will have to *use* them." Or, at most, the government would require no greater measure of compulsion that "half a dozen naval vessels . . . [to] blockade southern ports." In short, with proper preparedness, the process of suppressing a southern rebellion would be as simple as "putting down an ordinary fireman's riot in Philadelphia, or a plug ugly muss in Baltimore." Hence it was a misuse of language to speak of "war" as a possible consequence of existing difficulties. The crisis could result in nothing more serious than "the hanging of a score or two of the fools" who had "plotted their own certain destruction."

Preparedness advocates overlooked the fact that their measures, rather than overawing the disunionists, more likely would drive them to similar military exertions. Every Yankee regiment would have its southern counterpart. The psychology of fear would eliminate the last vestiges of caution in the South. The adversaries would come to grips sooner, but the consequences would be no less bloody. No rememdy for secession could have been more insidious than this.

But whether it was a matter of mobilization to frighten the South, or coercion as the sad but inescapable result of disunion, or force as a desirable remedy in itself, the use of military power had emerged as a distinct and likely course. A vigorous minority championed it openly. Many more concealed a similar purpose behind a camouflage of legalistic technicalities derived from a careful combing of the Constitution.

The Civil War

On April 12, 1861, Confederates in South Carolina fired upon the United States garrison at Fort Sumter. Blood was shed, and three days later President Lincoln called for volunteers to preserve the Union. This precipitated war, and each state and each individual American now had to choose sides.

The beginning of the Civil War in the spring of 1861 ended a decade of bitter debate over the issues of slavery, sectionalism, and finally, the right of secession. For the next four years the nation was a battlefield. The Civil War was the most wrenching emotional experience in the Republic's history and the culmination of the most severe crisis it had ever faced. The physical devastation of vast areas was incalculable; especially in Virginia's Shenandoah Valley, the destruction was nearly complete. Countless personal fortunes were lost as untold millions of dollars of Southern property, including slaves, were never recovered. Southern commerce and industry would need decades of rebuilding. Although perhaps military necessities, episodes such as "Sherman's march to the sea" left behind not only a swath of unprecedented physical desolation, but also a legacy of bitterness that passed from one Southern generation to the next.

Although material losses can be measured in dollars, human losses and suffering cannot. Nearly 600,000 Americans were killed or died from wounds or disease in the Civil War—almost as many as have been lost in all the nation's other wars combined. There were thousands more who came out of the war permanently mained in body or in spirit. The Civil War was a terrible calamity, perhaps even a travesty when one reflects upon the abstractions rather than the corporeal reasons for which it was fought. It is a subject of lamentable regret rather than for the unthinking glorification and nostalgic interest it has often received. Perhaps no other contemporary understood the nature of the conflict more clearly than did Abraham Lincoln. As T. Harry Williams observes in the first article of this section, no sooner did the 16th President take office than he was confronted with a reality that no other American leader had had to face: the dissolution of the Union. And no one knew, not even his cabinet or closest friends, what his strategies and policies would be. Even by the time he had become president, Lincoln was still a relatively obscure figure. He was perceived as a Western lawyer, a decent stumpspeaker and above all, as a shrewd politician. Lincoln had shown a remarkable ability to find moderate positions about slavery which he had cleverly crafted into opinions in accord with the Northern voters who had elected him.

What no one would have predicted in 1861 was that four years later a dead Abraham Lincoln would leave the capital as the nation's greatest national hero. By 1865 Lincoln was no longer a mere political figure and leader. To Northerners especially, he had become a dedicated, heroic martyr who had managed to recast a bloody civil strife into a national crusade. By the time of his assassination, the Civil War had become a spiritual struggle for principles higher than the political unity of a nation. Though he remained ever the artful statesman, a part of Lincoln saw the war as something more than politics, battles, and suffering. He thought of the war as a religious experience in which God's chosen nation was now being put through a special trial and punishment. He insisted that the war was a kind of blood sacrifice demanded by God as an act of contrition for the sin of slavery. When at the war's end he paid with his own life, many Americans interpreted his death as proof that his redefinition of the war was correct.

As William Barney discusses in the second reading of this chapter, no sooner did the conflict begin that it became a harrowing educational experience that quickly eroded American illusions about war. Both sides painfully learned that modern war is also total war, and thus always a social process in which civilians as well as soldiers were affected. Initially both the Union and the Confederacy fought the war in pursuit of a political objective: restoration or division of the Union. But the conflict, by its very nature, rapidly generated its own motives and ideals. The South, especially, never anticipated the North's ultimate resolve to prosecute the preservation of the Union ruthlessly, regardless of ultimate cost. Only by adjusting his policies to the realities of the struggle could Lincoln lead the North to victory, and by finding generals who understood the concept of total war.

As Emory Thomas observes in the third essay of this section, the Confederate nation was conceived with the illusion that the South's struggle for independence was fundamentally the same political conflict Americans had fought in 1776 against the tyranny of the British Empire. Only the players had changed in 1861. This time it was Abraham Lincoln and his Black Republicans who were conspiring to destroy the essentials of Southern life. Similar problems called for similar solutions—secession and independence— justified by the Lockean theory of revolution. If in 1776 Britain's superior forces and resources could not put down the resistance of an American people determined to be free, then, Southern fire-eaters boasted, this Southern war for independence would inevitably end in a Rebel triumph.

Abraham Lincoln: Pragmatic Democrat

T. Harry Williams

When President Lincoln in May of 1862 revoked General Hunter's order freeing slaves in his department, Wendell Phillips exploded with frustrated wrath. "The President is a very slow man; an honest man, but a slow moving machine," cried the Boston abolitionist. "I think if we can nudge him a little, it will be of great advantage." But as the war continued, Phillips came to despair that the man in the White House could be nudged—fast enough or far enough. "Mr. Lincoln is not a leader," Phillips lamented. "His theory of Democracy is that he is the servant of the people, not the leader. . . . We pay dear today for having as President a man so cautious as to be timid. . . . As long as you keep the present turtle at the head of affairs, you make a pit with one hand and fill it with the other. I know Mr. Lincoln. . . . He is a mere convenience and is waiting like any other broomstick to be used."

I

There was more in the abolitionist attitude than merely a feeling that Lincoln was a good but not particularly bright man who had to be guided along the right path. To such abolitionists as Phillips such dedicated Radical Republican leaders as George W. Julian, Abraham Lincoln was a politician without principle. These men can be accurately classified under a term popular in modern thought as "ideologues." They had a definite and detailed ideology or philosophy, and they had a precise blueprint for social reform based on a preconceived abstract theory. They were prepared to put their design into effect without much regard for the opinions of those who opposed them and without much thought of the problems that abrupt change might create. In describing their methods and goals they used such phrases as "remorseless and revolutionary violence." Their motto was that of intellectual radicals in all ages: Let there be justice even though the heavens crumble down. To such men—grim, certain, doctrinaire—Abraham Lincoln seemed theoretically backward. So also must Andrew Jackson have seemed to the professional expositors of Jacksonian Democracy, Theodore Roosevelt to the advanced pundits of Progressivism, and Franklin D. Roosevelt to the social welfare philosophers of the New Deal. None of the great American political leaders has been a systematic thinker or an advocate of change for the sake of theory.

Lincoln believed deeply in certain fundamental political principles, but he never assumed to elevate his beliefs into a doctrine. And his opinions or ideas bore little if any resemblance to what is called ideology today. Lincoln would be patiently amused at the attempts of moderns to classify his thinking into some neat niche under some convenient label. We are familiar with and tolerantly scornful of the efforts of politicians and special interests to annex him for their own ends. He has been claimed by Republicans and Democrats, by parties from the far right to the distant left. He has been put forward as the spokesman of unbridled individualism—and of unrestrained statism. But the ax-grinders have not been the only classifiers. The academic scholars, perhaps influenced more than any other group in contemporary society by the concept of ideology and always convinced that a man's ideas can be arranged in a logical pattern, have tried their hand at pinning tidy thought tags on Father Abraham. Characteristically, they have come up with contradictory conclusions.

Some historians, noting Lincoln's tributes to equality of opportunity and the virtues of hard work, and his obvious caution in the face of change, have depicted him as the personification of the economic conservative. Other writers, impressed by the same evidence but giving it an opposite twist, have decided that Lincoln knew little about the economic trends of his times, that he was, in fact, almost an economic simpleton and possibly a folksy front for the industrial capitalism then rising to power. But most historians, responding to the intellectual climate of our day and reflecting their own beliefs, have made Lincoln a liberal, which by their definition means a modern Democrat. Citing his statements that human rights were above property rights, and his friendly words for labor, they have presented him as an early New Dealer, as a pre-Fort Sumter Franklin D. Roosevelt.

All these attempts to categorize Lincoln's thinking fall wide of the mark. Indeed, it is doubtful if easy, explanatory labels can be affixed to any of the American political leaders. The nature of our political system is so complex that no facile polarism can be imposed upon it, especially when the polarism employs such terms as conservative and liberal drawn from European usage. Lincoln, like Jefferson, Jackson, and the two Roosevelts, was a pragmatist. In his approach to social problems he represented the best tradition of British and American politics. The spirit of American pragmatic reform, Frederick Lewis Allen has suggested, may be illustrated by comparing society or the nation to a machine. If something goes wrong with the machine, what should one do? The reactionary might say, "Don't fool with it, you will ruin it." The radical might say, "It's no good, get rid of it and find a new one." But the pragmatist would try to fix the machine up, to remove the defective part and add a new one. Translated into political language, his attitude would be to make a needed change at the right time. American pragmatism has stressed the necessity for continuous, co-operative experimental reform—but it has also insisted, above all, that while changes are being made the machine must be kept running. A proposed change may be moral or theoretically right, but it has also to be demonstrably sound in the light of past experience and present realities.

Lincoln's political beliefs, or what might be termed his inner opinions, were based firmly on principle. His public or outer opinions were always restrained by his strong pragmatic sense, by his fine feeling for what, given the fact of human limitations, was politically possible. One of the keys to his thinking is his statement that few things in this world were wholly good or wholly evil. Instinctively Lincoln distrusted doctrinaire thinkers like the abolitionists who claimed to know what was good and evil, and who were prepared to act upon their opinions. He distrusted the abolitionists because they were blueprint people, because they proposed to make a change based on theory, because they would force this change over all resistance and without regard for social consequences. Lincoln was as much opposed to slavery as the abolitionists. "If slavery is not wrong," he said, "nothing is wrong." But he did not consider that he had the right, even as President, to translate his opinion into action and impose it on others. "I am naturally anti-slavery," he said in 1864. "And yet I have never understood that the Presidency conferred upon me an unrestricted right to act officially upon this judgment and feeling."

By temperament Lincoln was tolerant, patient, noncensorious. By nature he was practical, moderate, gradual. Being what he was, he preferred to see changes come slowly and after due deliberation and with the consent of all affected groups. Almost instinctively Lincoln inclined to a middle-of-the-road position on issues. A man who thought like this was definitely not the kind of leader desired by ideologues like Phillips—a leader who was ready to do what God would do if God had possession of all the facts.

II

The historians of intellectual life have emphasized that four primary principles formed the basis of American political philosophy in the middle years of the nineteenth century when Lincoln was growing into mental maturity. Americans might quarrel about the application of these principles to specific current issues, but to an extraordinary degree they were accepted as common beliefs, so much so that some writers have referred to them as articles of the national faith. The four ideas may be conveniently summarized:

(1) A supernatural power, God or a Guiding Providence or nature, exercised a controlling influence over the affairs of men. God had created a divine or higher law for the guidance of humans, and men could apprehend this law and should seek to approximate their own statutes to it.

(2) Man was not just another creature on the planet, but a being with a higher nature; or, as some put it, he had within him a spark of the divine. He had a mind, and hence could reason, and he had a conscience, and hence could distinguish right from wrong. This being true, he could govern himself through democratic forms and could achieve, if not perfectibility, a high degree of political maturity and a fair measure of happiness.

(3) The best economic system was one based on private ownership of property and one in which most people were property owners. The right to acquire property was a natural right, and all men should strive to secure property. Under the workings of the system, some would get more than others but no great inequities would result as long as equal opportunity existed. And no class or group should enjoy special privileges that gave it an artificial advantage over others.

(4) The American Union was a unique and precious experiment in government. As the most successful example of popular government in a big country, the United States was the supreme demonstration of democracy and the hope of world democracy. It made men free in America, and eventually by the sheer force of its example would make them free everywhere. Americans were profoundly conscious of the Union's value to themselves and of its universal mission. This consciousness was one of the strongest forces sustaining American nationalism.

Lincoln took over all four of the common beliefs of his time and made them a part of his own thought. This is not to say that he borrowed them blindly or adopted them without analysis. Such a procedure would have been foreign to Lincoln's nature. Every idea he ever held was the result of long and tough thinking, of introspective brooding during which he turned a proposition over and over in his mind. When he finally arrived at the formulation of a fundamental principle, it usually became a permanent part of his mental makeup. Nevertheless, Lincoln must be classified as a derivative rather than a seminal thinker, as an expresser—in superb words—rather than an originator of ideas. He did, however, give a significant extension to one of the four principles, the exaltation of the American Union.

Statements attesting Lincoln's belief that a supernatural force controlled human activities are sprinkled throughout his public and private papers, and they appear in practically every phase of his political career. Even in his early years he was intrigued by the concept of this compelling force, which he sometimes called history. As he grew older he came to call it God. For most Americans, the notion of a Guiding Providence meant only that a benign deity exercised a general influence over the affairs of men and that within the divine framework men had some freedom to work out their destinies. History was not a haphazard process tending to nowhere in particular, but a progressive movement that was being guided toward a definite and high goal.

But Lincoln, with a deep mystic strain in his nature and with a constant sense of fatalism, both public and personal, pushed this idea further than most. It is no exaggeration to say that during the Civil War he developed a mechanistic interpretation of history. The great event with which his name is associated, the destruction of slavery, was, he believed, an act of divine power of which he was but the instrument. In a remarkable letter written in 1864 he reviewed the course of wartime emancipation, and then he added, "I claim not to have controlled events, but confess plainly that events have controlled me." In 1861 nobody had "devised, or expected" that the war would end slavery but now the institution was approaching extinction. "God alone can claim it. Whither it is tending seems plain. If God now wills the removal of a great wrong, and wills also that we of the North as well as you of the South, should pay fairly for our complicity in that wrong, impartial history will find therein new cause to attest and revere the justice and goodness of God." Lincoln stressed this theme again in the Second Inaugural Address when he said that the war was God's way of removing the evil of slavery as a punishment to both the North and the South for having condoned it. He realized that his ascription of inexorability would offend some people. "Men are not flattered by being shown that there has been a difference between the Almighty and them," he told Thurlow Weed. "To deny it, however, in this case, is to deny that there is a God governing the world."

The corollary to the principle of a supernatural power, the existence of a supernatural law, also formed a part of Lincoln's thought, but in his application of the principle to current issues he parted company with some of his fellow workers in the antislavery movement. From a reading of his papers, it is obvious that Lincoln believed there was a moral or higher law. "I hold," he said in the First Inaugural Address, "that in contemplation of universal law, and of the Constitution, the Union of these States is perpetual." It is just as obvious that he thought the Constitution approximated the spirit of divine law and embodied the best experience of man in government. He saw, or as Carl Sandburg has said, he sensed, that in a democracy there must be a balance between freedom and responsibility. The great merit of the American federal system was that it provided a balance between the government and the individual and between the nation and the states. Lincoln addressed himself to one of the fundamental problems of political science when, with his own government in mind, he asked: "Must a government, of necessity, be too strong for the liberties of its own people, or too weak to maintain its own existence?" The American system of divided powers, he thought, provided the only answer. "A majority, held in restraint by constitutional checks, and limitations, and always changing easily, with deliberate changes of popular opinions and sentiments, is the only true sovereign of a free people. Whoever rejects it, does of necessity, fly to anarchy or to despotism."

Lincoln accepted the principle of a higher law, but he refused to give it the logical extension, logical in theory, that some opponents of slavery gave it. If the supernatural law was perfect, it followed that human statutes that contravened it were illegal and must be changed. And if they could not be changed, they should not be obeyed. Some of the antislavery people persuaded themselves that the divine law concept justified the violation of any law protecting slavery. This was what William H. Seward meant when, in hurling defiance at the Fugitive Slave Act, he said, "There is a higher law than the Constitution." Lincoln also disliked the fugitive slave measure, but he could never have agreed to the idea that individuals could flout it, or any other law, merely because it conflicted with their interpretation of higher law. In some countries it might be necessary for men to defy the law, but in the United States, where change was easy and deliberate, such action was unnecessary and irresponsible. It constituted a flying to anarchy.

Rather than believing in the perfectibility of man, Lincoln thought that man was imperfect but was, nevertheless, the best instrument with which to accomplish the divine purpose. Rejecting the dream of unlimited social progress, Lincoln still believed that man was capable of improving himself and of increasing his political competence. His analysis was closer to the practical ideas of the Founding Fathers than to the romantic ideals of the thinkers of his own time. Lincoln readily grasped that the Fathers had not tried to establish a system of government based on human perfectibility but instead had created one that would enable men to raise progressively the level of their political maturity. In one of those "Fragments" in which he was wont to record his thinking, Lincoln wrote: "*Most governments* have been based, practically, on the denial of equal rights of men . . . ; *ours* began, by *affirming* those rights. They said, some men are too *ignorant,* and *vicious,* to share in government. Possibly so, said we; and, by your system, you would always keep them ignorant and vicious. We proposed to give *all* a chance; and we expected the weak to grow stronger, the ignorant wiser; and all better, and happier together. . . ."

It is Lincoln's economic thought that has provoked the widest differences of opinion among students of his life. The confusion derives from an attempt to apply labels, liberal and conservative, that have little applicability to the American scene, at least to the nineteenth century, and to a tendency of authors to project their own ideas and their images of the economic institutions of their day backward into time. Actually, Lincoln's views cannot be called either liberal or conservative in our sense of the words. Economics-wise he belongs to no party or group today, certainly not to the Republican and positively not to the New Deal. His economic concepts were completely the product of the economic system that he knew, and that system bears little resemblance to our own.

Lincoln grew to maturity during the preindustrial age of America's history; he became President when the nation stood at the threshold of the era of big business. Industrial combinations in the form that developed in the years after Appomattox did not exist. It is true that there were substantial aggregations of capital, especially in the Northeast, but these organizations and their future economic implication did not impress Lincoln and most Americans. (The opinion of some writers that Lincoln had only a very general understanding of economic matters is probably correct.) In the system that Lincoln saw about him—and this was particularly true of his own section, the Northwest—a large number of people owned property, in the shape of farms, factories, and shops, and made their living from the operation of their holdings. Unlike the present system, relatively few people worked for other people for wages or salaries. Many owners of property were also laborers in the sense that they worked in their own establishments. In short, this was a capitalistic economy that contained a lot of capitalists.

Lincoln's economic ideas were those of the average small capitalist of his time. It might be said that Lincoln and most Americans were "men on the make." That is, they wanted to raise their material standing by exercising the virtue of acquisitiveness. They saw nothing wrong with the drive to acquire property; indeed, they tended to glorify the property-getting process as a social good. In Lincoln's opinion the great merit of the American economic system was that it offered an equal opportunity to all men to secure property. And in his view equal opportunity would result in a system in which most men owned property. Lincoln respected labor, and he attested his respect in notable words on a number of occasions. Thus in his annual message to Congress in December, 1861, he said: "Labor is prior to, and independent of, capital. Capital is only the fruit of labor, and could never have existed if labor had not first existed. Labor is the superior of capital, and deserves much the higher consideration." But Lincoln's tributes to labor are usually misunderstood and misapplied today. They were not delivered to labor as a rival power to capital but to labor as a means of creating capital. Through his labor a man could become an owner or an employer. Lincoln always vehemently denied that American society was divided into two rigid classes of employers and employees. Most men, he argued, neither worked for others nor hired others to work for them; rather, they worked for themselves and were both capitalists and laborers. "There is no permanent class of hired laborers amongst us . . . ," Lincoln contended. "The hired laborer of yesterday labors on his own account to-day; and will hire others to labor for him to-morrow. Advancement—improvement in condition—is the order of things in a society of equals."

III

Of the four principles comprising the current creed of his time, the one that aroused Lincoln's deepest devotion was the exaltation of the American Union. This idea, or this image, of nationalism elicited the most frequent and the most eloquent passages in his writings, and to it he gave a significant extension that constitutes his only original contribution to political theory. It may be added that as a political actor Lincoln's chief concern was with nationality. When we say that as President he saved the Union, we are also saying that he preserved the nation—as both an abstraction and a physical reality. Perhaps Lincoln's truest title is not the Great Emancipator but the Great Nationalist. Three ideas stand out in Lincoln's concept of the nature and the significance of the Union. They, too, may be conveniently presented in itemized form:

(1) The nation was an organic whole, an entity that could never be artificially separated by men. The realities of geography—rivers, mountains, ocean boundaries—demanded that the United States remain united. Where, he asked the South in 1861, could a satisfactory line of division be drawn between two American nations? "Physically speaking, we cannot separate. We cannot remove our respective sections from each other, nor build an impassible wall between them." In his message to Congress in December, 1862, he gave a moving and also an exceedingly realistic description of the oneness of the United States, of what he called the "national homestead." The outstanding American geographical fact, he emphasized, was the great interior heartland of the Mississippi Valley dominating the whole nation. Did anyone really believe, he asked, that the Mississippi River could be permanently divided by a man-made line? The present strife between the North and the South had not sprung from any natural division between the sections, he insisted, but from differences among people, "the passing generations of men." The land, the national homestead, "in all its adaptations and aptitudes . . . demands unity, and abhors separation. In fact, it would, ere long, force reunion, however much of blood and treasure the separation might have cost."

(2) The American nation was uniquely different from all others in the cementing bond that held it together. Some nations were united by race, some by culture, some by tradition. But the United States, said Lincoln in his most original piece of thinking, was bound by an idea, the principle of equal opportunity for all that was pledged in the Declaration of Independence and embedded in the national consciousness. In a speech at Independence Hall in Philadelphia while on his way to Washington in 1861 to be inaugurated President, Lincoln tried to express what he thought was America's great idea. "I have often inquired of myself, what great principle or idea it was that kept this Confederacy so long together," he said. "It was not the mere matter of separation from the motherland, but that sentiment in the Declaration of Independence which gave liberty not alone to the people of this country, but hope

to the world for all future time. It was that which gave promise that in due time the weights would be lifted from the shoulders of all men, and that *all* should have an equal chance."

(3) American nationality was not a narrow thing intended only for the benefit of Americans. The Union and the idea it represented made men free in America and sooner or later by the power of its example would make them free everywhere. Lincoln was supremely conscious of the world mission of his country. Always during the Civil War he tried to lift the Northern cause to a higher level than victory for one section or even the nation. Always he attempted to show that the preservation of the Union was important for the universal family of mankind. The was was "a people's content" to maintain "in the world, that form and substance of government, whose leading object" was "to elevate the condition of men." The "great republic . . . the principles it lives by, and keeps alive" represented "man's vast future." It was "the last, best hope of earth."

IV

The great problem that faced the men of Lincoln's time was slavery. In his thinking about slavery Lincoln applied to the problem all four of the principles that formed the substance of his general political faith. He was opposed to slavery on moral, democratic, and economic grounds. He thought that it was wrong for one man to own another. He feared that the presence of slavery in American society would subvert the idea of equal opportunity. If the notion that Negroes did not possess equal economic rights became fixed, he said, then the next easy transition would be to deny the same rights to white laborers. He believed that slavery gave a tone of hypocrisy to the claim that the United States symbolized the democratic cause and thus endangered the success of America's world mission.

Yet in his approach to the problem of slavery, Lincoln was completely pragmatic and practical. He outlined his position as early as 1837 in resolutions which he and a colleague presented in the Illinois legislature declaring that slavery was founded on "injustice and bad policy" but that Congress had no power to interfere with it in the states where it existed. To Lincoln one fact in the situation—a fact that the abolitionists and other sincere antislavery people ignored—was of vital importance: slavery existed in the United States and millions of people believed in it. The physical presence of slavery and the feelings of its Southern supporters, he argued, had to be taken into account by the opponents of the institution. "Because we think it wrong, we propose a coarse of policy that shall deal with it as a wrong," he said. But, he immediately added. "We have a due regard to the actual presence of it amongst us and the difficulties of getting rid of it in any satisfactory way and all the constitutional obligations thrown about it."

Again differing with most antislavery men and showing a keen awareness of social behavior, Lincoln refused to criticize the Southern people for supporting slavery. "They are just what we would be in their situation," he said at Peoria in 1854. "If slavery did not now exist amongst them, they would not introduce it. If it did now exist amongst us, we should not instantly give it up." In this Peoria speech Lincoln dealt with the racial problems that would inevitably follow the destruction of slavery. The question of racial adjustment was inextricably connected with emancipation. If the Negroes were freed, what would be their place in society? The abolitionists favored, at least abstractly, a status of complete equality for the colored people. But most antislavery men, particularly if they were politicians, which was usually the case, hardly ever discussed the position of the Negroes *after* freedom. They had not thought the problem through, probably did not want to think it to a conclusion. Perhaps this was one of the tragedies of the antislavery movement.

Lincoln admitted at Peoria, as he did on other occasions, that he did not know any absolutely satisfactory way of dealing with slavery and the related racial problem. If all earthly power were given him, he said, he would not know what do do. His first impulse would be to free the slaves and remove them outside the United States, but he conceded that this "colonization" plan was impractical and impossible. What of the proposal to give the freed slaves an equal place in society? This would not do, Lincoln thought, because the mass of white people South *and* North would not agree to such a status for colored people. And whether the feelings of the whites were just was beside the point, he said, because "A universal feeling, whether well or ill founded, cannot be safely disregarded." Lincoln's own feelings about race are not easily comprehended by modern men. Personally, he had no color prejudices, as his relations with Negroes while President amply attest. But like perhaps ninety-nine percent of Americans in the nineteenth century, he believed that the colored race, either by nature or by cultural inheritance, was inferior to the white race. Under any system of racial relations and even if the Negroes were free, the superior whites would seek to oppress the lesser race. Immediate emancipation, Lincoln feared, would not therefore benefit either race and would create for the Negroes problems almost as troublesome as those of slavery. As Professor Donald has pointed out, Lincoln's views may not be palatable to the modern reformer but they were an accurate analysis of current American opinion.

Lincoln opposed slavery, but he also opposed the abolitionists—the ideologues who wanted to destroy it immediately and who were certain that they had an absolutely satisfactory way of solving race relations. He disliked their readiness to impose their inner opinions on others, their eagerness to enforce a great social change based on a moral theory. He distrusted their abstract approach to a complex situation and their refusal to admit that all kinds of practical problems would result from a sudden change in that situation. Above all, he was appalled by their willingness to give up the Union if they could not make it over in their image. To him the preservation of American nationality was infinitely more important than the accomplishment of immediate emancipation. "Much as I hate slavery," he said, "I would consent to the extension of it rather than to see the Union dissolved, just as I would consent to any great evil, to avoid a greater one."

At the same time that he attacked the abolitionists' solution, Lincoln put forward his own plan to deal with the problem of slavery. It was to prevent slavery from expanding into the national territories, to pen it up in the states where it already existed. His proposal, he liked to say, would place slavery where the public mind could rest in the assurance that it was in "the course of ultimate extinction." If slavery could not grow, he argued, it would eventually wither and die a natural death. During the interim years, as the institution declined in social health, plans could be worked out for its orderly demise. The slaveholders themselves, perceiving the inevitable, would consent to emancipation and would receive financial compensation from the national government for the loss of their property. This kind of patient abolition, Lincoln thought, would bring in its wake no unfortunate results for either whites or blacks. Lincoln's plan would have taken years to effect, possibly a generation or more, but, and this is often forgotten by some of its critics, it was intended as a fundamental settlement of a problem that had to be settled finally. Lincoln's whole position on the slavery issue was in the finest American pragmatic tradition. He opposed immediate abolition because it would make a right change at the wrong time, would wreck the machine of the Union. He proposed to keep the machine going and to make the change later when the time was right.

Lincoln's plan for a gradual solution of the slavery problem never had a chance. There were too many men in the North and the South who could not wait that long, who were determined to settle the issue immediately, even if they had to resort to force. And so the Civil War came, and Lincoln became the President of a divided Union. He became also the leader of a divided North, of a people who differed among themselves as to the objectives of the war they were fighting. Specifically the question in issue was whether emancipation should be made one of the war aims. The discord in Northern opinion was reflected in Lincoln's own Republican party in the struggle between the Radical and the Conservative factions. The Radicals wanted to use the opportunity of the war to strike down slavery; they demanded that the Union be restored without slavery. Lincoln and the Conservatives hoped to avoid turning the war into a crusade for social change, he and most Conservatives preferred to restore the Union with slavery still intact.

To Lincoln the preservation of the Union, of American nationality, was the great overriding object of the war. The Union dwarfed all other issues, including slavery. Lincoln intended to save the Union by whatever methods he had to use. As he told Horace Greeley, to accomplish his purpose he would, if necessary, free all of the slaves or free none of them or free some and keep others in bondage. At the same time he understood cleraly the dynamics in the war situation. He knew that slavery was the provoking cause of the conflict. Slavery was "the disturbing element" in "the national house," he said, and it would continue to generate strife until it was removed. He knew, too, that the antislavery impulse would receive a tremendous impetus from the war. Lincoln approached slavery during the war in the same pragmatic spirit with which he had dealt with it before the war. He was ready to end it, as he would any other social evil, if he was convinced that the time was right and that greater evils would not result from its destruction.

At the beginning of hostilities Lincoln proposed that the sole objective of the war should be restoration of the Union. His immediate purpose was to bring all parties and factions in the North together in support of a war for the nation. This required a statement of war aims so simple and so national that all groups could unite behind it. But beyond the exigencies of public opinion, Lincoln did not want emancipation to become one of the war aims. He did not want slavery to be destroyed suddenly in the anger of civil conflict. If slavery was uprooted as a part of the war process, the change would be too violent; such a change would make it difficult, if not impossible, to solve the related problem of race relations. At the same time he realized that the situation created by the war demanded a more urgent approach to emancipation; a plan had to be worked out *now* to place slavery in the course of extinction. In an effort to provide such a plan, Lincoln, on several occasions, asked the border states congressmen to join with him in initiating a scheme for compensated gradual emancipation. With singular blindness they ignored his ideas.

Inevitably the facts of the war made Lincoln's hopes and plans for a gradual, orderly reform of the slavery problem impossible. Only in a short war, as he probably realized, could he have carried his policy. The longer the struggle continued, the more hostile Northern opinion became to slavery. It was unnatural that the Northern people would fight and sacrifice, for any period, to preserve an institution that in the opinion of most was the cause of the war. By the summer of 1862 every political sign indicated that the Northern masses wanted slavery destroyed as a result of the war. Now Lincoln faced a dilemma. If he opposed the popular will, if he persisted in postponing a settlement of the slavery issue to some future date, he would divide Northern opinion and perhaps wreck the entire war effort. He would, and this was the vital point, defeat his larger objective of preserving American nationality. If he wanted to keep the machine running, he had to make a change; if he did not, the machine might break down.

For Lincoln there could be only one response and one action. It was at this time that he decided to issue the Emancipation Proclamation and to make emancipation a second aim of the war. He changed his position because the impelling dynamics of war had created a new situation that demanded a new policy. To the theoretical moralist, to the intellectual reformer, to the prophet of blueprints, his shift may seem unprincipled and opportunistic. Actually, Lincoln's stand on slavery was always completely moral. Before the war he had opposed abolition because it would destroy the Union. During the war he used abolition to save the Union. He opposed a right change at the wrong time and supported the same change at the right time. His course is the supreme example in our history of the union of principle and pragmatism in politics.

Foundations of the Southern Nation

Emory Thomas

John Locke had been dead a long time in 1861. Southern secessionists, however, resurrected him and the American revolutionaries of 1776, for whom he was the essential political patriarch. Southerners perceived their political circumstances as being parallel to those of the Founding Fathers: both sets of revolutionaries believed that they were dissolving Lockean compacts—the British Empire and the United States of America. For a time, the secessionists argued, these compacts had served the best interests of the contracting parties. Then, just as George III and his Parliament threatened the well-being of the American colonies, so Abraham Lincoln and his Republican Congress threatened the essentials of the Southern way of life. Similar problems called forth similar solutions—secession and independence—justified by the Lockean theory of the right of revolution.

In both cases catharsis came only after a prolonged period of radical activity. It has been the fashion to speak of the Southern secessionist leaders as "fire-eaters." Applied to Edmund Ruffin and men like him, the term is accurate to a point. Yet Ruffin and company were more than side-show performers; they were dedicated revolutionaries as well. With no less zeal and skill than James Otis or Sam Adams, the fire-eaters pursued their radical cause. Secession was not just a spontaneous restatement of Lockean theory; it was the culmination of years of radical tactics and revolutionary propaganda.

By February 1, 1861, seven Southern states had reenacted, they believed, the revolutionary "secession" of the Founding Fathers. In the process, Southerners had been preoccupied with a political philosophy whose end was revolution and with radical agitation whose goal was dissolution of the Union. In February 1861, however, the time for rending a nation was past; the time for making a nation from independent republics had arrived. Secession was basically a negative process. Once secession was accomplished Southern leaders faced the challenge of doing something positive: creating the Confederate States of America. To do this, representatives from six seceded states—South Carolina, Mississippi, Florida, Alabama, Georgia, and Louisiana (Texas completed the secession process late and her delegates arrived later)—gathered in Montgomery, Alabama, on February 4, 1861.

The choice of Montgomery as the site of the secessionists' convention revealed a great deal about the process of disunion just completed by the states of the deep South. The seven separate secessions which took place during the forty-three days between December 20, 1860, and February 1, 1861, were not spontaneous risings of an untutored mass of people. However fundamental and unreconcilable were the issues which provoked the Southern separation, the break with the Union did not just happen; people had to make it happen. In every Southern state were radical secessionists whose agitation transformed Southern ideology into Southern nationalism. Their zeal was genuine, and in the minds of fellow Southerners their cause was authentic; otherwise, they would have become generals with no armies. Yet the task of the radicals, as they perceived it, was more than educating and agitating; it was to plan carefully the process of their revolution as well as to proclaim its substance.

For many years the radicals had debated among themselves the tactics of their hypothetical coup. Two basic problems confronted them. First, should the Southern nation originate from concerted action by all or most of the Southern states, or should the states secede separately and then act in concert? Second, should the slaveholding border states be a part of the original Southern nation; or would it be wiser to induce the upper South to act as a buffer against reprisals from the North and then allow time to tell just how Southern the border really was? As it happened, partly by design and partly by accident, the radical leadership followed a compromise course in solving both of these tactical problems.

South Carolina seceded alone, but not quite as separately as it appeared. "Cooperationists," as the advocates of concerted action called themselves, were numerous and well placed in South Carolina. Actually "cooperationist" was an ambiguous label; some adopted it literally and believed in Southern unity before all else; others were cooperationists out of the fear of rash action and wished to explore with other Southerners all avenues of obtaining Southern rights before rending the Union; still others assumed a cooperationist stance to conceal from themselves and/or others unionist sympathies in hopes that "cooperation" would slow, then stall the secession band wagon.

The radicals' tactic, as it emerged, was to convene as many disunited states as possible as soon as possible. If the states of the upper South should choose to secede with the cotton South, well and good. If they should choose to wait, perhaps even better. Yancey probably stated this view best in a letter to Virginia newspaper editor Roger A. Pryor. "A well conducted Southern policy," Yancey wrote, "would seem to demand that, when such a movement [secession] takes place by any considerable number of Southern States, Virginia and the other border States should remain in the Union, where, by their position and their councils, they would prove more effective friends than by moving out of the Union, and thus giving the Southern Confederacy a long, hostile border to watch. In the event of such a movement being successful, in time Virginia and the other border States, could join." The Southern radicals were not clairvoyant; yet the selection of Montgomery as the convention site was an accurate prediction of the new nation's geographical center and an index of how carefully the radicals had managed their coup.

The assembly at Montgomery of fifty delegates from seven seceded states represented a great victory for Southern radicals. But much remained to be done—nothing less than the creation of a Southern nation.

To all appearances, the Montgomery Convention did its work well. There was at Montgomery, according to one delegate, a perfect "mania for unanimity." And in just five days the delegates adopted a provisional constitution, elected a provisional president and vice-president, and resolved themselves into the provisional Congress of the new nation. Appearances, however, were deceiving. Even in the midst of their triumph, the Southern radicals found themselves called upon to compromise their Southernism and to calm their ardor. The Confederacy created at Montgomery was not exactly what the super-Southerners like Rhett, Ruffin, and Yancey wanted. The convention's moderate majority was interested in preserving what it believed was the Southern status quo in the new nation; it was not willing to expand or intensify that status quo. The differences were subtle but important. The fire-eating radicals who had devoted much of their lives to Southern nationalism found themselves suddenly elevated to roles as irrelevant elder statesmen in the Southern nation. In the end few if any of them made any significant contribution to the Confederacy. Having worked and planned so long to give birth to it, more than one of the radicals became disillusioned with the infant nation; thus in response to the Confederacy's constitutional prohibition of the African slave trade, South Carolinian L. W. Spratt lamented, *"our whole movement is defeated. It will abolitionize the Border Slave States—it will brand our institution. Slavery cannot share a government with democracy—it cannot bear a brand upon it; thence another revolution. It may be painful, but we must make it."*

To understand the subtle schism between what the Confederacy was supposed to be and what it became, it is necessary to look at some of the men who assumed leadership at Montgomery and during the processes of secession which brought them to the convention. The mechanics of disunion were important because they significantly affected the actions and attitudes of the Montgomery delegates and they revealed most clearly the tension between the rival themes of radical theory and constructive action coexisting in the Southern political mind.

South Carolina's situation was especially instructive. The Palmetto State had both a long tradition of secessionist notions and a heritage of unionism and moderation. In the spring of 1860 South Carolina radicalism seemed to have reached a low ebb; the National Democrats, who proposed to save the South and the Union through the Democratic Party, gained control of Carolina polity. As a result, when the Democrats refused to adopt a platform containing strong guarantees for slavery, the state delegation to the Democratic Nominating Convention followed, rather than led, the Southern walkout in Charleston.

The subsequent sectional division of the Democratic Party and the strong probability of Lincoln's election in the fall of 1860 discredited South Carolina's National Democrats and gave radical secessionists the leverage they needed. Even so, South Carolina might not have been the first state out of the Union had it not been for its conservative constitution, which required the legislature instead of the voters to select presidential electors. When the legislature convened on November 5 to choose electors, a national Republican victory appeared certain. Accordingly, Governor Gist kept the solons in session to await the election results. Once Lincoln's victory was sure, Gist requested a secession convention, and his legislature issued a call for elections. From this point the die was cast. Unionists made poor showings when they dared to run for convention seats, and most of the cooperationists, convinced that ultimately South Carolina would not secede alone, supported separate state action. The convention met on December 17, and three days later by a unanimous vote of the delegates South Carolina seceded. Had an outbreak of smallpox not forced the body to move from Columbia to Charleston, the process would have been even shorter.

The Palmetto Republic made not one, but two declarations of independence, in which the convention attempted to explain and justify disunion. The "Declaration of the Immediate Causes of Secession," drafted by Memminger, focused on threats to slavery and slavery expansion made by the North during the recent past and likely to be made by the Republican Party in the near future. The "Address to the Slaveholding States," drafted by Rhett, was an extended dissertation which began with the Constitutional Convention of 1787 and rambled through a long catalog of sectional issues and crises, demonstrating Southern righteousness and Yankee perfidy at every point.

Rhett and Memminger shared a zeal for disunion; both were sincere Southern nationalists, yet the difference in the documents they produced was revealing. Rhett had been dreaming of a separate Southern nation for more than half of his sixty-one years. An austere, reserved man, he abstained from liquor and comradeship. About the South, though, Rhett had no reservations and exercised little control over his emotions. Rhett's vision of what the South had been and should be was deep and fixed; Southern ideology had made him an idealogue. All this came through in his "Address"; it was a fundamental appeal to Southern nationalism.

Memminger, on the other hand, although he had absorbed the Southern life style as deeply as Rhett, had come late to Southern nationalism. Born in Germany and orphaned in Charleston at a very young age, Memminger had acquired the education and background to go with his native abilities and had become a successful lawyer in his adopted city. His mind was flexible; he was a tactician instead of an idealogue. Once convinced that moderation was suicidal and cooperation futile, Memminger became a straight-out secessionist. He shared his countrymen's hopes and, more important, he knew their fears. Thus, while Rhett's "Address" appealed to hopes for a neo-Greek democracy, Memminger's "Declaration" dwelt upon fears for the sanctity and expansion of slavery. Both Carolinians were hyper-Southern; but while Rhett espoused eternal principles, Memminger sought successful strategems. Georgian T. R. R. Cobb expressed the difference. "Rhett," Cobb wrote to his wife, "is a generous hearted and honest man with a vast quantity of cranks and a small proportion of common sense." "Memminger," he added, "is as shrewd as a Yankee, a perfect—metamorphosed into a legislating lawyer."

The Mississippi experience was similar to that of South Carolina. Radicals in both states had tried to provoke secession in 1850 and 1851. Both had seen their hopes founder when the other Southern states failed to unite on the issue and their fellow Carolinians and Mississippians shrank from seceding alone. The events of 1860 renewed secessionist hopes, and Mississippi radicals were quick to seize their opportunity. In the 1860 presidential election John C. Breckinridge, the Southern Democrat, received 59 percent of the vote in Mississippi; John Bell, the Constitutional Union moderate candidate 36.2 percent; and Northern Democrat Stephen A. Douglas only 4.8 percent. Shortly after Lincoln's election, Governor J. J. Pettus called a special session of the Mississippi legislature to debate the fate of the state, and the solons called for elections to a convention.

Mississippians elected a strong secessionist majority to the state convention. The radical leadership was composed of relatively young lawyers and planters, men on the make who had the most to lose if the slave-plantation system were to die or fail to expand. The cooperationists and unionists were older men and politically more conservative (Whiggish) than the secessionist-democratic majority. On January 9, 1861, an ordinance of secession carried the convention, 84 to 15; eventually, ninety-eight of the convention's one hundred members signed the ordinance.

The Mississippians at Montgomery faithfully reflected the radical leadership of their state. For the most part they were young planters and lawyers who held few slaves and whose greatest service and status appeared to be in the future. Although the Mississippi delegation was representative and capable, it is interesting to note who was *not* included. None of the really great cotton planters was there; the old line secessionists, Pettus, John A. Quitman, and L. Q. C. Lamar, were noticeably absent; and those who were in Montgomery proved to be less doctrinaire than expected. Perhaps there was a hint of nascent moderation in Mississippians at the secession convention. In the aftermath of secession, that body passed (66 to 13) a resolution against renewing the African slave trade. Significantly, Mississippi and Mississippi Senator Jefferson Davis had been among the leaders of the movement to reopen that trade as recently as 1859. Davis, however, was now pursuing an ambiguous course; in the aftermath of Lincoln's election he had advised against immediate secession. Having accepted the risks and dangers of secession, Mississippians seemed more concerned about tactics designed to solidify their revolution than about doctrinaire proposals designed to carry the revolution to its logical extreme.

Alabama secessionists had a far more difficult task than their counterparts in Mississippi and South Carolina, much to the chagrin of the state's foremost secessionist, William Lowndes Yancey. Born in Georgia in 1814, Yancey grew up in Troy, New York, attended Williams College, then returned south to "read law" with South Carolina unionist Benjamin F. Perry. After some experience as a lawyer and newspaper editor in South Carolina, he moved to Dallas County, Alabama, where his reputation as a courtroom orator quickly led him into politics. Yancey soon forsook the unionist persuasions of his legal preceptor and during the 1840s became a strong advocate of Southern rights. To answer the Wilmot Proviso of 1846, which proposed making land gained in the Mexican War free soil, he formulated the Alabama Platform, insuring the protection of slave property in the territories, and walked out of the Democratic convention of 1848 when his platform was not adopted. During the 1850s Yancey abandoned hope of seeking the South's salvation in the Democratic party or the Union, and thereafter he devoted his skill and influence to Southern independence. The next time he walked out of a Democratic convention, in Charleston in 1860, most of the delegates from six other Southern states followed. This triggered the sectional split in the party which facilitated Lincoln's election and led to South Carolina's secession. Then, in November, Breckinridge carried Alabama; but the candidates of moderation, Bell and Douglas, had a combined vote total of 41,526, which compared respectably to Breckinridge's 48,831.

Governor Andrew B. Moore was a strong secessionist, more than willing to comply with his legislature's authorization to call a state convention in the event a "Black Republican" was elected president. Campaigns for delegate seats were brisk. Alabama cooperationists divided sharply in their response to the secession question—some favored eventual secession, others were covert unionists, and many wavered between these poles. Consequently the cooperationist cause lacked unity and direction.

Geographical conditions and political heritage complicated the situation. North Alabama was traditionally the home of small farmers and Jacksonian Democrats. Holding few if any slaves and revering the political memory of Andrew Jackson as frontier nationalist, north Alabamians were almost solidly cooperationists. Alabama urbanites, the few there were, also generally voted cooperationist moderation. In Mobile and Montgomery, however, the influence of planter residents and large slave populations added to the radical count. South and central Alabama had the geographical hallmarks of secessionism: plantations, cotton, and slaves. In 1850 and 1851, however, the north Alabama Democrats had joined the central and south Alabama Whigs to squelch the radicals. In 1860 the Whigs went over to secession, and united with the state's secessionist Democrats, they produced a working radical majority in the Alabama convention.

As in Mississippi, the secessionist leaders in the state convention were young planters and lawyers with relatively few slaves—men with a stake in the continuance of the Southern status quo. Cooperationists, as a group, were older, less wealthy and held even fewer slaves than the strong secessionists.

In 1860 the state of Florida was essentially an extension of Alabama and Georgia. In terms of population it was quite small; the entire population, approximately 78,000 whites and 63,000 blacks, was less than that of New Orleans. On the heels of Lincoln's election, Governor Madison S. Perry charged his legislature to call a state convention and the members complied. Perry was present in Charleston when South Carolina seceded, and presumably shared with other radical leaders in Florida the object lesson in disunion he had learned. On December 22 the voters chose secession convention delegates, electing forty-two secessionists and twenty-seven cooperationists. There was no marked difference in the backgrounds of the two factions. Apparently the best index of secession or cooperation in Florida was proximity to Georgia and Alabama. Northern counties were more likely to elect cooperationists because their voters wanted to wait and see what Georgia and Alabama did about secession. Florida cooperationists, as a group, favored united secession.

Georgia had the most land and the most people of any state in the deep South and was therefore crucial to the secessionist cause. Moreover, that state was the vital hinge between the seaboard and the gulf South. Back in 1850 a convention of Georgians had frustrated the radical secession scheme by agreeing to wait and test the Compromise of 1850 rather than attending a Southern convention and concerting secession. The Georgia Platform, a strong ultimatun to the North to abide by the 1850 Compromise, had dealt a death blow to the secessionists' hopes at the time. By 1860 circumstances and minds had changed. On December 6, Howell Cobb, President James Buchanan's secretary of the treasury and acknowledged leader of Georgia Democrats, resigned his national office and publicly announced his support for secession.

Cobb's brother T. R. R. Cobb had long been among the radical leaders, and Robert Toombs, Whig senator and erratic genius, also joined the campaign for immediate secession. To counter this powerful secessionist triumvirate were three highly respected Georgia moderates: Alexander H. Stephens, who believed immediate secession unwise but agreed to abide by his state's decision, Herschel V. Johnson, Douglas' Democratic running mate in 1860, and Benjamin Harvey Hill, who lent strong Whig support.

In November, Georgia Governor Joseph E. Brown, a staunch secessionist, requested from his legislature a million-dollar appropriation with which to arm the state and a convention to vote secession. The legislature debated two weeks before agreeing to call the convention. The delay was an accurate indication of the division in Georgia's political mind. Campaigns for 301 delegate seats at the convention was intense. The radicals used every tactic at their disposal. Howell Cobb, not himself a candidate, traveled throughout the state campaigning for straight-out secessionists. Toombs returned to Washington to see for himself whether compromise was possible, then on December 23 dispatched dramatic telegrams to Georgia's leading newspapers reaffirming his support for immediate secession. Results of the delegate elections on January 2 promised a close but clear secessionist majority in the convention. Still, Governor Brown apparently juggled the vote totals supplied to the press to make it appear that the popular vote overwhelmingly favored immediate secession. Authorized by the convention to keep the actual count a secret, Brown reported the vote as 50,243 to 37,123 for secessionists; an accurate count shows that a slim majority of Georgians in fact voted for cooperationists (42,714 to 41,717).

Georgians were the most numerous and probably the most talented of the delegates at Montgomery. Both Cobbs were there; Howell Cobb was elected president of the convention, and T. R. R. Cobb was an active member of the committee that drafted the permanent Constitution. Stephens, who attended although he had expressed some reservations when chosen by the Georgia convention, was a moderating force in the debates, and his election as Confederate vice-president was an index of the convention's moderate temper as well as Stephens' new-found loyalty. Toombs was a somewhat enigmatic figure at Montgomery. Originally he had hoped to become president of the Confederacy; when the hope proved illusory, he made his peace with Stephens and led a "loyal opposition" to the Cobbs.

The Georgia delegation well reflected the secession process which brought them to Montgomery. Of the ten delegates, three were Democrats and seven Whigs, four had been cooperationists, and six had been leaders of the straight-out secessionists. Most of the time this diverse group acted together—a significant commentary upon the convention's determination to present a united front.

In Louisiana secessionist sentiment was slow to form until the crisis of 1860 and 1861. The radicals had made little headway in the state, whose principal city, New Orleans, was a national trading and transportation center and whose most characteristic crop, sugar, was protected by the national tariff. When the fever of disunion struck, however, it became an infectious contagion. In the 1860 presidential election, Breckinridge Democrats carried Louisiana by only a narrow plurality. Lincoln's election, though, disenchanted many of the Whiggish supporters of the Constitutional Unionist moderate Bell. Thus when Governor Thomas O. Moore called for a convention to consider secession the legislature complied.

On January 7, Louisianians elected eighty straight-out secessionists, forty-four cooperationists, and six undecided delegates to the state convention. As in Georgia, the radicals reported a greater popular vote margin for secessionist delegates than was actually cast. The New Orleans *Daily Delta* gave secessionist candidates 54.2 percent of the vote; the actual returns indicate secessionists received 52.3 percent. Louisiana cooperationists, however, were more inclined toward secession than their counterparts in other states, especially since the convention met after five states had already seceded. Louisiana secessionists tended to be richer and larger slaveholders than their brethren elsewhere and to come from parishes where cotton was the principal crop. The cooperationists came either from the farmer class of the northern parishes or from the sugar-planting regions in he southern part of the state.

The convention voted secession on January 25 by a majority of 113 to 17. Louisiana then accepted the South Carolina Program and chose six delegates to the Montgomery Convention. These delegates, like Louisiana's radical leaders, were wealthy slaveholders committed to the Confederacy. Men of means, they determined that a Southern nation could best protect those means; well satisfied and well treated by the status quo, they went to Montgomery to preserve it.

Texas was exceptional. Governor Sam Houston, an unalterable foe of secession, refused to call the legislature into session or to heed radical demands for a convention. In the impasse a number of influential secessionists took it upon themselves to call an extralegal convention. Houston countered by calling a special session of the legislature, hoping it would denounce the proceedings; but it did just the opposite, approving the idea of a convention. Relying upon the right of Texans expressed in the state constitution to alter or abolish their government and upon this belated legislative approval for legitimacy, the Texas secession convention met in Austin in late January and passed 152 to 6 a resolution favoring secession. On February 1, Texas formally voted to secede (166 to 8); included in the ordinance was the provision that it be referred to the voters for final approval. The popular vote confirmed the convention's actions by more than three to one, and in time even Houston acquiesced in the action and coexisted with the Confederacy.

Because of the necessary referendum and the relative tardiness of the state's secession, the Texas delegation arrived in Montgomery too late to debate the provisional Constitution or to help elect the president and vice-president. Indeed the delegation did not officially claim its seats until the permanent Constitution was in its final stages of debate. Most colorful among the Texans was Louis Trezaunt Wigfall, a South Carolina native who had moved to Texas because he owed too much money and had fought too many duels in South Carolina. A staunch fire-eater, Wigfall persisted in his doctrinaire Southernism as senator in every Confederate Congress. Among the less colorful Texans was John H. Reagan, who became postmaster general of the Confederacy.

Including the Texans, fifty men served in the Montgomery Convention. Although two-fifths of them had been cooperationists in their home states, it is safe to say that with one or two exceptions all of the delegates endorsed by their presence the *fait accompli* of secession and wished their new nation well.

Secession was a radical act, and the process of disunion was the product of radical men and tactics. The Montgomery Convention, on the other hand, was a moderate, even conservative, body. This paradoxical sequence of radicalism followed by moderation is understandable only in the context of the delegates' background and recent experience. Even the most radical delegates realized that disunion had been not the unanimous choice of the Southern people, but often the tenuous choice of an emotional moment. And most of the delegates realized that if the Confederacy were to survive, it needed the good will and support of at least its own people and if possible people in the upper South, Europe, and even the North. The Confederates made a revolution to preserve and protect the Southern status quo from encroachment. At Montgomery they attempted to frame a government which would do precisely that.

Having agreed upon their mission, delegates next voted to conduct much of their business in secret sessions which promised fewer public poses from the delegates, encouraged free debate, and still allowed the convention to present a united front. With these preliminaries behind them, the delegates began the substantive business of drafting a provisional Constitution.

A committee of twelve chaired by Memminger worked steadily for two days and nghts and on the afternoon of February 7 presented their results. Next day the delegates debated the document and about midnight unanimously adopted it.

Memminger's committee used the United States Constitution as its model. The common assumption was that the work done in Philadelphia in 1787, with a few adjustments, would serve the Southern nation well enough—as long as Southerners were free to construe it properly. There were significant differences, however. The preamble of the new Constitution spoke of "sovereign and independent states" instead of "we, the people" and invoked "the favor of

Almighty God." The delegates passed over potentially divisive points about tariffs and slavery and agreed to deal with them at more leisure when they took up the permanent Constitution. The provisional Constitution provided for an item veto by the president, thus eliminating the practice of attaching unrelated riders to legislation; included a procedure to be followed in the event of presidential disability; and combined district and circuit court systems into a single district system in which each state constituted a district. Aside from these adjustments, the provisional government was little different in structure from that of the United States.

After adopting the provisional Constitution, the convention adjourned late on the night of February 8 and agreed to hold elections for provisional president and vice-president the following day. So far there had been amazingly little politicking on the subject. Rhett believed he had earned the honor. However, since honor must be bestowed rather than grasped, Rhett had not sought it openly, and his fellow South Carolinians did not put him forward. Howell Cobb was a contender but had said he did not want the job; and some, including his brother T. R. R. Cobb, believed him. A few delegates favored Toombs, and so did Toombs; but support for the fiery Georgian never grew, as his erratic statesmanship and hard drinking made him unacceptable to those delegates who demanded propriety and respectability. According to Stephens, Toombs was "tight every day at dinner" and "about two days before the election" Toombs was "*tighter* than I ever saw him." Yancey was unacceptable for some of the same reasons. He had so long been identified with radicalism that many were afraid of him. Stephens was the third Georgian under consideration, but although he was an energetic member of the convention, his eleventh-hour conversion to the Confederacy was a strong point against him, and in his own delegation were men whose political memories of Stephens were long and unpleasant. From the beginning the name most often mentioned was Jefferson Davis.

Davis had many of the qualifications which the Montgomery delegates sought. He had been a strong Southern rights man—but not too strong, like Yancey and Rhett. His public experience had been broad; he had been congressman and senator, had graduated from West Point, fought with distinction in the Mexican War, and served the Pierce administration as secretary of war. This military background was important; for even though the Southerners repeatedly told themselves and others that the North would not fight to restore the seceded states to the Union, their words were more hopeful than confident, and just in case they might be wrong, they wanted a constitutional commander-in-chief who would command. Few delegates knew Davis well; few people ever did. In time many of them would make judgments of Davis the man; but for the moment his public record was more important than his private life. And if Davis seemed a bit aloof, so much the better—dignity was important in the government of a revolutionary nation, and Davis looked like a president.

By the time the convention could turn its full attention to the choice of a president, three state delegations (Florida, Mississippi, and Alabama) favored Davis. Louisiana and South Carolina were uncommitted; Davis and Cobb had supporters in both delegations. Georgia was the least committed, having three serious contenders in its own delegation. At this juncture Cobb repeated his disclaimer and "immediately announced his wish that Davis should be unanimously elected." Accordingly every delegation except Georgia met in caucus and agreed upon him. The Georgians met at ten o'clock on February 9, an hour before the convention was to reassemble to vote. To the Cobbs' chagrin, Stephens emerged as Georgia's choice for vice-president, and the other state delegations agreed to vote for him. Thus Howell Cobb's magnanimity in refusing to contest the presidency not only cost him the opportunity of leading the Confederacy; it also advanced the career of his Georgia rival.

When the convention gathered on the ninth, the election, which had beeen so uncertain the night before, became a *pro forma* ceremony. The convention elected Davis and Stephens unanimously, thus preserving the appearance of unity and harmony. In the process delegates effectively snubbed the old radical secessionists in favor of "safe" Southerners.

President-elect Davis arrived in Montgomery on February 16. A large crowd followed him from the railroad station to the Exchange Hotel. There Yancey welcomed him and proclaimed that "the man and the hour have met!" As Davis offered his thanks, the symbolism of the moment was perfect. Yancey, the fire-eater, surrendered the stage to Davis, the statesman. The radicals' hour was over; sensible men had come to Montgomery to carry out a revolution made by others.

Two days after his arrival, Davis was inaugurated provisional president. An estimated ten thousand people, more than the town's population, watched the procession to the steps of the capitol, then thronged in front of the building to witness the ceremony. Before taking the oath of office, Davis delivered an inaugural address. Davis was known as a logician; but his address strained logic. He began by drawing the common parallel between what Southerners had done and what their grandfathers had done in the American Revolution. Then after invoking "the right of the people to alter or abolish governments," he abruptly asserted, "it is by abuse of language that their act [forming the Confederacy] has been denominated a revolution." Only in the context of the moment in Montgomery did Davis' revolution-no-revolution non sequitur make sense. The new President was supposed to allay fears, and he knew it; consequently most of his speech was a recital of how unchanged was the Southern status quo. "We have changed the constituent parts," he said, "but not the system of our Government." Davis' message was clear: we have exercised the right of revolution, he was saying, but we did so only to preserve the Southern life style. Davis believed what he said, and none of his listeners seemed to question his logic.

Now the convention turned to its final task as a constituent assembly, the permanent Constitution. While a drafting committee worked, the convention took up its role as provisional Congress and began debating and enacting legislation. Committee members worked long and hard at their assignment and sandwiched their labors on the Constitution between sessions of Congress. T. R. R. Cobb, for example, spent mornings with his congressional committee, afternoons in sessions of Congress, and nights with the constitutional committee.

On the last day of February the draft was ready for debate. For ten days the delegates doubled as members of the provisional Congress in the morning and of the constitutional convention in the afternoon. Finally, on March 11, they unanimously adopted the Constitution. In just thirty-five days, less than half the time it took the Founding Fathers to write the United States Constitution, the delegates had laid the foundation of the Southern Confederacy.

Like the provisional Constitution, the permanent document was an altered version of the United States Constitution. Some of the basic changes from the United States Constitution included in the provisional framework reappeared in the new document: the item veto, prohibition of the slave trade, strictures against tariffs, a district court structure, and a procedure to be followed in case of presidential disability. Rhett and some of the South Carolina delegates were bitterly disappointed about the prohibition of the slave trade but found themselves almost alone in this matter.

As might be expected, the Constitution expressly protected slavery in the Confederacy and its territories—"No . . . law denying or impairing the right of property in negro slaves shall be passed." The Constitution also forbade "internal improvements" and restricted the Congress from making appropriations not specifically requested by the executive branch unless the appropriations received a two-thirds majority vote in both houses. Congress was authorized to grant seat and voice to cabinet members so they might join debates over bills which concerned their departments. The Confederate Post Office was required to become self-sustaining within two years. The Confederate president was to serve six years but could not succeed himself. These provisions were adjustments in the old Constitution designed to realign its checks and balances and make the government as responsive and efficient as possible.

Significantly, the convention retained the "three-fifths clause" about the counting of slaves when determining a state's population for the purposes of taxation and congressional representation. The "necessary and proper" clause (Article I, Section 8, of the U.S. Constitution), too, remained, as did the theoretical basis of judicial review implied in the authorization of Congress to create a Supreme Court. On balance and in theory, the Confederate executive was probably stronger than his United States counterpart. Although he could not serve more than one term, that term was six instead of four years, and he had the power of item veto and strong control over appropriations.

Ironically, the most striking feature of the Confederate Constitution was not its Southern orientation. The permanent Constitution prescribed for the Confederacy much the same kind of union which the Southerners had dissolved.

Although the Montgomery Convention spent only ten days debating the Constitution before adopting it unanimously, it was during these deliberations that the sacred harmony of the convention came closest to shattering. Just as the Philadelphia Convention in 1787 had had a crucial "Great Debate" over state representation in Congress, so the Montgomery delegates had a great debate over admission of new states into the Confederacy. Led by Rhett, William P. Miles of South Carolina, and T. R. R. Cobb, convention radicals proposed to exclude nonslave states from the Confederacy. The moderates, Toombs, Stephens, and the president, who expressed his opinion privately, wished to leave the door open. The radicals feared reconstruction and even suggested that there was a move afoot to restore the old Union under the Confederate Constitution. Moreover, they feared that if nonslave states were admitted, free soil in the South would lead to "free-soilers" and doom the Confederacy to battle abolitionists all over again. The moderates argued that trade and transportation systems (the Mississippi River, for example) might in time attract free states to the Confederacy; they did not wish arbitrarily to exclude them and, with them, the hope of expansion into the west and perhaps into Mexico. The Montgomery Great Debate ended in compromise, as had the debate in Philadelphia in 1787. John G. Shorter of Alabama proposed that new states be admitted to the Confederacy by a vote of two-thirds of the House of Representatives and the Senate, with each state casting one vote in the Senate. The convention adopted Shorter's compromise, thus keeping the door open to free states, while the radicals found some comfort in the fact that free states would have to secure more than simple majority vote to enter the slaveholders' union.

The Great Debate at Montgomery was the last real obstacle in the way of the convention. When the delegates completed the Constitution, they could consider the Confederacy founded and themselves founding fathers. During the Great Debate, the radicals had made their last stand to extend and intensify the slaveholders' ideology, while the moderators resisted because they were satisfied to retain the Southern status quo and because they believed that in the real world nothing more than that was possible. The moderates won, as they had won other essential points at Montgomery, because the fundamental goal of the Southern revolution was the preservation of the Southern life style as Southerners then lived it. Southerners generally had adopted radical rhetoric and tactics to transform their ideology into nationalism; but once that transformation had occurred in secession, the radicals became superfluous. Confederates did not believe they needed to make new worlds; they were more than content with the world they already had. At Montgomery the moderate majority tried to codify the Southern status quo and to present a favorable image to the South and the rest of the world, and with the founding of the Confederacy they believed they had succeeded.

The People's War

William Barney

Ironies come cheaply in writing about the Civil War. The North, which went to war initially to preserve the Union as it was, with slavery intact, found that the war could be won only by restructuring the Union, with slavery destroyed. Southern whites, who went to war in large measure because they could not conceive of granting equality to their region's black population, found themselves at the end of the war in a position of inequality as regards the victorious North. As Lincoln noted in a speech in Baltimore in April, 1864, the nature and the impact of the war had been unforeseen. "When the war began, three years ago, neither party, nor any man, expected it would last till now. Each looked for the end, in some way, long ere today. Neither did any anticipate that domestic slavery would be much affected by the war. But here we are; the war has not ended, and slavery has been much affected."

The war was a grim educational experience that gradually eroded the illusions that had defined and sustained the initial responses of both the Union and the Confederacy to mobilization. Americans painfully learned that war is always a social process, and in so doing, they eventually had to face the central ambivalence of their conflict. On the one hand, the war was fought in pursuit of a political objective: restoration or division of the Union. On the other hand, the war, by its very nature, generated its own purposes and values. Lincoln finally led the North to victory only by adjusting his policies to this insight and by finding generals whose military strategy embodied a concept of total war.

Conquest Versus Maintenance

The most puzzling military aspect of the Civil War is not why the North finally won but, rather, how the South held out for so long. Given its immense economic disadvantages in war-making potential (the North in 1860 had over 90 per cent of the nation's industrial output), the ability of the Confederacy to survive a modern industrial war for four years is truly remarkable. Aside from the question of home-front mobilization, the prolonged defense of the Confederacy can be traced to the military and social realities of the war.

The North clearly had no choice but to adopt the offensive. Its objective of restoring the seceded states to the Union was, in effect, an imperial task of conquest, for it involved the reimposition of political authority over a vast territory controlled by a competing government. But the Confederacy, to achieve victory, had to hold what it already possessed; that is, it had only to maintain itself. Adding to the military problems of the North was the fact that the conflict evolved into a total war, in which victory or defeat was measured not so much by military statistics of battles won or lost as by the ability of one of the combatants to destroy the social fabric of its opponent. The South could be defeated only by bringing the war home to its individual citizens through a scorched-earth policy. Thus the Confederacy was able to sustain a war effort until it was literally overrun.

The "difficulty" rested in the exigencies of conducting a massive military offensive for which the Union was almost wholly unprepared. Nothing in the background of the Union generals had readied them for the modern total war they would have to wage. Tactics, logistics, intelligence, and medical services were all rooted in a strategic concept of limited war with fixed objectives to be secured by small armies suffering minimal casualties. The railroad, the telegraph, and the minié ball were to revolutionize the scope of war. Mass armies were now a logistical possibility, just as mass destruction was a military fact.

Although the forces of nationalism and revolutionary republicanism had spawned mass citizen armies in Europe in the Napoleonic era, no Civil War officer had had any experience with this new sociomilitary phenomenon. Many Civil War generals had read the writings of the Baron de Jomini, the most popular interpreter of Napoleonic warfare, and most were fascinated with the Napoleonic image of smashing, decisive battles, but for a practical guide the American officer corps naturally turned to its experience in the Mexican War. Despite the immense territorial gains wrested from Mexico in that war, the campaigns had been pre-Napoleonic in their stress on maneuver and avoidance of massive, bloody battles. Moreover, the armies had been small by Napoleonic standards. The main American army, Winfield Scott's invasion force, which had marched from Vera Cruz to Mexico City, had never exceeded 10,000 men. In contrast, Napoleon and his opposing generals had often commanded armies larger than 100,000. As training for the Civil War, the chief effect of the Mexican War was to confirm for American generals the military axiom that frontal infantry assaults in massed columns could consistently carry a defensive position. After all, the tactic had worked at Palo Alto and elsewhere: The Americans had attacked; the Mexicans had fired and then retreated.

In retrospect, it is hard to determine which was more responsible for the staggering casualties of the Civil War—the generals' infatuation with climactic battles or their inability to adjust to the suicidal obsolescence of traditional frontal assaults by infantry. While the generals overestimated the strategic importance of battles, so much that they often did not know what to do after a battle, whether a victory or defeat, they tragically underestimated the revolution in warfare wrought by the new rifled firearms.

Shock tactics could succeed before the Civil War because of the inaccuracy of smoothbore muskets, the standard arm of the infantry. Concerning these muskets, Ulysses S. Grant noted, "At the distance of a few hundred yards a man might fire at you all day without your finding out." Civil War armies, however, were equipped with rifled muzzleloaders, usually the .58-caliber Springfield or the .577-caliber Enfield rifle. What made these rifles both practical and devastating was the introduction in the 1850's of the minié ball, an elongated bullet with a hollow base that expanded upon firing. This expansion permitted the bullet to fit snugly into the rifle's grooved barrel, thereby greatly increasing its range and accuracy. Rifles now had an effective range of 400 to 600 yards, and they could kill at a distance of up to 1,000 yards. Such a withering fire could be laid down that artillery gunners could no longer close in for effective support of the advancing infantry. Artillery, rather than aiding the offense in Napoleonic fashion, now functioned best as another murderous defensive weapon.

The minié ball had shifted the advantages of warfare heavily, usually decisively, over to the defense, which now had a normal edge of 3 to 1 over its attackers. This ratio increased to 5 to 1 if the defense was entrenched behind breastworks or supported by artillery. Although it was clear why only one out of eight frontal assaults succeeded in the Civil War, the generals persisted in their outmoded tactics, formations, and battle plans. The results were murderous. Nine Confederate brigades attacked the fortified Union position on Malvern Hill during the Peninsular campaign.

> As each brigade emerged from the woods, from fifty to one hundred guns opened upon it, tearing great gaps in its ranks; but the heroes reeled on and were shot down by the reserves at the guns, which a few squads reached. Most of them had an open field half a mile wide to cross. . . . It was not war—it was murder.

This account of Malvern Hill by Confederate general D. H. Hill could stand as well for numerous other engagements. "We were lavish of blood in those days," remarked James Longstreet, one of Lee's generals, "and it was thought to be a great thing to charge a battery of artillery or an earth-work lined with infantry." The Confederacy, of course, had no monopoly on such suicidal grandeur. About sixty Union regiments suffered battlefield casualties in excess of 50 per cent in a single engagement. A Union soldier put it best: "This, then, is what an assault means—a slaughter-pen, a charnel-house, and an army of weeping mothers and sisters at home. It is inevitable."

Fighting for two respective democracies, the generals also had to be responsive to popular expectations. The sanguinary stalemate that characterized so much of the war frustrated both sides, and both Lincoln and Jefferson Davis were under pressure to find some offensive key to a quick victory. While Davis usually had to be convinced by his generals to order an offensive, Lincoln was constantly urging his generals to attack. Slow to perceive the military realities of the war, Lincoln often made unreasonable demands. Oblivious to the decided advantage enjoyed by the defense, he could not understand why McClellan failed to take Richmond in the spring of 1862. Yet McClellan, the attacker, had less than a two to one manpower edge over Lee. McClellan needed nearly three times as many troops to equalize the odds against a defender armed with the new rifled muzzleloaders. Lincoln was continually frustrated by what he felt were missed opportunities to deal a death blow to Lee's army after a Union victory, such as at Antietam or Gettysburg. In fact, very few Civil War battles ever resulted in a decisive victory for either side complete with the near destruction of the opponent's army. The cost of battle was almost as high for the victor as for the defeated. McClellan, often criticized for being overly solicitous of the welfare of his troops, was nonetheless correct when he noted that battlefield casualties alone did not measure the exhausted state of an army after a major battle. There would also be "many thousands unfitted for duty for some days by illness, demoralization, and fatigue."

The cost of conducting an offensive measured by the destructiveness of the minié ball was perhaps the prime factor behind the rather tortuous advance of the Union armies. However, political and logistical demands placed on the invading Union forces also slowed the offensive. As they moved into formerly Confederate territory, the Union armies had to disperse. Because their task of conquest meant occupation and pacification of rebel areas, federal troops had to be detached for garrison duty. Regiments were needed for patrol duty, to serve as provost guards, and to shield overrun areas from a counterattack by Confederate armies or guerrillas. Pacification required patience and the deployment of troops away from the combat cutting edge of the armies.

As much as the offensive capabilities of the Union armies were reduced by casualties and guard and garrison assignments, the immense number of soldiers immobilized by disease was a crucial and often overlooked factor in the military sluggishness that so exasperated Lincoln. To be sure, both armies suffered from grossly inadequate medical services, the Confederates probably more so, but the military impact was usually greater on the army that consistently had to assume the offensive.

For every battlefield death in the Civil War, two soldiers died of disease. Through disease nearly half of the effective strength of a regiment was lost in the first year of its existence; without fresh recruits, regiments tended to vanish as a result of illness alone within three years, by which time they would have been consolidated or discontinued. No wonder General William T. Sherman told his wife, "Our armies disappear before our eyes. [They] are merely paper armies."

Even when the losses were not so spectacular, the result was still a continual loss of combat efficiency. The straggling of those too weak to stand a hard march, the details of soldiers necessary to nurse and service the sick, and the puzzling, often paralyzing, problems of the generals in trying to cope with the chimerical size of their forces—all dulled the fighting edge of the armies.

Clearly, as Lincoln had begun to appreciate in the fall of 1862, the military dimensions of the war were complex and unprecedented. Still, generals who understood this war had to be found, and it is no accident that they emerged from the Western theater.

Union commanders in the West had two critical advantages over their Eastern counterparts. Perhaps most importantly, they had the time and independence to learn their craft. The Western armies were never the public's or the politicians' armies to the same extent as the Army of the Potomac, which was everybody's concern. The proximity to Congress and to newspaper correspondents, the simultaneous need to protect Washington and to capture Richmond, and, above all, the glaring publicity and high expectations that made this army the focus of attention subjected its commanders to unrelenting pressure.

Lincoln was well aware of the incalculable political importance of protecting Washington, and he was very sensitive to the Northern demand for a quick victory. Impatient with McClellan, he ran through several generals for the Army of the Potomac before he settled on Grant. In each case, a general had been promoted beyond his capacity. Whether it was John Pope, fresh from his victories on the Mississippi River, or Ambrose Burnside and Joseph Hooker, competent corps commanders in the Army of the Potomac, these men were simply overwhelmed by their new responsibilities. George Meade, in command at Gettysburg, was acceptable but too slow and methodical, to Lincoln's way of thinking. Although Lincoln cannot be blamed for his excessively close supervision of the main Eastern army, the result was often, as a Maine soldier put it, that "the farther our armies are from Washington the better success they have."

In the West, Grant and Sherman, each of whom began the war as colonel of a volunteer regiment, were able to learn from their mistakes. Promoted step by step in accordance with their ability, by 1863 they had emerged as truly outstanding leaders. Yet it is doubtful whether the Grant who was surprised at Shiloh in April, 1862, and who took the better part of a year to seize Vicksburg by July, 1863, would have survived in the hothouse atmosphere of the East, where McClellan was expected to capture Richmond within a few months. Similarly, the Sherman who feuded with the press and failed so badly in the assault on Chickasaw Bluffs in the Vicksburg campaign of December, 1862, might well have become a scapegoat in the East.

Conditions in the Western theater were strategically and tactically more favorable to the Union offensive than was the situation on the Eastern front. The sheer scope of the Western theater, plus the Union advantage of control over the rivers, gave the federal commanders an offensive advantage and room to probe and attack that were lacking in the East.

The loss of the Mississippi was equally disastrous for the South. The upper valley had been opened up by the Union in early 1862, just before New Orleans fell to Admiral David Farragut's fleet in April. Vicksburg and Port Hudson, the last two Confederate strongholds on the river, were taken in the summer of 1863, giving the Union undisputed control of this critical north-south axis. Foodstuffs from the trans-Mississippi region and blockade-imported war materials from Mexico continued to be smuggled across the river in small amounts, but the Confederacy had been effectively cut in two.

Federal successes in the West were a product of geography and technology as much as of the leadership capabilities of Northern generals. The Union gunboats were steam-driven and hence fast enough in most cases to maneuver out of the range of Confederate batteries. Moreover, these boats were armed with the new, heavier rifled guns, which rendered obsolete the traditional masonry and earthwork fortification encasing the shore batteries.

Not only did the Confederacy lack the industrial and naval facilities to neutralize the Union gunboats with fleets of their own, but its entire Western defense was thin and porous. From the battle of Mill Springs in January, 1862, which forced the Confederates out of eastern Kentucky, to the fall of Port Hudson in July, 1863, the Confederacy had neither the men nor the material to defend its land mass between the Mississippi and the Appalachians. In early 1862, at the start of the great federal offensive, the Confederate general Albert Sidney Johnston was attempting to protect a 300-mile frontier across Kentucky with forty-three thousand troops. His men were scattered, his communications were inadequate, and the two linchpins of the defensive line, Forts Henry and Donelson, were undermanned, badly constructed, and highly vulnerable to any determined federal push.

Once these forts fell, the Confederate defenses began to crumble in a domino effect. As essential areas of political, military, and logistical support were lost, the defense of the remaining regions became more difficult. Federal armies, astride the major rivers and railroads, had secure bases from which to launch raids, to outflank Confederate armies, and eventually to initiate major offensives.

Necessity forced the South to adopt the defensive. Strategically, an offensive policy was out of the question because of a lack of manpower and industrial resources to sustain an invasion of the North. Logistics also ruled out such a policy. An invading army in the North had to be supplied by either rivers or railroads, neither of which the South controlled. Lee did cross the upper Potomac on two occasions in 1862 and 1863, but his actions were more large-scale raids than prolonged offensives.

In formulating what defensive posture would characterize its military strategy, the Confederacy, while commissioning partisan rangers and resorting to partisan warfare wherever necessary, nonetheless intuitively rejected a full-scale guerrilla resistance. Although the need to keep open a lifeline to the outside world through blockade runners for war supplies was certainly an important factor, especially in the first two years of the war, rejection of partisan warfare was rooted even more in the nature of Southern society.

The guerrilla has to be extremely patient and willing to surrender large chunks of territory to the enemy while he retreats back into the interior. Unable to meet the enemy on the enemy's terms in modern warfare, the guerrilla must pick his time and terrain for the irritating and unsettling counterattacks that sap his adversary's will to continue the war. To function at all, however, the guerrilla must be protected and supplied by the agrarian masses. In the phraseology of Mao Tse-Tung, "guerrillas must swim like fish in the sea of the people." Here was the crux of the Confederate problem. In the Deep South nearly half the people were slaves whose support could not be relied upon. True, the slaves did not rise up in mass rebellion during the war, but they fled to Union armies at the first opportunity and provided those armies with invaluable scouting and intelligence sources. Without complete popular support, Confederate guerrillas would have been severely handicapped.

The class outlook and social values of Confederate war leaders also made unthinkable a defense limited to guerilla resistance. To have retreated into the mountains would have meant yielding not only the lush lowlands and black prairies that sustained plantation agriculture, but also most of the slaves. The South would have been sacrificing the very racial controls and way of life for which it was fighting. The twentieth-century guerrilla can make such sacrifices because his land and society are already controlled by an imperial outsider. In the South the situation was reversed, and the would-be guerrillas were not landless peasants but a mature, property-holding elite.

Thus, the real Southern debate hinged on whether it would conduct a passive or an aggressive defense (also known as an offensive-defense). The former course was favored initially by Jefferson Davis. By waiting for the North to attack, the South could reap the benefits of the 3 to 1 advantage enjoyed by the defense. Since federal armies had in the aggregate but a 3 to 2 manpower edge over the Confederate armies, the North conceivably could have been bled white in an exhaustive war of conquest. Moreover, the South would have had the propaganda benefit of casting itself as the assaulted and injured party in the conflict. Early in the war Davis explained that "the Confederate government is waging this war solely for self-defense." Not a war of aggression but a war to defend the right of self-government was the Confederacy's self-defined mission.

Yet, a passive defense was politically untenable. Davis could not emulate George Washington's strategy during the American Revolution of withdrawing his forces into the interior and leaving open vast stretches of uncontested territory to the enemy. Washington could conserve his army in this manner because the American rebels were not accustomed to the security and protection of their own central government. Southerners, of course, were, and they bitterly resented any policy that smacked of leaving them alone to face the federal invaders without the protection of a Confederate army. Faced with this political reality, Davis attempted to salvage his passive defense by scattering his armies along a wide defensive perimeter. When the inevitable federal break-throughs occurred, first in the western Virginia mountains and along the South Atlantic seaboard, and then, in early 1862, across the Kentucky-Tennessee line, Davis was receptive to the demands of his generals and the public for a more aggressive strategy.

Robert E. Lee was the most persistent and brilliant Confederate general in his application of the aggressive defense. He argued persuasively that the Confederacy had to choose either inaction, and the constant danger of being outnumbered wherever the Union decided to attack, or a bold policy of seizing the initiative by concentrating troops to meet the enemy at chosen points. The federal troops could be prevented from invading everywhere only by being pinned down and forced to fight at a time and a place selected by the Confederacy. Concentration, maneuver, and the climactic battle—these were the essence of Lee's conception of warfare, and his Virginia campaigns until 1864 were masterful examples of swift, unexpected offensive strokes that paralyzed the enemy and exploited his divided forces.

Lee, more than any other individual, exemplified this dominant theme of Confederate strategy—the concentration of armies through the use of the railroad and telegraph for surprise counterattacks against the exposed salients of the multiple federal lines of advance. It was this strategy that blocked the Union forces in the East throughout most of the war and at least slowed their advance in the West. Despite its apparent success, however, the aggressive defense could not stave off Confederate defeat. On the contrary, the inability of nearly all Confederate generals, Lee included, to accent defense rather than the offense, hastened the Southern collapse.

Popular frustration and anger over having the war fought on Southern soil, the inability of the generals to adjust to the destructiveness of the new minié-ball rifles, and the frantic desire to knock the North out of the war in one great battle—all reinforced the obsession with offense. Even Lee, for all his brilliance, succumbed. His stated objective was not merely to check or defeat the Army of the Potomac but to destroy it in Napoleonic fashion. In pursuit of this unattainable goal, he could be reckless with manpower, as during the Seven Days battles in front of Richmond in June, 1862, when he stubbornly attacked fortified positions. Failing to destroy the enemy's army, Lee took as his objective victories on Northern soil. The results were his bloody repulses at Antietam in September, 1862 (11,700 casualties), and at Gettysburg in July, 1863 (22,600 casualties). Lee's army which would confront Grant in Virginia beginning in May, 1864, already had been drained of its offensive power.

The South lacked more than the self-restraint necessary for a successful, long-range application of the aggressive defense. It also lacked the means of effectively coordinating its armies and command structure for concentration against the weakest points of the federal advance. Full exploitation of the aggressive defense required the close cooperation of scattered armies. This was hampered by the administrative and organizational problems inherent in the Confederate departmental system.

Appointed general in chief of the Union armies in March, 1864, Grant explained that his "general plan now was to concentrate all the force possible against the Confederate armies in the field. . . . Accordingly," he said, "I arranged for a simultaneous movement all along the line." Here was a sound, if obvious, strategy that Lincoln in fact had urged from the start of the war. The critical differences by 1864 were a Northern public more inured to accepting the heavy casualties that such a strategy necessarily entailed and a new command structure, which, while far from unified in the modern sense, nonetheless achieved a greater coordinated concentration of Union forces than had hitherto been possible. In criticizing the federal war effort prior to 1864, Grant noted that the various Union "armies had acted separately and independently of each other, giving the enemy an opportunity, often, of depleting one command, not pressed, to reinforce another more actively engaged." He added, "I determined to stop this." By applying massive, unrelenting pressure on the last two major Confederate armies, Lee's Army of Northern Virginia and Johnston's Army of the Tennessee, Grant kept the Confederacy from redeploying its troops for surprise concentrations and counterattacks.

The success of the offensive directed by Grant can easily be exaggerated. Lee still had sufficient cunning and manpower to stymie during most of 1864 the separate invasion armies advancing across West Virginia, through the Shenandoah Valley, and up the Yorktown peninsula. An integral feature of Grant's original plan, the occupation of Mobile, Alabama, to be followed up by a movement north toward Atlanta, was stillborn because the troops required were shifted to the politically inspired Red River campaign in Louisiana. Still, Grant's essential objectives, the destruction both of the South's two largest remaining armies and of its people's will to fight, were accomplished.

In Virginia, Grant, like a bulldog, clamped Lee's army in a death grip and chewed it to pieces. He was seeking victory not through some decisive battle but through the attrition of day-to-day battles. The entire Virginia campaign from May, 1864, to the end of the war was one continuous flanking action between two interlocked armies. Grant incessantly probed Lee's right flank and, in a series of rasping, brutal maneuvers, slowly forced Lee to extend it, until the flank was turned and the Confederate army was trapped in the entrenchments of Petersburg. For Lee the very worst had happened. He had lost his maneuverability and been forced to wage a war of attrition. As he had predicted to General Jubal Early, once he was besieged, it was a "mere question of time."

Grant succeeded, but at a terrible cost. In moving his army through the heavy forests and undergrowth north of Richmond known as the Wilderness to a base on the James River in May, 1864, he suffered fifty-five thousand casualties, the equivalent of Lee's total strength. Grant's response to the understandable charge that he was a butcher was simply that it was better to lose troops in a campaign to end the war than in a continuation of the prolonged stalemate that previously had marked the Virginia theater. And victory could be achieved, he concluded, only by undermining the morale of Lee's army "by desperate and continuous hard fighting." The elementary logic of Grant's position is undeniable, though it escaped most other Union Generals. Lee's soldiers, however, had grimly appreciated what Grant was doing. George Cary Eggleston recalled:

> We had been accustomed to a programme which began with a Federal advance, culminating in one great battle, and ended in the retirement of the Union army, the substitution of a new Federal commander for the one beaten, and the institution of a more or less offensive campaign on our part. [But with the coming of Grant] the policy of pounding had begun, and would continue until our strength should be utterly worn away. . . . We began to understand that Grant had taken hold of the problem of destroying the Confederate strength in the only way that the strength of such an army, so commanded, could be destroyed.

While Grant was taking the Confederacy out of the war by destroying its most fabled army, Sherman was accomplishing the same end by the indirect means of demolishing economic resources and subverting civilian morale. The horror and fascination with which Sherman has always been regarded stem from the fact that he stripped warfare down to its basics. He had no illusions about modern warfare. Because well-equipped mass armies depended on home-front mobilization of economic resources and moral support, war clearly had become a contest between peoples just as much as, if not more than, between rival armies. To win such a contest, Sherman concluded, his armies "must make old and young, rich and poor, feel the hard hand of war, as well as the organizing armies." Readily admitting that this policy necessarily entailed cruelty and barbarity toward civilian populations, he still felt it to be the quickest way to achieve victory. As he pointedly told the citizens of Atlanta when he ordered the evacuation of their city as a military necessity, "Now that the war comes home to you, you feel very different. You deprecate its horrors, but did not feel them when you sent car-loads of soldiers and ammunition, and moulded shells and shot, to carry war into Kentucky and Tennessee." In a letter to his wife Sherman was more succinct: Southerners "have sowed the wind and must reap the whirlwind."

Sherman's march in the fall of 1864 from Atlanta to Savannah and then up the coast into the interiors of the Carolinas was one extended exercise in destruction. His troops foraged liberally off the countryside, ransacked plantations, tore up railroads, and gutted factories and anything else of conceivable value to the Confederate war effort. A Georgia girl, Eliza Andrews, recorded in her diary what Sherman left in his track: "There was hardly a fence left standing. . . . The fields were trampled down and the road was lined with carcasses of horses, hogs, and cattle. . . . The dwellings that were standing all showed signs of pillage. . . . Hayricks and fodder stacks were demolished, corncribs were empty, and every bale of cotton that could be found was burnt by the savages."

With its main armies pinned down under constant poundings and with Sherman bringing the war home to civilians and leaving them nothing to fight for, the Confederacy was bludgeoned into submission by the early spring of 1865. The war, despite all earlier efforts to the contrary, had become a total war—in Lincoln's words, a "people's contest." Given the stakes involved, and the near-absolute involvement of the civilian populations, it could have become no less.

Total War

"The greater and the more powerful the motives of a war, the more it affects the whole existence of a people. The more violent the excitement which precedes the war, by so much nearer will the war approach to its abstract form." Americans had to learn through bitter experience the relevance of this observation by Carl von Clausewitz, the German military theorist.

Until 1863 the North officially fought the war as a limited conflict with the objective of restoring the Union as it was. In this way, Lincoln sought to control the conflict and prevent it from degenerating, in his phrase, "into a violent and remorseless revolutionary struggle." He assured Southerners that he did not want to strike at the foundations of their society and that "the utmost care will be observed [consistent with saving the Union] to avoid any devastation, any destruction of, or interference with, property, or any disturbance of peaceful citizens in any part of the country." But implicit in Lincoln's policy was the assumption that the failure to suppress the rebellion through conciliation would necessarily lead to a harsher policy of punishment. "Such as may seem indispensable, or may obviously promise great efficiency towards ending the struggle, must and will come," warned Lincoln in March, 1862.

Despite Lincoln's reluctance to declare emancipation as a war aim, the conflict could not be kept within its original bounds. By its very nature a civil war is very difficult to control, because it involves the fundamental issue of sovereignty, which, by definition, cannot be compromised. The rebels "cannot voluntarily reaccept the Union," remarked Lincoln; "we cannot voluntarily yield it." This ideological battle over absolutes was far different from most foreign wars, which are fought over fairly specific political or economic objectives. The comparison with a foreign war also highlights the inherent difficulties in undertaking peace negotiations during a civil war. A nation at war rarely denies the right of its foreign opponent to rule and hence has no compunction about recognizing its legal existence during negotiations. But with whom could Lincoln or Davis negotiate when each rejected the other's claims to sovereignty? The Confederacy denied the legitimacy of the Union's claim to rule over the seceded states, and the U.S. government denied the legitimacy of the Confederate claim to separate nationhood.

Had the Civil War not been fought between two democratic societies and between two military organizations that still had to call upon civilians for a wide range of vital support services, the war conceivably could have been more manageable. As it was, very few Americans, whether Unionists or Confederates, soldiers or civilians, could escape involvement in the war. Both sections shared a democratic culture that stressed the equal right of all adult white males to participate in the governmental decision-making process. Although this theoretical egalitarianism better describes the style and tone of politics than the actual distribution of political power, the result was nonetheless a striking, vibrant sense of individual identification with government. It was this feeling that the government in some real manner belonged to them that underlay the emotional identification of Northerners and Southerners with their governments' respective war efforts.

Americans demanded to know about *their* war not only because their sons were fighting in a holy cause but also because civilians themselves contributed so much to the war effort. The noncombatant populations, free and slave, male and female, manned the war-related industries, to be sure, or grew the crops that fed the armies and the industrial laborers, but it was the massive, voluntary response to the medical needs of the armies that most dramatically marked civilian involvement.

Civil War armies, whether Union or Confederate, had to depend on civilians for most of the food, clothing, and medical supplies that their governments were unprepared or unable to provide. With the exception of Southerners subject to intensive foraging by both armies, civilian support was voluntary. Individual households, under the direction of women, fraternal organizations, soldier-aid societies, and churches sent a stream of clothing, food packages, and hospital supplies to the front. In the North a major degree of centralization emerged with the creation of the U.S. Sanitary Commission. An outgrowth of various women's relief societies, the Commission was the largest private relief organization of the war. Relying solely on private donations, it rendered services worth about $25 million. The Commission stockpiled huge warehouses in the major Northern cities and had a small army of several hundred field agents who distributed the supplies. Its other main functions included policing sanitary arrangements in the army camps and maintaining soldiers' homes and convalescent centers. None of this would have been possible had not countless farmers responded to appeals for fresh vegetables, had not public schools held "onion days" and "potato days," and had not thousands of women given their time and services voluntarily.

Because so much of the South was itself the war front, a correspondingly centralized organization did not emerge in the Confederacy. But, for that very reason, the exposure of Southern civilians to the war was even more direct. With armies in their backyard subsisting off of civilians and with battlefield casualties having to be cared for on the spot, Southerners were in the midst of the war's anguish. During the Peninsular campaign in the late spring of 1862, the streets of Richmond were aptly described by a resident as "one vast hospital." The distinction between home front and battlefield dissolved as "ambulances, litters, carts, every vehicle that the city could produce, went and came with a ghastly burden. . . . Women with pallid faces flitted bareheaded through the streets searching for their dead or wounded." Churches, public offices, homes, any unused buildings, were thrown open to the wounded as makeshift hospitals.

Nothing brought the war home so indelibly as this personal involvement with death and the dying. Field hospitals after a battle were first and foremost the homes and barns of civilians in the surrounding area; bedding was often little more than straw gathered up from the nearby stables. The harried and undermanned medical staffs called on civilians as nurses and orderlies. Everyone was pressed into emergency service. A resident of Shepherdstown, Maryland, which served as a makeshift medical center for those wounded in Lee's Maryland invasion of September, 1862, recalled that "even children did their part."

After the initial shock had worn off, those who experienced the horrors of a field hospital with its screams and amputations were left both numb and embittered. A Union nurse, Mary Phinney, in remembering the men she cared for, said simply, "I'll never forgive the Rebels who kill[ed] them." Of course, even those Northern civilians distant from the battlefront were deeply affected by the casualties. "You could not forget the war, even if you had wished," noted Edward Dicey, an English correspondent writing from the North in 1862. "Every carriage on the railway trains was laden with sick or wounded soldiers, traveling homeward to be nursed, and, if I could judge their faces rightly, to die." Many Northerners undoubtedly agreed with Jefferson Davis when he argued late in the war that peaceful reconciliation was impossible because of a "sea of blood that freemen cannot afford to bridge."

A more persistent factor in limiting the nature of the war until 1863 was Lincoln's approach to the ultimate objective of somehow, someday restoring the rebel states to the Union as permanent, peaceful members. Wanting to avoid not only the social disruption of forced emancipation but also the possibility of unending, debilitating guerrilla warfare, Lincoln sought in the first years of the war to have federal armies re-establish political harmony and social stability as they advanced. Although extremely patient in pursuit of this goal, he gradually realized that his hopes conflicted with political and military realities. The rebellion was too strong to permit any compromise based on the maintenance of the Union. Its strength clearly rested on the Confederate military, which, as Lincoln noted, "dominates all the country, and all the people, within its range." To destroy that army required federal advances, and if the Union armies were to protect themselves within Confederate lines, let alone advance, they had to be agents of chaos and destruction.

The experience of most Union officers and soldiers, however, paralleled that of Grant. These men brought to the war no fixed ideas save the vague belief that after a few sound thrashings the Confederacy would see the folly of further resistance and capitulate. But when the supposedly decisive victories did not bring the expected outcome, when, on the contrary, the Confederacy fought back to regain what had been lost, the result was a new conception of the war and how it would have to be waged. For Grant, the turning point was the Confederate counterattack at Shiloh in the spring of 1862.

> . . . I gave up all idea of saving the Union except by complete conquest. Up to that time it had been the policy of our army . . . to protect the property of the citizens whose territory was invaded, without regard to their sentiments, whether Union or Secession. After this, however, I regarded it as humane to both sides to protect the persons of those found at their homes but to consume everything that could be used to support or supply armies. . . . Their destruction was accomplished without bloodshed, and tended to the same result as the destruction of armies. I continued this policy to the close of the war.

Throughout 1862 the rationale of total war gained momentum. Major General Henry W. Halleck, Lincoln's chief military adviser before Grant was brought East in 1864, cited 1862 as the year in which the character of the war had changed. In outlining Union military policy for Grant in March, 1863, Halleck insisted, "There can be no peace but that which is forced by the sword. We must conquer the rebels or be conquered by them." This was the same Halleck whose antebellum writings had always disdained a war directed at the enemy's civilian population and its resources. Such a policy, he felt, would lead to a breakdown of military discipline and convert the noncombatants into embittered partisans. By 1864, however, he was urging on Sherman just such ruthless warfare. Mildness had resulted only in a nest of "spies and guerrillas in our rear and within our lines." Strip the countryside, he advised, and send the civilians deep into the interior to seek the protection of their own armies. The South's ability to wage war must be ended. "I would destroy every mill and factory within reach which I did not want for my own use."

The basic federal tactic of sending slashing raiding parties supported by gunboats up the rivers and inlets of the Carolinas, Georgia, and Florida had exposed Southerners to a war of subjugation. The purpose of these marauding expeditions was painfully apparent. General David Hunter, at the time commander of the Federal Department of the South, explained in 1863 that they were designed to force the South to sue for peace or else withdraw its slaves from the region, thus abandoning one of the most fertile districts in the South. Mass destruction was clearly the means to achieve such ends. The June, 1863, Combahee River expedition in South Carolina was typical. The *New York Tribune* reported, "The soldiers scattered in every direction and burned and destroyed everything of value they came across. Thirty-four mansions known to belong to notorious Rebels, with all their rich furniture and rare works of art, were burned to the ground."

For over three years, rice mills, cotton gins, foodstuffs, and occasionally entire towns were burned. Slaves who had not already fled behind Union lines or who had not been evacuated by their owners were brought back to the Union bases. The Southern responses were helpless rage and a determination never to submit to what they saw as fiendish warfare. Many demanded that any captured Yankee soldiers be executed under state law for inciting slaves to revolt. A young aristocrat and lieutenant from Georgia, Charles C. Jones, Jr., believed that no other punishment was fitting for "the lawless bands of armed marauders who will infest our borders . . . subvert our entire social system [and] desolate our homes."

As early as June, 1862, the Yankees, operating from bases north and west of Vicksburg, began seizing slaves to assist in military-related work. Throughout the summer federal raids increased in tempo; plantations were ransacked and often burned. Planters sent as many slaves as possible back to the interior bayous or as far away as Texas. By fall in 1862, the delta country from Madison Parish in northeastern Louisiana up to Vicksburg was abandoned. The desperation of the few rebels who remained can be sensed in the plantation journal of Kate Stone. She decried her family's "miserable, frightened" condition and a life of "constant dread of great danger, not knowing what form it may take, and utterly helpless to protect ourselves." Just before her family finally fled in late March, 1863, Kate accurately summarized the Vicksburg campaign up to that time: "The enemy have now been three months before Vicksburg doing nothing against the city, but scourging this part of the country."

The scope of this social dislocation was exacerbated by economic devastation. The Union garrisons had to supply themselves. Although rail line had to be kept open to bring in foodstuffs, as well as replacements and war materials, the armies increasingly turned to the ready expedient of living off the countryside. In the first year of the war, efforts were made to keep this practice under control, but by 1862 federal commanders increasingly followed the example of General John Pope, whose much publicized order from northern Virginia in July, 1862, authorized his troops to forage for their supplies. Pope made a distinction between rebels and loyalists, with the latter group ultimately to be reimbursed. Even in 1862, however, this distinction was a hazy one that was very difficult to enforce. By 1863 it had lost all practical significance as applied to those civilians still behind Confederate lines, for the "Instructions for the Government of Armies of the United States in the Field," issued in April, 1863, had legitimized total war.

This general order declared that military necessity "allows of all destruction of property . . . and of all withholding of sustenance of means of life from the country," as well as "the appropriation of whatever an enemy's country affords necessary for the subsistence and safety of the Army." The military authorities in Washington had caught up with the kind of war that many of their field commanders had already been fighting. The main difference in 1863 was that the generals now had official sanction for extending the concept of the raid from a diversionary tactic or an attack on enemy communications to a systematic effort at destroying the agricultural and industrial resources of the Confederacy.

In the last two years of the war small detachments of Union cavalry swarmed over the nearly exhausted Confederacy in quick-striking, ravaging expeditions. Most of these raids have been forgotten, but their cumulative impact was staggering. A single minor expedition into northern Alabama in the spring of 1863 destroyed 1.5 million bushels of corn, 500,000 pounds of bacon, and huge quantities of grains and fodder; wrecked numerous small industrial establishments; and brought out 1,500 slaves. The federal commander reported that his men had "left the country in such a devastated condition that no crop can be raised during the year." In the last major raid of the war, in the spring of 1865, three cavalry divisions under General James Wilson demolished the remaining industrial base of the Confederacy by razing the ordnance and foundry centers of Selma, Alabama, and Columbus, Georgia.

Such warfare invariably spawned guerrilla resistance and, in turn, harsh retaliatory measures by federal forces. As could be expected, martial laws, fines, imprisonments, and the burning of houses and crops only stiffened resistance. How to cope with the guerrillas was an exasperating problem. The dilemma was epitomized by conditions in Missouri as late as February, 1865.

"It seems that," Lincoln wrote, "there is now no organized military force of the enemy in Missouri and yet that destruction of property and life is rampant everywhere."

Guerrilla warfare characterized the fighting in at least three major areas: Missouri, West Virginia, and eastern Tennessee. Although the Unionists here were in the majority, the attitude of many was probably best captured by Mark Twain, who said of his fellow Missourians, "It was hard for us to get our bearings." There was "a good deal of unsettledness, of leaning first this way, then that, then the other way." Loyalties were divided, and both the Union and Confederacy tried to convert the undecided and win back those who had gone over to the other side. The guerrilla, whether a Confederate sympathizer in Missouri or West Virginia or a Unionist in eastern Tennessee, relied on harassment by means of ambushes and sniping attacks. These tactics, plus the response they provoked, resulted in a warfare that knew no rules save those of survival. The sickening brutality was measured by the smashed-in skulls and mutilated bodies of the ambushed soldiers, by the summary executions in reprisal, and by the efforts of both military authorities to depopulate regions of the enemy's sympathizers.

In the lower South, guerrilla resistance, while never the official policy of the Richmond government, was nonetheless pervasive. It was directed at slowing the federal advance and undermining the new sociopolitical order based on free labor that the Union armies were trying to impose after the midpoint of the war. Although this resistance was often organized by the military under the Confederate Partisan Ranger Act of 1862, much of it was a spontaneous civilian reaction. In either case, the enraged federal response intensified the war's destruction. Villages were burned in retaliation for raids on Union supply depots; property was seized to indemnify Unionists for guerrilla-inflicted losses; and, by 1864 in the lower Mississippi Valley, for every lessee of a federally leased plantation who was killed by partisans, a fine of $10,000 was levied, which was to be collected by confiscating property within a thirty-mile radius.

As the war ground to a conclusion, Southern civilians were as prostrate as their armies. For most, their commitment to the Confederacy had been as total as the Union war effort that finally vanquished them. But, in fact, neither army spared the civilians. To the Union commanders, Southern civilians were the unrepentant enemy who either fought as guerrillas or furnished the essential home-front support for the Confederate armies. To the Confederate commanders, the same civilians were their one sure source of supplies. Whereas federal armies increasingly stripped the countryside by design, Confederate armies did so by necessity. And both armies destroyed public and private property to keep it out of the hands of the other.

The war had been a learning experience. Militarily, as well as ideologically, Americans discovered that there could be no middle ground. As much as Lincoln wanted to believe at the start of the war that the two sides were "not enemies, but friends," four years of bloodshed belied this idea. To win its war of conquest, the Union turned to a theory of war that made civilians as well as armies its target. To stave off defeat, the Confederacy was increasingly willing to sacrifice almost everything. As the wife of a Georgia minister and planter expressed it, "I can look extinction for me and mine in the face, but *submission* never!" For both sides victory had been defined as the continued existence of their respective nations. Defeat, no less than victory, would be total in the people's war.

On April 12, 1861, a state senator announced to the Ohio legislature that Fort Sumter had just been fired upon. The reaction of stunned, painful silence was broken by the cry of "Glory to God," uttered by abolitionist Abby Kelly Foster. Mrs. Foster had immediately embraced the war as a divinely inspired opportunity to free the black man by the sword. A far more typical Northern reaction was that of Jacob D. Cox, a Republican politician in Ohio and a future Union general. For Cox, civil war "seemed too great a price to pay for any good [except for] yielding what was to us the very groundwork of our republicanism, the right to enforce a fair interpretation of the Constitution through the election of President and Congress."

Foster and Cox epitomized the fundamental problem facing Lincoln as he strove to unite the North. The majority saw the war's sole objective as the perpetuation of the Union; a small, and often despised, minority passionately believed that the Union must also be regenerated through the war. Military necessity finally convinced Lincoln that the Union could be saved only by transforming it. Only after he was so convinced could he formulate the North's rationale of victory.

Reconstruction

Immediately following the Civil War (1861 to 1865) occurred one of the most difficult and evocative periods in American history, the Reconstruction era. Between 1865 and 1877 some of the most fundamental problems concerning the American political and social enterprise were explored, especially the race problem, and several key questions asked. What, if any, recriminations should be taken against the Southern white power structure to atone for the crime of secession? What civil and political rights were black Americans going to have and how could their freedoms be protected and maintained? When, and according to what criteria, were the states of the defunct Confederacy to be readmitted to the Union? Would the previously estranged and intractible Deep South ever again participate fully in the American political system? What was the economic future of the war-ravaged South already so backward in terms of industrial plant and infrastructure in comparison to the North before 1861?

The initial impetus to answer these questions came from the White House. President Lincoln, concerned to expedite the transition from war to peace, extended a lenient program of amnesty to the South in December 1863. Following Lincoln's assassination the Tennesseean Andrew Johnson maintained this executive generosity. The new President proposed that each of the ex-Confederate states convene a constitutional convention to adopt the thirteenth amendment ending slavery, nullify the secession ordinances, and repudiate state war debts. Upon completion of these uncontroversial demands Johnson would be comfortable welcoming southern senators and representatives back to power in Washington.

Almost from the start however, dissenting opinion assailed the executive approach. Operating from their Congressional power base, the ultimately successful Republican leaders, known as Radicals, began to organize their own plans for reconstruction which envisioned far more fundamental change for the South than either Lincoln or Johnson had anticipated. The First Radical

379

plan included the fourteenth amendment which established that freed men were citizens of the United States and thus eligible for all constitutional rights and privileges. When the Southern states resisted acceptance of this the Radicals shifted, in 1867, to a more forceful plan wich involved Southern states receiving new constitutions guaranteeing racial equality before the law and military occupation measures to enforce this change. Between 1868 and 1871 all the ex-Confederate states were re-admitted into the Union according to the provisions of this second Radical plan.

Despite the enthusiasm of the Radical effort, over time their reconstruction experiment fizzled out. One by one the states of the Old Confederacy began to fall under the dominance of unreconstructed, white, conservative governments. In the face of unrestricted Ku Klux Klan intimidation, the economic boycott of white Republicans, President Grant's lethargic ambiguity, a lack of conviction among the Northern masses toward the Radical cause, and the white South's unabashed bigotry, Radical reconstructionists learned the painful lesson that while laws and constitutions can readily be reconstructed social attitudes and emotions cannot. Sculpting a fair and just social order from the clay of the Old Confederacy would be impossible so long as the only tool was legislative pronouncement. In the wake of the Hayes-Tilden Compromise of 1876 came the Deep South's concerted effort to disenfranchise black voters and "redeem" Dixie from the carpetbaggers and the scalawags. In 1877 Georgia adopted its poll tax, just as the federal input into the reconstruction effort was ending, and in so doing heralded a return to the repression of black political and civil rights that was not to be seriously challenged until the 1960s.

The following articles have been selected to illustrate and amplify some of the key issues of reconstruction. Leon Litwack in "Slaves No More" dramatizes the conflicting emotions with which slaves greeted emancipation. Of course there was jubilation and celebration but there was also fear, apprehension, foreboding and a certain ambiguity in the hearts and minds of the newly free. How were black people going to fit into the post-war social structure of the Deep South? What was in store for black American children for whom a lifetime of freedom lay ahead? Would the burning sun of Dixie shine more kindly on black Americans now that the "slavery chain done broke at last", or would Babylon rise again as soon as the Yankee presence diminished? Litwack's prize-winning writing explores these and other critical concerns of America's blacks during the reconstruction era.

In the second selection Kenneth Stampp is less concerned with social history than with reconstruction politics, specifically the motivation and tactics of the Radicals. How would Radical measures be legislatively enacted? How would the Radicals preserve their unity following Johnson's defeat? How would the Radicals demolish the prestige of the Southern ruling class? These questions, along with the issues of land redistribution, the Freedmen's Bureau and the Fourteenth Amendment are all touched upon in Stampp's discussion.

The final selection deals with interpretations of reconstruction amongst historians. Since passions traditionally run high about the reconstruction era, events of the period have been distorted and misrepresented by professional historians as well as by Hollywood, yielding the simplistic stereotypes of the parasite carpetbagger, or the virtuous redeemer, or the base and venal black Republican. Louisiana historian T. Harry Williams in this 1946 essay was concerned to inject a measure of sobriety and objectivity into the debate. Reviewing and critiquing several of the leading interpretations of the day and combining this with a discussion of the attitudes of the Southern planter-business class towards reconstruction, Williams not only reveals the great complexity of the period but also demonstrates a commitment to the search for the truth in the past which should be the cornerstone of the historians' craft but is all too often forgotten in the heat of partisan debate.

Radical Reconstruction

Kenneth Stampp

After their victory over Johnson, the congressional radicals were suddenly forced to play a role they had never played before: that of responsible men exercising substantial power. Prior to 1866, though having considerable influence, they had always been a minority, and they now found the transition from uninhibited critics to makers of policy far from an easy one. When the radicals and their moderate allies decided to liquidate the Johnson governments in the southern states and to make an entirely new beginning, they had reached the point where they could no longer deal with reconstruction in vague and broad generalities. The time had come for specific legislative enactments and, equally important, for careful assessment of the obstacles they would encounter in striving to achieve their goals. Since the obstacles were sometimes greater than they had anticipated, their enactments were not always successful and occasionally led to unexpected results.

President Johnson, in spite of his defeat, continued to be a formidable problem. Though his vetoes of congressional legislation could be easily overridden, he alone could enforce the laws after they were passed; and in doing so he might give them the narrowest possible interpretation and exploit every defect. A second problem involved the moderate Republicans who presumably had been converted to radicalism. It still remained to be seen how complete and how durable the conversion would be. A third problem was the preservation of unity among the radicals now that the victory had been won; for radicals showed a disturbing tendency toward fragmentation and self-destruction. A final problem was the continued prestige of the old, experienced ruling class of the South, whose success in winning control of the Johnson governments demonstrated its enduring economic and political power. To offset its power the radicals relied upon the four million southern Negroes to create a new political force. Without effective Negro support, their program was bound to fail.

Since the Negroes were crucial figures in radical reconstruction, it is essential to understand their condition at the time they gained their freedom. Most of them had by then lost all but a tiny fragment of their African culture. Though in slavery they had been denied full participation in the white man's culture, their ambition was to become an integral part of American society. They knew how to make a living as free men, because they had experience as farmers, as skilled craftsmen, as domestic servants, or as unskilled urban laborers. What they still needed were economic opportunities, training in the management of their own affairs, and incentives for diligent toil.

Because the ante-bellum slave codes had prohibited teaching slaves to read or write, only a small minority of Negroes were literate. In this respect, as in most others, slavery had been a poor training school for the responsibilities of citizenship. It gave Negroes few opportunities to develop initiative or to think independently; it discouraged self-reliance; it put a premium on docility and subservience; it indoctrinated Negroes with a sense of their own inferiority; and it instilled in many of them a fear of white men that they would only slowly overcome. A writer in *Harper's Weekly* reminded friends of the Negroes that the freedmen were but "the slaves of yesterday . . . with all the shiftless habits of slavery [to be] unlearned. . . . They come broken in spirt, and with the long, long habit of servility."

Yet there is little evidence that slavery had developed in many of its victims a fondness for bondage. Masters liked to think that their slaves were contented with their lot—and no doubt some of them found it not too painful to adapt to their condition. But the behavior of the slaves during the Civil War removed any doubt about whether the majority of them understood the meaning of freedom and were eager to enjoy its benefits. For as the federal armies advanced, the slaves fled from the plantations by the thousands, and the southern labor system collapsed. A Georgia planter spoke for many others when he complained bitterly about what he regarded as the "ingratitude evinced in the African character." "This war," he wrote, "has taught us the perfect impossibility of placing the least confidence in any Negro. In too numerous instances those we esteemed the most have been the first to desert us. . . . House servants . . . are often the first to have their minds polluted with evil thoughts."

In short, most Negroes, to the dismay of their former masters, joyfully accepted their freedom; and for a time many of them took special pleasure in making use of one of its chief prerogatives: the right to move from place to place without the consent of any white man. An agent of the Freedmen's Bureau gave several reasons for the restlessness of the Negroes immediately after emancipation: they wanted to see new things; they looked for relatives from whom they had been separated in slavery days; they went to the cities in search of work or to find schools for their children. "The shackles suddenly falling off," explained Carl Schurz, "it is by no means wonderful that their first impulse should be to have a holiday. Some felt inclined to use their freedom first in walking a little away from their plantations."

This was precisely what the radicals proposed that the Negroes should do. The radicals, to reconstruct the South on a firm foundation, would throw out the Black Codes, which were hardly designed to prepare the Negroes for freedom anyway, given the Negroes civil rights and the ballot, and get white men accustomed to treating Negroes as equals, at least politically and legally. Aid to the freedmen was thus at the very heart of radical reconstruction; it was this aspect of the program, and litle else, that justified designating as radicals the Republican leaders in Congress. Their attempt to give full citizenship to southern Negroes—in effect, to revolutionize the relations of the two races— was the great "leap in the dark" of the reconstruction era.

Some of the radicals believed that it would be essential to give the Negroes not only civil and political rights but some initial economic assistance as well. These four million people had emerged from bondage in complete destitution, without land, without shelter, without a legal claim even to the clothes on their backs. Neither Lincoln's Emancipation Proclamation nor the Thirteenth Amendment had required masters to make any settlement with their former slaves for past services, or provided for economic aid from the public treasury. In the words of Frederick Douglass, the freedmen "were sent away empty handed, without money, without friends, and without a foot of land to stand upon. Old and young, sick and well, they were turned loose to the open sky, naked to their enemies."

This condition of economic helplessness, some radicals thought, was what threatened to make Negro freedom purely nominal; it was this that enabled the white landholders, with the aid of the Black Codes, to re-establish bondage in another form. The congressional Committee on Reconstruction heard a great deal of convincing testimony about the use of southern vagrancy laws and various extra-legal coercive devices to force Negroes back into agricultural labor under strict discipline. This testimony suggested that there was a close relationship between the securing of civil and political rights on the one hand and the establishment of economic independence on the other.

Near the end of the war, Edwin M. Stanton, Lincoln's Secretary of War, and General Sherman had a conference with twenty Negro leaders in Savannah. During the conference the question arose of how the freedmen could best be prepared to stand on their own feet. The reply of the Negroes was: "The way we can best take care of ourselves is to have land, and . . . till it by our own labor." They were doubtless right, for in the agricultural society of the South white landholders had become so accustomed to exploiting Negro labor that nothing less than a sweeping program of land reform could have changed things very much. Land reform might have been accomplished by assisting the Negroes to take advantage of the Homestead Act as it was applied to the public lands of the South after the war; or by federal land purchases and resale to Negroes on long-term credits; or by the seizure of land from the former slaveholders.

Though all of these methods were considered, most of the drive for land reform centered on the third alternative, that is, confiscation. Those who favored confiscation justified it, first, as a penalty for treason and, second, as fair compensation to the Negroes for their many years of unrequited toil. This matter of land redistribution, whether achieved through confiscation or in some other way, was one of the most momentous questions the Republicans had to decide. They made their decision before the end of 1867, and it proved to be a crucial one in the development of their program.

Early in 1865, General Sherman, faced with the problem of destitution among the masses of Negroes who had escaped from the plantations, took the first step toward a wholesale redistribution of land in one area of the Deep South. By his Special Field Order Number 15, he set aside the South Carolina and Georgia sea islands south of Charleston and the abandoned rice lands along the rivers for a distance of thirty miles inland for the settlement of Negroes. These lands were to be divided into farms of not more than forty acres, and Negro families were to be given "possessory titles" to them until Congress should decide upon their final disposition. General Rufus Saxton, a friend of the radicals with a genuine concern for the welfare of the freedmen, was appointed Inspector of Settlements and Plantations and placed in charge of the program. Saxton colonized some 40,000 Negroes on the lands under his control, and he presented evidence to the congressional Committee on Reconstruction that the program was a success. But President Johnson saw to it that most of these lands were returned to their original owners, and in January 1866 he removed Saxton.

The debate over land redistribution was resumed when Congress met in December 1865 and continued until early 1867 when that body finally passed a series of reconstruction measures. Sumner insisted that confiscation was a logical part of emancipation; the plantations, he said, "so many nurseries of the rebellion, must be broken up and the freedmen must have the pieces." Stevens, the strongest advocate of confiscation, reminded his colleagues that "when that wise man the Emperor of Russia set free twenty-two million serfs, he compelled their masters to give them homesteads upon the very soil which they had tilled; . . . 'for,' said he, in noble words, 'they have earned this, they have worked upon the land for ages, and they are entitled to it.' " Stevens wondered whether America would do less for its emancipated slaves. "The whole fabric of southern society *must* be changed," he said, "and never can it be done if this opportunity is lost. How can republican institutions, free schools, free churches, free social intercourse exist in a mingled community of nabobs and serfs? . . . If the South is ever to be made a safe Republic let her lands be cultivated by the toil of the owners, or the free labor of intelligent citizens. This must be done even though it drive her nobility into exile."

In elaborating his confiscation plan, Stevens proposed to apply it to about 70,000 of the "chief rebels" who owned some 394,000,000 acres of land. Thus confiscation would affect less than five per cent of the South's white families. He would dispose of the land in this manner: give forty acres to every adult freedman and sell the rest to help pay the public debt, provide pensions for disabled veterans, and compensate loyal men for damage to property suffered during the war. To the objection that it would be inhuman to treat 70,000 southern landlords in this fashion, Stevens recalled Lincoln's proposal to remove the Negroes from the country. "Far easier and more beneficial," he concluded, "to exile 70,000 proud, bloated, and defiant rebels than to expatriate 4,000,000 laborers, native to the soil and loyal to the government."

The congressional radicals won limited popular support for a program of confiscation. "Given two things," predicted the New York *Independent,* "the negro question solves itself—the easiest of all difficult problems: Land and the Ballot—land, that he may support his family; the Ballot, that he may support the state. Grant these to the negro, and . . . he will trouble the nation no more." In defense of Stevens, *Harper's Weekly* declared that "every reflecting man" knew that without land the Negroes lacked "a vital element of substantial citizenship."

But in the end, in spite of arguments such as these, the program of land reform was defeated. The moderate Republicans would not accept it, nor would some Congressmen who were normally counted as radicals. Not even the powers of Sumner and Stevens were great enough to force confiscation into the reconstruction acts of 1867. And this was a severe defeat for radicalism; or at least it defined some rather narrow boundaries within which the radicals could operate. It meant that their program would have only the most limited economic content; that the Negroes' civil and political rights would be in a precarious state for many years to come; and that radical influence in southern politics would probably collapse as soon as federal troops were removed. For the economic degradation of the Negroes strengthened the white man's belief in their innate inferiority, as well as the white man's conviction that for Negroes to possess substantial political power was unnatural, even absurd. The failure of land reform probably made inevitable the ultimate failure of the whole radical program—probably meant that, sooner or later, the southern white landholders and other propertied interests would regain control and reestablish the policies of the Johnson governments.

Why did confiscation—indeed, land reform of any kind—fail to pass Congress? In part it was due to the fact that many of the radicals did not understand the need to give Negro emancipation economic support. Most of them apparently believed that a series of constitutional amendments granting freedom, civil rights, and the ballot would be enough. They seemed to have little conception of what might be called the sociology of freedom, the ease with which mere laws can be flouted when they alone support an economically dependent class, especially a minority group against whom is directed an intense racial prejudice. Even William Lloyd Garrison, the most militant of the old abolitionist leaders, was ready to dissolve the American Anti-Slavery Society after the Thirteenth Amendment had been adopted. To Garrison legal emancipation and civil rights legislation were the primary goals, and the economic plight of the Negroes concerned him a good deal less.

Moreover, confiscation, or even the purchase of land for the Negroes, would have violated what most Republicans, radical or moderate, regarded as sound economic morality. Government paternalism of this sort would have a blighting influence on the initiative of those who received it. Since the Negro was free, his economic status must be determined by his own enterprise. "Now, we totally deny the assumption that the distribution of other people's land to the negroes is necessary to complete the work of emancipation," declared the *Nation*. Whether the ownership of land will prove a blessing or a curse depends on how the holder has acquired it. "If he has inherited it from an honest father, as most of our farmers have, or has bought it with the proceeds of honest industry, it is pretty sure to prove a blessing. If he has got it by gambling, swindling, or plunder it will prove a curse. . . . A large fortune acquired by cheating, gambling, or robbery is almost sure . . . to kill the soul of him who makes it—to render all labor irksome to him, all gains slowly acquired seem not worth having, and patience and scrupulousness seem marks of imbecility."

In addition, confiscation was an obvious attack on property rights—so much so that it is really more surprising that some of these middle-class radicals favored it, even when applied only to rebels, than that most did not. "A division of rich men's lands amongst the landless . . . would give a shock to our whole social and political system from which it would hardly recover without the loss of liberty," warned the *Nation*. A proposal "in which provision is made for the violation of a greater number of the principles of good government and for the opening of a deeper sink of corruption has never been submitted to a legislative body."

Finally, many business friends of the Republicans saw the propertyless Negroes as a labor reservoir for northern industry, or for southern industry or agriculture in which they might invest. Without exception, Northerners who had purchased southern cotton lands were opposed to confiscation. As a result, the land reformers were outnumbered even in the ranks of the radicals. John Binny told Stevens that the northern states "in monster public meetings would lift their voice in thunder against it. . . . You would lose your majority in Congress."

The Republicans did, however, make one less ambitious attempt to give the freedman federal assistance. The disruption of the plantation system, caused by the war and the abolition of slavery, created such widespread destitution among the Negroes that private benevolence was unable to cope with it. In March 1865 Congress created, as an agency of the War Department, the Bureau of Refugees, Freedmen, and Abandoned Lands, commonly known as the Freedmen's Bureau. It was to provide food, clothing, and medical care for both white refugees and Negro freedmen; to settle them on abandoned or confiscated lands; and in general to help the freedmen in the period of transition from slavery to freedom—to get them back to work, to aid them in their dealings with the landholders, and to provide them with schools. But according to the original act, the bureau's work was to terminate within a year after the end of the war.

The congressional Committee on Reconstruction, however, collected much evidence indicating that the bureau needed not only to have its life extended but to be given additional power. The committee found that landholders were using the Black Codes to take advantage of the Negroes and were combining to keep down the wages of agricultural labor. Sometimes they bound Negroes to unfair labor contracts; sometimes they refused to pay them wages at all. The committee also found that Negroes were not always receiving fair trials in state and local courts, and that they were often maltreated by individual whites or by organized bands of "regulators." Therefore Congress, in February 1866, passed a new Freedmen's Bureau bill indefinitely extending the agency's life, increasing its power to supervise labor contracts, and authorizing it to establish special courts for Negroes when they were unable to get justice in the regular courts. In his veto message President Johnson argued that the bill was unnecessary and an unconstitutional violation of the rights of the states; but Congress eventually overrode the President's veto.

The bureau, though competently and conscientiously directed by General Oliver O. Howard, was highly unpopular with most white Southerners and has since been subjected to severe criticism. Its critics accused it of meddling in matters that were not properly within the jurisdiction of the federal government; of stirring up discontent among the negroes and filling them with false hopes; of employing corrupt or incompetent administrators who wasted federal money; and of acting as a political agency for the Republican party. There was some truth in several of these charges. Some of the bureau agents did tell the Negroes that they were going to get land, not for the purpose of deceiving them but because the agents believed, or hoped, that Congress would actually give them land. Some of the agents were incompetent, some were corrupt, and some used the bureau's power to win Negro votes for the Republicans.

Such criticism, however, does not comprise a full appraisal of the bureau's work. Those who objected to it on the ground that the plight of the southern Negro was no concern of the federal government were, in effect, objecting to assistance of any kind; for Negro destitution was clearly a national problem which the individual southern states had neither the resources nor the desire to deal with. Actually, the most valid criticism that can be made of the Republican majority in Congress in this respect is that it failed to give the bureau sufficient power and funds to perform efficiently its manifold duties. As for the complaint that bureau agents stirred up discontent among the Negroes, the basis for it in most cases was that they encouraged Negroes to demand land, civil rights, and political enfranchisement. No doubt some agents did incite the freedmen in this fashion, and no doubt they distressed those who preferred to regulate race relations with some form of Black Code. White men who were accustomed to the humble, subservient Negro of slavery days were bound to find any change in his character unpleasant, any claim to equality almost intolerable. Insofar as the Freedmen's Bureau contributed to this result, it played a constructive role in the transformation of the Negro from salve to citizen.

The tradition that the bureau was rife with corruption and incompetence is also an exaggeration. In 1866, President Johnson, seeking ammunition to use against the radicals, appointed a commission, consisting of General Joseph S. Fullerton and General James B. Steedman, to make a thorough investigation of the bureau's activities. The commission was as hostile to the bureau as Johnson himself. In North Carolina it uncovered a major scandal, but a scandal of little use to Johnson, for it involved the cheating and mistreating of Negroes, not whites. Elsewhere the commission turned up so little that would help the President that its tour of the southern states was cut short and finally abandoned. In the words of a recent scholar: "President Johnson . . . had gained from the Steedman-Fullerton investigation . . . little but laughter from the Radicals. . . . His best efforts to discredit the Freedman's Bureau had failed."

A balanced evaluation of the Freedmen's Bureau, therefore, must stress its constructive achievements. First, while trying to make the Negroes self-supporting as soon as possible, the bureau provided emergency relief for those who were in desperate need. During its brief existence it issued more than fifteen million rations and gave medical care to a million people. Second, it spent more than $5,000,000 for Negro schools, a pitifully inadequate sum but as much as Congress would grant. Usually the bureau furnished buildings and other physical facilities, while private benevolent societies provided teachers and books; together they established the first schools for Negroes in the southern states. Third, the bureau tried to prevent landowners from taking advantage of the Negroes. It set aside some of the provisions of the Black Codes, saw to it that Negroes were free to choose their employers, fixed the conditions of labor, and supervised the mixing and enforcement of labor contracts. Finally, the bureau tried to protect the Negroes' civil rights. Because of the legal discriminations of the Johnson governments, local administrators either established special freedmen's courts to handle their cases or sent observers into the regular courts to make sure that trials were conducted fairly. Though a system of special courts for Negroes was obviously undesirable as a permanent arrangement, there seemed at the time to be no other way in some localities to avoid flagrant injustice.

But in 1869, with its work scarcely begun, Congress provided for the termination of the bureau's activities, and soon after it ceased to exist. Even a Congress dominated by the radical-moderate coalition could support an experiment in social engineering for only a few short years, and it had to be justified on the grounds of an unprecedented emergency. Thus ended the one modest federal effort to deal directly with some of the social and economic problems confronting the postwar South.

The liquidation of the Freedmen's Bureau also meant that Congress had lost its most efficient agency to protect Negroes in the enjoyment of the civil and political rights they had recently been given. Congress had provided federal guarantees of civil rights to all persons, first by the Civil Rights Act passed over Johnson's veto in 1866, then by the Fourteenth Amendment ratified by the states in 1868. The Civil Rights Act clearly conferred citizenship on American Negroes: it declared that "all persons born in the United States and not subject to any foreign power, excluding Indians not taxed," are citizens of the United States. This act removed the doubts about the Negroes' status which had been raised before the war when the Supreme Court, in the Dred Scott case, held that Negroes were not citizens, and when the State Department sometimes refused to give Negroes passports. In addition, the Civil Rights Act provided that citizens "of every race and color" were to have equal rights in all states to make contracts, to sue, to testify in court, to purchase, hold, and dispose of real and personal property, and were to enjoy "full and equal benefit of all laws and proceedings for the security of person and property." Finally, all citizens were to be subjected "to like punishment, pains and penalties, and to none other." Violations of this law carried penalties of fine and imprisonment, and the Executive Department and fedeal courts were given ample powers to enforce it.

For many years after reconstruction, as we know, the Fourteenth Amendment was almost a dead letter as far as the civil rights of Negroes were concerned; but the federal courts enforced it vigorously when any state tried to regulate railroads or other corporations. In law, corporations are "persons," and the courts repeatedly invalidated regulatory legislation as violations of the "due process" clause of this amendment. With this in mind, historians who stressed an economic interpretation of radical reconstruction insisted that the real, though secret, motive of the authors of the amendment was to protect corporations rather than Negroes. They based their case on the testimony of two members of the Joint Committee on Reconstruction who helped to frame the amendment.

Of course, we cannot read the minds of those who framed the Fourteenth Amendment, but there is no contemporary evidence—nothing in the records of the Joint Committee or in the congressional debates—to indicate any thought at the time of giving protection to private corporations. The case for an economic interpretation of Republican motivation must be regarded as unproved. There is, in fact, no reason to reject the explanation that Thad Stevens gave when the amendment was being discussed in Congress. Its purpose, he said, was "to correct the unjust legislation of the states [that is, the Black Codes], so . . . that the law which operates upon one man shall operate *equally* upon all. . . . Whatever law punishes a white man . . . shall punish the black man precisely in the same way and to the same degree. . . . Whatever law allows the white man to testify in court shall allow the man of color to do the same."

A far more significant question is how the framers of the Fourteenth Amendment defined civil rights and precisely which ones they intended to protect—a question that pro- and anti-segregationists are still debating today. It is reasonably clear that they intended to prohibit the states from governing Negroes by special Black Codes, from making certain acts felonies for Negroes but not for whites, from providing more severe penalties for Negro felons than for white, and from excluding Negro testimony in cases involving whites. It is doubtful, however, that most of them regarded the exclusion of Negroes from jury service, or anti-miscegenation laws, or the segregation of Negroes in public places as violations of civil rights. Few of the moderates would have thought so, and apparently not even all of the radicals did.

Actually, neither the radicals nor the Negroes of the reconstruction era considered social segregation to be the most urgent immediate issue. Though resenting it and occasionally speaking out against it, most Negro leaders acquiesced in segregation for the time being, in order to concentrate upon obtaining security of person, equality in the courts, and political rights. In the South the informal pattern of social segregation established for free Negroes in prewar years and enforced under the Johnson governments was challenged only sporadically. Nearly all of the schools subsidized by the Freedmen's Bureau were racially segregated. When Congress, in 1866, appropriated money for the schools of the District of Columbia, it again either approved of, or acquiesced in, a system of segregation. In fact, Senator Henry Wilson, a radical, admitted that a special system of Negro schools had been established and explained that the appropriation bill simply provided that "those in the colored schools will receive the same benefit that those receive who are in the white schools"—a fairly clear statement of the doctrine of "separate but equal." In short, most of the Congressmen who voted for the Fourteenth Amendment, and the states that ratified it, probably did not intend to outlaw state-enforced racial segregation. But the terms of the amendment, as we have seen, are broad and vague; and when the Supreme Court outgrew the sociology of the nineteenth century, it began to discover new meaning in the loose phrase "equal protection of the laws."

At least a few of the radicals, notably Senator Charles Sumner, believed from the start that they were proscribing segregation. Beginning with the reconstruction acts of 1867, Sumner tried, unsuccessfully, to require the southern estates to establish "public schools open to all without distinction of race or color." For the next seven years, until his death in 1874, he urged his colleagues to subsidize biracial public schools, to desegregate the schools of the District of Columbia, and, above all, to adopt a Civil Rights Act that would outlaw all forms of racial segregation as violations of the Fourteenth Amendment. The debate on Sumner's numerous bills ran the gamut of arguments that have been heard ever since. The segregationists, North and South, denied that a separation of the races was a violation of civil rights, or that the Fourteenth Amendment was designed to interfere with matters that are purely social; and they warned that an attempt to integrate the public schools would simply destroy the system altogether. Sumner replied that segregated schools were "an ill disguised violation of the principle of equality," and that they injured the personalities of white children as well as Negro. "Pharisaism of race," he said, becomes an element of character, when, like all other Pharisaisms it should be stamped out."

The Civil Rights Act of 1875 was significant nonetheless, because it was the first federal attempt to deal directly with social segregation and discrimination by the states or by private enterprises established to serve the public. "It is the completion of the promise of equal civil rights," said *Harper's Weekly*. "Honest legislation upon the subject will not at once remove all prejudice, but it will clear the way for its disappearance." In 1883, however, in a group of civil rights cases, the Supreme Court invalidated the act. It endorsed the position of the segregationists that the Fourteenth Amendment had not given Congress jurisdiction over the social relationships of the two races. There matters stood for the next seventy years.

On the question of Negro suffrage, the Republicans eventually took a bolder and less ambiguous stand than they did on the question of segregation, but only after several years of hesitation and evasion. In the autumn 1865 even Thad Stevens was noncommittal when he spoke to his constituents: "Whether those who have fought our battles should all be allowed to vote, or only those of a paler hue, I leave to be discussed in the future when Congress can take legitimate cognizance of it." But in most cases the radicals' early timidity resulted less from their own doubts than from their fear of public opinion in the North. Radicals were embarrassed by the fact that in most of the northern states the Negroes were then disenfranchised, and that in recent years the voters in several of them had rejected proposals to give Negroes the ballot.

As a result, few radicals made an explicit demand for Negro suffrage during the congressional elections of 1866, and the Fourteenth Amendment got at the matter only by indirection. The second section of the amendment simply provided that when a state denied adult male citizens the right to vote for reasons other than participation in rebellion or other crimes, such state was to have its representation in Congress reduced proportionately—a provision, incidentally, which in subsequent years was totally ignored. This weak and ineffective approach to Negro suffrage—the result of another compromise between radicals and moderates—caused Stevens privately to call the Fourteenth Amendment a "shilly-shally bungling thing," and finally, in 1869, after another relapse into timidity during the presidential election the previous year, the Republicans passed the Fifteenth Amendment, which unequivocally declared: "The right of the citizens of the United States to vote shall not be denied or abridged by the United States or by any State on account of race, color, or previous condition of servitude." The amendment was ratified by 1870; and thus, said the *Nation,* "the agitation against slavery has reached an appropriate and triumphant conclusion."

On reflection, however, the *Nation,* like many others, thought it would have been better to admit the Negroes to the franchise gradually, "and through an educational test." Some had suggested that Negro suffrage be postponed until 1876. Representative Julian presented the ablest defense of the almost immediate enfranchisement of the Negroes even though the great mass of them were illiterate. A literacy test, he argued, is "a singularly insufficient measure of fitness. Reading and writing are mechanical processes, and a man may be able to perform them without any worthiness of life or character. . . . If penmanship must be made the avenue to the ballot, I fear several honorable gentlemen on this floor will be disfranchised."

When the Republicans turned from the Negroes to the white men of the South who had supported the rebellion, their reconstruction measures were remarkably lenient. The fourth section of the Fourteenth Amendment prohibited the southern states from paying any Confederate debt or any claim for emancipated slave property. This amendment, in its third section, also withheld from the President the power to restore, by presidential pardon, political rights to Confederate leaders. As it was reported by the Joint Committee on Reconstruction, this section would have excluded those who had supported the Confederacy from voting in federal elections until July 4, 1870. "Here is the mildest of all punishments ever inflicted on traitors," said Stevens. "I would be glad to see it extended to 1876, and to include all State and municipal as well as national elections." Instead, the Senate softened it. In its final form it provided that persons who had held state or federal offices before the rebellion, and who had then supported the rebellion, were to be ineligible for public office until pardoned by a two-thirds vote of Congress. This disability applied to virtually the entire political leadership of the ante-bellum South; but for most of them it lasted only until 1872, when Congress passed a sweeping amnesty act. After that, all but a few of them were eligible once more to run for public office.

On March 2, 1867, the Republicans passed an act outlining their general plan of political reconstruction. Three subsequent acts, adopted on March 23 and July 19, 1867, and March 11, 1868, cleared up points left vague in the first act, provided machinery for the program's implementation, and established safeguards against presidential obstructionism. President Johnson, of course, vetoed these measures, but Congress passed them quickly and easily over his vetoes. Thus, two years after the end of the war, the process of reconstruction was begun anew. That Thad Stevens and the radicals now had their way may be attributed, first, to Johnson's recalcitrance to the very end; second, to the refusal of ten southern states to accept the terms of the Fourteenth Amendment; and, third, to the continued mistreatment of southern Negroes and Unionists.

These reconstruction acts were based on the assumption, as stated in the preamble of the first act, that "no legal State governments or adequate protection for life or property now exists in the rebel States." The purpose of the acts was to enforce "peace and good order . . . in said States until loyalty and republican State governments can be legally established." To this end, the Johnson governments were repudiated and the ten unreconstructed southern states divided into five military districts. The district commanders were given broad powers to "protect all persons in their rights of person and property, to suppress insurrection, disorder, and violence, and to punish . . . all disturbers of the public peace." They could, when necessary, remove civil officeholders, make arrests, try civilians in military courts, and use federal troops to preserve order.

The district commanders were also given the responsibility of putting the new program of political reconstruction in motion. They were to enroll the qualified voters, including Negroes but excluding those barred from holding office by the Fourteenth Amendment, and to hold elections for delegates to state constitutional conventions. Each convention was to frame a new constitution providing for Negro suffrage; and when the constitution was ratified by popular vote, a governor and state legislature could be elected. The first legislature was to ratify the Fourteenth Amendment. Finally, after Congress had approved of the new state constitution and after the Fourteenth Amendment had become part of the federal Constitution, the state would be entitled to representation in Congress. Meanwhile, however, the civil government of the state was to be deemed "provisional only, and in all respects subject to the paramount authority of the United States." When elections were held under such provisional government, those disqualified by the Fourteenth Amendment were not to be entitled to vote.

By 1868, six of the southern states had completed this reconstruction process and were readmitted. Four states—Virginia, Georgia, Mississippi, and Texas—delayed until after the Fourteenth Amendment had been ratified and the Fifteenth Amendment had been adopted by Congress. They were therefore required to ratify the Fifteenth Amendment as well. The Republican terms were then fully defined, and by 1870 political reconstruction had been completed in all of the southern states.

An Analysis of Some Reconstruction Attitudes

T. Harry Williams

In late years revisionist historians have done much to correct the existing and often distorted picture of the Reconstruction period in American hsitory. Earlier writers on Reconstruction, whether they were Republican politicians or southern polemicists, journalists, or historians, exhibited a number of historical deficiencies, but in general it may be said that they told a story that was too simple and naïve. It was simple in that the terrible complexities of Reconstruction were presented in the easy terms of stereotypes—the good white Southern Democrats fighting against the bad colored Republicans and their insidious northern allies, or vice versa. It was naïve in that virtually no analysis was made to explain why people acted as they did. Thus carpetbaggers were dishonest because they were bad men or Republicans, but no attempt was made to describe the forces which contributed to their dishonesty. The revisionists have forced several modifications in the Reconstruction story. They have demonstrated, among other things, that the corruption of the Reconstruction state governments has been exaggerated and that in any case corruption was a national, not a purely southern, phenomenon, with an expanding capitalism as the chief corrupting agent; that Democrats were quite as willing as Republicans to be bought by business; that the supposed astronomically high appropriations of the Reconstruction government seem so only in comparison with the niggardly budgets of the planter-controlled governments of the antebellum period; that although the Reconstruction governments were corrupt and dishonest, they must be credited with definite progress in the fields of popular education and internal improvements; and that the national reconstruction program was radical only in a superficial sense in that it gave political power to the Negro but failed to provide economic power through the promised confiscation and ownership of land, and thus that because the position of the Negro had no lasting basis his rule was easily overthrown.

These new viewpoints have provided a desirable balance and proportion to the traditional historical treatment of Reconstruction. Still debated and in part unexplored in research are the motives of the northern and southern people during this period. Who supported Reconstruction and why; and who opposed it, and why? In analyzing the motivation of Reconstruction, historians have devoted most of their attention to northern political and economic groups and have produced certain conclusions which have been generally accepted. What may be termed the Beale thesis, because it has been most competently developed by Professor Howard K. Beale, offers a sectional-class explanation of Reconstruction. According to this thesis, Reconstruction was a successful attempt by northeastern business, acting through the Republican party, to control the national government for its own economic ends: notably, the protective tariff, the national banks, a "sound" currency. To accomplish its program, the business class had to overthrow from the seats of power the old ruling agrarian class of the South and West. This it did by inaugurating Reconstruction, which made the South Republican, and by selling its policies to the voters wrapped up in such attractive vote-getting packages as northern patriotism or the bloody shirt. Another student of the period, while accepting the Beale thesis, points out that northern business men supported Reconstruction not only because of national issues but also because they thought it would enable them to exploit the South through protected capital investments, and that Republican bosses supported Reconstruction because they believed that if the South could be made Republican they could stay in power.

The Negro author W. E. Burghardt Du Bois, conceding the part played by industry in formulating the Reconstruction program, contends that there was in the North a substantial mass opinion of liberal idealism, which he calls "abolition-democracy," that stood for a democratic reconstruction plan, including equal rights for Negroes. This group, he insists, represented in politics by men like Thaddeus Stevens, was equally influential with business in determining the nature of Reconstruction. The existence of such a body of opinion cannot be disputed. That it was as extensive as Du Bois thinks or that it was animated by as much idealism for the Negro may well be doubted; unfortunately there is no way to document accurately its numbers or influence. One thing is certain. The leaders of abolition-democracy did not succeed in incorporating their ideas into the Republican reconstruction scheme. They demanded universal suffrage, universal amnesty, and confiscation of the land of rich Southerners and its distribution among the freedmen. The Republican politicos, being economic reactionaries, discarded confiscation because they had no interest in bringing about a social revolution, and they rejected universal amnesty because it would have made a Republican South improbable. It would seem that the party bosses, instead of being influenced to any considerable degree by abolition-democracy, used it for whatever it was worth to marshal support for a program designed to benefit a plutocratic minority.

An interpretation of northern motivation that differs in part from both Beale and Du Bois has come from Marxist historians and writers. The Marxian thesis has been elaborately presented by James S. Allen, who regards Reconstruction as a plan formulated and carried through by big business to enable it to dominate the nation. Up to a point, this is only the Beale thesis dressed up in Marxian jargon. Allen, however, proceeds to advance the claim that the business program was "democratic," because industry, in achieving power, smashed the old, feudal planter class of the South and thus helped prepare the way for the coming of the industrial state which, after business itself was smashed, would evolve into a perfect democracy of the Marxist variety. In recent years writers of Marxist persuasion have dropped Allen's emphasis on the class struggle, and have presented Reconstruction as a straight-out plan of equalitarian democracy. The new departure has been most strikingly expressed, in fictional form, by Howard Fast, who flatly states that the Reconstruction acts of 1867 were intended "to create a new democracy in the South." The Marxian thesis in any of these forms has little validity. No amount of historical legerdemain can transform the economic reactionaries of the Republican party into great liberals or make the protective tariff and the gold standard into items of the democratic faith. Furthermore, as will be shown, the Marxists are wrong when they try to develop the corollary that Reconstruction was also a democratic process in the South.

The sectional-class thesis of Beale would seem to be the most nearly correct analysis of northern motivation, although Beale did not fully explain how northeastern business persuaded agrarian Republicans from the Middle West to support industrial measures and a reconstruction policy designed to insure the rule of business in the South. It has since been demonstrated that this was done in part by giving the Middle West exceptionally generous appropriations for internal improvements and in effect buying its support; and to this should be added such other inducements as free land, pensions, and railroads, as well as such emotional and psychological appeals as habitual use of the bloody shirt. Du Bois was also undoubtedly correct in contending that idealistic forces played a part in shaping reconstruction policy, and his point is a good, although minor, corrective to the purely economic analysis. But the major fact remains that the men who made Reconstruction were moved by issues of economic and political power far more than by democratic idealism.

While the question of northern motivation has been fairly well established, there has been little attempt to prepare a systematic analysis of southern attitudes toward Reconstruction. Most of the professional historians writing on southern reconstruction have been members of or followers of the so-called Dunning school. They are largely responsible for the familiar stereotypes of Reconstruction. According to their interpretation, Reconstruction was a battle between two extremes: the Democrats, as the group which included the vast majority of the whites, standing for decent government and racial supremacy, versus the Republicans, the Negroes, alien carpetbaggers, and renegade scalawags, standing for dishonest government and alien ideals. These historians wrote literally in terms of white and black. This is not to say that they did not recognize the fact that there were differences between Southerners on such issues as Negro suffrage. But they explained the differences in terms of individual motivation. Thus Southerners who advocated the vote for Negroes were either bad men, or wartime Unionists who hated "rebels," or kindly planters who knew Negroes well and wanted to control their votes in the right direction. Although the Dunning writers sensed an apparent disagreement between the planter-business class and the small farmers on the Negro question, with the planters being willing to accept a position of greater equality for the Negro, they did not explore the difference or try to ascertain whether there were economic and social causes for its existence.

No such reluctance characterizes Du Bois. He boldly proclaims that Reconstruction was a labor movement, an attempt by the whtie and black proletariat to control the South, "a vision of democracy across racial lines." A basic error invalidates most of his thesis. There was no white proletariat of any significant numbers; the great mass of the whites were yeoman farmers who thought in terms of racial supremacy instead of class solidarity. Furthermore, he exaggerates the readiness of the former non-slaveholding whites to unite with the Negroes. He himself recognizes that there are factual weaknesses in his theory. He knows that the common whites furnished the power by which the Republican state governments were overthrown; but he explains this disturbing fact by claiming that the planters cut off the developing interracial co-operation of the proletariat by appealing to the prejudices of the poorer whites and organizing them on the color line. Closely paralleling Du Bois' interpretation, and even going beyond it, is that of the Marxists. They, too, present Reconstruction as a biracial movement of the laboring class which was finally destroyed by a counter-revolution of the planters. According to Howard Fast, the Negroes and poor whites joined hands in the Republican party and created "a fine, a just, and a truly democratic civilization," but the reactionary planter class refused to permit this experiment in social democracy and wiped it out with force. That the validity of such assertions is open to serious question can be shown by examining the attitude of the planters and business men in Louisiana toward Reconstruction and the Negro and placing the results in the larger setting of what is known about the general attitudes of the southern whites in other parts of the region.

First of all, despite the opinions of the Marxists, the overwhelming mass of the people—the yeoman farmers, middle class whites, and poor whites—were fiercely opposed to Negro suffrage and to any condition of equality for the Negro. The evidence on this point, while not voluminous because of the general inarticulateness of the common whites, is strong; it is best expressed by the fact that the small-farmer, white-belt areas of the southern states voted heavily against Republicans and Republican measures in election after election. As Horace Mann Bond puts its, the farmers hated equally slavery, planters, and Negroes. The attitude of the common whites of Reconstruction is consonant with the known attitude of the poorest whites, economically, today; that is, racial antipathy toward Negroes is always sharpest when accentuated by economic competition. The teachings of social psychology can be adduced to support the generalization concerning the reaction of the whites. In a caste system based on a fixed status for groups, any attempt by a subordinated element—in this case the Negroes—to achieve a higher status unlooses feelings of tension and fear in the next higher group, which will exert itself, often violently, to keep the subordinated group down.

The most powerful group in the South was the planter-business class and its professional allies; its position on Reconstruction was of decisive importance. In the beginning days of Reconstruction, the planters and business men strongly opposed the central proposal of the Radical Republican program—suffrage for the Negro. But they opposed it for economic rather than racial reasons. This fact is crucially important in understanding their reactions. To use modern terms, they feared that the grant of the ballot to the Negro would add to the strength of the liberal or progressive vote. This is not to say that they did not regard the Negro as an inferior being of an entirely separate race. But it is to say that they reacted to a proposal to enfranchise a laboring class as would any propertied minority in any society—they opposed it because they believed it would lead to an attack upon property. A few quotations selected from many statements appearing in conservative New Orleans newspapers which were spokesmen of the planter-business interests will demonstrate the point. Terming universal suffrage a menace to property, the New Orleans *Times* said: "The right to vote should be given to those only who can use it with discretion and sound judgment, and as our electoral privileges are already too wide, it would be the maddest folly to extend them at once to a class who have always been under control, and who—without the ability to form a correct judgment for themselves—would be left to the tender mercies of party tricksters." Let the Negro wait until he acquired property before he became a voter. In a fuller and more philosophical exposition of its views, the *Times* stated:

> Wherever voters greatly outnumber property holders, property will assuredly be unsafe. When voters have property and intelligence, there is some hope that they may "find their interest in the interest of the community" and be anxious to secure a consistent, honest, economical and straight-forward administration. But the selfish interest of the non-property holding voter lies in an altogether different direction. He wishes to secure rich pickings, and, too frequently, soils his fingers by base bribes. Were universal negro suffrage to be added to the white universal suffrage now existing in the South, the security of both life and property would be greatly weakened. . . . With our

present too widely extended suffrage it is difficult even now to steer between the rocks of the political Scylla and the whirlpool of its Charybdis, and with universal negro suffrage added, the task would be wholly hopeless.

Becoming frankly specific, the *Times* later declared that "If representative institutions are to be preserved in this country, the control of taxes must be left to those who pay them, and the protection of property to those who own it." The New Orleans *Crescent,* endorsing the proposal of South Carolina's planter leader, Wade Hampton, to extend the vote to Negroes who had acquired property and an education, asserted: "Southern conservatives ask nothing more on the subject of suffrage than that its distribution shall be determined by the test of character and intelligence. They have asked for nothing more from the time that, by one of the irreversible results of war, the Southern negroes became a part of the free population of the country. It is not their fault if such a test has been rejected in favor of another that proscribes a large proportion of the highest intelligence on the one hand, and opens all political functions to the maximum of ignorance on the other." Expressing the conservatives' fear of the economic implications of Negro suffrage, the *Crescent* said: "It seems to be practically absurd and dangerous to commit the decisions of those difficult questions to numbers of extemporized citizens incapable of forming any accurate or rational opinions; and likely to imagine that the right to vote means the right to live without work, and to rob the industrious classes for the benefit of the idle and thriftless." The *Picayune* denounced Negro suffrage because it did not believe that common men of any color should vote; manhood suffrage was "the unlimited suffrage of the ignorant, landless and lawless." "We look upon it [voting] as a duty rather than a right," said the *Picayune,* "and regret that there is so much of it among the whites." To the *Picayune,* Reconstruction was a process that proscribed "intelligence, probity and property" and elevated propertyless nobodies to power.

To the testimony of conservative newspapers can be added representative statements of conservative planter-business leaders. In 1867, when Congress was considering the radical reconstruction acts, various southern newspapers asked prominent individuals to give their reactions to the proposed measures. More frank and philosophical than most was J. W. Robb of Mississippi. He warned conservatives that all republics in history had fallen when they had extended the ballot to a laboring class, "an ignorant horde of stupid and besotted men." "I believe," he continued, "that from the introduction of negro suffrage, the worst form and spirit of agrarianism will arise to distrub the peace and order of the State, and that it will require our utmost exertions to keep it down, and retain for ourselves political existence and individual security." Francis T. Nicholls, who became governor of Louisiana in 1877 when white supremacy supposedly was restored, told a Congressional committee that conservatives were opposed to Reconstruction because it had endangered property interests by placing ignorance in power. Before Reconstruction, he said, there had been a relatively small group of ignorant white voters whom the rich could control, but Reconstruction had made ignorance "the dominating power." He favored a law that in the interest of property would disfranchise the ignorant of both races.

Congress ignored the opposition to Negro suffrage of the planter-business class, based primarily on economic grounds, and of the common whites, based primarily on racial grounds. In 1867 it passed the reconstruction laws of the Radical Republicans; and Negro suffrage and, in many states, Negro rule became a reality. There followed a period of years, varying in different states, in which the Republican party, led by white carpetbaggers and scalawags and composed predominantly of the Negro masses, controlled the South. The political record of its rule was a compound of blatant corruption and forward social legislation. It was an expensive program. Money was needed to gratify the desires of the white and colored politicans for graft and of the colored masses for social services furnished by the state. The Republicans had to resort to higher and higher taxation, and necessarily they laid the heaviest taxes upon real property. While taxation affected all property holders, large and small, the brunt of it fell upon the large holders. This, as Du Bois points out, is a crucial fact in Reconstruction history—a war-impoverished propertied class was being compelled by the votes of poor men to bear an almost confiscatory tax burden.

Faced with extinction by taxation, the planter-business class reacted again and characteristically in economic rather than racial terms. Negro votes had imposed the tax burden. Negro votes could lift it. If in order to persuade the Negroes to do so it was necessary to grant them political and civil equality or even to let them run the state, well and good. Get the tax rate down, cried one New Orleans conservative, "even if every office in the State, from Governor to the most insignificant constable, were filled by a negro." Urged another: "We must get rid of party hacks and political jobbers, and satisfy the reasonable demands of the negroes. This accomplished, Louisiana will again blossom as the rose. It is our only salvation." A prominent merchant declared: "I am in favor, in case we ever have another election, of giving to the colored people the bulk of the lucrative positions. . . . I am not afraid that they will, in any considerable degree abuse their privileges, and, for ourselves, we want nothing but peaceful government." "You want civil equality; you shall have it," a leading business man pledged the Negroes, "if you forsake the Northern adventurer who has plundered poor Louisiana until she is penniless." On with political co-operation with Negroes, exclaimed a property holder, "for God's sake if it will give us an honest government; our present lot is insupportable." A blunt Natchitoches planter asserted that it was imperative that the whites detach the Negroes from the Republicans: "When the war was over we wouldn't have anything to do with the niggers, and let the Radicals gobble them up. . . . I am in favor of anything to get them. Drop the name of Democracy, I say, and go in for the niggers."

What practical political action did the planter-business class take during Reconstruction to protect itself from excessive taxation and to foster its economic interests? In local elections in New Orleans, for example, the business men contemplated putting up Negro candidates for Congressional and city offices to compete with white Republicans. On Carondelet Street, the City's great business center, it was planned to nominate a colored foreman of one of the leading cotton presses for Congress. Such a man, asserted the business reporters of the New Orleans *Times,* "Will protect and do more for the South than any white Radical which can be selected to run against him. Carondelet street will go for the gentlemen with the cotton press." The business men, this journalist explained, "are taking an unusual interest in being represented in Congress by a representative born in the South. The nearer approach to a real African, black in color, the more confidence will be placed in him." Since the records do not show that the Carondelet magnates got their foreman nominated, it is probable that the Democratic leaders in New Orleans refused to take a Negro candidate, or even more probable that the cotton press gentleman, if he had political ambitions and an eye for the future, became a Republican. Regardless of the outcome, however, the episode demonstrated that these hard-headed business men placed their economic interests above racial differences and that they preferred to entrust those interests to an understanding and amenable Negro rather than to an untried white.

A second device adopted by the conservatives was to enter the Republican party and seek to control it. A recent study by David H. Donald illustrates how this was done in Mississippi. After Radical Reconstruction went into effect most of the former Whigs, in antebellum times the party of the big slave-holders, became Republicans. "Such action is not hard to understand," writes Donald. "The Whigs were wealthy men—the large planters and the railroad and industrial promoters—who naturally turned to the party which in the state as in the nation was dominated by business interests." At first these planters, or scalawags, to use a familiar term, dominated the party, but they lost their leadership to the carpetbaggers who, in the struggles for power within the party, were willing to promise more to the Negroes. Donald points to the planters' fruitless opposition to the Republican program of big budgets and high taxes and their revulsion against the social equality claimed by the Negroes as sources of their difficulties. Finally, repudiated by people they could not control, they drifted "slowly and reluctantly over to the Democratic camp."

Still a third device employed by the planters and business men was to invite the Negroes to leave the Republicans and join with them in a new political organization separate from the Democratic party. The conservatives promised in such case to respect the Negro's civil equality and his right to vote and to hold office. Such movements were tried in several states, the most elaborate being the so-called "Louisiana Unification Movement." Inaugurated in 1873, this movement was headed by General Pierre G. T. Beauregard and was supported by the flower of the wealth and culture of New Orleans and South Louisiana. Its platform advocated complete political equality for the Negro, an equal division of state offices between the races, and a plan whereby Negroes would become landowners. The unifiers denounced discrimination because of color in hiring laborers or in selecting directors of corporations, and called for the abandonment of segregation in public conveyances, public places, railroads, steamboats, and the public schools. The Louisiana movement, like the others, failed for lack of support from the white masses. The unification program was popular in New Orleans and in the plantation belt of South Louisiana, but in the small-farmer areas of other parts of the state it was received with loathing and execration.

It is evident that a basis existed for an alliance of the planter-business class and the Negroes. "If they [the planters] had wished," writes Du Bois, "they could have held the Negro vote in the palm of their hands." Why did such an alliance fail to materialize? In the first place, the leaders of the unification movements could not persuade any significant number of whites to support the concessions which the planters were willing to accord the colored people. The common whites, animated by racial motives, refused to follow planter leadership, and without any mass white support the unification movements could not succeed. In Louisiana the movement failed to develop much mass support even from the Negroes because professional Negro politicians, secure in their place in the Republican party, advised their followers to shun co-operation and because those Negro leaders who favored co-operation could not suppress their suspicion of the sincerity of the planter-business class. "We know that, by an alliance with you, we can have more privileges than we now enjoy," one Negro spokesman told the conservatives. "We will not then have to cling to the carpet-baggers for protection, but can ourselves take whatever share of office and representation falls to us fairly. Still, we have *some* rights now, and we don't intend to give them up. Rather than do that, we will cling to the carpetbagger forever, and let him share our power."

In the second place, the planters and business men, while willing to make far-reaching concessions to the Negroes, did not make them because they believed in the principles of racial equality. They made them because of pressing economic reasons and because they wanted to control the Negro vote. They never ceased to regard the Negroes as inferior creatures who by an unfortunate turn of fate had become politically powerful in the state. Hence there was a limit to their concessions, its line marked by anything that seemed to suggest social equality. The carpetbaggers, unhampered by such reservations, could always outbid the conservatives. Thus in states like Mississippi, where the planter tried to dominate the Republican party, the carpetbaggers took the leadership of the Negroes away from the scalawags. Finally, the differing economic aspirations of the wealthy whites and the Negroes prevented any lasting alliance of the two. The Negroes demanded a program of social services financed by the state, which meant high taxes. The planters wanted to control the colored vote in order to reduce these services and lower taxes which they considered almost confiscatory. The Negroes wanted higher wages and shorter hours; the planters wanted a serf-like system of sharecropping. The planters simply lacked the capital to finance the Negro's social or labor program; but in view of the obvious conflict between the desires of the two groups it is doubtful whether such a program would have received support from the planters even if they had possessed the necessary means for financing it.

And so the planters and business men, unable to prevent the establishment of Negro suffrage and unable to control it after it was established, joined with the common whites to overthrow the Republican state governments. By 1877 the Democrats controlled every southern state, and what the textbooks call white supremacy was restored. Actually, Negroes continued to vote, although in reduced numbers, and white supremacy was not restored until the 1890's. As Professor C. Vann Woodward has ably demonstrated, the men who came to power after Reconstruction were not in the old agrarian, planter tradition. They were often of the planter class, but in reality they were industrialists or would-be industrialists. They preached the industrialization of the South through the importation of Yankee capital, a policy of low taxes to attract business, and a political alliance with the Northeast instead of with the South's traditional ally, the West. These men reacted to Negro suffrage as had men of their class during Reconstruction. As the vote of labor, it was something to be feared and kept in hand, but as the vote of an inferior people, it was also something that might be manipulated for the benefit of the wealthy. As events developed, the bosses of the New South sometimes found that they could use the colored vote to beat down attempts of the farmers to take over control of the Democratic party. In the election of 1880 in Georgia, for example, the rich defeated the farmers through a combination of a minority of the white votes and a majority of the colored ones. The southern champions of industrialism, therefore, took no action to disfranchise the Negro; they used him to maintain the supremacy of a few white men over other white men. Disfranchisement finally came as a result of the efforts of small-farmer leaders like Ben Tillman.

Placed in the general setting, therefore, the interests and activities of the Louisiana planter-capitalist group serve to confirm the fact that the Reconstruction period was one of the most complex in American history. It witnessed the ending of a great civil struggle and the travail of postwar adjustment, the consummation of a momentous economic revolution, and a wrenching change in race relations. No less complex than the times were the motives that impelled people—northern and southern, white and black, rich and poor—to act as they did. No simple or generic explanation cast in the form of sectional stereotypes will supply the key to what happened. Economic, social, and political stimuli affected groups in the South in different ways, and Southerners differed among themselves on the issues of Reconstruction in about the same degree as did groups in the North. The planter-capitalist class of the South thought and acted in terms of economic self-interest in a fashion similar to the industrial magnates of the North. The important difference was that the business men carried the northern people with them while the planters were unable to convince the white masses in the South that economics transcended racial supremacy.

Slaves No More

Leon Litwack

Slavery chain done broke at last!
Broke at last! Broke at last!
Slavery chain done broke at last!
Gonna praise God till I die!

Way up in that valley,
Pray-in' on my knees,
Tell-in' God a-bout my troubles,
And to help me if He please.

I did tell him how I suffer,
In the dungeon and the chain;
And the days I went with head bowed down,
An' my broken flesh and pain.

I did know my Jesus heard me,
'Cause the spirit spoke to me,
An' said, "Rise, my chile, your children
An' you too shall be free."

If done 'p'int one mighty captain
For to marshal all my hosts;
An' to bring my bleeding ones to me,
An' not one shall be lost.

Now no more weary trav'lin',
'Cause my Jesus set me free,
An' there's no more auction block for me
Since He give me liberty.

On the night of April 2, 1865, Confederate troops abandoned Richmond. The sudden decision caught Robert Lumpkin, the well-known dealer in slaves, with a recently acquired shipment which he had not yet arranged to sell. Desperately, he tried to remove them by the same train that would carry Jefferson

Davis out of the Confederate capital. When Lumpkin reached the railway station, however, he found a panic-stricken crowd held back by a line of Confederate soldiers with drawn bayonets. Upon learning that he could not remove his blacks, the dealer marched them back to Lumpkin's Jail, a two-story brick house with barred windows located in the heart of Richmond's famous slave market—an area known to local blacks as "the Devil's Half Acre." After their return, the slaves settled down in their cells for still another night, apparently unaware that this would be their last night of bondage. For Lumpkin, the night would mark the loss of a considerable investment and the end of a profession. Not long after the collapse of the Confederacy, however, he took as his legal wife the black woman he had purchased a decade before and who had already borne him two children.

With Union soldiers nearing the city, a Confederate official thought the black residents looked as stunned and confused as the whites. "The negroes stand about mostly silent," he wrote, "as if wondering what will be their fate. They make no demonstrations of joy." Obviously he had not seen them earlier that day emerging from a church meeting with particular exuberance, "shaking hands and exchanging congratulations upon all sides." Nor had he heard, probably, that familiar refrain with which local blacks occasionally regaled themselves: "Richmond town is burning down. High diddle diddle inctum inctum ah." Whatever the origins of the song the night of the evacuation must have seemed like a prophetic fulfillment. Explosions set off by the retreating Confederates left portions of the city in flames and precipitated a night of unrestrained looting and rioting, in which army deserters and the impoverished residents of Richmond's white slum shared the work of expropriation and destruction with local slaves and free blacks. Black and white women together raided the Confederate Commissary, while the men rolled wheelbarrows filled with bags of flour, meal, coffee, and sugar toward their respective shanties. Along the row of retail stores, a large black man wearing a bright red sash around his waist directed the looting. After breaking down the doors with the crowbar he carried on his shoulder, he stood aside while his followers rushed into the shops and emptied them of their contents. He took nothing for himself, apparently satisfied to watch the others partake of commodities long denied them. If only for this night, racial distinctions and customs suddenly became irrelevant. From behind the barred windows of Lumpkin's Jail, the imprisoned slaves began to chant:

> *Slavery chain done broke at last!*
> *Broke at last! Broke at last!*
> *Slavery chain done broke at last!*
> *Gonna prise God til I die!*

The crowd outside took up the chant, the soldiers opened the slave cells, and the prisoners came pouring out, most of them shouting, some praising God and "master Abe" for their deliverance. Chaplain White found himself unable to continue with his speech. "I became so overcome with tears, that I could not stand up under the pressure of such fullness of joy in my own heart. I retired to gain strength." Several hours later, he located his mother, whom he had not seen for some twenty years.

The white residents bolted their doors, remained inside, and gained their first impressions of Yankee occupation from behind the safety of their shutters. "For us it was a requiem for buried hopes," Sallie P. Putnam. . . . The sudden and ignominious Confederate evacuation had been equaled only by the humiliating sight of black soldiers patrolling the city streets. Few of them could ever forget the long lines of black cavalry sweeping by the Exchange Hotel, brandishing their swords and exchanging "savage cheers" with black residents who were "exulting" over this dramatic moment in their lives. After viewing such spectacles from the window, a young white woman wondered, "Was it to this end we had fought and starved and gone naked and cold? To this end that the wives and children of many dear and gallant friends were husbandless and fatherless? To this end that our homes were in ruins, our state devastated?" Understandably, then, local whites boycotted the military band concerts on the Capitol grounds, even after Federal authorities, in a conciliatory gesture, had barred blacks from attendance.

Four days after the entry of Union troops, Richmond blacks assembled at the First African Church on Broad Street for a Jubilee Meeting. The church, built in the form of a cross and scantily furnished, impressed a northern visitor as "about the last place one would think of selecting for getting up any particular enthusiasm on any other subject than religion." On this day, some 1,500 blacks, including a large number of soldiers, packed the frail structure. With the singing of a hymn, beginning "Jesus my all to heaven is gone," the congregation gave expression to their newly won freedom. After each line, they repeated with added emphasis, "I'm going to join in this army; I'm going to join in this army of my Lord." But when they came to the verse commencing, "This is the way I long have sought," the voices reached even higher peaks and few of the blacks could suppress the smiles that came across their faces. Meanwhile, in the Hall of Delegates, where the Confederate Congress had only recently deliberated and where black soldiers now took turns swiveling in the Speaker's chair, T. Morris Chester, a black war correspondent, tried to assess the impact of these first days of liberation: the rejoicing of the slaves and free blacks, the tumultuous reception accorded President Lincoln when he visited the city, the opening of the slave pens, and the mood of the black population. "They declare that they cannot realize the change; though they have long prayed for it, yet it seems impossible that it has come."

It took little time for the "grapevine" to spread the news that Babylon (as some blacks called it) had fallen. When black children attending a freedmen's school in Norfolk heard the news, they responded with a resounding chorus of "Glory Hallelujah." Reaching the line "We'll hang Jeff Davis to a sour apple tree," one of the pupils inquired if Davis had, indeed, met that fate. The teacher told her that Davis was still very much alive. At this news, the pupil expressed her dismay "by a decided pout of her lips, such a pout as these children only are able to give." Still, the news about Richmond excited them. Most of the children revealed that they had relatives there whom they now hoped to see, several looked forward to reunions with fathers and mothers "dat dem dere Secesh carried off," and those who had neither friends nor relatives in the city were "mighty glad" anyway because they understood the news to mean that "cullud people free now."

When the news reached a plantation near Yorktown, the white family broke into tears, not only over the fall of Richmond but over the rumor that the Yankees had captured Jefferson Davis. Overhearing the conversation, a black servant rushed through the preparation of the supper, asked another servant to wait on the table for her, and explained to the family that she had to fetch water from the "bush-spring." She walked slowly until no one could see her and then ran the rest of the way. Upon reaching the spring, she made certain she was alone and then gave full vent to her feelings.

> I jump up an' scream, "Glory, glory, hallelujah to Jesus! I's free! I's free! Glory to God, you come down an' free us; no big man could do it." An' I got sort o' scared, afeared somebody hear me, an' I takes another good look, an' fall on de groun', an' roll over, an' kiss de groun' fo' de Lord's sake, I's so full o' praise to Masser Jesus. He do all dis great work. De soul buyers can neber take my two chillen lef' me; no, neber can take 'em from me no mo'.

Only a few miles from the Appomattox Courthouse, Fannie Berry, a house servant, stood in the yard with her mistress, Sarah Ann, and watched the white flag being hoisted in the Pamplin village square. "Oh, Lordy," her mistress exclaimed, "Lee done surrendered!" Richmond had fallen the previous week, but for Fannie Berry this was the day she would remember the rest of her life.

> Never was no time like 'em befo' or since. Niggers shoutin' an' clappin' hands an' singin'! Chillun runnin' all over de place beatin' tins an' yellin'. Ev'ybody happy. Sho' did some celebratin'. Run to de kitchen an' shout in de winder:
>
> > *Mammy, don't you cook no mo'*
> > *You's free! You's free!*
>
> Run to de henhouse an' shout:
>
> > *Rooster, don't you crow no mo'*
> > *You's free! You's free!*
> > *Ol' hen, don't you lay no mo' eggs,*
> > *You's free! You's free!*
>
> Go to de pigpen an' tell de pig:
>
> > *Ol' pig, don't you grunt no mo'*
> > *You's free! You's free!*

Tell de cows:

> *Ol' cow, don't you give no mo' milk,*
> *You's free! You's free!*

Despite the immediate gratification experienced by the black residents of Richmond, the death of slavery proved to be agonizingly slow. That precise moment when a slave could think of himself or herself as a free person was not always clear. From the very outset of the war, many slaves assumed they were free the day the Yankees came into their vicinity. But with the military situation subject to constant change, any freedom that ultimately depended on the presence of Union troops was apt to be quite precarious, and in some regions the slaves found themselves uncertain as to whose authority prevailed. The Emancipation Proclamation, moreover, excluded numbers of slaves from its provisions, some masters claimed to be unaware of the emancipation order, and still others refused to acknowledge it while the war raged and doubted its constitutionality after the end of hostilities. "I guess we musta celebrated 'Mancipation about twelve times in Harnett County," recalled Ambrose Douglass, a former North Carolina slave. "Every time a bunch of No'thern sojers would come through they would tell us we was free and we'd begin celebratin'. Before we would get through somebody else would tell us to go back to work, and we would go. Some of us wanted to jine up with the army, but didn't know who was goin' to win and didn't take no chances."

Outside of a few urban centers, Union soldiers rarely remained long enough in any one place to enforce the slave's new status. Of the slaves in her region "who supposed they were free," a South Carolina white woman noted how they were "gradually discovering a Yankee army passing through the country and telling them they are free is not sufficient to make it a fact." Nor was the protection of the freedman's status the first priority of an army engaged in a life-and-death struggle. When the troops needed to move on, many of the blacks were understandably dismayed, confused, and frightened. "Christ A'mighty!" one slave exclaimed in late 1861 when told the troops were about to depart. "If Massa Elliott Garrard catch me, might as well be dead—he kill me, certain." Even if Union officers assured him of his safety, the slave had little reason to place any confidence in the word of someone who would not be around on that inevitable day of reckoning. While encamped in the North Carolina countryside, the black regiment to which Henry M. Turner was attached had attracted nearly 700 slaves from the immediate vicinity. "To describe the scene produced by our departure," he wrote, "would be too solemn, if time and space permitted. Suffice it to say, many were the tears shed, many sorrowful hearts bled. . . . God alone knows, I was compelled to evade their sight as much as possible, to be relieved of such words as these, 'Chaplain, what shall I do? where can we go? will you come back?' "

Widespread dismay at the impending departure of the Yankees reflected not only the prevailing uncertainty about freedom but the very real fear that their masters or the entire white community might wreak vengeance on them for any irregular behavior during the brief period of occupation. In a Mississippi town near Vicksburg, a number of slaves had joined with the Yankees to plunder stores and homes, apparently assuming that the soldiers would be around to protect them. But now the troops were moving on, leaving the looters with their newly acquired possessions and all the slaves, regardless of what role they had played in the pillaging, at the mercy of whites who felt betrayed and robbed. With "undisguised amazement," the blacks watched the soldiers leave, and within hours one of them caught up with the Yankee columns and reported that a number of his people had already been killed. On a plantation near Columbia, South Carolina, the master and mistress waited until the Yankees departed and then vented their anger on a young slave girl who had helped the soldiers to locate the hidden silverware, money, and jewelry. "She'd done wrong I know," a former slave recalled, "but I hated to see her suffer so awful for it. After de Yankees had gone, de missus and massa had de poor gal hung 'till she die. It was something awful to see." With similar swiftness, a slaveholder who was reputedly "very good to his Negroes" became so enraged over the behavior of a black that the moment the Yankees left the area he strung him up to the beams of a shed.

Where slave misbehavior had been particularly "outrageous," as in northern Louisiana and the adjoining Mississippi counties, the Yankee raiding parties had no sooner returned to their bases than local whites demanded swift and severe retaliation. Not content to leave such matters entirely in the hands of the planters, a newspaper in Alexandria urged that public examples be made of "the ungrateful and vindictive scoundrels" who seized their masters' property, volunteered information to or acted as guides for the enemy, and "were seen armed or participated in any active demonstration."

> The uppermost thought in every one's mind before the Yankee invasion of our Parish was, what will be the conduct of the slaves. The most important consideration for all of us now that the invasion has swept by, is what conduct are we to pursue to them? . . . Some offences have been committed that cannot be atoned for but by death. Others may be safely expiated by the lash or other corporeal punishment. Others may safely be left to the milder discipline of the plantation. The punishment for each proper to its kind, should be inexorably and unflinchingly afflicted.

Nearly a year elapsed before the Union Army returned to these regions, and this time some of the slaves insisted that they be permitted to accompany the soldiers rather than be left behind. Near Alexandria, an elderly slave told a Union correspondent. "Oh, master! since you was here last, we have had dreadful times." Several other slaves who had gathered around him corroborated his narration of a reign of terror.

We seen stars in the day time. They treated us dreadful bad. They beat us, and they hung us, and starved us. . . . Why, the day after you left, they jist had us all out in a row and told us they were going to shoot us, and they did hang two of us; and Mr. Pierce, the overseer, knocked one with a fence rail, and he died next day. Oh, Master! we seen stars in de day time. And now we going with you, we go back no mo'!

Even if such stories were exaggerated for northern consumption, the fact remains that many slaves realistically perceived the degree to which their "freedom" rested on a Yankee presence. Once the troops moved on, despite the assurances of Union officers and regardless of how exemplary black behavior might have been, the status and conditions of labor of the slaves tended in many regions to revert back to what they had been, sometimes with painful consequences for those who insisted upon asserting their freedom or who were thought to have been "spoiled" by the Yankees. "The negroes' freedom was brought to a close to-day," a South Carolina white woman reported with relief, noting that as soon as the Yankees moved on, Confederate "scouts" assembled the slaves, told them the Union soldiers had no right to free them, and advised them to return to their usual tasks. Many former slaves recalled precisely that experience. "They tol' us we were free," an ex-North Carolina slave testified about the Yankees, but the master "would get cruel to the slaves if they acted like they were free." Although recognizing that he was free, a former Alabama slave knew better than to claim that freedom in the presence of his master. "Didn't do to say you was free. When de war was over if a nigger say he was free, dey shot him down. I didn't say anythin', but one day I run away." After Confederate troops briefly reoccupied several parishes in southern Louisiana, James Walkinshaw, an overseer, quickly made it clear to the blacks he supervised that the Yankee invasion had changed nothing. "Don't contradict me," he shouted at a slave who protested his order to work harder. "I don't allow anybody white or black to do that; if you contradict me again, I'll cut your heart out; the Yankees have spoiled you Niggers but I'll be even with you." Apparently the verbal reprimand was not sufficient, for the overseer terminated the incident by stabbing the "spoiled" slave in the breast.

The racial tensions exacerbated by black behavior during the Yankee invasion persisted long after the troops had moved elsewhere. With even greater vigilance, slaveholders and local whites scrutinized the remaining blacks, looking for any actions, words, or changes in their demeanor that suggested Yankee influences. Eliza Evans, a former Alabama slave, could recall quite vividly the day she first used the surname which a Yankee soldier had persuaded her to assume. "Jest Liza," she had told the soldier when he asked for her name. "I ain't got no other names." After ascertaining that she worked for a John Mixon, the Yankee had told her, "You are Liza Mixon. Next time anybody call you nigger you tell 'em dat you is a Negro and your name is Miss

Liza Mixon." The idea appealed to the young slave. "The more I thought of that the more I liked it and I made up my mind to do jest what he told me to." Several days later, after the Yankees had withdrawn from the area, Eliza was tending the livestock when her master approached. "What you doin', nigger?" he demanded to know. "I ain't no nigger," she replied. "I'se a Negro and I'm Miss Liza Mixon." Startled by her response and sensitive to any signs of post-Yankee insolence, the master picked up a switch and ran after her. "Law', but I was skeered!" she recalled. "I hadn't never had no whipping so I ran fast as I can to Grandma Gracie." She reached her grandmother about the same time her master did. "Gracie," he charged, "dat little nigger sassed me." When Eliza explained what had happened, revealing the conversation with the soldier, her grandmother decided to mete out the punishment herself. "Grandma Gracie took my dress and lift it over my head and pins my hands inside, and Lawsie, how she whipped me and I dassent holler loud either." Still, as she recalled the incident many years later, Eliza Evans suggested that she had derived considerable self-pride from this initial assertion of freedom. "I jest said dat to de wrong person," she concluded.

What, then, was "freedom" and who was "free"? The fluctuating moods of individual masters, unexpected changes in the military situation, the constant movement of troops, and widespread doubts about the validity and enforcement of the Emancipation Proclamation were bound to have a sobering effect on the slaves' perceptions of their status and rights, leaving many of them quite confused if not thoroughly disillusioned. The sheer uncertainty of it all prompted blacks to weigh carefully their actions and utterances, as they had earlier in the war, even in some instances to disclaim any desire to be free or to deny what the Yankees told them. "Sho' it ain't no truf in what dem Yankees wuz a-sayin'," Martha Colquitt recalled her mother telling her, "and us went right on living just like us always done 'til Marse Billie called us together and told us de war wuz over and us wuz free to go whar us wanted to go, and us could charge wages for our work."

Only with "the surrender," as they came to call it, did many slaves begin to acknowledge the reality of emancipation. The fall of Richmond and the collapse of the Confederacy broke the final links in the chain. With freedom no longer hanging on every military skirmish, slaves who had shrewdly or fearfully refrained from any outward display of emotion suddenly felt free to release their feelings and to act on them. Ambrose Douglass, who claimed to have celebrated emancipation every time the Yankees came into Harnett County, North Carolina, sensed that this time it was different, and he proposed to make certain. "I was 21 when freedom finally came, and that time I didn't take no chances on 'em taking it back again. I lit out for Florida." The day the war ended, Prince Johnson recalled, "wagon loads o' people rode all th'ough de place a-tellin' us 'bout bein' free." When the news reached Oconee, Georgia, Ed McCree found himself so overcome that he refused to wait for his master to confirm the report of Lee's surrender: "I runned 'round dat place a-shoutin' to de top of my voice."

In the major cities and towns, far more than in the countryside, the post-Appomattox demonstrations resembled the Jubilees that would become so firmly fixed in black and southern lore. If only for a few days or hours, many of the rural slaves flocked to the nearest town, anxious to join their urban brethren in the festivities and to celebrate their emancipation away from the scrutiny of their masters and mistresses. When news of "the surrender" reached Athens, Georgia, blacks sang and danced around a hastily constructed liberty pole in the center of town. (White residents cut it down during the night.) Although urban blacks had enjoyed a certain degree of autonomy in the past, military occupation afforded them the first real opportunity to express themselves openly and freely as a community, unhampered by curfews, passes, and restrictions on assemblages. Even before Appomattox, many of them made full use of such opportunities.

The largest and most spectacular demonstration took place in Charleston, less than a month after Union occupation. More than 4,000 black men and women wound their way through the city streets, cheered on by some 10,000 spectators, most of them also black. With obvious emotions, they responded to a mule-drawn cart in which two black women sat, while next to them stood a mock slave auctioneer shouting, "How much am I offered?" Behind the cart marched sixty men tied together as a slave gang, followed in turn by a cart containing a black-draped coffin inscribed with the words "Slavery is Dead." Union soldiers, schoolchildren, firemen, and members of various religious societies participated in the march along with an impressive number of black laborers whose occupations pointed up the important role they played in the local economy—carpenters, butchers, tailors, teamsters, masons, wheelwrights, barbers, coopers, bakers, blacksmiths, wood sawyers, and painters. For the black community of Charleston, the parade proved to be an impressive display of organization and self-pride. The white residents thought less of it. "The innovation was by no means pleasant," a reporter wrote of the few white onlookers, "but they had sense enough to keep their thoughts to themselves."

Less than a week after the end of the war, still another celebration in Charleston features the ceremonial raising of the United States flag over the ruins of Fort Sumter. Far more dramatic than any of the speeches on this occasion was the presence of such individuals as William Lloyd Garrison, the veteran northern abolitionist, for whom this must have been a particularly satisfying day. Robert Smalls, the black war hero who had delivered a Confederate steamer to the Union Navy, now used that same ship to convey some 3,000 blacks to Fort Sumter. On the quarterdeck stood Major Martin R. Delany, who had once counseled emigration as the only alternative to continued racial oppression and enslavement and who would soon take his post as a

Freedmen's Bureau agent in South Carolina. Next to Delany stood another black man, the son of Denmark Vesey, who some thirty-three years before had been executed for plotting a slave insurrection in Charleston.

Nearly a week after the fall of Richmond, the Confederate dream lay shattered. When the news reached Mary Darby, daughter of a prominent South Carolina family, she staggered to a table, sat down, and wept aloud. "Now," she shrieked, "we belong to Negroes and Yankees." If the freed slaves had reason to be confused about the future, their former masters and mistresses were in many instances absolutely distraught, incapable of perceiving a future without slaves. "Nobody that hasn't experienced it knows anything about our suffering," a young South Carolina planter declared. "We are discouraged: we have nothing left to begin new with. I never did a day's work in my life, and don't know how to begin." Often with little sense of intended irony, whites viewed the downfall of the Confederacy and slavery as fastening upon them the ignominy of bondage. Either they must submit to the insolence of their servants or appeal to their northern "masters" for protection, one white woman wrote, "as if we were slaves ourselves—and that is just what they are trying to make of us. Oh, it is abominable!"

Seeking "*temporary* relief" from the recent disasters, including the loss of "many of our servants," Eva B. Jones of Augusta, Georgia, immersed herself in fourteen volumes of history. But she found little comfort in a study of the past, only additional evidence of human depravity.

> How vice and wickedness, injustice and every human passion runs riot, flourishes, oftentimes going unpunished to the tomb! And how the little feeble sickly attempts of virtue struggle, an after a brief while fade away, unappreciated and unextolled! The depravity of the human heart is truly wonderful, and the moiety of virtue contained on the historic page truly deplorable.

If she found any consolation in her readings, it was only to know how often "these same sorrows and unmerited punishments that we are now undergoing [have] been visited upon the brave, the deserving, the heroic, and the patient of all ages and in all climes!" Returning to the history that was being acted out in her own household, she bemoaned the abolition of slavery as "a most unprecedented robbery," intended only for the "greater humiliation" of the southern people. "However, it *is* done,"she sighed; "and we, the *chained witnesses,* can only look on."

With such thoughts preying upon them, slave-owning families prepared to surrender their human property but not the ideology that had made such possessions possible and necessary.

Questions

Chapter One—The Colonial Period: Making It in the New World

Perry Miller: "The Errand into the Wilderness."

1. According to Miller, why did English Puritans emigrate to the New World? Were they coming for the same reasons other Englishmen came?
2. What was the Puritans' "errand?"
3. What was the covenant philosophy under which the Bay Colony operated?
4. No matter how determined and pure their intentions, the Puritans were destined to fail in their errand. Why? What factors beyond the Puritans control undermined their purpose?

Philip Greven: "Family Structure in Seventeenth-Century Andover, Mass."

1. How does Greven's methodology differ from that of Miller? What are the implications for the historian of Greven's approach?
2. What was the relationship between family structure and economic developments in Andover during the years of Greven's study?

Edmund Morgan: "The Jamestown Fiasco."

1. Even before leaving England, what sort of perceptions of the New World did most Englishmen have? How did these perceptions affect the Jamestown settlement?
2. What were the main failures of the settlement of early Virginia? Why does Morgan call his article the "Jamestown fiasco?"
3. What pivotal role did John Smith play in the history of early Virginia?
4. Despite incredible greed, stupidity and arrogance, England's first colony at Jamestown survived. Why?

Chapter Two—The American Revolution

James Martin: "A Most Undisciplined, Profligate Crew: Protest and Defiance in the Continental Ranks, 1776–1783."

1. What were the main sources of protest and resentment amongst the colonial militia according to Martin?
2. Assess the social composition of the rank and file of the colonial army. How did the class structure of the army affect morale?
3. What type of unity existed between the military and the larger colonial community? How did most non-combatants view the Continental Army?
4. From what types of backgrounds did most colonial officers come from? What sort of relationship existed between enlisted men and their officers?

Broadus Mitchell: "The War Within."

1. Who were the Whigs and Tories? What were the main causes of their conflict?
2. How were Loyalists treated during the war, and what were the implications of this treatment?
3. Why did many Americans remain loyal to "king and country," despite the danger to their lives?
4. In many ways the "war within" was a more significant conflict than the struggle between England and the colonies. Why so? Could the fighting between Whig and Tory be interpreted as a civil war? How so?

Gordon Wood: "Republicanism as a Revolutionary Ideology."

1. What does the author mean by the concept of republican ideology? What is republicanism in the context of Wood's thesis?
2. From what sources did the American revolutionary leaders derive their concept republicanism?
3. How do the ideas of public virtue and the rebellion of 1776 fit together in Wood's thesis?
4. Given the confines of Wood's argument, was rebellion against English authority inevitable? Why? In the American mind what had the English polity become?

Chapter Three—Confederation and Constitution

Merrill Jensen—Articles of Confederation "The Problems of Interpretation"

1. How does Jensen interpret the American Revolution? What is the significance of his statement that, "The American Revolution marks the ascendancy of the radicals in the colonies."?
2. Who were the "agrarian and proletarian elements" of Jensen's argument? What did they represent and who opposed them?
3. Why, according to Jensen, were the Articles of Confederation replaced by the Federal Constitution? What were the implications of this view for future constitutional debate?

Esmond Wright—The Fabric of Freedom—"The Constitution"

1. Does the Philadelphia Convention appear to you to represent a balanced cross-section of colonial life?
2. Identify and discuss the key issues and compromises confronted by the Philadelphia Convention. What techniques of persuasion did the Federalists use to secure acceptance of the document?
3. Review and assess Wright's discussion of constitutional historiography.

Federalist #10

1. What advice does Madison offer with regard to regulating first the causes then the effects of factionalism?
2. What does Madison have to say about the differences between a democracy and a republic?
3. How does the size of the political unit influence Madison's discussion of restricting factionalism? What flaws, if any, can you see in his argument?

Chapter Four—The New Nation, 1788–1815

Forrest McDonald—Hamiltonianism

1. What kind of "political economy" did Hamilton envisage for the United States?
2. How did Hamilton hope to accomplish his balanced economy?
3. To Hamilton and many of his Federalist associates, why was it deemed essential for the United States to become a nation of "shopkeepers" as opposed to a nation of farmers?
4. Although Hamilton's principal concern was the economic stability of the new nation, his programs were nevertheless politically motivated. What political objectives did Hamilton hope to realize with his monetary policies?

John C. Miller—Thomas Jefferson and the Philosophy of Agrarianism

1. According to Miller, Jefferson's agrarian and republican ideals were the total antithesis of his Federalist counterpart, Alexander Hamilton. How did Jefferson's political and economic philosophy differ with that of his adversary?
2. How did Jefferson perceive the American people which led to his conclusion that "the government that governs the least governs the best?"
3. Why was Jefferson so opposed to Hamilton's programs? What dangers did he see in them?
4. Why did Jefferson believe it was essential for the New Republic to remain principally agrarian?

Harry Coles—Prologue to War

1. Why did it seem that the United States was "destined" to fight another war with England in 1812?
2. What particular irritants pushed the United States to a declaration of war?
3. What effects did the French Revolution have upon Anglo-American relations? In fact, could it be said that had there not been that upheaval, there might not have been reason for war between England and the United States?

4. Not all Americans welcomed war with England. In fact, New Englanders in particular opposed hostilities with England. Why? On the other hand, Southerners and Westerners agitated for war. Why?
5. Could the United States have avoided another war with England?

Chapter Five—The Jacksonian Era

James Curtis—President and Defender

1. According to Curtis, what personality traits did Jackson possess that in many ways contributed to both his popularity and political ascendancy?
2. How did Jackson perceive his role as president? How did his activism challenge the notions of executive conduct established since the administration of George Washington?
3. Though he is considered by many to be one of this country's most significant "symbols", why, according to Curtis, is Jackson worthy of such acclaim?

Edward Pessen—The Jacksonian Character

1. According to Pessen, the true American character emerged during the 1830's and 1840's. What kind of unique, indigenous American personality developed during the Jacksonian Era?
2. In the hands of shrewd Jacksonian politicians, the common folk's crude and selfish behavior became a powerful political weapon. How so?
3. Have our basic assumptions and conduct changed much since the Jacksonian Era? Aren't our priorities similar? Don't we still display many of the same crass affectations and frenzied acquisitiveness as our Jacksonian predecessors?

Glyndon G. VanDeusen—Politics, a Tariff and a Bank

1. What did the Second Bank of the United States symbolize to its Jacksonian adversaries? Why did they feel so compelled to destroy it?
2. According to VanDeusen, what role did the Bank play in the nation's economy? Was it the "monster" the Jacksonians accused it of being?
3. Why were Southerners opposed to the tariffs of 1824, 1828?
4. What was the central theme of Calhoun's *Exposition and Protest?* Was it a legitimate constitutional argument or merely the partisan sophistries of a frustrated politician?
5. Why was Jackson so enraged by South Carolina's position on the tariff?

Chapter Six—Reform in Antebellum America

Merton Dillon—Goading the Monster

1. Who were the abolitionists? What was their background and motivation to purge the Republic of the evil of slavery?

2. What did slavery represent to many of the abolitionists?
3. Not all of the movement's members were "immediatists". What was the attitude of the crusade's other wing toward manumission?
4. How did the Northern public tend to view the abolitionists, their motives, policies and overall crusade?

David Rothman—The Well-Ordered Asylum

1. According to Rothman, regardless of the type of institution created for the deviant and dependent, they all had a fundamental purpose. What was that objective?
2. What were the assumptions all reformers shared regarding the asylum and its usefulness in rehabilitating the depraved and indigent?
3. Of particular concern to reformers was the moral and spiritual well-being of American youth. When placed in the appropriate reformatory, what did the caretakers hope to instill in these children? What kind of regimen was established and why?
4. Overall were the various asylums established during the Jacksonian Era successful in reforming individuals or were they created for the more effective and safer purpose of controlling those passions, vices and individualism perceived to be threatening the Republic's morality and virtue?

Gerda Lerner—The Grimke Sisters

1. According to Lerner, the various antebellum reform crusades provided women with their first opportunities to break the shackles of domesticity. How did that process occur?
2. Once "allowed" to become reform activists, how did women influence the various organizations they joined?
3. The Grimke sisters were especially prominent women reformers who had a very significant impact upon not only the abolitionists cause but the nascent feminist movement as well. How did their efforts help promote the cause of feminine equality?

Chapter Seven—The World of the Slaves

Winthrop Jordan—The Enslavement of Negroes in America to 1700

1. Why did racial slavery and discrimination replace general slavery and discrimination according to Jordan?
2. What characteristics of life in the New World uniquely qualified America to become a slave holding society?
3. What preconceived ideas and traditions about slavery and bondage did the English New World settlers bring with them? In what sense does the author describe the origins of New World slavery as an "unthinking decision"?

Sterling Stuckey—Through the Prism of Folklore: The Black Ethos in Slavery

1. What is the thesis of Stuckey's piece? What sources does Stuckey employ to reinforce his argument?
2. How does Stuckey link the history of American slaves to the existence of an Afro-American culture?
3. How do popular artistic or esthetic pursuits ease the burdens of everyday life or act as "a form of group therapy" as Stuckey suggests?

Peter Kolchin—Reevaluating the Antebellum Slave Community: A Comparative Perspective

1. What is the thesis of Kolchin's piece? What specific analytical techniques does he utilize and what is his criticism of the revisionist works of the 1970s?
2. Why, according to Kolchin, did America's slaves have little opportunity to develop independent economic activity and community solidarity?
3. How did America's slaves challenge their oppressors according to Kolchin and how did these techniques differ from those of other slave holding societies?

Chapter Eight—The Crisis of the 1850's

Otis Singletary—The Coming of the War

1. What beliefs and attitudes led to the notion of "manifest destiny?"
2. Once Americans had filled their heads with arrogance of manifest destiny, what did they determine to do?
3. Was the Mexican War the result of the rhetoric of manifest destiny or would such a conflict have occurred without such propaganda?
4. Was the Mexican War the Republic's first imperialist war?
5. What issues contributed to the outbreak of hostilities with Mexico?
6. Could the United States have accomplished its objectives without war?

David Potter—The Nature of Southern Separatism

1. What socioeconomic and environmental factors intensified Southern nationalism during the 1850's?
2. Unlike their Northern counterparts, how did the majority of informed Southerners perceive the structure and purpose of the Union?
3. Were Southerners correct in their contention that the majority of Northerners were abolitionists and were thus intent on destroying their peculiar institution?
4. Given the nature of Southern separatism, was war with the North inevitable?

Kenneth Stampp—The Search for Remedies

1. According to Stampp, once Lincoln had been elected, all hopes of sectional compromise were dashed. Northerners were then confronted with the reality of civil war. What other alternatives did the North have at this juncture?
2. Throughout the 1850's the majority of Northerners were mute to the clamoring of the Southern fire-eaters. Should they have paid closer attention to what the extremists were saying?
3. What were some of the prevailing Northern attitudes toward the fire-eaters? How did the majority of the Northern public perceive the impending crisis? Did they believe war was imminent? Or, was the latest secession threat simply more impassioned hyperbole?

Chapter Nine—The Civil War

T. Harry Williams—Abraham Lincoln: Pragmatic Democrat

1. According to Williams, what kind of "politician" was Lincoln?
2. How did Lincoln perceive the secession crisis and how did he handle it as president?
3. Once the war had started, how did Lincoln perceive the conflict? Did he regard it as war or rebellion? Why?
4. What sort of problems did Lincoln have throughout the war with Northern Public opinion? Why did he have such difficulties? How did Lincoln finally win public support for the Union cause?

Emory Thomas—Foundations of the Southern Nation

1. According to Thomas, how did the secessionists justify their right to leave the Union? What historical precedents did they call upon to substantiate their argument?
2. Once the Confederacy was established, what kind of confederation was it to be?
3. Assess the Confederacy's leadership. Who were the individuals who dominated not only the secession conventions throughout the South, but also the Confederacy's constitutional convention? What was their political ideology?
4. Does the Confederate constitution reflect Southern society and mentality as a whole? Or was it more of a reflection of the interests and attitudes of the planter elite?
5. According to Thomas, was secession and the formation of the Confederacy popularly endorsed?

William Barney—The People's War

1. Why does Barney call the Civil War the "people's war?"
2. In many ways, the American Civil War was the world's first modern, total war. How so?

3. Did either the North or the South envisage this kind of conflict? Why not?

4. Though the Confederacy put up a valiant resistance, what Southern shortcomings, both economic and political would inevitably lead to a Union triumph?

5. Given the overwhelming logistical and economic advantages the North had (at least on paper!) why did the war last so long? What factors contributed to the South's ability to hang on for four years? Could the South have won the Civil War?

Chapter Ten—Reconstruction

Leon Litwak—Slaves No More

1. What according to Litwak were the pressures placed upon southern blacks immediately after emancipation?

2. What was "freedom" for southern blacks during reconstruction? What did it mean to be a "slave no more"?

3. What role did the Union army have in securing black emancipation? Did northern soldiers seem particularly committed to southern racial equality?

Kenneth Stampp—Radical Reconstruction

1. What do you understand by the term "radical reconstruction"? What specific philosophy or agenda does it embrace? How can you assess its achievements?

2. Summarize the issue of land reform as treated by Stampp. Why did any meaningful land reform program—specifically one based upon confiscation fail to pass Congress?

3. What was the Freedmen's Bureau? Analyze the achievements, failures, possibilities etc. of this federal assistance program.

4. What does Stampp's article have to say concerning the relationship between the 14th Amendment and the issue of racial segregation? What according to Stampp was the main significance of the 1875 Civil Rights Act and what does he have to say about the black suffrage issue?

T. Harry Williams—An Analysis of Some Reconstruction Attitudes

1. Summarize the Beale thesis and the Marxist view of Reconstruction. How, according to Williams, do they differ?

2. Summarize what Williams has to say concerning southern white attitudes toward Reconstruction. What does Williams mean when he refers to the Dunning School.

3. Review the interests of the planter class with specific reference to Reconstruction issues. What practical political action did the planter class take during Reconstruction to protect itself from excessive taxation?

4. What do you understand by the term Revisionism? Why do you think the Reconstruction era has been particularly subject to stereotyping and oversimplification?